NATIONAL INFORMATION SYSTEM IN EDUCATION

CONCEPTS IN COMMUNICATION, INFORMATICS AND LIBRARIANSHIP (CICIL)

General Editor : S. P. Agrawal

For a list of titles in this series, see pp. 380-384 at the end of the book.

Dr. S.L. Verma possesses a Master Degrees in Economics and in Library and Information Science and Ph.D in Information Systems. He has entered the Library profession by choice and not by chance. He has nearly three decades of experience in the working of various libraries–special as well as academic ranging from School Libraries to University Libraries and has been responsible for collection and dissemination of Information during the last decade. He has also been closely associated with the organisation of workshops, seminars and training for the Librarians of schools and Teacher Training Institutes.

Presently, he is working as Deputy Librarian in the Department of Library, Documentation and Information, N.C.E.R.T. New Delhi.

ISBN 81-7022-571-X

Concepts in Communication,
Informatics & Librarianship-70

NATIONAL INFORMATION SYSTEM IN EDUCATION
A Comparative Study

S.L. VERMA
Deputy Librarian
National Council of Educational Research and Training
NEW DELHI 110016

CONCEPT PUBLISHING COMPANY, NEW DELHI-110059

Published with the financial assistance from ERIC [NCERT], New Delhi

ISBN 81-7022- 571-X
First Published 1996

Published and Printed by
Ashok Kumar Mittal
Concept Publishing Company
A/15-16, Commercial Block, Mohan Garden
NEW DELHI - 110059 (India)
Phones: 5554042, 5504042

GENERAL EDITOR'S INTRODUCTION

In view of the momentous global changes in almost every aspect of modern life brought about by the science and technology the role of education is increasing by being re-defined. In the new situation education has come to be recognised as a vital factor for human development which is the core of all developmental efforts. It is not only through conventional capital in the form of machinery and materials that rapid economic development can be achieved, the human factor also makes its own significant contribution to it. West achieved phenomenal socio-economic and technological progress because of the realization that education is an investment and that a sound educational system, which is capable of producing better human resources, could help realization of better economic and social goals. Of late, there has been a growing awareness among the developing nations that neglect of education by them is mainly responsible for their activity. India, which is vast and poor, and even so making concerted efforts for speedy industrialization, is too moving in this stream and this is reflected in India's Eighth Five Year Plan document. 'Expansion and utilization of employment opportunities', says the plan document, 'and increase in productivity are strongly influenced by education. In the process of development education is, therefore, an investment. This investment has to be made well in time to derive full benefits from the over all development effort'.

A number of factors influence building up of a sound and reliable educational structure. But the key factor, as is the information infrastructure which is a very weak link in India's educational scheme of things. Free flow of information is obviously an essential requirement for achieving educational goals and objectives. In any field of activity policy decisions cannot be judiciously taken in absence of full and reliable data, and access to the most diversified and comprehensive information. Hence, it cannot be over emphasised that for educational decision-making too we have to depend heavily on timely and reliable information flow. In India, where educational scenario is disquieting and economic growth tardy, it is necessary to develop proper national information system in education, to provide right type of information in right time to educational administrators and planners.

The present publication is based on Dr. Verma's research study conducted for doctoral degree in the Library and Information Science on the subject crucial for our educational progress, which despite a number of Committees and Commissions set up from time to time and governmental policies adopted on the basis of their commendations, has not made much headway and has not proved on effective instrument for social development and appreciable economic growth. The book underlies the importance of education for human resource development and pleads for evolving a national information system for desired change in the educational scenario.

Before making out a case for a national information system in education in India, the publication gives a broad over view of educational as well as information systems of U.K. and U.S. as also of the prevailing situation in India by way of necessary background and to their salient features indicating both the similarities and dissimilarities of these systems. Since the focus of the book is on information system, it makes a detailed examination of the national library, public and academic libraries, the library co-operation and the networking, the existing library and educational information networks. It also explains the concept, the design and functions of an information system to evolve a suitable model of National Information System for Education. In the light of the findings of the study, Dr. Verma makes a detailed analysis of the proposed model's objectives, planning and coordination, governance financial aspect, and emphasises its suitability in the Indian context.

It will certainly prove a boon to the educational planners, administrators and researchers.

S.P. AGRAWAL

PREFACE

The book is based on my Doctoral thesis entitled, 'A Comparative Study of the National Information Systems in Education in UK and USA with a view to Developing a model for India' submitted to University of Delhi under the supervision of Prof. D.S. Aggarwal.

The National Information System for Science and Technology (NISSAT) and National Social Science Documentation Centre (NASSDOC) have emerged sources of information to meet the needs in the areas of techno socio-economic concern. No similar information system exists in vital field like education. This book is a modest attempt to fill the gap.

Firstly, I should express my deep sense of gratitude to Prof. D.S. Aggarwal, University of Delhi without whose able guidance the genesis of this book would not have been possible. I am also indebted to Sh. B.V.S. Sastry, IAMR, New Delhi whose continuous guidance has steered the book at every stage. For guidance in analysis and interpretation of data, I am extremely grateful to Dr. C.L. Kaul, NCERT.

I am grateful to ERIC (NCERT) for extending financial support for the publication of this book. Dr. P.L. Malhotra former Director, NCERT Prof. A.K. Sharma, Director, NCERT and Dr. A.N. Maheshwari, Jt. Director, NCERT have been sources of great inspiration and encouragement. I am indebted to them.

I would like to record deep appreciation for the interest evinced in the speedy publication of this book by Shri Ashok Kumar Mittal, Concept Publishing Company, New Delhi.

I am, also thankful to a host of individuals and organizations who have helped me in some way or the other in bringing out this book.

S.L. VERMA

CONTENTS

LIST OF FIGURES

LIST OF TABLES

1

INTRODUCTION

Education for National Development

Education has always been accorded a lofty place in Indian society. The great leaders of Indian freedom movement realised the fundamental role of education and stressed its unique significance for national development. Gandhiji formulated 'The Scheme of Basic Education' seeking to harmonize the intellectual and manual work. This was a great step forward in making education directly relevant to the life of the people.

In the post-independence period, a major concern of the Government of India and of the States has been to give increasing attention to education as a factor vital to national progress and security; problems of educational reconstruction were reviewed by several Commissions and Committees, notably the University Education Commission (1948-49), the Secondary Education Commission (1952-53) and Education Commission (1964–66).

Since the adoption of the 1968 policy, there has been considerable expansion in educational facilities all over the country at all levels. The most notable development has been the acceptance of a common structure of education throughout the country and the introduction of the 10+2+3 system.

Educational objectives, during these years, lay more stress on further democratisation of education, improving access to education, better educational opportunities of the disadvantaged, achieving more regional equity, increasing the range of educational opportunities, introducing increased vocational bias in the curricula, more relevant to socio-economic needs, developing alternate strategies, broadening the concept of continuing education, increasing access of women to all level of education and awareness of environmental problems. The progress and prosperity of a society largely depends on the availability of knowledge and extent of its use at any time.

EDUCATION – A RESOURCE

As a Human Capital

Education is an important factor in achieving rapid technological progress and economic development and in creating a social order founded on the values of freedom, social justice and equity. Economic growth is generated not only by conventional capital in the form of tools and machinery, but also by men. And just as technological improvements increase the efficiency of machinery, so also education increases the efficiency of manpower. Indeed, recent statistical investigations show that the improvement in the 'human factor' accounts for a major part of economic growth.

The renowned American economist T.W. Schultz has viewed education as investment for building up human capital. He emphasised the role of education in economic growth in the following statement:

> "Although it is obvious that people acquired useful skills and knowledge, it is not obvious that skills and knowledge are a form of capital, that this capital is in substantial part a product of deliberate investment, that it has grown in Western Societies at a much faster rate than conventional (non-human) capital, and that its growth may well be the most distinctive feature of the economic system. It has been widely observed that increases in national output have been large compared with the increases of land, manhours, and physical reproducible capital. Investment in human capital is, probably, the major explanation for the difference". [1]

Improvement in the quality of manpower and of machinery go hand in hand; both of them reflect the greater effectiveness of the human factor which is, or should be, the good education. The role of the educated leadership in production has led to the theory of education as investment. This is an important reason why society as a whole should contribute to investment in education.[2] For the realization of this, educational system and programmes have to be directed towards a set of goals and tasks. Human resource development is both an important national goal and an essential means of achieving rapid socio-economic progress in the Indian context. The Seventh Five Year Plan points out how a narrow view of resource mobilization, limiting to financial sphere fails to do justice to the complexity of the development process in which the human factor plays the most important part. It declares that without adequate development of human resources in its widest sense, we cannot avoid setbacks to the process of development itself and that education in all its aspects holds the key to rapid and sustained social and economic advance. The National Policy on Education (NPE) 1986 states that it should now be possible to further intensity the nation-wide effort in human resource development with education playing its multi-faceted role.[3]

Traditional Indian way of thinking views a human being as a positive asset and a precious national resource which needs to be cherished, nurtured and developed with tenderness and care. Each individual's growth presents a different range of problems and requirements, at every stage from the womb to tomb. The catalystic role of education in this complex and dynamic growth process needs to be planned meticulously and executed efficiently.

Education – As a Factor of Production

Education develops manpower for different levels of the economy. It is also the substrata on which research and development flourish, and is the ultimate guarantee of national self-reliance.

Education is a unique investment for the present as well as future.[4] Indeed, statistical investigations show that improvement in the "human factor" accounts for a major part of economic growth. Describing education as a factor of production, the American economist Schultz states: "I noted that the unexplained increases in U.S. national income have been especially large in recent decades. On one set of assumptions, the unexplained part amounts to nearly three-fifth of the total increase between 1929 and 1956." (Real income doubled, rising form $ 150 to $ 302 billion in 1956 prices. 89 billions of the increase or about 59 per cent of the total increase in real income is taken to be unexplained). "How much of this unexplained increase in income represents a return to education in the labour force? A lower limit suggests that about three-tenth of it and an upper limit does not rule out that more than one-half of its came from this source." (In terms of percentages the lower estimate

TABLE 1.1: Mean Income (or Earnings) by Level of School Completed, 25 years old and over, for the United States: 1939, 1946, 1956 and 1958

Year	Elementary-High School Average Income		Differential percent Difference	High School-College Average Income		
	Elementary	High School		High School	College	
1939	(a)*	$ 1661	(a)*	$ 1661	$ 2607	57
1946	$ 2327	2939	26	2939	4527	54
1949	2829	3784	34	3784	6179	63
1956	3732	5439	46	5439	8490	56
1958	3769	5567	48	5567	9206	65

(a)* Not available

came to 29 per cent and the upper estimate to 56 per cent). "These estimates also imply that between 36 and 70 per cent of the hitherto unexplained rise in the earnings of labour is explained by returns to the additional education of workers."[5] Continuing further, he states, "The fact that the return to high school and to higher education has been about as large as the return to conventional forms of capital when all the costs of such education including income foregone by students are allocated to the investment component."[6]

Numerous studies, conducted under varying economic conditions, have shown that persons with more schooling tend to earn more. This is well illustrated in the table 1.1 given above by Miller.[7]

Need for Information

Information is considered to be a basic resource for national development. Organised generation, transfer and use of information is helpful in shaping the socio-economic development of any nation. In the modern context it is evident from experience, study observation and discussion that not only educationists, scientists and technologists but also managers, planners and policy-makers have recognised the necessity of information in the performance of their respective tasks. Decision-makers are realising that information is the basis of gainful decision, governments recognise its importance for bringing about social change.

In order to make this information useful, one has to develop a system of information flow in a society. The right information should be made available to the right person at the right time. Every citizen must have the fundamental right to obtain the information he needs irrespective of his physical, social and economic condition.

What is Information

Now let us understand the term information. The terms data and information are easily understood intuitively, but their precise definition is bedevilled by the problem of distinguishing between the two. Data refers to a string of symbols and is used in the form-oriented sense. On the other hand, information is perhaps more often used in the context-oriented sense. Information is often defined as data useful for decision-making.[8]

Data consist of a set of characters or signals to which a significance can be assigned. Information is processed to make them meaningful.[9]

The data are information when processed i.e. decoded and related to other data. This selected aspect of information has also been emphasized by Schoderbek, "Information concerns selected data – data selected with respect of problem, user, time, place and function. He also emphasizes the role of information as an "evaluated data in a specific situation."[10]

Information plays significant role in improving educational standards and quality of research. Access to precise and reliable information at the right time to the right person in a form most conveniently usable by him, can help to minimise the wastage of resources.

Needs of Educational Information System for India

The preceding section shows the importance of education for human resource development leading to socio-economic development and the crucial role information plays in all areas of human activities. There is no gain-saying the need for information in the field of education particularly in a vast and poor country like India. The human resource development in India is critically dependent upon the right information at the right time. Against this background, the need for an efficient educational information system for India is felt.

This concept of education as a basic input for human resource development is the guiding principle for educational development in the Five Year Plans. This underscores the responsibility of the State to provide educational opportunities to all and to relate education to work and development. There has been a tremendous expansion of educational facilities in the country. The number of institutions has gone up from 1,65,000 to 7,40,000.[11]

With about a hundred million students, three million teachers and more then half-a-million educational institutions, India has one of the largest educational systems in the world. In the management of such a large system, the information plays a very significant role.[12]

The size of the country is big. India consists of diverse peoples speaking different languages in different parts of the country. The Constitution recognised 15 major languages, and there are about a dozen more languages which are spoken by substantial number of people. The product of literature in all these languages has been continuously increasing. The ratio between the titles published in English language and in other Indian regional languages on subjects dealing with development is estimated to be 40:60.[13] This vast information needs to be collected, stored, organised, preserved and served to different groups of people spread all over the country.

India is a federal country with 25 States and 7 Union Territories. The Constitution of India has placed the responsibility of development of 'Libraries' partly with the Centre and partly with the States. It gives the Central Government power to run institutions of National character. But libraries in colleges and schools form part of the responsibility of States and Union Territories. The 42nd amendment to the Constitution transferred 'Education' to the Concurrent List and thus academic libraries have come under the joint responsibility of the Central and State Governments.

Notwithstanding the nearly four decades of planned development, there exist wide inter-regional disparities, a huge backlog of unenrolled children, increasing number of illiterates and a growing number of educated unemployed. The absence of a proper information system to provide access to the data available even within the existing system has also been responsible for this state of affairs. The data base for policy making has been found insufficient; only a limited amount of data is being tabulated and much less utilised by the planners and administrators.

To have rapid economic growth and to place social democracy on sound footings, India requires a well-planned educational system and for such a well-planned and programmed educational system, the planners, administrators, policy-makers, teachers and researchers need right types of information at the right time. To achieve all this, we require a national information system in the field of education.

India has a considerable stock of information resources located at different places and institutions. The resources are often wasted due to inaccessibility, poor organisation and lack of system.

Information has been developing at an exponential rate. The fields of knowledge are expanding. It has been observed that knowledge is doubling itself in a decade. The traditional disciplines are undergoing fragmentation and new disciplines are emerging. On the other hand, the fields of knowledge are increasingly becoming inter-dependent requiring multi-disciplinary approach in education and research.

Explosion of information has created problems regarding the organisation of the materials. Individual libraries cannot cope with this as no library can acquire all the materials it needs for its readers. It is therefore essential that the information generated and stored at various geographical points in the field of education has to be integrated into a network of data bases to form a National Information System for Education in India.

Rationale of the Study

'Education' is multi-disciplinary, incorporating several areas of study like philosophy, psychology, sociology, science, management, development, economics, statistics, etc. Given its broadest interpretation, the information needs of educationist would have to encompass the information needs in almost all areas of study.

In most of the libraries the collection is not comprehensive in the form of subject in the field of education. There is no evidence of a systematic development of collection in the libraries. There seems to be an overemphasis of monographs and journals at the expense of other primary resources like government documents, research reports, theses, seminars/ conference proceedings, Commission /Committees' reports or commentaries thereon etc.

In terms of subject coverage too, there seems to be a predominance of certain areas over others, for example, the coverage on educational psychology and educational sociology tends to dominate over areas like educational planning, educational administration and educational technology.

The reasons for the inadequate collections in the libraries to meet the educational information need are as follow:

Vastness of the Country

India covers an area of 32,87,263 sq. kms. According to the 1991 census the total population was 84,39,30,861. The literacy percentage is 52.11. A number of languages and dialects are spoken in India. For the Seventh

Plan (1985-1990), the Planning Commission has approved an outlay of Rs. 6,383 crore and the outlay for education in 1991-92 is Rs. 1805.30 crore. We had in 1983-84 110 million students, 2.5 million teachers; 7,75,000 primary schools, 50,000 secondary schools, 5,000 colleges and 120 Universities. There is the Central Government and 32 State and Union Territory Governments. There are several national level and state level research and training institutions in the field of education. A large number of educationists are engaged in the non-formal, adult and continuing education. The educationists engaged in vocational/professional and technical education constitute a big number. All these are the end-users of educational information. To take care of this phenomenal demand, a well-knit programme of coordination among the educational information centres and libraries is a must.

Weakness of Educationists as a Pressure Group

Next to defence, education commands the highest allocation in the national budget. It is ironical that while it is now acknowledged that education is crucial to national development and commanding priority, there is no national information system for meeting the requirements of the educationists. A national set-up needs to be established that is characterised by the following:[14]

(i) A positive policy on information collection and dissemination functions in the field of education with clearcut objectives and task requirements;

(ii) A well-developed collection of India resources incorporating all types of materials – printed and non-printed–on all aspects of Indian education;

(iii) A corps of well-qualified librarians, qualified in both education and librarianship with a working knowledge of computer technology; and

(iv) The existence of a data bank with input of local (raw and processed) data. This data bank should have access to the world's data banks of educational information via computer link-ups and should be accessible to all units within the Central and State Departments of education, to educationists, researchers and other agencies involved in educational activities.

The acuity of information need in education in not realised both by the users and the government as much as in other fields such as science and technology because the contribution of education to socio-economic development is being recognised only recently. Further, the users of educational information in India are not articulate in expressing their needs and make do with the available resources unlike the other pressure groups which compel the government to cater to their needs.

Difficulty in Understanding User Needs

This is one problem that is easy to identity but difficult to define. It is easy to see whether or not user needs are effectively met because dissatisfaction can be seen and heard but cannot be accurately measured.

Determining user needs is not an easy task. Several factors must be considered:[15]

(a) Why they need the information;
(b) The type of information they need;
(c) The sources from which they obtain their information;
(d) The methods they use to obtain information;
(e) How useful is the information obtained.

Considering all these aspects user needs can be translated into programmes of action. Resources and services can be planned or developed on the basis of user needs.[16] It requires constant surveying to know the ever changing needs of the users in the field of education, which may not be possible for a single library. It requires the collective effort to know the needs to the users and hence a net-working is the solution.

The Constraints of Library Collections

In library collections the emphasis is on conventional materials like books, monographs, journals, and other printed materials. There is an obvious lack of newer forms of materials.

Educationists find the library collections inadequate, because they do not reflect the teaching and research needs. The collections are not systematically developed but are generally allowed to develop along the lines of 'he who wants to order books can order books'. In most of the libraries, there is no policy governing the ordering of books mainly because ordering of books is undertaken by the interested few. This has led to a few active people constantly ordering books while the apathetic majority of educationist do not express their needs. This is the reason why the collections do not reflect the real 'needs' of educationists. By catering to the 'wants' of the few active educationists, the collection is built upon the basis of perceived needs–the librarian perceives the needs of the few educationists as the needs of all educationists.

The collections do not contain materials which are directly relevant to their teaching and research needs either in form or subject coverage. While most collections are abundant in the secondary sources like monographs and journals, primary sources like government documents, research reports, seminar/conference reports, educational statistics and data, theses and policy statements are not easily available. Since the teaching and research activities undertaken by the educationists are mainly oriented towards the Indian situation, and Indian materials constitute the primary service and hence the need for such sources in the collection is obvious.

The collections are also lacking in variety. There is a tendency for them to be mainly stocked with printed materials at the expense of other materials like films, slides, tape-cassettes, video-cassettes, charts, maps, simulation games and test materials. Educational information that is available in the new media has flooded the foreign markets but is almost non-existent in educational libraries. The information in these formats may not be as good as that in the monographs or journals in quality in content but an exposure to a variety of information resources is itself an educational experience for the educationists.

The collections are considered inaccessible because;

(i) Membership of each library is strictly limited to its institutional members, although permission may be granted to other educationists on the basis of specific requests. In this way, although there are many educational libraries, the educationists cannot get access to most of the collections;

(ii) Inter-library loans, although available, are too slow and expensive to be effective due to the vastness of the country and postal charges. Books borrowed on inter-library loans are not substitute for one's own collection;

(iii) Educational information produced by the government departments, particularly the Ministry of Education and State Governments' departments of education is usually for limited circulation and is therefore not available for public consumption for years. It is mostly in the form of memeographs and is cyclostyled. Some of the documents, especially statistics and primary data take a long time to be published, and are rendered obsolete when obtained. Some materials like theses and seminar reports, commission/committee reports are available only in certain libraries and since membership is the basic requisite for loans, their accessibility is limited to a few; and

(iv) The location of most of the good collections is not advantageous to many educationists. Most libraries are concentrated in Delhi and other capital cities of the States while most of the teachers of the schools, colleges and teacher-training colleges and many of the post-graduate researchers reside outside Delhi and State capitals. Distance, time and money invariably restrict their search for information.

Library Staff

Most of the library staff servicing the needs of educationist are not knowledgeable in the subject area. As a result, the educationists do not have confidence in the information-retrieval skills of the librarians. They may refer to the librarians for advice on library usage but would prefer to retrieve the materials themselves.[17] (Educationists are mainly served either by librarians who do not have qualifications in education or by educationist-Teachers-Incharge in school libraries–who do not have the qualification in librarianship.)

Since it has not been envisaged that libraries would employ staff on the basis of subject specialization, the only alternatives would be on-the-job training or encouraging further studies to enable them to acquire a working knowledge of the subject area of the users.

With areas of studies getting wider even as they get more specialized –librarians cannot keep up with the number of new disciplines that emerge as off-shoots of older disciplines.[18] Employing librarians for every discipline would not only be uneconomical but also absolutely irrational.

This problem is difficult to solve. The solution, at best, can only be through the establishment of a national information system for education. The libraries' staff who are academically competent to acquire other skills, while competent in one, should be given in-service training. Intelligence, alertness, willingness to learn and job commitment may be developed through the in-service training conducted by the system which would turn non-specialist librarians into a corps of librarians who are capable of rendering specialist services. In-service training is the most important factor for librarians to acquire competence in serving the needs or specialists.

Outdated Methods of Retrieval

Libraries serving as information centres cannot afford to be passive in their approach to information retrieval. Judging from their activities, the existing libraries seem to be passive repository libraries rather than action-oriented libraries in that:[19]

(a) they retrieve documents rather than information;
(b) they have restrictive information activities; and
(c) they have no sense of urgency in their retrieval activities.

Apart from an inadequate collection and unsuitably qualified staff, information retrieval in these libraries in hampered by outdated methods of retrieval. Most of the functions in these libraries tend to be operated manually. Lack of mechanized functions tends to burden librarians with tasks that are tedious and time-consuming. Labour-intensive functions like cataloguing, acquisition and circulation should be mechanized to save time and effort–thus leaving librarians free to concentrate on serving educationists. Educationists' need for certain materials (mainly local primary sources)–and facilities (mechanized/computerized searches) must be noted and must be made available to the librarians to comply with. However, as librarians must work within the financial and administrative constraints, not all user needs can be complied with as in the case of computerization of literature search/information retrieval methods. The cost of providing and maintaining computer services is prohibitive even in the developed countries. So priorities would have to be established. Such type of ventures will have to be taken on a cooperative basis.

From the above we find the inadequacy and weakness of the library information resources, facilities and services to educationists. In the light of all these problems, there is only one way and that is, libraries in the field of formal sector or non-formal sector, whether they are in school or in higher education, whether they are serving planners/administrators or researchers, will have to resort to net-working systems to provide the information required by the reader, in the manner in which he wants and at the place where it is required.

Title of the Study

The present study has been entitled as:

"A Comparative Study of National Information Systems in Education in U.K., U.S.A and India with a view to developing a Model for India."

Scope of the Study

The scope of the study has been limited to the following:

(i) To study in brief the existing Educational Systems of U.K. U.S.A. and India. To find out the similar and disimilar points in the three systems of education;
(ii) To study the existing Educational Information System of U.K., U.S.A. and India;
(iii) To examine the ineffectiveness and deficiencies in the Indian Educational Information System vis-a-vis that of U.K. and U.S.A;
(iv) To identity and agency that may function as a focal point both for the national educational information network and as a co-ordinator with international agencies in the field of education;
(v) To establish vertical and horizontal linkages among the sub-systems and between the system and its components;
(vi) To indicate the information services, products and programmes for the system; and
(vii) Evolving a model on the basis of views of potential users, ascertained through a questionnaire and personal interview.

Objectives of the study

The study has been carried out with the following objectives:

(i) To study in brief the existing educational systems of India, U.K. and U.S.A.;
(ii) To study the existing information systems of these three countries in the field of education;
(iii) To make a study of user needs and preferences and on the basis of these to evaluate the effectiveness of the existing information services, programmes and products in India,

keeping in view the availability of such facilities in U.K. and U.S.A.; and

(iv) To evolve a model for the National Information System for Education in India.

Hypotheses

Following are the hypotheses of the study:

(i) The information centres in the field of Education in India are decentralized and scattered;

(ii) These decentralized and scattered educational information centres cannot meet the needs of different categories of users *viz.* planners, administrators, teachers, teacher educators, researchers and librarians/documentalists etc. in the field of education;

(iii) There is a need for National Information System for Education in India;

(iv) The vertical and horizontal coordination among the existing educational information centres, and hence their net-working is possible;

(v) The National Education Information Centres working in the developed and developing countries are useful; and

(vi) An efficient National Information System for Education in India does not exist.

Limitations of the Study

The study has been delimited to the following:

(i) The literature survey is limited to published material only in English language;

(ii) Literature on U.K. and U.S.A. is limited to its availability in Delhi libraries including British Council Library and British High Commission and American Information Centre and U.S. Embassy located in Delhi;

(iii) The questionnaire responses are limited to mail and subsequent reminders. However, in Delhi and ILA and IASLIC Conferences, personal pursuation is used; and

(iv) Personal interviews from experts are limited to those staying only in Delhi.

Selection of U.K. and U.S.A. as Countries of Comparison-Rationale

The reasons for selecting these countries for the present study are as follows:

The Educational Information System of any country depends upon the system of Education of that country. Keeping this in view the selection of United Kingdom and United States of America have been made for developing the proposed model of National Information System in Education for India.

Why is U.K. Selected?

(i) The U.K. is a developed country. In this country education has been given its right place in planning and economic development of the country. India also has to give proper attention to the education policy and the linkage of education to the economic development of the country;

(ii) England has ruled over India for about two hundred years and the development of educational institutions like schools, colleges, universities etc. is on a similar pattern of the educational institutions in U.K. The University Grants Committee of U.K. and the University Grants Commission of India, the All India Councils for the Technical Education, Agricultural Education, Medical Education, Teacher Education and Central Advisory Board for Education (CABE) are developed on a similar pattern of the corresponding institutions of U.K. in the field of education. The educational administration and financing of education are also of similar nature in both the countries;

(iii) In U.K. the Parliament is supreme. The Country has unitary form of Government. The pattern of education is almost similar in Wales, Scotland and Northern Ireland. In India, also, the Parliament is supreme. Though the country does not have the unitary Government in form, it does not have a strictly federal form also. The education is in the concurrent list of the Constitution. The 10+2+3 pattern of education is prevalent in almost all the States and Union Territories. The higher technical and professional education is controlled by the National Bodies which administratively and financially are controlled by the Central Government and thus we also have a similar pattern of educational system all over the country. The 'Central Schools' and 'Navodaya Vidyalayas' spread over the length and breadth of the country have further minimized the differences in the educational pattern of the country; and

(iv) Some of the racial traits of the English people are reflected in their educational system. The English people are conservative by nature, though they are progressive in science. A judicious mixture of the old and new is found in their character.

The English people can never tolerate a total annihilation of their old traditions in order to give place to anything new. The people may accept something new, but they do not do that replacing totally their past traditions.

Individual freedom is another trait of the British character. So, a prominent part has been played by the voluntary (private) agencies in the field of education. The love of religion is another unique feature of the British character. This feature is reflected in the activities of many Religious Bodies which have greatly contributed to the development of education in the land. Consequently, Religion has become an inseparable part of education, though the secular character of education is maintained, at the same time.

In our country also, the traditions, old beliefs about education and the religious base have affected the educational development to a great extent.

The above mentioned factors gave a solid ground to the investigator to make the selection of U.K. for the study of educational information system of U.K. and develop a model for India.

Why is U.S.A. Selected?

The selection of U.S.A. is based on the following reasons:

(i) The country is large in size. This country has an advantage of rich natural resources and is a nation of immigrants. The country has democratic ideals and education is treated as a State subject;

India is also a large country consisting of 25 States and 7 Union Territories. The country is rich in resources and is a land of many religions and languages. Our country also cherishes the ideals of democracy and treats education as a means of achieving the democratic ideals. Though the education is in the concurrent list, it is a State subject for all practical purposes;

(ii) Each State in U.S.A. keeps in mind the needs of the local people and forms its own policy. As a result, the educational expenditure is shared by the local people and the Government. The people of U.S.A. are always forward-looking and they accept readily what is good for the nation. In a democratic country, one should always remember that the nation is more important than an individual. In other words, the existence of an individual is due to the nation. Therefore, the people are democraticized through education. The nature of these problems may be of some interest to an underdeveloped country like India. India needs that her people put the nation before the self and believe in true and real democracy. This can be achieved through education only;

(iii) Americans are the people who, meeting with constant danger and hardships, learned to solve empirically the real-life situations that faced them, and who developed a flexibility and versatility of outlook and an adaptation to constantly changing circumstances that led them increasingly to discard traditional or outmoded behaviour of thought and ways of life;

It has been rightly said that the Americans are engaged in an experiment in universal education which they think is the democratic way of life. The first requirement of American public education is that it must be democratic. Education must develop the child's whole personality–try to fit him adequately to fulfil his role in that democracy. The American people have always thought that it is the duty of a free country to provide every citizen with general education. Education is necessary for turning out good citizens.

This is the attitude which is required to be developed in Indians to give up traditional or out-moded ways of life, behaviour and thought. We also want every Indian to be a good citizen who fulfils his role in the country's democracy; and

(iv) King opines that "Education is for the development of individual qualities, for making first-class citizens who will have splendid careers and will be well adjusted members of the community."[20]

Americans believe in the integrity and worth of the individual and the right of every one to "life, liberty and pursuit of happiness." In U.S.A. education is given, along with training in commercial and industrial subjects, to citizens so that each person may offer his creative cooperation in the progress of the country. America is the country that realised at a very early stage that education is a factor of production and it contributes very significantly towards economic growth.

On the anology of USA, India also is required to pay more attention towards its vocationalization of education. All technical and vocational institutes should have close links with commerce and industry of the country.

The above mentioned reasons justify the investigator to select U.S.A. for the purpose of comparison for this study. The investigator is of the view that study of the educational systems and the educational information systems of U.K. and U.S.A would give a useful and meaningful perspective for developing an educational information system for India.

REFERENCES

1. Schultz, T.W., 1961, Investment in human capital. *American Economic Review,* 51, pp. 1-17
2. OECD, 1966. Policy conference on economic growth and investment on education, Washington, 1961. Paris: OECD, pp. 23-25
3. India, Ministry of Human Resource Development 1987, Annual report 1986-87. New Delhi: Ministry of Human Resource Development, p.1
4. India, Ministry of Human Resource Development, Department of Education 1986, National Policy on Education-1986. New Delhi: Department of Education, p. 3
5. Schultz, T.W., 1961, Investment in Human Capital, *op.cit.*, pp. 1-17
6. *ibid*
7. Miller, Hermein P., 1960, Annual and life time income in relation to education 1939-1959. *American Economic Review,* 50, p. 969. Table 3.7
8. Soergel, Dagobert, 1985, *Organizing Information: Principles of data base and retrieval systems.* New York: Academic Press, p.17
9. Hussain, K.M., 1973, *Development of Information System for Education.* New Jersey: Prentice-Hall, p.81
10. Schoderbek, P.P., ed. 1968, *Management Systems: A Book of Readings.* New York: John Wiley, p. 44
11. India, Ministry of Education and Culture 1984, Report on educational development in India 1981-83. New Delhi: Ministry of Education and Culture, p. 2

12. Kapoor, M.M., 1986, Information system for educational management in India. p. 196. In *Handbook of Libraries, Archives and Information Centres in India* edited by B.M. Gupta and others. New Delhi; Information Industry Publications, vol.3
13. Biswas, Subhash, 1986, South East Asian collections in India-problems and prospects, with emphasis on exchange of publications. pp.179-180 In *Library and Information Science Horizon* edited by B.Guha, New Delhi: Allied
14. Osman, Zaiton Binti, 1983, Library and information needs of and services to Malaysian educationists, pp.450-462 In *Library in the Information Revolution: Proceedings of the Sixth Congress of South East Asian Librarians*, 30 May-3 June 1983, Singapore: Maruzen Asia
15. Weisman, Herman M., 1972, *Information Systems, Services and Centres.* New York: Becher and Hayes, pp.35-37
16. Adam, Ralph, 1975, Meeting the information needs of social scientists. *Information Scientists*, 9 (4), pp. 141-148
17. Hanson, C.W., 1964, Research on users' needs: where is it getting us? *ASLIB Proceedings,* 16(2), pp.64-78
18. Menzel, Herbert, 1964, Information needs of current scientific research. *Library Quarterly*, 34 (1), pp. 4-19
19. Osman, Zaiton Binti, 1983, Library and information needs. – *op. cit*
20. King, Edmund J., 1963, *Other Schools and Ours*. New York: Holt, Rinehart and Winston, p. 3

2

EDUCATIONAL SYSTEMS

U.K. EDUCATIONAL SYSTEM

(Objectives:– An overview of the salient features of the educational systems of U.K., U.S.A. and India are depicted in this chapter with a view to having a proper perspective of the issues involved in devising a national educational information system. The present chapter is divided into three parts: the first part dealing with the educational system of U.K. and the next two parts with the educational systems of U.S.A. and India respectively).

Britain comprises Great Britain (England, Wales and Scotland) and Northern Ireland and is one of the 12 member States of the European Community. Its full name is the United Kingdom of Great Britain and Northern Ireland.[1]

Physical Features

Area

Britain constitutes the greater part of the British Isles, a geographical term for a group of Islands lying near the North-Western cost of mainland Europe. Britain's area is some 2,44,100 sq. kms of which nearly 99 per cent is land and the remainder inland water. It is 1000 kms from the south coast to the extreme north of Scotland and just under 500 kms across in the widest part. There are numerous bays and in-lets and no place in Britain is more than 120 km away from tidal water. The prime Meridian of 0^0 passes through Greeenwich (London).

Climate

Britain has a generally mild and temperate climate. The prevalent winds are south-westerly and the day-to-day weather is mainly influenced by depressions moving eastwards across the Atlantic. The weather is subject to frequent changes but it is rarely above 32 0° or below 10 0° C. The average annual rainfall is more than 1,600 mm in the mountainous areas of the west and north but less than 800 mm over central and eastern parts. Rain is fairly well distributed throughout the year, but, on average, March to June are the driest months and September to January the wettest. [2]

Demographic Aspects

The total population (usually resident at the Census of 1981) of the country was 53,556,911 out of which Males were 26,053,190 and Females were 27,503,721.[3] For every 1,000 Males, there are 1,055 Females. The birth rate was 1.8 per cent in 1985 and death rete was 1.2 per cent. [4] The expectation of life for a man is about 70 years and for a women 76 years.[5]

Encyclopaedia Britannica, Book of the Year 1988 gives the following data on demographic aspects :-

Population (1987): 56,878,000
Density (1987): persons per sq. km. 233.0
Urban-rural (1985): Urban 91.5 per cent rural 8.5 per cent
Six Distribution (1987): Males 48.7 per cent Females 51.3per cent[6]

Constitution

The Constitution of United Kingdom, unlike that of most other countries, is not contained in any single document, formed partly by Statute, partly by common law, partly convention, it can be altered by Act of Parliament, or by general agreement to create, vary or abolish a convention. The Constitution thus adapts readily to changing political conditions and ideas.

The organs of Government are clearly distinguishable although their functions often intermingle and overlap. The Legislature, Parliament is the supreme authority. The Executive consists of: (1) the Government–Cabinet and other Ministers who are responsible for initiating and directing National Policy; (2) Government Departments, which are responsible for National Administration; (3) Local Authorities, which administer and manage many local services; and (4) Public Corporations responsible for operating particular nationalized industries or, for example, a social and cultural service, subject to ministerial control in varying degrees. The Judiciary determines common law and interprets Statutes, and is independent of both the Legislature and the Executive.

Monarchy

The monarchy is the most ancient secular institution in the United Kingdom. The British people look to the Queen not only as their Head of State, but also as the symbol of their Nation's unity. Despite interruption in the direct line of succession, the hereditary principle upon which it was founded has always been preserved.[7]

The Queen personifies the State. In law, she is Head of the Executive, an integral part of the Legislature, and Head of the Judiciary, the Commander-in-Chief of all armed forces of the Crown and the Supreme Governor of the established Church of England. As a result of a long process of evaluation, the monarchy's absolute power has been progressively reduced. The Queen acts on the advice of Her Prime Minister, which She cannot ignore. The United Kingdom is governed by Her Majesty's Government in the name of the Queen.[8]

Thus we can say that in Britain, there is parliamentary form of government with limited Monarchy as Head of the State.

Parliament

Parliament is the supreme legislative authority. Its three elements, the Queen, the House of Lords and the elected House of Commons, are outwordly separate, as they are constituted on different principles. But then, Parliament usually requires the concurrence of all its parts.[9]

The Polity

Britishers have many a contradiction in their behaviour. It is believed that Britishers are conservative as they take quite some time to accept a change. They are in fact proud of bold ventures and are not afraid of experimental uncertainty. Their emphasis is to go forward even when the path is not so smooth. It is perhaps why their revolution has brought more changes than most of the revolutions of the world.

Class distinctions are strong and suitably graded from the highest to the lowest yet money and family prestige alone do not buy other people's respect and compliance in Britain.[10]

The way of life of the people of Britain has been changing rapidly from the second half of the twentieth century. As in many other countries underlying causes include a lower birth rate, longer expectation of life, a higher divorce rate, widening educational opportunities, technical progress and higher standard of living.[11]

Every one in Britain has the right of religious freedom (in teaching, worship and observance) without interference from the Community or the State. Churches and religious societies may own property, conduct schools, and propagate their beliefs in speech and writing. There is no religious or denominational bar to the holding of public office.[12]

Britain has a long tradition of religious tolerance, a feature which has been much in evidence with the acceptance of a wide variety of religious beliefs and traditions brought in by substantial numbers of immigrants of different nationalities. There are now large and growing communities of Muslims, Hindus and Sikhs, and arrangements have been made in places of work to allow the members of non-Christian religions to follow their religious observance.[13]

Economy

Britain has an open economy, in which international trade is vital part of economic performance. In 1985, exports of goods and services accounted for about one-third of its Gross Domestic Product (GDP). In 1985, GDP at current factor cost totalled £ 304,400 million while National Income (NNP) was £ 264,019 million and per capita income in 1984 was £ 4614.[14]

The economy is primarily based on private enterprise, and government policy is aimed at encouraging the private sector, which accounts for three-quarters of GDP and a similar proportion employment. The underlying rate of growth has been some 3.0 per cent a year.[15]

Britain has an employed labour force of some 24 million. Percentage of employees in (June 1985) agriculture, forestry and fishing 1.6; energy and water supply 2.8; manufacturing 25.8; construction 4.5 and service industries 65.3.[16]

U.K. Education System: Objectives

The decentralized character of the educational system and the long tradition of non-interference by Central Government in most aspects of education is the hallmark of a passive role of Government in the British Education System. One of the recent detailed statements appeared in a government consultative document issued by the Secretary of State for Education and Science in 1977 which tentatively proposed the following aims for schools: [17]

(i) To help children develop lively, enquiring minds, giving them the ability to question and to argue rationally, and to apply themselves to tasks;
(ii) To instill respect for moral values for other people and for oneself, and tolerance of other races, religions and ways of life;
(iii) To help children understand the world in which we live, and the interdependence of nations;
(iv) To help children to use language effectively and imaginatively in reading, writing, and speaking;
(v) To help children to appreciate how the nation earns and maintains its standard of living and properly to esteem the essential role of industry and commerce in this process;
(vi) To provide a basis of mathematical, scientific, and technical knowledge, enabling boys and girls to learn the essential skills needed in a fast-changing world of work;
(vii) To teach children about human achievement and aspirations in the arts and sciences, in religion, and in the search for a more just social order; and
(viii) To encourage and foster the development of children whose social or environmental disadvantages cripple their capacity to learn, if necessary by making additional resources available to them.

The higher education system is seen by government as having a triple role of developing knowledge, applying it to contemporary problems, and training highly skilled human resources; recently a fourth role, that of providing for updating of knowledge for adults in science, technology, and business subjects, has been given prominence.

Educational Administration

Despite the rapidly growing importance of education and training in people's lives, the UK does not have a single body responsible for the education system– it has many systems funded by many different bodies in different places, and doing different things in different ways for different reasons.

This decentralization which characterizes education policy begins at the Central Government level where each part of the UK has a separate body responsible for most of its education policy. In England this is Department of Education and Science (DES), in Wales the Welsh Office (Education Department) in Scotland the Scottish Education Department (SED) and in Northern Ireland the Department of Education for Northern Ireland (DEN). Although these bodies are important, they are not the sole controllers of education in their areasbodies actually responsible for providing schools, colleges and courses are Local Education Authorities (LEAs) and, in Northern Ireland only, Education and Library Boards. This partnership between Central Government and local authorities has been a feature of UK education since public education provision began in 1870.

Such an arrangement, described by the DES as a national system, locally administered, is intended to give a coherent overall national system which is also responsive and flexible enough to meet specific local needs.[18]

It was only in 1870 that, for the first time, the community began to take a much more direct part in the education of its children, Forester's Act in that year created 'School Boards' (elected for the purpose) and these remained in existence until 1902, when the Local Education Authorities (LEAs), large and small came into being.[19]

The 1944 Act strengthened the central authority by replacing the Old Board, with its vague superintendent role by a new Ministry of Education charged with the duty of promoting the education of the people and of controlling and directing the Local Authorities to that end.

Education Act 1944

Section 1 of the Education Act 1944 provides as follows:

"It shall be the duty to the Secretary of State for Education and Science to promote the education of the people of England and Wales and the progressive development of Institutions devoted to that purpose, and to secure the effective execution by local authorities under his control and comprehensive educational service in every area." While the part II of the Act, is concerned with the statutory system of education, the first part (Section 6.2) deals with the local administration.

The local administration of the statutory system of public education provides that:

(i) "Every local education authority shall, in accordance with arrangements approved by the Secretary of State, establish such education committees as they think it expedient to establish for the efficient discharge of their functions with respect to education; and

(ii) Every local education committee of a local education authority shall include persons of experience in education and persons acquainted with the educational conditions prevailing in the area for which the Committee acts."

The authority of educational administration clearly establishes the central and local areas of the system and the interdependence of the two, although the position of Central Government as the senior partner is implied by the duty imposed on the Secretary of State to secure action by Local Authorities, and by the unequivocal responsibility to promote the education of the people.

(iii) The third statutory element of educational administration is the Chief Education Officer. Section 88 of the 1944 Education Act laid upon a Local Education Authority the duty of appointing a fit person to be the Chief Education Officer. This duty was retained by specific provision under the Local Government Act 1972.[20]

The Department of Education and Science (DES)

Its direct line of descent is the Committee or Council for Education 1839-56, the Education Department 1856-1900, the Board of Education 1900-44 and the Ministry of Education 1944-64.

Powers and responsibilities of DES were considerably increased by the 1944 Act which emphasised the mandatory duties (rather than permissive powers) of the Local Education Authorities.

(i) Under Section 99 of the Act, the Minister has the right to declare any local authority in default of its obligations, to issue appropriate directions and to enforce them, if necessary, by legal action;

(ii) Under the Section 68 of the Act, the Minister was given the power to decide that a local education authority is acting unreasonably, or proposes to do so;

(iii) Under Section 13 of the Act (as amended) the Minister has the negative power of approving or disapproving the opening, closure or transposition of individual schools;

(iv) Under Sections 100 and 111 of the Act, which authorise the Central authority to classify its broad legislative provisions by means of issuing standing rules and orders, the Minister has the power to control by regulation; and

(v) Traditionally the Central authority has wielded power through the process, facilitated by the local authorities' heavy dependence upon Central financial support.

The Head of DES of the Secretary of State of Education and Science (who is member of the Central Government responsible for education).

The Local Education Authority (LEA)

There are at present 104 LEAs in England and Wales. The main grouping are:

(i) London (21)
(ii) Metropolitan Districts (36)
(iii) Shire Counties (47). (In England 39 LEAs and in Wales 8 LEAs).[21]

The Education Committee

Members of an Education Committee are mainly of two kinds. A majority must be drawn from the elected members of the Council itself and they are normally chosen to reflect in the Committee the balance of party political interest in the Council itself. The other main body of members are those who are co-opted from outside the ranks of Councillors. These are to be persons of experience in education and persons acquainted with the educational conditions prevailing in the area for which the Committee acts.

An Education Committee wili appoint sub-committees to conduct much of the business (*e.g.* Primary Sub-Committees, Secondary Sub-Committee, Further Education Sub-Committee, Sites and Building Sub-Committee etc.). A total of five or six Sub-Committees is common.

The Chief Education Officer

Section 88 of the 1944 Education Act required each LEA to appoint 'a fit person' to be its Chief Education Officer. There are at present 104 Chief Education Officer in England and Wales, of whom 103 are men and only one is a woman. Some broad generalisations about the work of a Chief Education Officer can be:

(i) First and foremost he is the principal educational adviser to the Council as local educational authority; and
(ii) The second broad area of work lies in implementing with care and accuracy the decisions and policies of the authority as expressed in meetings of the Council and Education Committee.[22]

He is, generally, a person with an arts degree who is trained as a teacher and taught full-time for five or six years, nearly always in a secondary school.[23]

Education Department

Each LEA has a Central Education Department under the direction of the Chief Education Officer.

Financing of Education

Local education authorities are directly responsible for the funding of most non-advanced further education courses. In order, however, to make training and vocational education more relevant to employment needs, responsibility for a quarter of the budget spent in England and Wales on work-related curses has been placed with the Manpower Service Commission.

An education support grant scheme introduced in England and Wales in 1985 enables the government to support local authority expenditure on educational activities of national priority, such as improving the school curriculum, methods of assessment, records of achievement and school management. In 1986-87 it is intended to provide £28 million out of total expenditure of £40 million on 16 such projects

Support for the universities and certain other higher education institutions, and grants to students, account for most of the direct expenditure by Central Government. About 80 per cent of universities' income comes from public funds, the major part being recurrent grant paid by the Government of the University Grants Committee, which allocates the funds to individual universities and certain other institutions. (However, the independent University of Buckingham receives no assistance from public funds although its students can apply for mandatory grants).

Funds for advanced courses in polytechnics and other colleges of further education maintained by local authorities are allocated centrally. The National Advisory Body for Public Sector Higher Education advises the government on how these resources should be allocated in England. The Wales Advisory Body has a similar function. There is no equivalent organisation in Scotland but the Scottish Territory Education Advisory Council has general advisory functions.

Many universities, polytechnics and other higher education institutions undertake training, research and consultancy for commercial firms and get funds from these sources. A number of institutions have endowments and receive grants, gifts from foundations and benefactors. Local education authorities are empowered to sell goods and services arising as by-products of educational activities through their further education institutions.[25]

The proportion of the gross national product devoted to education reached a postwar peak of 6.2 per cent in 1974-75. It had dropped to 5.4 per cent by 1977-78; at this time, education expenditure was approximately 13 per cent of total public expenditure and it remained at about this level until 1980-81.[26]

(*Note*:- No estimates of the proportion of private resources devoted to education are available).

In 1984-85 public expenditure on education in England, and on Universities in Great Britain, was about £13,411 million, compared with £12,920 million in 1983-84. Table 2.1 sets out the main heads of expenditure for these years in cash.

Planned spending education in 1986-87 is some £17,500 million, about 10 per cent of public expenditure. More than four-fifths of this expenditure is incurred by local authorities, which plan their spending according to local needs and circumstances.[28]

General Structure

The basis of modern education was laid down in the Act of Parliament 1944 which is a land mark in the educational history of the nation. Every

TABLE 2.1: Public Expenditure on Education and Related Services within the Area of Responsibility of the Secretary of State for Education and Science

£ million (cash)[27]

	1983-84 Current	out-turn Capital	Total	1984-85 Current	Provisional Capital	Out-turn Total
Schools (England)						
Under-Fives	296			310		
Primary	2,416			2,531		
Secondary	3,735			3,912		
Others	821			868		
Total Schools	7,268	322	7,590	7,621	299	7,920
Post-school						
Further education (England)	1754	120	1874	1829	111	1940
Universities (Great Britain) including student support	2176	118	2294	2226	121	2347
Total Post	3930	238	4168	4055	232	4287
Other Expenditure (England)						
Other educational services	711	25	736	745	34	779
Schools meals and milk	426	–	426	425	–	425
GRAND TOTAL	12,335	585	12,920	12,846	565	13,411

child in UK is to be provided facilities for education, irrespective of his social and financial position, the education suited to his abilities and aptitudes. There are three stages of education: (i) Primary; (ii) Secondary; and (iii) Further Education.[29]

Primary Education

Primary education is divided into three stages:

(i) nursery school and Kindergarten upto 5 years

(ii) infant school - 5 to 7 years

(iii) Junior School 7 to 11 years. The term "elementary" has disappeared.

Nursery Schools

The 1944 Act did not make education in a nursery school or class compulsory, but it did lay upon the Local Education Authority a duty to have regard to the need for securing that provision for pupils who have not attained the age of five years by the provision of nursery schools, or alternatively of nursery classes attached to infant schools. [30]

EDUCATION ACCORDING TO AGE

PRIMARY	Nursery Schools (2–5) or Nursery Classes (3–5)		
	Infant Schools (5–7) and Junior Schools (7–11)	*or* Primary Schools (5–11)	
SECONDARY	Grammar Schools (11-19) *or* Technical Schools (11-19) *or* Modern Schools (11-17)	*or* Comprehensive Schools (11-19)	*or* High Schools (11–14) (*or* 11–16) and Upper Schools (14–19) *or* Colleges (16–19)
FURTHER	Technical Colleges - National - Regional - Area - Local Colleges of Commerce Art Schools and Colleges Agricultural Institutes and Colleges	15-16 and upwards	
EDUCAT	Teacher's Training Colleges Colleges of Advanced Technology Universities	18 and upwards	
ION	Adult Education, including Evening Institutes, Workers' Educational Association classes, University Extension and Extra-Mural courses.		

Source: Pedley, F.H. *Educational System in England and Wales.* Oxford, Pergaman Press, 1964. p.2

Nursery schools are provided for children between the ages of two and five; nursery classes for children between three and five. There are usually a head teacher and three nursery assistants in a school for forty children. In England, 43 per cent and in Scotland 36 per cent of three and four year olds receive education in nursery schools or classes or in infants' classes in primary schools. In addition, many children (at least 40 per cent of three and four year olds) attend informal pre-school play groups organised by parents and voluntry bodies such as the Pre-school Play Groups Association.[31]

The Plowden Report on Children and their Primary Schools (1967) made the recommendation that the immediate expansion of nursery education is necessary "so that all the three to five-year old group could attend on a half-time basis, whilst some 15 per cent could attend full-time where the need was demonstrated".[32]

In 1984-85 there were 561 schools and 50,000 pupils in the maintained schools relating to public sector in England.[33]

Infant Schools

These schools admit children at about the age of five and keep them until the end of the school year in which they reach the age of seven. But by no means all children are educated in separate infant schools. The infant education forms a part of the pre-primary education.

With a few exceptions, infant schools are independent units with independent staff and building. At times, infant school is a part of a Junior School. Almost 100 per cent of infant school teachers are females. All infant schools with the exception of one per cent are co-educational. Numbers with such schools vary greatly depending upon the demands of the catchment area. The infant school has a reception class which provides an adjustment of settling-in period to school. It may then have several more classes depending on its size. The structure of these classes varies greatly from school to school.[34]

Junior Schools

Junior schools are of relatively recent growth. They appeared for the first time between the two World Wars as a result of the creation of separate senior schools, following the recommendations contained in the Hadow Report of 1926.

The considerably significant part of primary education between the ages of 7 and 11 years is handled in junior schools.

Almost all of them are co-educational and law of the land demands compulsory education of the children of this age group. The education at this level is quite well-planned and is technically quite in accordance with the latest techniques of teaching and learning. The junior school is characterised by an atmosphere in which experiment and inquiry beyond the bounds of conventional subjects is encouraged. Many new ideas in subject teaching are being introduced into the curriculum. The curriculum includes language development, science, mathematics and environmental studies. The provision for teaching English to immigrants is also there. The number of students in each class is about 40.[35]

Junior schools are usually exciting, pulsating with the thrill of discovery and the pleasure which children derive from being completely involved in their work. There is encouragement of creative activity in all its forms. New methods are encouraging children to discover the relationship between numbers rather than to learn to calculate by rote. Experiments are going on in the teaching of modern languages at the junior stage.

Secondary Education

The system of secondary education which had taken shape from the 1944 Education Act was strongly influenced by the recommendation of the preceding White Paper which envisaged that there would be three main types of secondary schools to be known as 'grammar', 'modern' and 'technical' schools.

Until the early sixties, the great majority of secondary schools maintained by local education authorities were of these three types. Entry to the different types generally depended on the results of tests taken at about the age 11. But the new government which took office in 1974, however, announced its intention of developing a fully comprehensive system of secondary education in the maintained as well as the assisted schools and of ending selection according to ability for different types of secondary school at the age of 11 or at any other stage.[36]

About 90 per cent of the maintained secondary school population in England and Wales attend comprehensive schools, which take pupils without reference to ability or aptitude and provide a wide range of secondary education for all or most of the children of a district. The schools can be organised in a number of ways including those that take the full secondary school age-range from 11 to 18; middle schools whose pupils move on to senior comprehensive schools at 12, 13 or 14, leaving at 16 or 18; and schools with an age-range of 11 or 12 to 16 combined with a six-form or a tertiary college for pupils over 16. Tertiary colleges provide a full range of vocational courses for students over 16, as well as academic courses. Most other children, still, receive secondary education in 'grammar' or 'secondary modern' schools.

Scottish secondary education is almost completely non-selective and the majority of schools are six-year comprehensive. Because of local circumstances there are some comprehensive schools at which courses may last only four years or less; pupils may transfer at the end of their second or fourth year to a six-year comprehensive.

In Northern Ireland secondary education is organised largely along selective lines, based on a system of testing. There are, however, certain areas where secondary schools operate on non-selective basis.[37]

Independent Schools

Independent schools are outside the publicly maintained sector, but they must register with the appropriate education department and are open to inspection. There are about 2,500 independent schools educating 550,000 pupils of all ages. They charge fees, varying from about £ 100 a term for day pupils at nursery age to £ 2,000 a term for senior boarding pupils. Many offer bursaries to help pupils from less well-off families. Such pupils may also be helped by local education authorities, which give assistance according to parental income (over 230 schools participate in the scheme). The government also gives income-related help.

A number of independent schools have also been established by religious and ethnic minorities. The normal age range is from seven-plus to 11, 12 or 13 but many of the schools now have pre-preparatory departments for younger children.

Independent Schools for older pupils-from 11, 12 or 13 to 18 or 19—include about 500 which are sometimes referred to as 'public schools'. They should not be confused with the state-supported public schools in Scotland.[38]

Further Education : A Post-School Education

Vocational Education

Children over the age (16) of compulsory school attendance may continue in the same school in what is known as the "Sixth Form", usually for two further years, or they may transfer to a separate institution such as sixth-form college (catering mainly for full time 16 to 18 year-olds), tertiary colleges, college of further education or technical college. These three are essentially similar and cater to all ages over 16, and offer a wide range of vocational and academic courses, full time and part time.[39]

Every local education authority (LEA) has one or several further education (FE) colleges. They provide the biggest single part of post-school education and training. These courses include General Certificate of Education (GCE) and Vocational Courses for the 16 to 19 year old. In some areas all the education for this group is provided by FE Colleges when they are called tertiary colleges. They also provide a large amount of vocational training in conjunction with local industry.[40]

A group of courses called 'Vocational Preparation Courses' for young people who want to improve their general education without taking traditional academic courses are usually one or two years full-time at college or school. Bodies offering qualifications or curricula for vocational courses include City and Guilds, Royal Society of Arts, Certificate in Further Education and the Scottish Certificate in Vocational Studies.[41]

A growing recognition of the need to equip pupils of all abilities with the skills needed by modern commerce and industry led the Government to launch the Technical and Vocational Education initiative in England and Wales in 1983 and in Scotland in 1984. The scheme, consisting of a series of pilot projects devised and managed by local education authorities, is funded and administered by the Manpower Services Commission.[42]

Education for those who have left school can be divided into two categories: non-advanced further education (NAFE) which consists of courses provided upto the standard of the General Certificate of Education (GCE) at Advanced (A) level and higher education. Post-school education is provided at universities, polytechnics, the Scottish Central Institutions and other publicly maintained or assisted colleges. The latter have a variety of titles including colleges of higher or further education, colleges of technology, colleges of art, agricultural colleges and adult education centres. Many education and training schemes are run by public or private organisations, or firms. A first degree in the United Kingdom usually requires three years of full time study but some courses require four years or more.[43] More than a third of young people receive some form of post-school education.

The term 'further education' is generally used to define all post-school education other than higher education, and comprises non-advanced courses (of A-level standard or below). Non-advanced and some advanced courses are provided by 740 colleges of further education, almost all of them controlled by local education authorities. Non-advanced courses are also provided by adult education centres. Much of the provision outside the universities is broadly vocational in purpose. A large proportion of students of non-advanced courses attend part-time, either by day release or block release from employment or during the evenings.

Polytechnics and other Institutions

A major contribution to post-school education in England and Wales is made by the 30 polytechnics which have been established since 1967. They provide courses in a wide range of subject at all levels, though the trend is towards a concentration on advanced work-courses. Polytechnics have close links with commerce and industry. Similar provision is made in Scotland in the 16 central institution and a number of further education colleges, and in Northern Ireland by the University of Ulster.

Universities

There are now 46 universities in Britain, including the Open University, compared with 17 in 1945. They are governed by royal charters or in some cases by Act of Parliament, and enjoy complete academic freedom, appointing their own staff and deciding which students to admit, what and how to teach and which degree to award. Admission to universities is by examination or selection. Of the 2,92,000 full-time university students in 1984-85 (excluding those at the Open University and the University of Buckingham) about 47,500 were post-graduate. There are some 30,000 full-time university teachers paid wholly from universities' funds. The ratio of staff to students is about one to ten, one of the most favourable in the world.

Except at the Open University, first degree courses are mainly full-time and usually last three or four years. Medical and Veterinary courses usually require five or six years. Degree titles vary according to the practice of each university. In England, Wales and Northern Ireland the most common titles for a first degree are Bachelor of Arts (B.A.) or Bachelor of Science (B.Sc.) and for a second degree Master of Arts (M.A.), Master of Science (M.Sc.) and Doctor of Philosophy (Ph.D). In Scotland Master is used for a first degree in arts subjects.

Research is an important feature of university work; many staff combine research with their teaching duties and about half of post-graduate students are engaged on research projects.[44]

Teacher Education

All entrants to teaching in England and Wales must have taken a recognised course of teacher training. Courses are offered by institutes of higher education, mostly universities, many polytechnics and by certain other colleges. Non-graduates usually qualify by way of three or four-year courses leading to the Bachelor of Education (B.Ed) degree: graduates take a one-year Post-graduate Certificate of Education.

In Scotland all teachers in education authority schools must be registered with the General Teaching Council for Scotland. It is Government policy that all entrants to the teaching profession in Scotland should be graduates. Now, primary teachers qualify either through a four-year B.Ed course or a one-year post-graduate course of teacher training at a college of education. Teachers of academic subjects at secondary schools must hold a degree containing two passes in the subject which they wish to teach. In certain non-academic subjects, a relevant specialist diploma has been acceptable in place of a degree, but this provision is being phased out.

In Northern Ireland teacher training is provided by the two universities and the two colleges of education. The principle courses are B.Ed. (three or four-year honours), B.A. and B.Sc. with education (three-four or five years) and the one-year Certificate of Education for graduates.

The Government is taking steps to improve the quality of teaching by revising selection, training and placement procedures for new teachers, and by providing more in-service training opportunities.

Measures taken to strengthen initial teacher training in England and Wales have included the establishment of a Council for the Accreditation of Teacher Education to review all existing courses and to issue new criteria against which courses can be assessed. The Education Bill gives the Government powers to require local education authorities to appraise the performance of teachers. In Scotland post-graduate courses are being revised. All new pre-service and major in-service courses provided by colleges of education must be approved both by the Scottish Education Department and a validating body.

Non-Formal and Adult Education

It is becoming increasingly recognised that education is a process which continues throughout adult life. The scope of adult and continuing education has widened in recent years and now includes in addition to the development of the individual through cultural, physical and craft pursuits, such subjects as basic education (in literacy and numeracy), consumer education, and health education. Continuing education also includes training for those in employment to enable them to keep pace with technological changes. In 1982 government launched a professional, industrial and commercial updating programme (PICUP), designed to help colleges, polytechnics and universities to meet the need to update and broaden the skills of those in mid-career in industry, commerce and the professions.[45]

Courses of adult and continuing education are provided by LEAs, the extramural departments of universities, and certain other bodies such as the Workers' Educational Association. Most of the courses are part-time (day or evening), but a few are for short residential periods, and a very few are in publicly financed long-term residential colleges. A wide range of subject is on offer, from basic education (such as literacy) and examination courses in academic or vocational subjects to education in artistic or cultural pursuits. Fees are charged and are often expected to cover the full cost of the course.[46]

The Open University

In 1986 some 1,40,000 students were following Open University courses, more than half at degree level. The Open University is a non-residential university which provides part-time degree and other courses, using mainly a combination of correspondence courses, television and radio broadcasts, and summer schools, together with a network of study centres for contact with part-time tutors and counsellors and with fellow students. The standards of the university's degrees are the same as those of other universities. Its first degree, for which courses began in 1971, is the B.A.(Open). The University also has a programme of higher degrees, B.Phil. M.Phil and Ph.D. available through research, and M.A. and M.Sc. through taught courses. A continuing Education Programme, including short courses of community education, in service training for teachers and other staff and up-dating courses for managers, scientists and technologists, is the fastest growing aspect of the university's work.[47]

Special Education

Special education needs emanate from learning difficulties arising from emotional or behavioural disorders as well as physical or mental handicaps. Education Act of 1981 states that a child is in need of special education "if he has a learning difficulty which calls for special education provision to be made for him".[48]

Before the 1981 Act, two per cent of all children were singled out as in need of special education, which usually meant they went to a special school. Special schools cater for children with physical, mental or emotional disabilities or a combination of all these. Some special schools are day schools, others are boarder schools and some have a mixture of the two. They may be run by a local education authority or by a voluntary organisation such as the Spastic Society or the Royal National Institute for the Blind (RNIB). A few are independent (i.e. private) schools. However, Warneck recommended that most children with special educational needs should go to ordinary schools.[49]

Now local education authorities in England and Wales must ensure that children with special needs are educated in ordinary schools provided that the parents' wishes have been taken into consideration and that this is compatible with meeting the needs of the child, with the provision of efficient education for the other children in the school, and with the best use of resources.

In Scotland, school placing is a matter of agreement between education authorities and individual parents, with the exception of mentally handicapped children. Children with special educational needs in Northern Ireland are provided for in the same way as in England and Wales.

There are almost 2,000 special schools (both day and boarding), including those run by voluntary organisations, which cater to a wide variety of handicaps.[50]

Examination And Awards

At present the principal examination taken by secondary school pupils in England, Wales and Northern Ireland at the age of 16 and over are those leading to the General Certificate of Education (GCE) at Ordinary (O) level and to the Certificate of Secondary Education (CSE). Both are normally taken after five years of secondary education. The GCE Advanced (A) level is normally taken after a further two years' study. The highest grade (grade 1) in the CSE is accepted as equivalent to the standard of a higher grade pass (grades A to C) at GCEO – level, and these are the qualifying grades for entry to further education and training. The A-level examination is the standard for entrance to university and other higher education, and to many forms of professional training.

In order to improve examination courses and raise standards of performance, the Government decided to replace GCEO-level and CSE examination by a single qualification, the General Certificate of Secondary Education (GCSE): two-year courses leading to the new qualification were introduced in England, Wales and Northern Ireland in the autumn of 1986.

The Certificate of Pre-Vocational Education, a new qualification awarded for the first time in 1986, is intended for those at school or college who wish to continue in full-time education for a year after the age of 16 to prepare either or work of vocational courses.

The public examination system in Scotland is different from that in other parts of Britain. Scottish pupils take the Scottish Certificate of Education at ordinary grade at the end of their fourth year of secondary education. Pupils in the fifth and sixth years sit for the SCE Higher grade, and passes at this grade are the basis for entry to university, college of education or professional training.[51]

The system of examination in further and higher education is complex but it provides for a variety of modes and levels of study.[52]

In England, GCE examinations are organised by independent examining boards, most of them connected with a university, and the CSE examinations are controlled by regional examination boards.

An increasing proportion of students on advanced courses in Great Britain outside the universities are taking courses leading to the qualifications of the Council for National Academic Awards (CNAA). The Council awards degree and other academic qualifications are comparable in standard with those granted by the universities. Other examining bodies may include the Business and Technician Education Council (BTEC) which plans and administers courses for students in industry commerce and public administration in England, Wales and Northern Ireland. Courses leading to BTEC awards are available at polytechnics, colleges of further and higher education, and in some schools. The Scottish equivalent of the Council is the Scottish Vocational Qualifications Council.

Educational Research

Educational research in the United Kingdom originated about a century ago, when some universities established chairs of education, the occupants of which emphasised the need for the systematic study of education and for a scientific approach to such study. Early work was focussed on psyhology, history, and comparative studies. Between 1900 and 1945, the effort devoted to educational research in the United Kingdom was small. Nevertheless, research in such areas as mental testing and child development had important influences on educational practice.

In 1947 National Foundation for Educational Research was established with financial assistance from Local Education Authorities. With the establishment of this foundation, educational research received the impetus.

Educational research has drawn on psychology, philosophy, history and sciology, among other disciplines, in its development. The Register of Educational Research in the United Kingdom lists research projects being undertaken in more than some 250 bodies.[53]

The Department of Education and Science is the single largest source of funding for the educational research. The main areas of research projects are: Pre-school; pupil performance, children with special needs (including learning difficulties, the handicapped, and ethnic minorities); the transition from school to work; the curriculum, teacher training; and management in education and further and higher education.

U.S.A. EDUCATIONAL SYSTEM

The foremost nation in the Western Hemisphere in population and economic development, the United States of America is a Federal Republic comprising 50 States. It is often referred to simply as the United States and, colloquially, as America. The 48 contiguous States occupy the central one-third of the North American continent, bounded on the West by the Pacific Ocean, on the north by Canada, on the east by the Atlantic Ocean, on the South by Mexico and arms of the Atlantic Pacific. The newest States, Alaska and Hawaii, lie at the North-Western extremity of the continent and in the mid-Pacific, respectively.[54]

Physical Features

Area

A nation of 9,529,063 sq. km., it encompasses several outlying territories (Puerto Rico and the Virgin Islands, Hawaii and the Pacific Islands, and Alaska) but is for the most part a compact territory extending about 3865 km. from the Atlantic to the Pacific Oceans, and 2576 km. from Canada in the north to Mexico in the South.[55]

Climate

The conterminous United States lies entirely between the Tropic of Cancer and 50^0N latitude a position that confines Arctic Climates to the high mountain tops and genuine tropics to a small part of the Southern Florida.

The climate varies with latitude, distance from the sea and the effect of relief, ranging from polar conditions in North Alaska through cool to warm temperate climates further South. In Mountain States it is very cold in the north in winter, with considerable snow fall. In the south, such higher temperatures and aridity produce desert conditions. Rainfall every where is very variable as a result of rain-shadow influences. In High Plains a continental climate with a large annual range of temperature and moderate rainfall, mainly in summer, although unreliable. Duststorms are common in summer and blizzards in winter. In Central Plains a temperate continental climate, with hot summers and cold winters, except in the extreme south. Rainfall is plentiful and comes at all seasons, but there is a summer maximum in Western parts. In Mid-West, continental with hot summers and cold winters. Rainfall is moderate, with a summer maximum in most parts.56

So we can say that it contains great variations in physical geography, seasonal climate, and flora and fauna.

Demographic Aspects

U.S.A. is a country of immigrants, first from Britain and then from Germany, Scandinavia, Southern and Eastern Europe. Immigrants continue to enter the United States, though on a relatively reduced scale, not only from Europe but also from Asian countries and Central and South America. In addition, descandants of slaves imported from Africa during colonial and early post-colonial years and migrants from the Caribbean island form a substantial black minority. The ethnic origin of the majority (87 %) of the United States population is white, black comprise some 11 per cent, while Asians account for about 1.5 per cent.[57] Total population (excluding armed forces overseas, US population abroad and outlying areas) in 1980 was 226,545,945 and comprised 110,053,161 males and 116,492,644 females; 167,054,638 were urban and 59,491,167 were rural.[58]

Britannica book of the year 1988 gives the following data on demographic aspects for U.S.A.[59]

Population (1987): 243,773,000
Density: persons per sq. km. 25.6
Urban-Rural (1980): Urban 73.7; rural 26.3 per cent
Sex distribution (1986): male 48.68 per cent female 51.32 per cent
Composition by race (1986): white 84.8 per cent; black 12.2 per cent other 3.0 per cent
Birth rate per 1,000 population (1987): 15.5
Life expectancy at birth (1986): white male 72.0 years, black male 65.5 years, white female 78.9 years, black female 73.6 years.

Constitution

The form of Government of the USA is based on the Constitution of 17 September 1787 and subsequent amendments. By the Constitution the Government of the nation is composed of three co-ordinate branches, the executive, the legislative and the judicial.

The United States Constitution sets up and defines a federal system of government in which certain powers are delegated to the national government and all other powers to the states. The national government consists of executive, legislative and judicial branches designed to check and balance each other, all inter related and overlapping, yet each quite distinct.

The 5th Article mentions the procedure for making an amendment into the Constitution. Amending the Constitution requires a proposal by a two-thirds vote in Congress or by a national convention, followed by ratification by three fourths of the state legislatures or state conventions.

Executive Branch

The executive branch of the government is headed by the President, whose formal responsibilities include those of chief executive, treaty maker, Commander-in-Chief of the army, and head of state. In practice, they have grown to include the drafting of legislation, the formation of foreign policy, personal diplomacy, and leadership of his political party. The members of the President's cabinet are called Secretaries.

Legislative Branch

The legislative branch of the government is the Congress, which has two houses: the Senate and the House of Representatives. Powers granted to Congress under the Constitution include the power to levy taxes, borrow money, regulate interstate commerce, declare war, seat members, discipline its own membership and determine its rules of procedure.

The House of Representatives is chosen directly, by the electorate in each State, the number of representatives allotted to each State being based on population. They serve for a two-year period.

Each State elects two senators. Each terms of service is for six years, and terms are so arranged that one-third of the members are elected every two years. Treaties made by the president with other governments must be ratified by a two-thirds vote of the Senate.

Judicial Branch

The United States Supreme Court, the third, or judicial branch of the government, interprets the meaning of the Constitution and of federal laws. It consists of nine justices (including the Chief Justice) appointed for life by the President with the consent of the Senate. It has appellate jurisdiction for the lower courts and from state courts of last resort if a federal question is involved. It has original jurisdiction over cases involving foreign ambassadors, ministers, consuls, and cases to which a state is a party.[60]

State Governments

The governments of the 50 states have structures closely paralleling those of the federal government. Each State has a governor, a legislature, and a judiciary. Each State has its own Constitution.

The Polity and Economy

The Polity

A majority of the people of the United States has achieved a relatively high level of material comfort, prosperity and security. However, they are worried about crime, racial injustice, urban decay, environmental pollution, narcotics, alienation among the young, and the high cost of living. Social unrest and tensions and division among the citizens have shattered what is traditionally called the 'American dream' of equality to all its people, particularly to those who are members of minority groups. The traditional spirit of U.S. society had characterised the nation as a democratic "Land of Opportunity", in which social, political economic and religious freedom prevail, one man is as good as another, and every man can achieve if only he wills.

The population of the United States is the most widely diverse of any nation in the world. The United States is not homogeneous, it is a pluralistic society, a nation of groups. The long cherished belief that the United States has been a great "melting pot" in which people from all nations and cultures have blended into what are called "Americans" is a myth.

Churches and synagogues in the United States claimed 131,000,000 members in 1970. Of these, more than 40,000,000 nearly 24 per cent of the population were Roman Catholics and about 5,900,000 were Jews. The Protestants were about 72,000,000. Religious inter marriage is still not common.[61]

The Economy

Rich in land, population, and natural resources, and highly developed technologically, the population of the United States enjoys a high standard of living. It leads the nations of the world by the conventional indicators of consumption such as protein intake and energy consumption per capita. The Gross National Product (GNP) was 3662.8 billion dollars in 1984 and per capita income was 12726 dollars in 1984.[62]

Socio-economic trends reveal a continued decline in the proportion of the labour force employed in farming, a reduced blue-collar cadre, and over 50 per cent of the population employed in white-collar occupations ranging from clerical workers to professional and technical jobs. The number of people employed in technology and the distributive trades has increased substantially in a proportion to the labour force. Since the 1960's, the size of the labour force and the participation of females in it have increased substantially.[63]

Objective of the Educational System

The general goals of education of a country are influenced by the history, geography and demography of a country and so is the case with U.S.A.

Americans are the Western pilgrims, who are carrying along with them that great march of arts, sciences, and industry which began long since in the east. The Americans were once scattered all over Europe; in U.S.A. they are incorporated into one of the finest systems of population which has ever appeared, and which has become distinct by the power of the different climates they inhabit.[64]

A high level of shared education is essential to a free, democratic society and to the fostering of a common culture, especially in a country that prides itself on pluralism and individual freedom.

Emphasising the importance of education, President Reagon said, "Certainly there are few areas of American Life as important to our society, to our people, and to our families as our schools and colleges."[65] To have excellence in education means to have excellence in many related things. At the level of the individual learner, it means performing on the boundary of individual ability in ways that test and push back personal limits, in school and in the work place. Excellence characterizes a school or college that sets high expectations and goals for all learners, then tries in every way possible to help students reach them in order to respond to the challenges of a rapidly changing world. Americans want to excel in the world to provide equality to all its people and to have a learning society.

In a world of ever-accelerating competition and change in the conditions of the workplace, of ever-greater danger, and of ever-larger opportunities for those prepared to meet them, educational reform should focus on the goal of creating a learning society. At the heart of such a society is the commitment to a set of values and to a system of education that affords all members the opportunity to stretch their minds to full capacity, from early childhood through adulthood, learning more as the world itself changes. Such a society has a basic foundation, the idea that education is important not only because of what it contributes to one's career goals but also because of the value it adds to the general quality of one's life. In Americans' view, formal schooling in youth is the essential foundation for learning throughout one's life. But without life-long learning, one's skills will become rapidly dated.[66]

The American educational system has therefore set the following general objectives:

(i) to create unity out of diversity;
(ii) to foster democratic ideals and practices;
(iii) to assist individual development;
(iv) to ameliorate social conditions; and
(v) to improve national progress.[67]

Educational Administration

Education and Government

Education is a state subject. Even this was declared through the 10th amendment declaring education to be a state and local responsibility. The omission of education from express inclusion of the Constitution has often been the focus of the debate concerning the extent of the Federal Government's role in the educational system. Despite its absence, the framers and other leaders of the time repeatedly called for such a Federal role in education. Most of the proposals, however, were directed at higher education. According to the President Washington, a federal role was important for the following three reasons. First, there was a desire to encourage a strictly American rather than European education. Second, he perceived that nationally sponsored education would eliminate sectional and local prejudices. And third, as indicated in his Farewell Address, Washington considered "the promotion of political intelligence as a national safe-guard".[68]

In 1642, the Masachusetts General Court passed the Massachusetts Bay Law establishing a precedent of local responsibility for education. This Act and the subsequent legislation of 1647, the Old Delunder Law, which called for the creation of local public schools according to population size, were extended on a national scale in 1785 by the passage of Land ordinances. Through these ordinances, the first Federal aid to education was given.

In 1862, the Morrill Act was enacted to respond to the growing educational need for practical higher education in the areas of science, agriculture, and industrial training.

The next significant Federal initiative was the creation of the Office of Education in 1867. The education department was empowered to collect educational data and statistics, to disseminate information concerning education, and to encourage educational endeavours. In 1864, the Department of Education was relegated to bureau status and was transferred to the Department of the Interior. By 1930, the bureau was affiliated with the Federal Security Agency and later with the Department of Health, Education, and Welfare.[69]

In 1917 a vocational education act called the Smith-Hughes Act of 1917, was passed to reorient local education programmes to meet the needs of changing labour markets.

The continuing debates concerning an appropriate Federal role led to President Eisenhower's establishing a White House Conference on Education in 1954. The task force recommended that the Federal Government should provide financial aid to State and local communities for educational purposes. It concluded that there was an appropriate role for the Federal Government in educational matters.

The National Defence Education Act (NDEA) of 1958 was passed as a consequence of the widely held belief that the educational system was inadequate in mathematics, science and foreign language instruction. This belief was directly related to the successful launching to the Soviet Spacecraft, Sputnik. The passage of NDEA resulted in a substantial increase in Federal aid to education.

The next major educational act, the Elementary and Secondary Education Act (ESEA), was passed in 1995. Its passage signalled and unprecedented entry by the Federal Government into educational affairs. ESEA provided funds for educational R&D, for promoting educational innovation, and for assisting State agencies to establish there programmes.

With the passage of education legislation in the1960's and 1970's, the role of the Federal Government in education is, generally speaking, five-fold:

(i) Promotion of equal opportunity as exemplified by ESEA, the Education Amendments of 1972, by grants and legislation for the handicapped, by desegregation efforts and bilingual decisions, and by others;

(ii) Innovation and stimulation of education reform through research grants, teacher training, vocational education, reading improvement programmes and others;

(iii) Provision of grants in support of educational research the results of which could have broad applications in the Nation's schools;

(iv) Promotion of educational preparation for employment, which can be traced to the Smith-Hughes Act of 1917. "The School's potential contribution to economic productivity was thus the first, and for a long time, the only expressed national interest in education;"[70] and

(v) Provision of Limited Funding targeting specific needs areas such as planning grants for management purposes on the State level, equalization reforms for State finance mechanisms, instructional equipment, and others.

The judiciary has also played a very key role in extending the influence of Federal Government in the field of education.

Administrative Structure

Historically, education has been considered a state and local responsibility, but the Federal Government has been involved at all levels since the 1872 grant of public land to the States to establish colleges of agriculture and mechanical arts.

The U.S. Constitution contains no direct mention of education. One of the provisions of the Constitution that affects education indirectly is found in Article 1 establishing the powers of Congress – the legislative branch of the Federal Government Article 1, Section 8 is commonly called the general welfare clause. The general welfare clause of the Constitution has been used by the U.S. Supreme Court to allow expansion of the Federal role in education.[71]

Department of Education

The Federal organization directly concerned with education is the Department of Education. The Department functions with the divisions and sections.

Basic Functions : The basic function of the Department of Education has remained unchanged since its creation to collect and disseminate information and statistics on education. But under its mandate to promote the course of education and under specific legislation, the Department now has five other essential functions.[72]

(i) Administering grants to the States according to the regulations and procedures established by the Office of Education;
(ii) Contracting with colleges, universities, States and private agencies for studies and research on educational problems;
(iii) Providing consultative services, largely to State departments of education, professional societies, colleges and universities, and other Federal departments, including international organisations;
(iv) Operating educational programmes under agreement and in cooperation with other Federal agencies; and
(v) Collecting educational information and dissemination in three broad categories: (a) vital statistics, sometimes tabular, without comment or analysis, (b) reports containing statistics; and (c) publications not printed but otherwise duplicated.

State Government Administration

Responsibility for education of the State level lies in the hands of the State department of education, consisting of the State board of education, the Chief State School Officer and the staff of the education department. The department of education has several responsibilities for providing education at all levels. Curriculum, graduation requirements, teacher certification and working conditions, school finance, are among its more important responsibilities.

Local Control of Education

As a rule, the practical responsibility for running the schools is in the hands of smaller units such as counties or districts. The schools are managed by local school district boards. School districts vary in size from the small ones in rural areas, with a single one-room elementary school, to those in metropolitan areas with hundred of schools of various kinds and thousands of teachers.

Role of Parents Teachers Associations

The Parent Teacher Associations work with the school officials in determining educational goals. Through these associations the parents assess the work of the schools and confer regularly with the teachers and take appropriate steps for the progress of their children.

Private Schools Administration

About 11 per cent of enrolled children are in private schools. The private schools are mostly controlled by Catholic institutions. The private schools must meet the same basic standards as those set for public schools, but are free to add to the curriculum whatever else they wish and to choose their own teachers. A few of the States grant financial aid to the sectarian schools, but most of the States prohibit such aid.

Higher Education Administration

Most States have a separate board responsible for public higher education and for the licensing of private colleges and universities. Higher education institutions are managed by a president appointed by the trustees and staff. Faculties have major responsibility for the educational programme and selection of academic staff subject to the approval of administration.[73]

Financing of Education

Total annual expenditure for public and private education from Kindergarten to graduate school was estimated at about US$166.2 billion for 1979-80. US$ 107 billion went for elementary and secondary schooling and US$ 59.1 billion for institutions of higher learning. Public schools and colleges spent about US$ 135.3 billion, nearly two-thirds of it on higher education. Expenditure on education represents about 7 per cent of GNP. The expenditure varies among States and among local districts within a State.

Public school revenues derive mainly from county and other local sources, largely in the form of real estate taxes and from state taxes which comes to near about 90 per cent. The rest is met by the Federal Funds. The largest increases in federal funding during this period were in higher education, vocational-technical schooling and continuing education. Student fees, private grants and endowments etc. constitute a major source of funding for higher education.[74] The Federal contribution to all higher education, both public and private, is about 13.7 per cent, with the States paying about one-third of the total.

Tuition and living costs for students in higher education have been rising sharply in recent years. It is estimated that half of all entering students receive some form of financial aid in the form of scholarships, partial or complete remission of fees, or long-term, low-interest loans. In addition, it is common practice for students to supplement their resources through part-time and vacation employment.

General Structure

Each of the States provides a system of free public schools covering Kindergarten plus 12 years. Though laws vary among the States. Schooling is generally compulsory from the age of 6 or 7 to 16. There are three structural patterns in common use; the K 8-4 plan, meaning Kindergarten plus 8 elementary grades followed by 4 high school grades; the K 6-3-3 plan, Kindergarten plus 6 elementary grades followed by a 3-year junior high school and a 3-year senior high School; 6-6 plan, Kindergarten plus 6 elementary grades follow by a 6-years high school. Thus for school education there are courses covering 12 years plus Kindergarten. All plans lead to high-schools graduation, usually at age 17 or 18 and vocational education is an integral part of secondary education.[75]

Primary Education

The word 'Primary Education' is not used in U.S.A. Here the word "Elementary Education; is in vogue. Education in the United States is not merely free but it is also compulsory. In general, youngster from seven to sixteen years of age must attend school, although the exact requirements vary from State to State. Ninety-nine per cent of all elementary school age children are enrolled in schools. The vast majority of these pupils attend public schools.

Despite early interest in education, public schools in America got off to a slow start. Though the "Old Deluder Satan" Act of 1647 required the establishment of elementary and secondary schools, various factors, however, delayed the actual development of public schools for almost two centuries. The factors responsible for the delay are: many people saw little practical value in education; members of ethnic or religious factions feared that a public system of schools might threaten their identity, and the general reluctance to pay taxes to educate other people's children. Wealthy families sent their sons and daughter to private schools and consequently did not feel the need for publicly supported institutions.[76] Gradually, however, the idea of free public education gained acceptance for the public schools and the first organisations which could be recognized as public schools appeared in the early nineteenth century. Cincinnati founded its public schools system in 1825 and Chicago opened its first public school in 1830.

Early Childhood Education

The pre-primary education institutions (the nursery school and the kindergarten) constitute so to speak the preliminary units of the "elementary school" and consequently it is considered more appropriate to speak of "early elementary education" or "early childhood education" than of "pre-primary education". The Office of Education, a Federal agency founded in 1867 to promote and encourage educational development throughout the country, has given leadership to programmes of early childhood education and has had on its staff specialists to help the States and local school districts in the development of educational programme for young children.

The nursery school is for children aged 3 to 5 years and the Kindergarten for children aged 4 to 6 years; the term "primary school" comprises the nursery school, the Kindergarten and the first three grades of the elementary school; the term "elementary school" usually embraces the education given in the nursery school, the Kindergarten and the six or eight grades of the elementary school (that is, children up to the age of 11 to 13 years).

The following are the different types of establishment for the education of children aged from 3 to 6 years.

(i) The Kindergartens an establishment operated under public or non-public auspices; and usually enrolling children 5 years of age for a year prior to their entry to the first grade of the elementary school. Some establishments admit children at 4 years of age and keep them for two years. The kindergarten, now more than a hundred years old, was established under private auspices and by 1870 certain States had incorporated it in their education systems and today all States have Kindergarten;

(ii) The Nursery School; an establishment also public or non-public, enrolling prior to the Kindergarten, children 3 and 4 years old. It was introduced in the United States towards 1920. Originally child development centres which were financed by private grants and were later developed by means of federal funds;

(iii) The Cooperative Nursery School of Cooperative Kindergarten; a nursery school or Kindergarten adopted to serve parents in guiding the education of children in a continuous group experience under a specially qualified teacher. The school is administered by parents who participate in various ways;

(iv) The Nursery School and Kindergarten in a Child Development Laboratory; a child development centre operated by a college or university for the purposes of research, which later often enables new methods to be evolved and demonstrates how, in such fields as psychology, education, home economy, sociology and medicine, and knowledge of human growth and behaviour is inter-related;

(v) The Play Group or Play School; a neighbourhood group meeting under a teacher, who guides the children's early socialising experience through play and learning is the essence of the play school;

(vi) The Nursery School and Kindergarten for Exceptional

Children; a place for meeting specific phsycial, mental or social needs of special children which may asist in early diagnosis; and

(vii) The Guided Observation Nursery School/Kindergarten for parent Education; a place where parents bring their children for a morning and the children have a group experience with other children of the same age while the parents watch teachers guide their learning. Then follows a discussion with a parent education leader on aspects of child development.[77]

As a great percentage of nursery schools and kindergartens are under private auspices, it has become necessary to establish standards governing the organization of these establishments. Many States have a plan of state registration and accreditation and their State Departments of Education give consultant services and have responsibility for evaluating the quality of private and public nursery and kindergartens.

Elementary Education

The period of elementary education is six or eight years. It is followed with six years by six-year secondary education or eight years by four-year secondary education.

The aims of elementary education are stated in the curricula. In United States educators think in terms of continuity of objectives throughout the entire programmes for education at all levels. However, specific goals are defined in the courses of study for each of the subject areas.

Despite the fact that curricula are worked out separately in the States and at the local level, the objectives set are basically the same Nation-wide: (i) to develop physical and mental health; (ii) to prepare for life in a community which recognizes family and social values; (iii) to give moral training and education for citizenship; (iv) to impart basic knowledge and skills; (v) to develop inteliigence and individual aptitudes; and (vi) to prepare for practical life.

Study guides or teachers' guides usually contain suggestions, but no single method is prescribed. Emphasis is laid upon the need to adopt the method to the class and to the teaching situation. Flexibility and creativity on the part of the teachers are encouraged.

Curricula are not built on a fixed pattern. Related subject matter is frequently grouped as social studies (Geography, History, Civics), as language arts (reading and literature, handwriting, spelling, oral and written expression) and as arithmetic and science and as the arts.

For the most part curricula are suggestive rather than mandatory. In some States the law required that certain subjects – State history, for example–be taught in the school.

In the situation one may wonder how the student gets admission in another school of the same State or school of a different State in the event of transfer of his parents or due to some other reason when there is so much diversity in the curricula. The solution lies in the fact that the receiving school usually accepts him, at least on a trial basis, at the grade level indicated by the records of the sending school, whether or not the curricula of the two schools are exactly comparable; adjustments are made after studying child in the new situation.

As already stated, curricula are not issued by a Federal Authority; the system is very decentralised and courses of study vary from State to State, from community to community and to some extent from school to school. The education authorities of each State make available, curriculum guides for the use of local authorities which develop their own curricula within the framework of State-wide requirements. In the preparation of curricula the State Superintendent for Public Instruction appoints a committee consisting of members of the profession, businessmen, and community leaders. It includes teachers and administrators also. The concept of continuous curricula revision is generally accepted throughout the United States as essential to a dynamic education programme which makes possible due consideration of changes in living conditions. Curriculum research is carried out by a large number of institutions such as American Educational Research Association of the National Education Association; the U.S. Office of Education; the State Departments of Education, the Local School Authorities; the National Committees, the Professional Organisations; the Research Institutes; the Research Laboratories; the Institutions of Higher Education and the Independent Foundations etc.[78]

In U.S.A. 99 per cent of 6 to 13-year-olds (grade 1-8) are enrolled. The major points of dropout in flow through the system occur at about 18 (end of high school) and at about 20 years (completion of junior or community college).[79]

The total enrolment of K-8 in 1985 was 31,347,000 out of which 27,047,000 were in public schools and 4,300,000 were in private schools.[80]

Secondary Education

Generally secondary level education is from grades 7 to 12. Pupils normally enter these grades at the age of 12 years and graduate at the age of 18 years. Some of the secondary schools enroll pupils from grades 9 to 12 and the age for entering and for graduating is respectively 14 and 18 years. There is no minimum or maximum age.

About 90 per cent students go to supported public schools, and 10 per cent attend schools which are privately supported, most frequently by the Churches.

The school systems are different in different States and are organized to provide schooling on a 6-3-3, 6-6 or 8-4 basis and, therefore, the secondary schools are of four types: (a) the three-year junior high school; (b) the three-year senior high school; (c) the six-year secondary school; (d) four-year high school. The trend is towards an increase in the number of secondary schools organized on the 6-6 or 6-3-3 pattern.

Education is generally provided for all children upto the statutory age (mostly 16 years). By "all" is meant that no child is excluded for reasons of race, creed, colour or physical or mental ability. Secondary education is the responsibility of the States and each of the fifty States controls its own school system, delegating many controls to local school districts. Each local school district has its own educational philosophy in accordance with which its aims are determined. Guidance in regard to aims is also supplied by regional associations, national subject matter organizations, national educational organizations as well as by colleges, universities and the Office of Education.

In U.S., Secondary education "comprehensive high school" requires special mention. The comprehensive high school is a distinctive feature of American secondary education. It offers all types of special education, combined in the same school. All students take required core courses, such as English, social studies, science and mathematics and as electives they choose the courses required to meet the needs of commercial, technical, agricultural or home economics training. James B. Conant, former President of Harvard University has said :

> "The comprehensive school is characteristic of our society. It offers in one spot secondary education for almost all the high school children of one town or neighbourhood. It educates the boy who will be an atomic scientist and the girl who would marry at 18; the prospective captain of a ship and future captain of industry. It educates the bright

and the not-so-bright. It provides good and appropriate education, both academic and vocational, for all young people within a democratic environment which the American people believe serves the principles they cherish".[81]

Curricula and syllabuses are left to the freedom of principals and teachers. States have the power to issue curricula but the responsibility is usually delegated to the local school authorities. Curricula and syllabi vary greatly from State to State and from place to place within States. These differences in curricula bear no relation to pupils' sex or to ethnical or denominational groupings, in all of which matters of freedom are protected. Supreme Court decisions have eliminated religious instruction from public schools, and have declared illegal segregated public schooling. The great differences in curricula are between small and large schools as well as between rural and urban ones.

There is no authority responsible on the national level for preparing syllabuses; each State has the authority to impose observance of its recommendations concerning curricula. This authority is generally used by the board for education through superintendent of schools.

The Local School Systems develop their own syllabuses with aid from State Department of Education, Universities etc. A Planning Council is constituted consisting of representatives from different groups such as teachers, city and county superintendents, curriculum consultants, parents teachers association etc.

Various ways have been adopted for achieving liason between primary and secondary syllabuses. The Central Curriculum Planning Committees are composed of both elementary and secondary school representatives. Curriculum prepared by the representatives at one level is reviewed by the representatives of another level. Sometimes representatives of primary level serve on the committees of secondary level and *vice versa*. Similarly the requirements of higher education also affect the programme of the secondary schools to a considerable degree. In this way a continuum is maintained in the curriculum of the entire educational system.

Secondary schools provide a core curriculum for the students of grades 7-9 and this provision is made to include all subject matter pertinent to the development of broad units of work. For other grades, syllabuses are developed subject by subject and, in addition to the minimum subject objectives teachers provide educational experiences appropriate to the maturity level of the pupils.[82]

The total enrolment of Elementary and Secondary education in fall 1985 was 45,113,000 out of which 39,513,000 students were in public schools and 5,600,000 were in private schools; the strength of students for grades K-8 was 31,347,000 (27,047,000 in public schools and 4,300,000 in private schools) and for grades 9-12 was 13,767,000 in public schools and 1,300,000 in private schools.)[83]

Post-School Education

The Community College

This institution imparts education to students in the age group of 18-20 for two years after passing their secondary examination and adults in the age group of 28-30.

Summarizing the philosophy of educational liberals, the Joliet Illinois Board of Education said: "The basic function of public education should be to provide educational opportunity by teaching whatever needs to be learned to whoever needs to learn it".[84]

Acceptance of this position has led to the growth of the community college in all fifty States. Joliet Junior College in Illinois is the oldest community college, dating from 1901. By 1921 the Nation had 207 two-year colleges out of which only one-third were tax-supported institutions. Today, the public colleges enroll 95 per cent of all two-year colleges students.

Public Community Colleges are opening at the rate of more than 50 a year. In 1971 the nation's 873 public community colleges had 2.5 million students and their enrolment increase has been spectacular.[85]

The public junior college appeared when various educational leaders advocated creation of separate lower-division institutions to relieve the universities of offering courses to freshman. These educationists wished to free the universities to concentrate on upper division and graduate education.[86] Their plan advocated increased educational opportunities beyond high school and the transfer of the most able junior college graduate to universities.[87]

The community college performs five main functions:

(i) It provides for students to transfer to a baccalaureate programme at a four-year college of university;
(ii) It provides vocational training for people who are already working or expect to be working in the near future;

(iii) it gives remedial instruction to adults who did not learn basic skills in elementary or high school;
(iv) It offers recreational, cultural activities for adults who are not seeking regular vocational or academic skills; and
(v) It diverts inept students away from a transfer, four-year programme into a lower-status vocational programme.[88]

Curriculum

The curriculum for the community colleges are prepared to fulfil the objectives and functions of a community college. The curriculum is prapared flexible so that it can meet the changing needs of the society and keep pace with the development of technology. The curriculum is based on the following five functions to be performed:

(i) Two-year curricula which are equivalent to freshman and sophomore years at a university or college;
(ii) Curricula in preparation for immediate employment in a number of semi-professional, industrial, business, and technical fields... designed to meet the employment needs of the area served;
(iii) A general education programme for personal enrichment and cultural development;
(iv) Courses designed to make up high school deficiencies permitting further eduction and training at the cultural level;
(v) A programme of guidance and orientation to make the individual aware of his special abilities and aptitudes.[89]

In 1965, 14 per cent of the community college credit enrolments were in occupational education programmes.

By 1980 this had grown to 63 per cent of the credit enrolment. Community Colleges prepare students for work in more than 1400 occupations. A typical community college has approximately 30 to 50 different occupational programmes.[89]

Vocational Education

Vocational education means different things to different people. Generally by vocational education is meant that: education is vocational when it is designed specifically to improve the efficiency of an individual in a specific occupation. It is related to actual job requirements, whether the job is at the entry level or at some advanced level.

Vocational education is training for jobs which do not require a baccalaureate degree. Higher education, however, is not excluded by this definition. Vocational education is growing rapidly in community colleges, where academic credit is awarded for the Associate of Arts and the Associate of Science Degree.

Vocational education takes place in many different organizations - public and private, profit making and non-profit making. Among these are community colleges, high schools, occupational training centres, skill centres, technical institutes, jobs corps camps, and neighbourhood centres as well as business and industrial firms.

Freedom of occupational choice is very important. Emphasis upon equality of opportunity suggest that every child regardless of origin, should be allowed to choose between being a doctor or an automobile mechanic, a taxi driver or a test pilot. Americans expect schools to support all pupils' job aspirations and to develop their vocational capacities to the fullest. This has resulted in the multiplication of vocational curricula and students. Thus vocational education has reached a more heterogeneous clientele with a variety of curricula.

The conceptual foundation for vocational education was forged in the late nineteenth and early twentieth centuries. The first manual training high school in the United States was established in 1880 by Colvin M. Woodward. This manual training, however, was not designed to prepare workers for a vocation. Instead, it provided them with general knowledge, skill and attitudes that would enable them to derive satisfaction from their lives and fulfil their responsibilities as citizens. These non-vocational, practical arts evolved into industrial arts, general home economics, general business, and general agriculture.

The vocational emphasis was popularized in the twentieth century by the Douglas Commission appointed by the Governor of Massachusetts (1905), the National Society for the Promotion of Industrial Education (1906), the Commission on National Aid to Vocational Education (1914), the Federal Board of Vocational Education (1917), the American Vocational Association (1926), the Panel of Consultants on Vocational Education (1961), the Advisory Council on Vocational Education (1966) and the State and National Advisory Councils (1968). Congress promoted vocational education through the Smith-Hughes Act of 1917, which set the basic pattern for vocational education for almost half a century and through the Vocational Education Act of 1963. The Manpower Development and Training Act of 1962 and the Comprehensive Employment and Training Act of 1974 have emphasized the need for remedial job training programmes in addition to the traditional programmes of the public schools.[91]

Occupational programmes in 1971 were 17,460 in secondary schools out of which 16887 were public (15469 local, 1363 State and 55 Federal) and 573 private (364 Religious and 209 others schools, and 8182 post-secondary schools.[92]

Higher Education

As has already been stated, in the United States, the Constitution makes no reference to education, but it confers upon the States powers in those areas which are not specifically denied to the States or reserved to the Federal Government. Power over education and legal responsibility for the maintenance of educational system, therefore, vests in each of the 50 States. Because of these legal and constitutional circumstances, there are many different types of higher education in the United States.

There are two main types of institutions of higher education: State (or public) and private. Certain private institutions are religious institutions. About 30 per cent of the total number of students attend private institutions. The main difference between the two is a financial one: private institutions have only limited financial help from the State authorities. State institutions may be the responsibility of the State they are situated in, or of local authorities. The Federal Government plays an important part in their financing.

Given the very large number and variety of institutions of higher education and high level of student attendance, there are considerable differences in the quality of the teaching provided in them. There are several non-governmental regulating organisations. Accreditation system is there to foster co-operation between the various institutions and to harmonise the methods, structures and norms of the teaching programmes in these institutions.

The accreditation system is characteristic of American higher education. Universities have founded six regional accreditation organizations to ensure the high level of higher education by recognising through accreditation those institutions in their regions who fit their required standards. There are also another 50 national accreditation organizations which are established within the framework of various professions and which establish standards and guidelines within their professional subjects for the specialised and professional institutions of higher education as well as university departments. Apart from these specific organizations, there are a number of coordinating organizations for higher education, such as the American Council of Education, Association of American Universities, the National Association of State Universities and Land-Grant Colleges, the Association of Urban Universities, etc.[93]

The official name of an institution does not necessarily indicate the level of teaching it provides. Certain institutions designated as 'universities' do not provide courses beyond those leading to the bachelor's degree, while others designated as 'colleges' offer programmes leading to the doctorate and enjoy great prestige.

In a general way, institutions of higher education in the United States can be classified into four main categories:

(i) Technical institutions and 'semi-professional' schools: offering two-years or three-year courses, leading to an 'associate' qualification and preparing students for employment in semi-professional occupations such as medical, dental and engineering technicians or skilled employees for commerce, accountancy, nursing etc. Programmes resemble those in junior colleges;

(ii) Junior colleges or community colleges: providing two year courses which may lead to studies in the two categories mentioned below at Nos. (iii) and (iv);

(iii) Liberal arts colleges, state colleges and independent professional institutions: awarding the first degree (bachelor's degree) and sometimes the master's degree and the doctorate. Independent professional institutions include teacher-training colleges, institutes of technology (of a higher level than institutions providing short courses in category 1), schools of theology, art, etc; and

(iv) Universities: awarding the highest degree (Doctor's degree). There is in every State at least one college (or university) called a Land-Grant College, created originally to train agricultural technicians and engineers. Most of these institutions have become very large universities where students can study all subjects, from humanities to applied sciences. Various programmes offered by different types of institutions often overlap considerably. A university, for instance, usually comprises institutions of professional education as well as those offering courses similar to those of a technical institutions.

Access to higher education is based on the high school diploma (primary and secondary school-leaving certificate) awarded around 18 years of age, after 12 years of primary and secondary studies. Adults who have not completed work for a traditional high-school diploma may earn a high-school equivalency certificate or diploma by means of the 'tests of general educational development' (GED). These equivalency awards are accepted in lieu of a high school transcript by most institutions of higher education. Many institutions of higher education select candidates either on results in the high-school diploma or through an entrance examination.

Candidates may apply to several universities or colleges at the same time. A straight-forward high-school graduation is not now considered to be specific enough for the admission to the institution of higher education. As a consequence, a number of colleges now rely on the college board examinations, the Educational Testing Service, psychological tests, aptitude tests or on their own admission procedure. This is the national policy on acceptance applicable to all American colleges or universities.

In universities and colleges, the first two-year phase (feshman year and sophomore year) almost always consists of broadly-based studies in humanities, social sciences, applied and natural sciences, fine arts. This phase is aimed for more specialized studies. This phase represents the first half of the first stage of studies. It is given in arts and science junior colleges, State college, and universities. It is a prerequisite to more specialized studies and then devoted to more specialized studies, and culminates in the bachelor's degree, which is the first university degree. In the table 2.2 the Preliminary studie –the duration of preliminary studies before entering a professional faculty is varied (one to five years). In fact candidates often obtain a full Bachelor of Arts or Bachelor of Science degree[94] are given. Professional course is frequently conditional on the candidate first undertaking all or part of a Bachelor degree in a non-professional field e.g. bachelor of arts or science before being allowed to specialize.

In colleges, in the first stage, four-year courses in technology train higher technicians.

The second stage of higher education leads, after one or, more often two years' study in a university or in some colleges, to the Master's degree. Candidates usually have to submit a thesis.

The third stage of higher education is reached after three years' study in a university or college, either in faculties providing traditional teaching (arts, law, science, etc.) or in specialized schools of engineering, agriculture, architecture, economy, veterinary medicine, etc. This culminates in the doctor's degree, which is the highest university degree. Candidates for the doctor of philosophy usually have to take an examination as well.

In several subjects, but mostly in the scientific ones, post-doctoral studies of one to three years' duration enable holders of a degree of doctor of philosophy to acquire further specialized knowledge in their fields. These studies are often financed by such central organizations as the National Science Foundation or the Public Health Service or some other related organizations to the specific field of specialization.

In fall 1985, the total enrolment in higher education was 12,247,000 out of which 9,479,000 students were in public institutions and 2,768,000 were in private institutions.[95]

Teacher Education

In 17th century, the missionaries in USA based on their European experience, started seminars for school masters. The first pedagogical seminar was opened at Kaethen in 1619, it was followed by one in 1684 at Rheims. Another seminar was held in 1696 at Halk.

The beginning of professional teacher training was made in the 19th century by opening of Normal schools. In the 20th century setting up of colleges and university departments for teacher training has brought out most of the reforms in teacher education.

There are four types of teacher education institutions in U.S.A.

(i) *Normal schools*: The first Normal School was established in the year 1823 by Samuel at Concord, Vermount followed by James in 1827 at Lancaster, Massachussets.
In the beginning, the training was of one year for elementary school teachers, then the course was changed to two and then three, then the schools became Teacher' Colleges and offered a four-year course leading to the Bachelor's degree and now leading to a Master's degree in education.

(ii) *Teachers' Colleges*: As a result of the improvement of professional courses and need for secondary school teachers, the normal schools have changed over to teachers' and awarded degrees from two to four, or in some cases five years. Some of the colleges award Master's and Doctoral degrees too. The teaching programme includes general education, professional education in teaching, practice in teaching, specialisation in the field of teaching;

(iii) *Departments of Education*: As a result of the expansion of school education, some arts colleges added a department of education for the preparation of adequate number of teachers. Some of the universities have also departments of education. University of Law was the first to start the department of education in 1873. These departments do research in methods of teaching and provide advanced courses for teachers and educational administrators; and

(iv) *Schools or Colleges of Education*: Most of the universities have established schools or colleges of education. In such institutions students are accepted from the first year and they pursue general course for B.A. degree along with the courses in education which includes some hours for practice of skill in teaching. Michigan University was the first to make such arrangements. At the end of the course the students are awarded B.A., M.A., Ph.D. or D.Ed. degrees depending upon the duration of the courses attended and the examinations passed.

Curricula

The curriculum programmes in teacher education have three parts: (i) general education, (ii) provision for specialization, and (iii) professional education.

The required course in most States lasts four years and culminates in a baccalaureate degree. The following is a sample of a programme for the training of teachers:

(a) *General education*: 65 credit hours. This is about one-half of the college programme, it includes English, history and social studies, science, art, music, health and physical education;

(b) *Subject concentration*: 20 credit hours. This encourages the

TABLE 2.2 : Profile of Higher Studies
Duration of Studies
(Previous education 12 years, high-school diploma)

Year	1	2	3	4	5	6	7	8	9	10	11
Education		A		B	M	ES	D				
Arts		A		BA		M		D			
Religion, theology *		A		BA			B/M		D		
Fine arts, applied arts			C	B		M		D			
Architecture *		A			B		M	D			
Law *		A		BA			B	M		D	
Economic and Social Sciences		A		BA	M			D			
Administration and Business Affairs		A		B	M			D			
Commercial Sciences		A		B	M			D			
Exact and Natural Sciences		A		B	M			D			
Engineering, technology *		A			B		M		D		
Medical Sciences											
Medicine *		A		B/BS			D(P)	M			D
Dentistry *		A		BS			D(P)	M			D
Pharmacy *		A				B	M		D		
Veterinary Medicines *		A		BS				D(P)	M		D
Agriculture, forestry, fisheries		A		B		M		D			

A associate degree or certificate
B bachelor's degree (mentioning the field)
BA bachelor of arts
BS bachelor of science
D Doctor's degree (Doctor of Philosophy)
D(P) Doctor's Degree (Professional title in medicine, etc.)
ES education specialist
M master's degree

* Preliminary studies - the duration of preliminary studies before entering a professional faculty is varried (one to five years) and in fact candidates often obtain a full bachelor of arts or bachelor of science degree.[96]

Unesco : World Guide to higher education. p. 315.

student to become especially well grounded in any one subject in order to give him a special feeling of competence in atleast one phase of the subject-matter;

(c) *Professional education*: 35 credit hours. This subject is usually distributed in increasing amounts from freshman to senior years; and

(d) *Free electives*: 10 credit hours. These are free, unrestricted electives over and above the 20 credit hours in the subject concentration.

The total of 130 credit hours includes physical education. Some institutions also have some special requirements such as the ability to play a piano and ability to pass a speech test.[97] Students preparing to teach in secondary schools usually make major preparation in one subject matter area and minor preparation in another.

Students preparing to teach in the elementary school are likely to take a series of courses centring around child development and the methods of teaching in the elementary school.

All colleges preparing teachers make some provision for professional education in courses which are aimed specifically at teaching as a profession. Although the exact content and sequences of courses vary greatly among institutions, there are common elements in the professional education for prospective teachers of both elementary and secondary schools.[98]

In 1979, 2.5 million teachers were employed in public and private schools, 2.185 million in the public sector. Of these 1.340 million were elementary classroom teachers and 1.120 million were in secondary schools. The pupil-teacher ratio in 1979 was 19.2 : 1.

Public schools teachers are better educated now a days than previously. Only one per cent of teachers in 1976 had not acquired a Bachelor's degree. Other 37 per cent had a Master's degree.

The majority of all elementary and secondary teachers are female. In 1978, the proportions were 17:83 and 54:46 in elementary and secondary schools respectively. The overall Male-Female teachers ratio is 40:60.

In colleges and universities faculty numbered about 820,000 (full and part-time) all-levels) in 1979. The private sector comprised 30 per cent of the total.

Graduate and in-service studies and encouraged by salary incentives and state licensing requirements. A Master's degree is required for a permanent high school teaching license in many cases.

Teacher salaries are determined by local school districts and vary considerably. The National average salary for public school teachers was approximately US $ 16,000. The average salary for college faculty (all ranks) is about US $ 23254 per year in 1979-80.[99]

Non-Formal and Adult Education

Non-formal education in the United States presents a bewildering array of different activities for adults. It is provided by public and private agencies, by employers and labour unions, by profit making individuals and religious and secular philanthropic groups as well as by schools and colleges in their extension or continuing education programmes for adults. They cover such activities as adult basic education (for literacy, and for high school equivalence), post-secondary (non-collegiate studies, business and consumer education, as well as a range of hobby, craft, artistic and recreational activities. Estimates of the number of persons involved in such lifelong learning activities are uncertain. A Federal study found that 7,500 firms with over 500 employes spent US $2 billion on direct personnel training and development activities in 1975. The Civil Service Commission reported half a million workers involved in some kind of education at an annual cost of US $ 125 million. But these figures represent only a small proportion of the numbers and kind of non-formal education.[100]

The reasons for this vague picture of adult education can be found in the following:

(i) The development has been largely invisible, partly because the education of adults is not considered a Central part of society's eduational venture;

(ii) Most of the adult education is sponsored by non-eduacational organizations–churches, business, industries, community groups, voluntary associations, and government (including military);

(iii) The instruction provided by these organisations is usually intended to further their own distinctive aims rather than to be a public eduational service;

(iv) Discrepancies between criteria of adulthood–a large proportion of college students both graduate and undergraduate, are married, have children and are in part self-supporting; and

(v) The use of formal eduational institutions as inservice training agencies for the professions.[101]

Therefore, it can be said that the distinction between the non-formal education for adults and formal education has become ambiguous in U.S.A.

In the United States, adult education has first roots extending back several hundred years. The best known organizations being the men's clubs organized by Benjamin Franklin in 1727 for the discussion of ideas and current events. By the 1830's there were hundreds of subscription libraries, reading rooms, debating clubs and other lecture services directed toward the education of adults. The first public evening school was established in 1810, followed by New York City in 1833 and, in the West, San Francisco in 1856 in Cincinnati.

In the recent past new programmes of adult education have emerged. They are located in all parts of the country. Among them some of the important are:

(i) The Free University of Berkeley was created in 1966 to offer educational experiences to students, drop-outs and adults as an alternative to the formal curriculum of the university between 1965 and 1967 at least twelve universities were organized across the country;

(ii) Helitrope, which offers programmes throughout the area. Teachers are employed on the basis of their competency in a particular area of study rather than by their academic qualifications. Class in photography, Russian Literature, body massage, theatre directing and Islam;

(iii) Entrophy–Under this programme the atmosphere is informal-more classes are held in people's homes. There is no pressure from examinations or grades;

(iv) Orphans–An experimental project for young people's between the ages of ten and seventeen;

(v) New ways–a college-level programme for college level students and adults; a clearing house for teachers and adults looking for alternative in education;

(vi) Liberation School–A politically oriented programme for adults. It offer courses and seminars on major political issues;

(vii) Every woman's village–Programme intended to develop educational opportunities for women who were otherwise not adequately served by either the formal system of education of the prevailing adult education programmes;

(viii) University without walls has been established by an association of twenty-five colleges and universities interested in promoting experimentation and research on the most effective ways of improving education in a rapidly changing society. This programme attracts students who have dropped out of conventional programmes and adults who were unable to enroll in such programmes because they work full-time. The university without walls seeks older students as well as the young "to build a new dialogue and trust between younger and older persons";

(ix) Open Universities – provide an opportunity for adults to pursue Bachelor's and Master's degrees, part-time and off-campus.

Growth in the number of older students has led to a system where by individuals may receive college credit for life experience. At the secondary level, too, alternative school programmes have developed. Their major characteristics include a combination of work with formal studies, student planning of individual programmes, an unstructured school day, and the use of learning contracts.

Special Education

Special education is necessitated by individual differences in the way children learn the skills. Difference, for purposes of special education, is a marked discrepancy between the performance of an individual and the performance of the majority (i.e. the average). Special education deals with children who are exception to the rule-special children for whom uniform educational procedure applicable to most children is clearly unsuitable. Exceptional children manifest performance that is superior or inferior to that of the average child.

The problem of special education was noted by John Lewis in 1924. Today special educators list mainly these categories of exceptionality - the mentally retarded; the emotionally disturbed; the learning disabled; the speech impaired; the crippled and other health impaired; hearing impaired; the visually impaired and the gifted and the talented.[102]

Since its inception in the early nineteenth century, special education has been concerned with both the handicapped and the gifted. However, a great deal more of special eduation's resources and much more of society's concern have gone into helping the handicapped than into special education for the gifted.

E.O. Seguin has reported the establishment of a State-supported experimental school for idiots at Albany, New York in 1851 and later other schools were established. He commented "Thus the United States has eight of these schools, in which nearly one thousand children are constantly in training."[103]

The U.S. Congress, recognising the need for special care of children established the Children's Bureau in 1912. Special public schools classes and recourse programmes for all types of exceptional children proliferated and then Council for Exceptional Children (1922) was founded. Training programmes for teachers of the handicapped were begun in teachers colleges and universities. One of the strong influences on special education beginning in 1950 with the organization of the National Association for Retarded Children (now the National Association for Retarded Citizens). The Association for Children with Learning Disabilities was founded in 1963.

Administration of Special Education

The following agencies are involved in the administration of Special Education in U.S.A

The Local Education Agency

The variety of instructional and related service alternatives constituting a free, appropriate, public education for which (Local Education Agency) LEA is responsible leads to a complex set of administrative relationships. Administration of supportive services, such as resource consultation to every regular classroom teacher is the responsibility of LEA.

The Intermediate Education Unit

The role of the Intermediate Education Unit (IEU) in education generally has been a mix of supportive and direct service functions. The IEU function in education of students with special needs uses a direct service model.

Institutional Schools

They are the schools operated within residential institutional settings. The institutional system as a whole is under a State Department of Health or other non-educational agency of State Government. Hence, the status of the educational programme within such structure is generally regarded as secondary to other functions of the agency.

University Affiliated Facilities

These facilities include training of professional personnel in education as well as all other human service fields.

Institutions of Higher Education

The major role of Institutions of Higher Education (IHE) remains one of personnel development and knowledge production. The impact of current trends on the administration of IHE units concerned with special education, is, however, considerable.

Federal Agencies

Federal agencies are minimally involved with the direct operation of service systems. The Federal level of government performs exclusively a support service function. The variety of agencies through which Federal support of education for the handicapped is channeled, is surprisingly great. While the Bureau of Education for the Handicapped (BEH) within the Department of Education contributes the major effort, other units within the Department of Education, as well as units in the Office of Human Development and in other subdivisions of the Department of Health Eduation and Welfare, also are involved in the indirect support of special education. Outside HEW, even the Department of Defence carries on programmes of education which caters to the special education needs.[104]

Educational Research

The establishment of the National Institute of Education, a network of regional research and development laboratories, and facilities for national assessment of school achievement testify to the considerable quantitative growth of educational research in the United States.

While basic and applied research are both evident, the latter predominates. Much effort has been devoted to outstanding and immediate public concerns such as the education of special groups (the socially and economically disadvantaged and the handicapped): reforming the arrangements for financing State and local school systems; and improving careers and vocational school programmes. Several social sciences disciplines and psychology are all represented in such efforts. Another sector in educational research is developing and testing instructional systems (not only books and other print materials, but computer software also). Teachers, professors and technician often collaborate with the support of publishers and electronic companies. Public and philanthropic agencies may support studies concerned with special or smaller groups such as the handicapped. Evaluation of current and experimental educational programmes is often included in the regular activities of State Education Departments and the larger urban districts.

In 1957 the Federal support to educational research was US$ 1 million and it rose to US $ 100 million in 1970s. Federal funds account, however, for only about one-quarter of the resources, the major portion comes from private foundations, universities and colleges, and State Education Departments.[105]

EDUCATION SYSTEM IN INDIA

Physical Features

Area

India has always attracted attention of the world as being one of the oldest civilizations with Kaleidoscopic variety and rich cultural heritage. It covers an area of 32,87,263 sq. km. extending from icy snow-covered heights of Himalayan ranges to tropical virgin forests of the south. Bounded by the great Himalayas in the north it stretches southwards and at the Tropic of Cancer, tapers off into the Indian Ocean between the Bay of Bengal on the east and the Arabian Sea on the West.

Lying entirely in the northern hemisphere, the main land extends between latitudes 8^0 4' and 37^0 6' north and longitudes 68^0 7' and 97^0 25' east and measures about 3,214 km. from north to south between the extreme latitudes and about 2,930 km. from east to west between the extreme longitudes. It has a land frontier of about 15,200 km. The total length of the coastline of mainland, Lakshadweep group of islands and Andaman and Nicobar group of Islands is 7,516.6 km.[106]

India is adjoined in the north by China, Nepal and Bhutan; in the east by Burma and Bangladesh; in the north-west by Afghanistan and Pakistan and in the south is Sri Lanka.

Climate

The climate of India may be broadly described as tropical monsoon type. There are four seasons in India: (i) winter season (January-February), (ii) hot weather season, summer (March-May), (iii) rainy season, south-western monsoon period (June-September) and (iv) post-monsoon period, known also as north-east monsoon period in the southern peninsula (October-December).[107]

Demographic Aspects

According to the 1991 Census, the total population of India was 84,39,30,861. The proportion of rural population to total population was 76.69 per cent and of urban population to total population was 23.31 per cent. Male-female ratio is 1000:929. The average density of population per sq. km. in 1991 was 267. It varied considerably from state to state, being as high as 747 in Kerala and as low as 57 in Sikkim and 10 in Arunachal Pradesh.[108]

In 1991, there were 43,75,97,929 males and 40,63,32,932 females. Thus for every 1000 males, India has 929 females, only Kerala has more women than men, that is 1040 per thousand men. The lowest female ratio is in Andaman and Nicobar Islands, where it is 820 per thousand men.[109]

Constitution

India, a Union of States, is a Sovereign Socialist Secular Democratic republic with a parliamentary system of government. The Republic is governed in terms of the Constitution, which was adopted by the Constituent Assembly on 26 November, 1949 and came into force on 26 January, 1950.

The Constitution which envisages a parliamentary form of government is federal in structure with unitary features. The Constitution distributes the legislative power between the Union Legislature and the State Legislatures and provides for vesting of residual powers in Parliament. The power to amend the Constitution also vests in Parliament. At present, India comprises 25 states and 7 union territories.[110]

The Polity and Economy

Polity

The composite culture of India is essentially an expression of the inner urges and cumulative beliefs of its people gathered through centuries of experience. It is the perennial flow of this cultural stream which determines the nation's strength, its character and its capacity to survive as an integrated living reality despite heavy odds and its continuous march forward on the path of progress.

Differences in languages, religion, culture and state of socio-economic development make India a land of contrasts. In the middle class urban situation, however, caste is being replaced by 'class' to same degree as a result of pressure generated by industrialization and modernization. Joint family still prevails in rural areas but is tending to be replaced by the nucleous family in the cities.

India is a country of many religions. The major six religious groups are Hindus (82.63%), Muslims (11.36%), Christians (2.43%), Sikhs (1.96%), Buddhists (0.71%) and Jains (0.48%) and the remaining (0.43%) contribute the people belonging to other religions.[111]

Economy

India is rich in natural resources and manpower. These resources have, however, not been exploited fully and are capable of greater utilisation. The Indian economy is still predominantly an agricultural, a little over one third of the country's national income being derived from agriculture and allied activities which absorb about two thirds of the working force. Since 1947, the aim has been to diversify the economy. Some of the important data are given below:

	At 1984-85 (price)	At 1970-71 (price)
Net national income	1,73,207 crores of Rs.	57,017 crores of Rs.
Per Capita Income	2348.8 Rs	771.5 Rs.[112]

Unemployment

The number of persons on the live registers of employment exchanges gives an idea of the trend of unemployment. The number of job-seekers on the live registers of employment exchanges was 262.699 lakh as on 31 December 1985. [113]

Objectives of the Educational System

Historical Perspective

Four distinct periods of development can be marked in the history of Indian education – Ancient, Mohammedan, British and Post-Independence periods. A singular feature of ancient Indian civilization was that it has been moulded and shaped more by religious than by political or economic influence. Indian philosophy asserted that the goal of life was to achieve self-fulfilment and therefore the purpose of education was to aid in this self-fulfilment, and not the acquisition of mere objective knowledge.[114] Education's chief concern was the individual. It flourished in the intimate relationship between the teacher and the pupil. The pupil lived with the teacher as a member of his family; he belonged to him and not to a school. "Here the personal touch, the living relationship between the pupil and teacher make educaiton."[115]

The advent of Muslims in India in the 11th century brought in the system of education based on Maktabs and Madarsas mainly for religious purposes. However, the Hindu systems of education continued to prevail in Pathshalas and in temples.

British influence: The Wood's Despatch (1854) recommending the spread of education through indigenous institutions, establishment of universities, cultivation of the mother tongue and provision of vocational education was the landmark of British influence on Indian education which led ultimately to the promotion of modern education. The year 1937 saw the transfer of education to the control of popular ministries under Provincial Autonomy.

Post Independence Period: The fourth Education Commission and the first to be appointed in the post-independence period, was the University Education Commission (1948-49) which reviewed the development of higher education in the country and made proposal for its future expansion and improvement. A similar function for secondary education was performed by the Secondary Education Commission (1952) which was the fifth in the series. All the five commissions looked at education in a compartmentalized fashion and moreover, no commission had ever been appointed for primary and adult education. There was a strong demand in the fifties and early sixties that Government of India should appoint an Education Commission to look at education as a whole, including primary and adult education. On this demand, Central government appointed the Education Commission, 1964-66 (under the chairmanship of Prof. D.S. Kothari and thus is popularly known as Kothari Commission) at the initiative of Mr. M.C. Chagla, the then Minister of Education who entrusted in with the task of looking at the entire spectrum of education except medical and legal education. This is, therefore, the first Commission in our educational history to look comprehensively at almost all aspects of education.[116]

A Committee of Members of Parliament was appointed in 1967 to consider the recommendations made by the Commission. In 1968, the Government issued a policy statement on education, the first National

Policy Statement on Education formulated by the Government of Independent India. It served as the basis for educational development so far until the recent efforts to formulate the educational policies of the country once again. This rethinking dates from 1977-78, and a draft policy document was issued in May 1979. However, before any effort towards its implementation could be made, it was given up.

The Central Advisory Board of Education, based on Kothari Commission's recommendations adopted a resolution in its meeting held in November 1974 recommending the introduction of the 10+2+3 pattern of education all over the country during the Fifth Plan period.

On January 5, 1985, the Prime Minister, Rajiv Gandhi in his broadcast to the nation promised a new education policy that would equip the country both scientifically and economically to enter the 21st century. Consequent to it, on 20th August 1985, Education Minister, K.C Pant presented a 'Status Report' entitled 'Challenge of Education – A Policy Perspective', to the Parliament. After a great deal of discussion, a National Policy on Education, 1986, popularly known as New Education Policy, was approved by the Parliament in May 1986.

Education is a pre-requisite, for progress and development. And, in the order of priorities, education has been accorded a high priority as an integral part of country's developmental process. Due to concerted efforts during the last four decades of independence, a four-fold increase has been registered the total number of literates. There has been a phenomenal increase in the number of schools, colleges and universities. In 1950-51 the schools were 2,30,683 while in 1990-91 the number has gone to 7,83,647. The colleges were increased from 578 to 5748 and universities gone from 27 to 146 in the same period. (Annual Report 1991-92 to Pt.1 MHRD, New Delhi, p. 297). Together with the quantitative expansion of educational facilities, there is now a greater emphasis on qualitative improvement.

Before 1976, education was exclusively the responsibility of the States, the Central Government being concerned with certain areas like co-ordination and determination of standards in technical and higher education, etc. In 1976, through a constitutional amendment, education became the joint responsibility of the Central and State Governments.

Besides policy formulation, the Department of Education, Ministry of Human Resource Development shares with the State Governments the responsibility for educational planning. Uptil the Sixth Plan, education was taken to be a social service rather than an input in the development process. There has been a change in the emphasis beginning with the Sixth

Plan, wherein it has been considered to be pivotal in the social and economic development of the country through development of human resources. Priority has been given to the programmes on universalisation of elementary education and eradication of adult illiteracy in the age-group of 15-35 by 1990.

An important focus of the Seventh Plan (1985-1990) would be to raise the quality and relevance of education. Non-formal education and open learning system would be encouraged at all levels. Priority has also been given to the technical and higher education, vocationalization of secondary education, developoment of regional languages, strengthening of monitoring and evaluation machinery for effective implementation of Plan programmes etc. Emphasis has also been laid especially in dynamic and beneficial linkages between education, health, social welfare and employment programmes.

During the Seventh Five Year Plan, an outlay of Rs. 6382.65 crore for education was approved by the Planning Commission.[117] For the Eighth Plan, the Planning Commission has approved an outlay of Rs. 16813.35 crore for General education and 2786.38 crore for Technical education.[118]

In the Directive Principles of State Policy it is envisaged under Article 45 that the state shall endeavour to provide within a peroed of ten years from the commencement of the Constitution for free and compulsory education for all children until they complete the age of 14 years.[14] This target has yet to be achieved.

Recapitulating the goals of education emphasised by the Indian Constitution and enunciated from time to time, by thinkers, planners, policy makers and educationists, the New Education Policy (1986) envisages the following aims of Indian Educational System:

(i) Emphasis on the Socio-economic Well-being Competence and Creativity of the Individual. This encompasses:

- (a) physical, intellectual and aesthetic development of personality;
- (b) inculcation of a scientific temper and democratic moral and spiritual valued;
- (c) development of self-confidence to innovate and face unfamiliar situations;
- (d) creation of an awareness of the phycisal, social, technological, econimic and cultural environment;
- (e) fostering a healthy attitude to dignity of labour and

hard work;

(f) a commitment to principles of secularism and social justice;

(g) dedication to uphold the integrity, honour and foster the development of the country; and

(h) promotion of international understanding.

(ii) Development of knowledge and skill in various areas. In addition to developing the personal attributes listed above, education has to assume the responsibility for imparting knowledge about concepts and facts relating to different subjects and for developing skills in the area of languages and communication also interest in hobbies, games and sports;

(iii) Development of knowledge and skill in Employment Opportunities: Education has to equip the pupils with competence, in term of knowledge and skills, in various combinations at different levels of understanding, relating to the opportunities of employment in the context of a particular pattern and pace of Devolpments;

(iv) Integration of Individual into the Social System: Education has to play an important role in integrating the individual into the social system. It is meant to inculcate suitable habits for health care, mental application, management of time and conservation of physical, mental and emotional energy;

(v) Education as a Means of Equalising Opportunities: Education can be the most effective means for equalising opportunities and reducing disparities between human beings;

In a democratic society, it is considered a fundamental right of citizens. In the ultimate analysis, therefore, the aim must be to enlarge the coverage and improve the quality of education in our institution so that a person, belonging to any religion, caste, creed, sex or economic strata, would have the opportunity of developing his or her potentials to the full.

(vi) Development of Sense of Right and Wrong: No law and order system can survive if educated people do not have respect for life or a sense of right and wrong. Democracy and civic life will degenerate beyond recognition if people do not understand the importance of tolerance and respect for viewpoints different from their own.

(vii) Development of Spirit of Adventure and Mass Participation in various Programmes: The spirit of adventure and the confidence to innovate and take risk has to be instilled in the minds of young people. The priority programmes requiring mass acceptance and participation for their success, like protection of the evironment, energy conservation and population control, cannot make a real headway unless a programme for the improvement of ecological conditions makes the students aware, right from their formative years, of the close interdependence of their own welfare with the outcome of these programmes.

It may be mentioned here that the goals of education listed above do not envisage the laying down of omnibus objectives for all levels of education on 'a priori' basis. Adult education would have different goals from those for school and university education. In different age groups relevant to elementary, secondary, vocational and higher education, the need as well as capacity for acquiring knowledge and skills varies considerably.[119]

Educational Administration

Administrative Structure and Processes

India is a Union of States with a written constitution. According to the Constitution, Central Government is solely responsible for the subjects mentioned in the Union List of the Constitution. Similarly, the State Governments are responsible for the subjects mentioned in the State List. There is also a Concurrent list which is the joint responsibility of Central and State Governments.

The system of educational administration in India follows by and large the constitutional provision. There are at present two levels of control in the area of education, i.e. Central Government and State Governments. States have to accept full responsibility for all school education, and in some of the states, the local bodies have also been associated so that day-to-day administration of schools be brought as close to the local community as possible. In the higher education, on the other hand, the states have to share the responsibilities with the universities, the University Grants Commission and the Government of India. In other words school education is predominantly local body-state partnership and higher education is a centre-state partnership.

By a Constitutional Amendment in 1976, education was placed in the Concurrent List. Prior to this Constitutional Amendment, the Central Government was directly responsible by virtue of entries in the Union List for several educational sectors including (a) co-ordination and determination of standards in institutions for higher education and research and scientific and technical institutions; (b) Union agencies and institutions for professional, vocational or technical training (c) promotion of special studies or research; and (d) Central universities and any other institutions declared by Parliament as institutions of national importance.

In discharging this constitutional responsibility, the Governments at the centre and the state, have enacted legislation to govern the educational institutions and administer the programmes at various levels and in different fields. The statute books of the states for example, cover legislations relating to schools education, State universities, Boards of Secondary Education, Compulsory Primary Education, etc. while those of the Centre include University Grants Commission Act, Acts governing the Central Universities and the five Indian Institutes of Technology, Apprentices Act etc.[120]

Educational enterprise in India is not only confined to government but to a large number of non-government organisations as is shown in diagram below:

Educational Enterprise

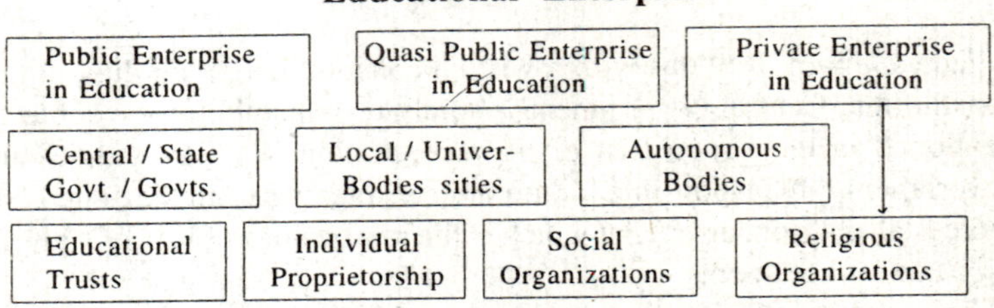

The Ministry of Human Resource Development, Department of Education plays a major role in ensuring a coordinated development of education all over the country and in developing national programmes in some essential areas like elementary, adult and secondary education and research.

Organisational Structure

The Department of Education, one of the constituents of the Ministry of Human Resource Development, is under the charge of Minister of State with overall charge of Minister for Human Resource Development. The Secretariat of the Department is headed by the Secretary and Educational Advisor (Technical). The Department is organised into Bureaux, Divisions, Desks, Sections and Units. Each bureau is under the charge of a Joint Secretary/Joint Educational Adviser assisted by Divisional Heads.[121]

Subordinate Offices/Autonomous Organisations

Over the years, a number of subordinate offices and organisations have come up under the Department. For coordination and determination of standards in education, some of the important organizations are:

(i) Central Advisory Board of Education;
(ii) University Grants Commission (UGC), New Delhi
(iii) National Council of Educational Research and Training (NCERT), New Delhi;
(iv) National Institute of Educational Planning and Administration (NIEPA), New Delhi;
(v) Indian Council of Social Science Research (ICSSR) New Delhi;
(vi) Indian Council of Historical Research, New Delhi;
(vii) Kendriya Vidyalaya Sangathan, New Delhi;
(viii) Indian Councial of Philosophical Research, New Delhi;
(ix) Navodaya Vidyalaya Samiti, New Delhi;
(x) Central Board of Secondary Education, New Delhi;
(xi) Central Hindi Directorate, New Delhi;
xii) Commission for Scientific and Technical Terminology, New Delhi; and
(xiii) National Book Trust, New Delhi.

All the states, with the exception of the very small ones, also oversee district administration. At the head of the district education administration is a district education officer with several deputies and sub–deputies who together inspect and supervise and sub–supervise the schools. The heads of schools prepare school time tables, attend to discipline among pupils and supervise the work of teachers.

Financing of Education

Educational financing in India has developed to be a multisource system although the state has been taking an increasingly commanding position in this behalf since Independence. Education is now financed by the Central Government, State Governments, local authorities and through fees and other sources that include endowments, donations and voluntary contributions.

Educational financing by the Central Government and the State Governments is of two categories, viz. Plan and Non-Plan. Plan allocations cover development expenditure while non-Plan allocation provides for maintenance. The Central Government, however, is directly responsible for the development programmes in the fields within its purview. It also takes up schemes known as Centrally Sponsored Schemes and Central Schemes administered by the States which are of common interest and utility to the State Governments and represent nationally identified objectives. The Central Government has in the post-independence period, been extending increasing financial assistance to the State Governments, besides incurring considerably direct expenditure on the Central and Centrally sponsored schemes.[122] Over the years, there has been a remarkable increase in expenditure on education, both as a percentage of Gross National Product (GNP) (3.2 per cent in 1980) and as a percentage of government expenditures (15.1 per cent in 1980). There is a wide difference in per student expenditure at different stages. The table 2.3 given below represents the facts.

The Budget expenditure on Education (Revenue Account) at the Centre and the States in 1982-83 was of the order of Rs. 52,000 million as against Rs. 47,000 million in 1981-82.

A comprehensive programme of scholarships exists to aid equalization of educational opportunity and to provide facilities for higher and specialized education and training. National Scholarships (26,000 in all) are given to talented students in rural areas. National Scholarships and

TABLE 2.3: Per Student Costs and Percentages of Education Expenditure Allocated to Different Levels in General Education.[123]

	Cost per student (rupees) 1981-82	% of educational expenditure allocated to different stages 1981-82*
Primary	168.9	48.1
Secondary	915.4	30.7
Higher	5807.1	13.3

* The total percentage of expenditure comes to 92.1 per cent. The balance is on administration and supervision, pre-primary education, adult education, etc.

national loan scholarships, 26,000 and 20,000 respectively are awarded on a merit and means basis. In addition, a large number of scholarships are awarded for research and for further studies overseas in science and technology. India also offers scholarships to students from the developing countries to pursue studies in Indian Universities.[124]

General Structure

Pattern of Education

There were some variations in the structure of education in different States. The recommendations of Education Commission (1964-66) led to a Resolution on the National Policy on Education which aimed at providing a broadly uniform educational structure in all parts of the country, the 10+2+3 pattern. This consists of ten years of schooling, two years of higher secondary education (either in schools or colleges) and a three-year period of higher education for a first degree. All the States and Union Territories have now switched over to the new pattern. The school year varies in different parts of India but usually runs from July to April with brief breaks in October and December. Generally speaking, the number of working days is 200.

Pre-Primary Education

Early Childhood (Pre-School) Education in rural and backward areas was suggested under the Sixth Plan. Early Childhood Education for children is designed towards improving their communication (language) and cognitive (social, emotional, intellectual and personality development) skills as a preparation for entry into primary schooling.

Pre-Primary Education is voluntary. Apart from private and self-help schemes it includes, in some instances, the provision of welfare facilities and is directed mainly to the under privileged sections of the community.

Seventh Plan provision is Rs. 2.5 crores for early childhood education.

Elementary Education

Elementary education in India is divided into a lower and upper stage, the latter sometimes being referred to as the middle school level. Children normally enter the lower primary school at the age of 6 years and complete this stage at the age of 11 (Standard I to V) Upper Primary consists of a three-year course for the 11-14 age band (Standards VI to VIII). Examination at the lower primary level are set by either individual schools or Municipal/District Boards and are usually held at the end of each term and the school year. This also applies to the Upper Elementary Education.

The enrolment of students in the age group 6-14 (Classes I-VIII) in 1983-84 was 10,60,75,000 (constituting 78.01 per cent of the population group) which increased to 12,43,99,000 in 1986-87 (consisting of 85.08 per cent of the population group).[125]

Secondary and Higher Secondary Education

Secondary education covers a period of four years (Standard IX to X and XI to XII) and caters to the 14 to 18 year old age bank. Various types of school leaving certificates are issued by the examination boards, including the Secondary School Leaving Certificate (SSLC), the Higher Secondary Certificate (HSC) and the Indian School Certificate (ISC). At the Secondary level, there are distinctions with respect to the curricula and standards between the schools in different States and schools affiliated to central bodies such as the Central School Organisation and Navodaya Vidyalaya Samiti.

Kendriya Vidyalaya Sangathan (Central School Organisation)

The scheme of opening Kendriya Vidyalayas with a common syllabus and medium of instruction to cater to the needs of the children of transferable central government employees was approved by the Government of India in November 1962. In 1963, twenty regimental schools then functioning in defence establishments were taken over as Kendriya Vidyalayas. Since then the demand for Kendriya Vidyalayas has been rising steadily and 633 Kendriya Vidyalayas have been opened till December 1986.[126]

Navodaya Vidyalaya Samiti

An autonomous organisation (registered under Societies Registration Act) known as Navodaya Vidyalaya Samiti has been set up to establish and run Vidyalayas with the funds coming from the Government of India. To provide equal opportunity to the talented children in the rural areas for development of their full potential to facilitate the process of school improvement and to promote national integration, residential schools to be called Navodaya Vidyalayas have been set up by the organisation. Education in Navodaya Vidyalayas, including boarding and lodging, as well as the expenses of uniform, textbooks, stationery, rail and bus fare from and to the homes, etc. would be free for all students. 60 schools have started functioning upto 26th January 1987.[127]

Post-School Education: Vovcational Education

The National Education Policy of 1986 has reiterated the 10+2 pattern emphasizing the importance of vocationalization of education. In view of the felt need in the country to provide middle level trained manpower, some vocational institutions have grown up. An All-India Survey of technical and vocational institutions published in 1977 revealed that there were 6052 technical, vocational and training institutions in the country where the admission requirement ranged from secondary to middle or class V examination.[128]

The scheme of vocationalization was started in 1976. The NCERT does have a vocational education unit but it is too small to accomplish the task.

To give a thrust to the vacationalization of education a conference of State Education Ministers held in April 1987 resolved that a massive programme of vocationalization of the +2 stage of education be undertaken all over the country and the Central Government should bear 50 per cent of the cost of this programme. It was also decided to set up a Joint Council of Vocational Education (JCVE) at the national level and the State Councils of Vocational Education (SCVE) as the state counterparts of JCVE.[129]

Work experience and vocationalization have been introduced in primary and secondary education, though the bulk of vocational training is conducted by Industrial Training Institutes at the craftsman level. There are 495 ITIs in India, 6 of them being exclusively for women and the others co-educational. There are also 306 private ITIs in 1976-77. The duration of training may be for one to two years. The entry qualifications depend on the trade the entrant wishes to pursue, but for technical subjects the entry requirement may be as high as a pass in the standard X or XII with mathematics and Science as a compulsory requirement. The language of instruction in ITIs is the local language, but in some trades such as radio servicing English is widely used. Approximately, 1,80,000 trainees pass out of the ITIs every year. There are also Polytechnics which enrol students for various diploma courses of three years duration in vocational subjects.[130]

Higher Education

Students enter higher education at the age of 17 or 18 years, after having completed Standard XII at school. Though there is some variation among different universities, many students spend two/three years reading for a general degree and three years for an honours degree. First degree courses are generally conducted in affiliated colleges, i.e. a network of private and State-sponsored institutes recognised by specific universities which undertake direct responsibility for post-graduate studies. The curricula and examinations are controlled by some 120 full-fledged universities. In addition to the traditional universities, there are specific institutions of higher learning which are recognised as having the status of universities e.g. Central Institute for English and Foreign Languages, Hyderabad, Institutes such as the five Indian Institutes of Technology, the Regional Engineering Colleges, Indian Institutes of Management etc. Various medical colleges also provide specialist education at the graduate and post-graduate level.

The student enrolment in universities and colleges was 35.71 lakhs in 1985-86. The number of students in university departments was 5.96 lakhs and in the colleges 29.75 lakhs.

Enrolment in the faculty of Arts constituted 40.3 per cent of the total enrolment. In the Faculty of Science and Commerce, the percentage was 19.7 and 21.5 respectively.

Curriculum Development

Curricula at the higher education level are the responsibility of the universities, which also prescribe them for the colleges affiliated to them. There is a board of secondary education in each State with responsibility for devising curricula and prescribing textbooks for secondary and higher secondary classes. For the primary and middle stages, the responsibility rests mainly with the State Education Departments. The geographical coverage of curricula in universities extends only to affiliated colleges, and there is a common curriculum for secondary and primary education throughout each State.

New Education Policy, 1986 envisages that there should be a national curriculum framework for the country. The organization of the content and process of education is being given the foremost priority in the implementation of the New Education Policy (NEP), 1986. NCERT has already developed syllabi in different subjects for the primary, upper primary and the secondary stage, based on the National Curricula Framework in terms of the objectives of teaching of different subjects.

Education Commission (1964-66) also called for increasing emphasis on work experience, national and social service, and ethical and moral valued.[131] The University Grants Commission, the boards of secondary education and NCERT continue to make substantial efforts to improve curricula at all levels. Particular attention is being paid to the question of restructuring courses and relating them to the needs of the rural and urban environments.

Examinations

Examinations occupy a dominant position in India's educational system. Traditionally, what has mattered is the score obtained in an examination rather than the quality of education, though it is believed that they are not necessarily related.

In all parts of the country, stages in the education system are divided into grades or classes. Promotion from one grade to the next depends on continuous pupil assessment through terminal tests, and invariably, an examination at the end of the school session. At the initial stages, examinations are flexible and are solely the internal concern of each school; but in the higher stages an external element in evaluation tends to increase, as do rigidities in the system. Certificates provided by the elementary school authorities are accepted for purposes of admission to secondary schools.

While examination of pupils at the end of grade 9 and 11 is the responsibility of schools, boards of secondary education conduct examinations at the end of the secondary (grade 10) and higher secondary (grade 12) stages. In setting question papers and practical tests in science and certain other subjects, and in the checking of answer books, the boards take the help of experienced school and university teachers. On the basis of the results of examinations, they award certificates which are required for admission to further courses or for employment. Examination at the higher education stage is the responsibility of universities. In some universities and other institutions of higher learning, the academic session is divided into semesters and evaluation is undertaken in each semester.

Educational thinkers and specialists in evaluation and measurement have, for a long time, been concerned about the system of examination. Reform of the examination system has been a continuous endeavour since independence. The Central Examination Unit was established in 1958 (it merged with NCERT in 1961) and a programme of systematic reform was started. These reforms cover external examinations as well as school evaluation and include a scheme for the intensive training of the various personnel responsible for examinations. The reforms have been adopted by all boards of secondary education.

Teacher Education

There are basically three types of training for teachers in India depending upon where they are likely to teach: in the lower primary, upper primary or secondary school. The minimum qualification for admission to the course for lower and upper primary school teachers is a pass in the standard XII and the course may last for one or two years. Teacher education institutes of these levels are controlled and financed by State departments of education. Secondary schools are staffed usually by graduates who have completed a one-year Bachelor of Education Course at a college affiliated to a university. In addition, there are certain centrally funded institutions, such as four Regional Colleges of Education which offer a combined four-year course leading both to a subject degree and a Bachelor of Education, and the National Institute of Education, in New Delhi which receives financial assistance from Central Government funds through the National Council of Educational Research and Training (NCERT). Studies at the M.Ed and Ph.D levels can be undertaken in a number of universities including the Centre of Advanced Studies in Baroda.

Most of the teacher appointments are made from among trained personnel. Table 2.4 given below presents the number of teachers in schools in 1947 and 1981-82.

TABLE 2.4: Number of Teachers in Schools and the Percentage of Trained Teachers in 1947 and 1981-82.[132]

	1947		1981-82	
	Thousands of teachers.	Percentage trained teachers	Thousands of teachers	Percentage trained teachers
Primary Schools	344	67.1	1365	87.1
Middle Schools	50	58.3	847	89.2
High/Higher Schools	93	54.9	942	88.6

On the recommendation of the National Council of Teacher Education (NCTE), most States have introduced a two-year certificate course for primary school teachers. There are summer schools for secondary and college teachers for in-service training. Under its faculty improvement programme, the University Grants Commission provides financial support for teachers wishing to pursue research.

NCERT in coordination with NCTE and the State Councils of Educational Research and Training, has endeavoured to upgrade the quality of teacher education. It supported the Intensive Teacher Education Development Programme in several States and has assisted State authorities in improving teacher training curricula. Central Government also provides financial support to primary teacher-training colleges for the improvement of their facilities.

Non-formal and Adult Education

The social demand since independence has been mainly for formal or institutional education. Nor-formal education is relatively an undeveloped sector. The non-formal education channel is being developed as a system complementary to the formal one. The programme envisages decentralisation in regard to course content, duration, place and hours of learning, and pattern of instruction.

To achieve the goal of universalization of elementary education in fulfilment of constitutional objective, non-formal education for the elementary age-group children has been developed as an alternative supportive system of formal schooling. During the financial year of 1986-87, a total grant of Rs. 712 lakh has been sanctioned.[133]

In the early 1960's universities established correspondence courses and departments of adult and continuing education. In 1978-79, 22 universities were organising courses with an enrolment of about 1,34,000.[134] A start has also been made with correspondence courses at the secondary level. Radio and television are also being used to supplement correspondence instruction, though in a very small way.

A wide variety of adult education programmes have been orgaised since independence. All the earlier programmes merged in the National Adult Education Programme (NAEP) which was launched in 1978. The National Adult Education Programme aims at involving all agencies (government, voluntary organisations, educational institutions, etc.) in programmes ranging from plain functional literacy to consciousness-raising education for illiterate persons in the 15-35 age-group.

Administratively, the programme works at State and District levels. Each State also has a State resource centre for the production of instructional material, training and evaluation. At its peak in 1979-80, there were approximately 1,00,000 adult education centres under the programme. The Sixth Five Year Plan (1980-85) continued the programme with a few shifts of emphasis and calls for universal literacy in the 15-35 age-group by the end of 1990.[135]

Special Education

Article 41 of the Indian Constitution lays down that the "State shall, within the limits of its economic capacity and development, make effective provision for securing the right to work, to education and to public assistance in cases of unemployment, old age, sickness and *disablement* and in other cases of deserved want". A little further, Article 46 adds that the "State shall promote with special care the educational and economic interests of the *weaker sections* of the people and shall protect them from social injustice and all forms of exploitation".[136]

Broadly speaking the handicapped persons are divided into four main categories, namely, (i) the blind, (ii) the deaf and the dumb, (iii) the orthopaedically handicapped, and (iv) the mentally handicapped.

Earlier, the physically handicapped were treated as a burden on society. They were either provided care by the joint family systems or supported by alms. Attitude to the handicapped has undergone a change and their rehabilitation in the normal stream of life is regarded as essential to the social and economic health of society itself.

India adopted the system of educating handicapped children largely through Christian missionaries who came from Europe. As a consequence, special residential school was the accepted pattern for most handicapped children.

In the early 19th century various forms of integrated education were introduced for certain categories of the disabled. The first school for the blind was set up at Amritsar in 1887 and the first school for the deaf was set up at Bombay in 1885. In 1947 when India attained independence, the country had only 32 schools for the blind and about 235 schools for the deaf. Schools for mentally retarded children began to be set-up in the late thirties and early forties. Special schools for orthopaedically handicapped children are by and large the product of the post-independence period.[137]

After independence, the subject "Education of the Physically handicapped" was entrusted to the Ministry of Education and the

Ministry initiated many programmes to tackle this problem. The subject was given to the Department of Social Welfare since June, 1964. At the State level, Departments/Directorates of Social Welfare handle this programme.[138]

Progress made in regard to different categories of the handicapped is as indicated below:

The Blind

A major project undertaken by Government of India for the education and training of the blind was the establishment of a National Centre for the Blind at Dehra Dun in 1950. The Centre provides a fairly wide range of services. It has (a) Training Centre for the Adult Blind, (b) Model School for a Blind Children, (c) Central Braille Press, (d) The Workshop for the manufacture of Braille Appliances, (e) The National Library for the blind started functioning in 1963, and (f) A School for the partially-sighted children was added for children between 5 and 12 years of age.

There were about 288 schools.

The Deaf

There are about 306 schools and other institutions for the deaf children. The Government of India established a Training Centre for the Adult Deaf at Hyderabad for imparting technical training to deaf adults. In 1962 a school for partially deaf children was added to the Centre.

Orthopaedically handicapped

There are about 134 institutions for the orthopaedically handicapped children in the country.

The Mentally Handicapped

There are about 128 schools for mentally retarded children. The Government of India started a model school for the mentally deficient children in New Delhi.[139]

The Government of India launched a centrally-sponsored scheme of Integrated Education for the Disabled Children (IEDC) in 1974 under the erstwhile Department of Social Welfare. The Scheme was transferred to the Department of Education in 1982. The States of Bihar, Karnataka, Kerala, Maharashtra, Nagaland, Tamil Nadu, Orissa, Mizoram and the

Union Territory of A and N Islands have started implementing the scheme. The scheme has not progressed according to expectations.[140]

Education for all being the goal, efforts are made to Universalize Primary Education (UPE). One of the difficulties in the realization of the UPE goal refers to non-enrolment and drop-out of special groups of children. It is, therefore, necessary that special groups of children receive greater attention to benefit from the expansion of educational facilities under the UPE input. The National Policy on Education (NPE) 1986, underlines the fact that despite the enormous expansion of primary education in the post-independence period, the population of disabled children has not been adequately served as a part of UPE. The Programme of Action (POA), 1986 provides the number of disabled persons in different age-groups based on the Nineteenth and Twenty-eighth National Sample Survey and total population in the Population Statistics Paper 2 of 1983, Government of India. The estimates are presented in the Table given below:[141]

TABLE 2.5: Population of Disabled by Nature of Disability in 1981

Disability	All ages		
	Rural	Urban	Total
(1)	(2)	(3)	(4)
Visually Handicapped	2856575	566159	3422734
Deaf	2818675	543364	3262039
Dumb	1362914	392262	1755176
Orthopaedically handicapped	4238428	1074138	5312616
Total	11276592	2575973	13852565

Note:- Based on prevalent rate given in nineteen and twenty-eighth of National Sample Survey and total population in the Population Statistics paper 2 of 1983, Series I India, A.G. Office.

School for the Disabled Children

Disability	All ages		
	Rural	Urban	Total
(1)	(2)	(3)	(4)
Blind	28	260	288
Deaf/Dumb	27	279	306
Orthopaedically Handicapped	16	118	134
Mentally Retarded	8	120	128

National Council of Educational Research and Training (NCERT) (1992) Fifth All-India Educational Survey, New Delhi, NCERT, Vol. 1, Table 49, p.380-81.

The total disabled children falling under the universalization of primary education age group comes to 4.3 million.[142]

Ensuring equal educational opportunities for the handicapped the NPE states that the objectives should be to integrate the physically and mentally handicapped with the general community as equal partners, to prepare them for normal growth and to enable them to face life with courage and confidence.[143]

Education Research

Systematic educational research is of recent origin in India. Research in universities leading to M. Phil/Ph.D. and post-doctorate degree in education began only after Independence. With socio-political changes in the country, interest in educational research increased rapidly and by 1972 about 50 universities provided facilities for Ph.D. level research in education.[144] In the 1950s, a number of institutions were set up by the Central Government for research in various aspects of education. In 1961, these institutions were amalgamated into NCERT. Within a few years of its establishment in 1961, NCERT published two comprehensive lists of dissertations, completed in Indian universities at the M.Ed. and Ph.D. levels. In the middle of the 1970s, the Indian Council of Social Science Research initiated a programme for surveying research in the social sciences. The Association of Indian Universities publishes at regular intervals, subject lists of all dissertations approved in Indian Universities. In the early 1970s, at the instance of University Grants Commission, the Centre of Advanced Study in Education of the Maharaja Sayajirao University of Baroda took up a project of abstracting all published and unpublished research studies and has since published two monumental surveys.[145] The third has been published by NCERT in 1987.[146] These surveys contain classified abstracts of nearly 2000 research documents.

An overview of the salient features of the educational systems of UK, USA and India are depicted in the preceding sections of this chapter. In the next few pages a comparison of the three education systems is attempted.

COMPARATIVE STUDY OF THE EDUCATION SYSTEMS OF UK, USA AND INDIA

The basic objectives of education in all the three countries i.e. UK, USA and India are almost common. In U.K. the emphasis is on a developing rationality; respect for moral values and instilling the importance of unity and interdependence of life on the planet whereas in U.S.A. the efforts are to provide an opportunity to all children to stretch their minds to full capacity, to develop the ability to adapt to the changes in the society and in general to increase the quality of life. In India the objective of education is intertwined with the goal of life itself i.e. the self-fulfilment and therefore, to develop all such human faculties which help to achieve this goal.

A comparison of the salient features of the educational systems in the three countries is given below:

Educational Structure

UK The education is divided into three stages *i.e.*, (i) primary, (ii) secondary, and (iii) Further. The primary education is upto the age of 11 years, secondary education upto 16 years and senior secondary education upto 18 years.

India India has adopted 10+2 system of education and divided the pre-college education into three stages i.e. (i) Middle, (ii) Secondary, and (iii) Senior Secondary. The Middle level education covers upto the age of 14 (class-1-8), the Secondary level upto the age of 16 (Class-9th-10th) and the Senior Secondary upto the age of 18 (classes 11th-12th).

USA In USA there are three plans covering 12 years of pre-college education:-

(i) K 8-4 Plan
(ii) K 6-3-3 Plan
(iii) K 6-6 Plan

Educational Policy

UK In UK 5 years of education is compulsory.

India In India though the Constitution provides 8 years of compulsory education, so far schooling for five years for about 90 per cent of the children has been provided.

USA In U.S.A. elementary education i.e. upto the age of 14 (Class-VIII) is compulsory.

Controlling Agencies

UK The control is in the hands of local educational authorities;

there are also private schools, aided and recognised by the locai agencies.

India The control is in the hands of Educational Committees of the District and Municipal Boards. There are also private schools recognised and aided by local educational authorities. In India local authorities do not levy educational cess and the assistance of the Government is the only source of their income.

USA The control is vested with the local authorities. The local organisations in USA are the township or County Boards of Educational Districts. Educational Units in USA are smaller than district boards in India. Both Private and Public schools are there. Though accredition of schools is done, yet it is not compulsory. Taxes are levied.

Religion

UK The 'religions agencies that maintain educational institutions in UK are secular and denominational bodies, but then, all the denominational bodies belong to one broad religious order, namely Christianity.

India In India, though the denominational bodies belong to several religions, Hindus form a majority of students even in Christian schools.

USA Some schools are on religious basis, and even belong to minorities.

Private Enterprise

UK In UK private enterprise is allowed in the field of education and the government grants aid to schools opened by private enterprise. There are not much private managed schools getting aids from the government. There are either government owned schools or private managed ones.

India India also admits the private enterprise in the field of education and grants aid to private managed schools.

In India a majority of private managed schools are getting grants-in-aid from the government.

USA The private schools of USA do not get grants in-aid from the state authorities.

Educational Finance

UK In England, all education, including technical, is financed by the Ministry of Education Department of Education and Science, (DES).

As it has already been mentioned, in England, DES is the sole body to finance, develop, organize and establish the technical and professional institutions.

There is a joint financing of the Central Government and the Local Education Authorities (LEA) with a fairly clear line of authority defined between them. Central Government does have a strong voice in the overall provision made for education locally, in buildings, in teachers' salaries and in setting up somewhat national goals of priority in education. Beyond that, the LEAs have the responsibility for education.

India In India some professional and technical institutions are financed by the Department of Education, Ministry of Human Resource Development while others are either under Ministry of Industry, or Ministry of Agriculture or even some are under the Ministry of Labour. This is also a reason for the uneven progress of technical and professional education in India.

In India, some institutions are under the State Departments, others are under the Centre and this creates a certain amount of confusion and is responsible for lop-sided development of the technical and professional education in the country.

Central Government in India assists state universities through University Grants Commission and also undertakes some programmes of school education through National Council of Educational Research and Training (NCERT), an autonomous organisation set up by the Ministry of Education, Government of India. In India, State Governments give grants-in-aids to private schools.

USA Though in USA Federal Government is not directly responsible for education, it has made efforts from time to time in the area. The System of Land Grants for technical and vocational institutions, is a very strong force behind the successful wide-spread network of technical and vocational institutions all over the country.

The Council for Financial Aid to Education gives encouragement and assistance to industrialists, schools, colleges and universities for the promotion and development of vocational education and brings about coordination and cooperation among the industrialists, and educational authorities.

Federal Government in USA looks after education of the Red Indians, military education and acts as a clearing house for information. State Governments in USA do not give grants-in-aids to private schools.

Admission

UK In UK students are admitted after a public examination at the age of eleven.

In UK those who aspire to enter a University are required to sit for the University entrance examination.

India In India admission is on the basis of the school tests.

In India, students are examined at every stage and every year. The quality of the student is determined only by the examination held at the end of the year and at his performance throughout the year or years. India is more examination ridden, and public examination determines the entrance eligibility.

USA There are no public examination at the close of High Schools in U.S.A In some universities and colleges, however entrance examinations are there.

Examination

UK In UK the Bachelor's degrees are awarded both in pass and honours, one with a general course and the other with a more specialized study in one branch. The pass degree is awarded after three years and honours after four years.

India In India also both types of degrees are awarded: the BA (pass) after three years and BA (Honours) also after three years. The Master degree is awarded after two years of Bachelor's degree.

USA In USA the first degree is awarded four years after the

high school, and Master degree is awarded after one year after the Bachelor's degree.

Cost

UK In England education is costly; yet there are larger number of scholarships and better endowments in British universities.

India In India too education is costly. But there are fewer number of scholarships and endowments. Universities are mostly dependent on fees and government grants.

USA In USA there are two types of universities; Private universities and State universities. Tuition fee is nominal in State Universities. In Private universities the tuition fee is high.

Course of Study

UK There is not many choices in combinations of a particular course of study.

India In India a limited choice of combination of a course of study is available.

USA In USA, studies are divided into units and a student can take a fixed number of units, not necessarily from cognate or allied fields. An American student can offer a major in Physics, with History, Spanish Language, Beauty Culture and Psychology as minors.

Vocational/Technical Education

UK In UK the drifting to vocational education is compulsory where the result is poor.

There are more openings for industrial and practical courses and therefore there is less crowding for an academic type of education.

There are more openings of technical education in UK in view of the degree of industrialization that Great Britain has achieved. A certain degree of prestige is also attached with technical education.

There is not any significant arrangement for vocational education of those already in employment, nor there exists a close relation between the institutions and the shop floor.

India In India, there is no drifting to vocational education. It depends upon the will of parents and not upon the result.

In India, more students follow the academic type of school courses, though some opt for vocational courses.

In India facilities for technical education are still poor. Efforts are now being made to increase the facilities for technical education.

In India, not much attention is paid to apprenticeship training. There is no close relation between institutions and the plant.

USA The American secondary schools train students both for university entrance as well as vocational streams.

There are elaborate procedures of vocational education in American high schools. Earning while learning is becoming increasingly common in USA.

As may be expected, USA has better provision for technical education which is given at various levels from high school to the doctoral stage. Technical schools are better equipped and have, perhaps, better qualified teachers. Emphasis is laid on practical work than on mere theory. Along with technical education, some courses on liberal arts are also taken. This prevents the student from being a narrow technician.

In USA the arrangement for vocational education of those already in employment is one of the important aspects of vocational education. There is a very strong cooperation among the institutions, farm and plant. Private and Public sectors play a very significant role in the training of the students.

Higher Education

UK UK has residential, unitary and non-residential, affiliating and federal types of universities. In UK examination is not the main function of the university and teaching functions of the universities are more emphasised than examining functions.

British universities enjoy greater autonomy owing to less dependence on government grants. Even in University Grants Committee, academics dominate and for academic courses and appointments, universities are almost fully independent.

The Chancellor or the Visitor in England is merely a dignitary who has limited functions to perform.

There is not much variation in standards among the different universities.

India

India has also the similar types of universities.

Indian universities were firstly examining bodies and teaching was started some sixty years afterwards; examinations still dominate the programmes of Indian universities.

Indian universities enjoy less academic freedom owing to a greater dependence on government grants.

In India, on the other hand, the Chancellor or the Visitor of the university is either President of India, Vice-President, Prime Minister or Governor, whose directives are to be carried out generally with the consultation and advice of the Central or State Governments. Here the Chancellor or the visitor enjoys large amount of residuary powers.

There is also not much variation in standards among the different universities of India.

USA

All universities can claim state grants in India.

The universities generally, have liberal arts colleges, undergraduate colleges and graduate schools under their Federal structure.

All examinations in American universities are integrated with teaching and class records are emphasised in awarding grades. There is hardly any external examiner in USA at any examination.

American universities enjoy more freedom. There is no organization like UGC in America. The President of a university is an elected representative of the trustees and enjoys all powers except in educational matters.

The President of the Board of Trustees, Dean of Faculty and the Committee work in a spirit of close co-operation and goodwill. There is no Federal interference in the working of universities. Grants are given.

In USA the powers are with the Board of Trustees and elected President formulates all policies except in academic matters. Universities perform their academic functions through faculties under a dean for each faculty. Due to this reason, standards vary in each university and there is no central authority for approval of the curriculum of universities. In American universities there is a great variation in standards of different universities. There even colleges award degrees upto the Doctorate level.

State grants are limited to state universities only in USA.

Adult Education

UK There is no problem of adult illiterates in England because of its tradition of compulsory education for nearly a hundred years. Adult education in England implies further education only to those adults who need it either to raise their vocational competence or to provide them with suitable leisure-time activities.

India In India illiteracy exists on a large scale and as such adult education programmes are primarily directed towards the spread of literacy in the country.

USA In USA, literacy is cent per cent. Literacy programmes are planned only for a few aged Negroes or Red Indians or New Mexicans. Adult education takes the shape of better vocational and recreational facilities.

Teachers

UK Teachers in UK love their profession very much and enjoy social status. They do not run after tuition but help poor students in extra time. They have close relations with parents of the children, they often visit them at their houses and discuss the social and psychological problems of the children. They give lot of care to behavioural development of the children.

In UK coaching is only through the institution and no private coaching exists.

UK offers good salary to the primary teachers who are mostly women.

In UK, an entrant to teacher training is required to have completed at least secondary school education and to have had two/three years' training afterwards. In England, three-year courses of intending teachers are provided mainly in colleges of education. Following a recommendation of the Robbins Committee, students of college of education are able to work for a degree of Bachelor of Education together with a professional teaching qualification by means of a 4-year course. University graduates can take up a one-year course at university departments of education or colleges. The bulk of the teacher training is conducted in institutes of education.

Much emphasis has been given to in service training. A good teacher is he who is himself always learning and always developing his knowledge and understanding of children and young people.

India In India teaching is not considered a profession but just a bread-earning occupation. School teachers pay more attention to private tuition rather than to their normal work in schools. They do not have close contacts with the parents of the children. They do not bother for the behavioural, emotional and psychological problems of the children. Their duty is limited to schools only.

In India salaries are less in comparison to the primary teachers of UK. The teachers are mostly men.

In India teachers of elementary schools are less equipped for their work. We have still untrained teachers. The minimum requirement of general education for teacher training is also low.

In India there is one-year course after graduation for intending teachers of secondary schools. Kurukshetra University started a four-year integrated course (combining academic and professional studies). After this, the four Regional Colleges of Education offer four-year Integrated course for secondary school teachers and two-year Master's degree programme. For untrained but experienced teachers correspondence-cum-summer schools, which may be regarded as sandwich courses, have been started.

In India also much importance, though in theory, has been given to in-service teacher education. University Education Commission stressed that experience needs to be supplemented by experiment. A teacher should become a learner from time to time. NCERT started arranging many teachers' training programmes after the announcement of the New Education Policy of 1986.

USA Teachers in USA take a lot of interest in extra curricular activities of the children. Poor students are given extra time. They divide the subjects into units and allow the child to go with his own speed.

Teachers are well paid and mostly are women. Although teachers' social status depends on the income, they do not engage themselves in private tuitions to supplement their income as is generally being done in India.

There is practically no difference in the professional qualifications between an elementary school teacher and a secondary school teacher in USA. The standards of efficiency in teaching are quite high. The teachers are moreover able to introduce latest psychological innovations even in elementary schools.

In USA general education is the foundation of any programme of professional education. Teachers are expected to have a rich cultural background. Specialised education in subjects, fields or levels is given to all teachers. Internship serves as a period of testing and probation. There, internships are often found in curricular patterns such as the five-year programmes.

The Commission on Teacher Education in USA states that the continued education of teachers means much more than what is normally realised. In USA, a good deal of attention is given to in-service teacher training. It is necessary to have the up-to-date knowledge about new developments to have a continuous growth of intellect and eliminate deficiencies.

The salient features of the educational systems of UK, USA and India delineated in this chapter would enable us to have a proper perspectives of the issues involved in devising a National Educational Information System. The National Information Systems in Education of the three countries are studied in the next chapter.

REFERENCES

1. Great Britain. Central Office of Information, (1987). *Britain: An official handbook*

1987. London: Central Office of Information, p.1

2. *Ibid.*, p.19
3. Paxton, John ed. (1987). *Stateman's Year-book 1987-88*. London: Macmillan, p.1285
4. Great Britain. Central Office of Information. (1987). Britain... *op. cit.*, pp.21-22
5. *Ibid.*
6. *Encyclopaedia Britannica,* Inc.(1988). Britannica book of the year 1988. Chicago: Encyclopaedia Britannica, p. 722
7. Great Britain. Central Office of Informaiton (1987). Britain... *op. cit.*, p.31
8. *Ibid.*, p.33
9. *ibid.*, pp. 34-35
10. Sodhi, T.S.(1975). *Comparative Education, Philosophy, Patterns and Problems of National Systems of UK, USA, USSR*, India. Ludhiana: Mukund Publications, pp.38-39
11. Great Britain. Central Office of Information.(1987). Britain... *op. cit.*, p.19
12. *Ibid.*, p.203
13. *Ibid.*, p.27
14. *Ibid.*, Table 13, p.217
15. *Ibid.*, p.210
16. *Ibid.*, p.6
17. Husen, Torsten and Postlethwaite, T.Neville. eds.(1985). *International Encyclopaedia of Education*. Oxford: Pergamon, vol.9 p.5353
18. Pates, Andrew ed.(1983). *Education Factbook: An A.Z Guide to Education and Training in Britain*. London: Macmillan, p.98
19. Padley, F.H.(1964). *Pergamon Guide to the Educational System in England and Wales*, Oxford: Pergamon, p.ix
20. Brooksbank, K. and Ackstine, A.E. eds.(1984). *Educational Administration*. 22nd edn. Essex: Councils and Education Press, pp. 4-5
21. *ibid.*, p.16
22. *ibid.*, pp.24-25
23. *ibid.*, p.20
24. *ibid.*, p.26
25. Great Britain. Central Office of Information. (1986). *Education in Britain* 1986. London: Central Office of Information, p.163
26. Husen and Postlethwaite. eds. (1985). *International Encyclopaedia of Education. op. cit.*, p.5355
27. Great Britain. Department of Education and Science. (1985). Annual report. London: HMSO, Table 19 p.75
28. Great Britain. Central Office of Information. (1987). Britain... *op. cit.*, p.162
29. Pedley, F.H. (1964). Educational System. *op. cit.*, p.2
30. Evans, Keith. (1975). *Development and Structure of the English Educational System*. London: University of London Press, p.175
31. Great Britain. Central Office of Information (1987) Britain... *op. cit.*, p.164
32. Evans, Keith (1975). Development and Structure.. *op. cit.*, p.197
33. Great Britain. Development of Education and Science. (1985). Annual report. *op. cit.*, p.110
34. Pates, Andrew ed.(1983). Factbook... *op. cit.*, p.110
35. Sodhi, T.S. (1975). Comparative education... *op. cit.*,pp.99-100
36. Great Britain. Central Office of Information. (1974). *Education in Britain. op. cit.*, p.18

37. Great Britain. Central Office of Information. (1987). Britain... *op. cit.*, p.164
38. *Ibid.*, p.165
39. Husen and Postlethwaite eds. (1985). *International Encyclopaedia of Education. op. cit.*, p.53-54
40. Pates, Andrew ed. (1983). Factbook... *op. cit.*, p.53
41. *Ibid.*, p.228
42. Great Britain. Central Office of Information. (1987). Britain... *op. cit.*, p.167
43. Husen and Postlethwaite. eds. (1985). *International encyclopedia of education. op. cit.*, p.5354
44. Great Britain. Central Office of Information. (1987). Britain... *op. cit.*, p.173
45. *Ibid.*, p.175
46. Husen and Postlethwaite. eds. (1985). *International Encyclopedia of Education. op. cit.*, p.5355
47. Great Britain. Central Office of Information (1986). Education in Britain. *op. cit.*, p.173
48. Great Britain. Development of Education and Science.(1981). Education Act 1981. London: HMSO, chapter 60 sec.1
49. Warneck, M. (1978). Special education needs: Report of the Committee of Enquiry into the Education of Handicapped Children and Young People. London: HMSO.
50. Great Britain. Central Office of Information. (1987). Britain., *op. cit.*, p.166
51. *Ibid.*, pp.168-169
52. Husen and Postlethwaite. eds. (1985). *International Encyclopedia of Education. op. cit.*, p.357
53. *Ibid.*, p.5358
54. Encyclopaedia Britannnica Inc. (1978). New Encyclopedia Britannica-Macropaedia. Chicago: *Encyclopedia Britannica,* Vol. 18, p.905.
55. *ibid.*, p. 915
56. Paxton, John. ed. (1987). *Statesman's Year Book 1987-88.* London: Macmillan, p.1374
57. Husen and Postlethwaite eds. (1985). International Encyclopaedia of education. *op. cit.*, p. 5359
58. Paxton, John ed.'1987' . Statesman's Year Book 1987-88, *op. cit.*, p.1368
59. Encyclopaedia Britannica, Inc. 1988. Britannica Book of the year 1988. Chicago: *Encyclopaedia Britannica,* p.724
60. Encyclopaedia Britannica, Inc. (1978). New Encyclopaedia Britannica-Macropaedia. *op. cit.*, vol.18, pp.937-38
61. *Ibid.*, p.929
62. U.S. Department of Commerce. Bureau of Census (1986). Statistical abstracts of the United States. Washington, D.C.: Superintendent of U.S. Documents, Table 721-23 p.433.
63. Husen and Postlethwaite eds. (1985). International Encyclopaedia of Education. *op. cit.*, p.5360.
64. De Crevecceur, Letters from an American farmer, (1782) *In Education in a free society* by S. Alexander Rippa. ;1984'. 5th edn. New York: Longman, p.3.
65. U.S. Department of Education. National Commission on Excellence in Education (1983). A nation at risk- a report. Washington, D.C.: Superintendent of U.S. Documents, p.6.
66. *Ibid.*, pp. 13-14
67. Husen and Postlethwaite eds. (1985). International Encyclopaedia of Education. *op. cit.*, p.5360.

68. U.S. Office of Technology Assessment (1982). Informational Technology and its Impact on American Education-an OTA Report. Washington, D.C. Office of Technology Assessment, p.152.
69. *Ibid.*, pp.152-153
70. Timpane, M. ed. (1974). *Federal Interest in Financing Schooling.* Cambridge, Mass: Balinger, p.4-7
71. Hessong, Arbert F. and Weeks, Thomas H. (1987). *Introduction to Education.* New York: Macmillan, p.343
72. U.S. Office of the Federal Register National Archives and Records Administration (1987). Government Manual 1987/88. Washington, D.C.: Superintendent of U.S. Documents, p.263
73. Husen and Postethwaite eds. (1985). International Encyclopaedia of Education. *op. cit.*, p.5363
74. *Ibid.*
75. Paxton, John ed. (1987). Stateman's Year Book 1987-88. *op. cit.*, pp.1417
76. Cubberley, Dilwood P. (1976). Public Education in the United States In *American Education: A Sociological View* edited by David W. Swift. Boston: Houghton Miffin Co., p.19
77. Unesco: Organisation of Pre-primary Education. Publication No.230. Paris: Unesco, pp.270-71
78. Unesco. Preparation and Issuing of the Primary School Curriculum. Publication No. 194. Paris: UNESCO, pp.141-43
79. Husen and Postlethwaite eds. (1985) International Encyclopaedia of Education. *op. cit.*, p.5361
80. U.S. Department of Education. (1987). Digest of Education Statistics. Washington, D.C.: Superintendent of U.S. Documents, Table 3, p.9
81. Sodhi,T.S. (1975). Comparative Education, Philosophy, Patterns and Problems of National Systems. *op. cit.*, p.175
82. Unesco. Preparation of General Secondary School Curricula-Publication No. 216. Paris: Unesco, pp.315-319
83. U.S. Department of Education. (1987). Digest of Education Statistics. *op. cit.*, Table 3 p.9
84. Blocker, Clyde E. and others. (1965). *Two-year College a Social Synthesis.* Englewood Cliffis, New Jersey: Prentice-Hall, p.32
85. American Association of Junior Colleges. (1972). Junior College Directory. Washington,D.C; *American Association of Junior Colleges,* p.89
86. Gleazer, Edmund J., Jr. (1967). *American Junior Colleges.* Washington.D.C.: American Council of Education, p.3
87. Carnegie Commission on Education. (1970). *Open Door Colleges.* New York: Mc Graw-Hill, p.10
88. Holan, William and Swift, David W. (1976). Community College In *American Education: A Sociologican View* edited by David W. Swift. *op. cit.*, p.98
89. Swift, David W. ed. (1976). *American Education. op. cit.*, pp. 102-103
90. Husen and Postlethwaite. eds. (1985). International Encyclopaedia of Education. *op. it.*, Vol.2 p.243
91. Reinhart, Bruce (1976). Vocational Education In *American Education - A Sociological View* edited by David W. Swift. *op. cit.*, p.270-71
92. National Centre for Educational Statistics (1971). *Directory of Post-Secondary Schools with Occupational Programmes.* Washington, D.C.: Government Printing Office, p.xix

93. Unesco. (1982). *World Guide to Higher Education : A Comparative Survey of Systems,* Degrees and Qualifications. 2nd edn., Paris: Unesco, p.312
94. *ibid.,* p.315
95. U.S. Department of Education (1987). *Digest of Education Statistics. op. cit.,* Table 3, p.9
96. Unesco. (1982). World Guide to Higher Education. *op. cit.,* p.315
97. Unesco. Primary Teacher Training. Publication No. 117. Paris: Unesco, p.242-43
98. Richardson, C.A. and others. *Education of Teachers in England, France and U.S.A. Paris:* Unesco, p.278-81
99. Husen and Postlethwaite eds. (1985). International Encyclopaedia of Education. *op. cit.* p.5364
100. *Ibid.,* p.5362
101. London, Jack and Wenkert, Robert (1976). Adult Education Definition, Description and Analysis In American Education edited by David W. Swift. *op. cit.,* p.236,245
102. Kauffman, James M. and Hallahan, Daniel P. eds. (1981). *Handbook of Special Education.* New Jersey: Prentice-Hall, p.3-4
103. *Ibid.,* p.6
104. Sage, Daniel. (1981). Administration of Special Education In *Handbook of Special Education* edited by Kauffman and Hallahan. *op. cit.,* p.328
105. Husen and Postlethwaite eds. (1985). *International Encyclopaedia of Education. op. cit.,* p.5365
106. India. Ministry of Information and Broadcasting (1987). India 1986-A reference annual. New Delhi: Publication Division, p.1
107. *ibid.,* p.4
108. *Data - A Reference Book.* Decin: B R Phs. corph. Table I.p.48
109. *Ibid.,* Table 2.p.49
110. *Ibid.,* p.11; Table 3,11.3,26.3
111. *Ibid.,* p.20
112. *Ibid.,* p.14
113. *Ibid.,* Table 12.1 p.249
114. *Ibid.,* Table 24.5 p.545
115. Mookerji, Radha Kumud. (1960). *Ancient Indian Education.* 3rd ed. Delhi: Motilal, p. xix
116. *Ibid.,* p. xxvi
117. Naik, J.P. (1982). *Education Commission and After* New Delhi: Allied, p. 1-2
118. India. Ministry of Information and Broadcasting (1991). India 1990 a reference annual. *op.cit.,* p. 370
119. Aggarwal, J.C. (1993). *Eighty Five Year Plan: Planning and Development in India.* Delhi; Shipra, table 10.p-72
120. India. Ministry of Human Resource Development–Department of Education. (1985). Challenge of Education a Policy Perspective. New Delhi: Department of Education, p.68-70
121. India. Ministry of Education and Culture (1984). Report on Educational Developments in India 1981-83. New Delhi: Ministry of Education and Culture, p.19-20
122. India. Ministry of Human Resource Development. (1987). Annual Report 1986-87 Part 1, Department of Education.New Delhi: Department of Education, p.1
123. Bordia, Anil (1985). India: System of Educaion In *International Encyclopaedia of Education* edited by Husen and Postlethwaite. *op. cit.,* p.2429
124. India. Ministry of Education and Culture. (1984). Report on Educational

Developments in India. *op. cit.*, p.22-23

125. India. Ministry of Human Resource Development. (1987). Annual Report 1986-87 Part 1 - Department of Education. *op. cit.*, p.5
126. India. Ministry of Human Resource Development. (1987). Annual Report 1986-87 part 1 - Department of Education. *op. cit.*, p.21
127. *Ibid.*, p.14
128. Institute of Applied Manpower Research (IAMR) - New Delhi (1977) Directroy of Technical in Vocational Institutions In *New Education Policy in India* by P.D. Shukla (1988). New Delhi: Sterling, p.74
129. Shukla, P.D. (1988). *New Education Policy in India*. New Delhi: Sterling, p.82
130. Institute of Applied Manpower Research (IAMR) - New Delhi. (1977). Directory of Technical and Vocational Education and Training Institutions. New Delhi: IAMR, 1018 p.
131. Bordia, Anil (1985) *India: System of Educaion. op.cit.,* p.2430-31
132. *Ibid.*, p.2430
133. India. Ministry of Human Resource Develpment. '1987'. Annual Report part 1 - Development of Educaion *op. cit.*, p.5
134. Buch, M.B. ed. (1987) Third Survey in Education 1978-83. New Delhi: NCERT, Abstract No. 1481
135. Bordia, Anil (1985) India: System of Education. *op. cit.*,p.2429
136. Nayar, D.P. (1981). Planing for the Physically Handicapped In *Third All India Conference on Educational Research* April 22-23, 1981 New Delhi: NCERT, p.1.3.2
137. Rege, A.G. (1981). Education and Rehabilitation of the Disabled In *Third All India Conference on Educational Research,* April 22-23, 1981 New Delhi: NCERT, p.1.4.10
138. Nayar, D.P. (1981). Planning for the Physically Handicapped *op. cit.*, p.1.3.5-6
139. *Ibid.*, p.1.3.10-11
140. National Council of Educational Research and Training (NCERT) - New Delhi (1987). Project Integrated Education for the Disabled - a document. New Delhi: NCERT. p.6
141. India. Ministry of Human Resource Development - Department of Education (1986). National Policy on Education 1986: Programme of Action. New Delhi: Department of Education. p.130.
142. Narasimhan, M.C. and Mukherjee, A.K. (1987) Disability a Continuing Challenge. New Delhi: Wiley Eastern, Table 1. p.116
143. India. Ministry of Human Resource Development - Department of Education. (1986). National Policy on Education 1986. New Delhi: Department of Education, p.6
144. Bordia, Anil. (1985). India: System of Education. *op.cit.*, p.2426-32
145. Buch, M.B. ed. (1974). *Survey of Research in Education. Baroda: Centre of Advanced Study in Education,* Maharaja Sayajirao University of Baroda, Vol. 1&2
146. Buch, M.B. ed. (1987). Survey and Research in Education. New Delhi: NCERT, Vol.3

3

EDUCATIONAL INFORMATION SYSTEMS

U.K. EDUCATIONAL INFORMATION SYSTEM

Libraries

Historical Perspectives

Before the fifteenth century, there was no 'general public' for books in the sense in which the phrase is used today. Books were for the most part in Latin: they were, therefore, for the learned, and learning was virtually the monopoly of the clergy. The ranks of the clergy, however, included not only the members of the religious orders, and the hierarchy of the secular church, but also many who would now a days be identified as stewards, laymen-clerks, secretaries, lawyers, teachers, physicians and civil servants. It was this body which constituted the 'public' for books, and its needs, though varied, were strictly professional.

Books were, by today's standards, fantastically expensive. In these circumstances, though some of the clergy managed to assemble small libraries of their own, most of them necessarily relied on institutional libraries. Libraries existed mainly in the monasteries and other religious houses, and in the universities. Apart from libraries, the collections of books were to be found also in the secular cathedrals, in collegiate churches, in parish churches and even, towards the close of the Middle Ages, in a few schools.

Though there were many libraries, there were very few books for all the libraries and were by modern standards very small. The universities benefited more than other institutions by the munificence of donors, but even here the largest collections recorded did not exceed 1,000 volumes. The Oxford and Cambridge University Libraries were substantially smaller than this, and none of the Scottish University Libraries attained any considerable size during the medieval period. It was estimated that if all the libraries in Britain put together, they could muster as many as 100,000 volumes.

All these medieval libraries, were, of course, basically theological. We find that the books were divided into nine classes or distinctions. The first distinction was devoted to Bible and books on the Bible; four were devoted to theology; two to civil and canon law; one to logic, philosophy, rhetoric, medicine, chronicles and romances; and one to poetry, grammar and dictionaries. Here we have the basic elements which are to be found in nearly all medieval libraries, but of course the emphasis on the subjects varied according to the use the library was intended to have.

Library Organization

In the fourteenth and fifteenth centuries a very large proportion of books came by way of gift or bequest. The university and college libraries in particular benefited in this way. The college libraries were often endowed by their founders.

In the early Middle Ages, as the books were few and the problem of storage presented little difficulty, they were kept in chests or cupboards. By the mid-fifteenth century, however, it was becoming increasingly common to have a special library room and fitted with lecterns to hold the books and provide accommodation for reading. Usually, it seems, the books were chained to the lecterns. Libraries of this kind became the general rule at the universities and in the secular cathedrals. It was particularly useful to name a central place where books could be readily consulted and at the same time adequately safeguarded. Some books were chained and some were kept in cupboards. The chained constituted, "a sort of reference library, available to members of the house, and very likely to the members of the public also, or at least to properly accredited persons".[1] The rest remained in cupboards and were available for loan.

Thus the distinction between the reference library and the lending library was established early. The libraries of the two universities of Oxford and Cambridge were generally for reference. However, at Oxford there was a separate set of books, kept in a chest which was available on loan to masters. The college libraries had loan collections as well as chained reference collections.

The growth of the size of libraries made it necessary to provide some kind of a catalogue. A remarkable example is the catalogue of the Benedictin priory of St. Martin at Dover compiled by its librarian John Whytefeld in 1387. This was a triple catalogue, comprising a shelf list, a list showing the individual works of each author and an alphabetical list by titles of all the works in the library. The first attempt at multi-library catalogue, now known as inter-library catalogue, or union catalogue, was a list known as the Registram Librrerum Angliae.[2]

Publis Libraries

The monastic libraries, it appears, were reasonably accessible for purposes of reference to all who desired to use them which meant, in practice, to clergy and students. It is in the secular cathedral libraries, rather than in the monastic libraries, that a resemblance closest to the modern concept of a public library can be found.

The fifteenth century saw not only the continued growth of institutional libraries of all kinds, and a rapid improvement in library facilities, but also a great increase in the number of books in private circulation. By the mid-fifteenth century literacy, in the sense of an ability to read and write in English, was almost universal among the gentry and the merchant class of London and south-east England, and was becoming increasingly common among the ranks of craftsmen and shopkeepers. It is against this background of increasing literacy that the first public libraries made their appearance. Three such libraries existed in the fifteenth century, the first being the Guildhall Library of London in 1423 and the other two public libraries were established later in the century, one at Worcester and one at Bristol. The libraries were attached to religious guilds and were open to both men and women.

The introduction of printing made possible the multiplication of books on a vast scale which laid the foundation for and extended public library service. However, in mid-century, the destruction of most of the old medieval libraries brought to an end such public facilities as these institutions were offering. Only in the closing decades of Elizabeth's reign the work of reconstruction was taken up and provision for public reading was made on a small scale.

Until the Reformation, libraries were almost all institutional in character. These libraries became numerous, especially in England from the late seventeenth century onwards. As time went on they became increasingly accessible to the public, and less exclusively religious in character, so that they came to form a bridge between the medieval libraries and the modern Public Library System which had its beginning in the mid-nineteenth century.

The first municipal foundation independent of either Church or school was at Norwich in 1608. In 1656 it was converted into a subscription library, for reference only, on the basis of a subscription of 12d per quarter. Another independent municipal library was that at Bristol, established in 1615, for the furtherance of learning.[3] In 1740 the library was transferred to a private subscription one and came into public possession in 1853. The movement for the establishment of town libraries continued in full swing until almost the eve of the Civil War.

More than one-third of the total number of endowed libraries were founded in the years between 1680 and 1720. Whereas in the period before 1680 the main concentration had been on the establishment of libraries in the larger towns, most of the new libraries were in small towns and villages. After 1720 the pace slackened and although libraries continued to be founded here and there well into the nineteenth century, only a few can be assigned to the period after 1770. Altogether about 160 libraries were founded between 1680 and 1800. The great majority of these post-1680 libraries were in the smaller centres of population, especially in rural areas. In the eighteenth century the lending of books became much more common.

The subject coverage of the libraries of this period varied according to the origins of the collection. Theology was always well represented. English books were common in most libraries. The subjects included not only theology and the classics but works of general literature, history, topography travel and natural science. They also included mathematics, astronomy, medicine, agriculture, philosophy, education, poetry and the fine arts.

Development of Public Libraries

The first Public Libraries Act was passed in 1850, which was subsequently amended several times. It empowered local authorities to provide Public Libraries and by 1900, most cities and towns had done so. However, inadequate financial resources restricted their spread. The limitation of the service to urban areas arose because of the fact that when the first legislation was passed there was no large unit of local government for rural areas: country councils did not exist.

The Act of 1919 attempted to remove some of the difficulties and deficiencies. It abolished the tax limitation: henceforth local authorities could spend what they wished on the public library service, but no money was forthcoming from national sources. It also gave country councils responsibilities for areas not already served. However, the responsibility was permissive–no library authority was compelled to provide a service.

There were no national standard, and no government department was responsible for supervision. There was no provision for co-operation between public libraries and no co-ordination of their services. There were over 600 public library authorities.

Notwithstanding all these difficulties caused by inadequate legislation, the public library service flourished. In 1925, it was said that over half the people living in county library areas were with library service and by 1958, the gap had been almost totally filled.

By 1958, there were over 12 million public library users in England and Wales. There was complete coverage. All potential library authorities had adopted the Libraries Acts, and the number of service points had grown from probably less than 5,000 in 1919 to over 25,000. Stocks of books had reached in 1958 over 60 million and book loans nearly 400 million. It was realised that public libraries were an essential factor in social progress.

Public Library Cooperation

Lacking statutory powers, local authorities had set up co-operative interloan bureaux on a voluntary basis and, by 1958, there were ten of these formal organizations of libraries on a geographical basis for interloan of books, with a national focal point in the National Central Library.

With the growing importance of general education, especially in the area of adult education, the public library was seen as an 'opportunity for bringing all classes together, and uniting them in the common bond of literary pursuits'.[4]

The Ministry of Education set-up a Committee under the chairmanship of Sir Sydney Roberts to consider the redistribution of public library functions.[5] The committee made it clear in its report of 1959 that there were two vital requirements for the reform of the public library service. One was the creation of large and more viable library authorities. The other was the formulation of detalied standards of service, with adequate supervision by a government department.

The Government accepted the report in principle, and appointed two working parties to examine details. One for co-operation and one for standards.

A minimum standard for book purchase was laid down of 7200 volumes annualy, to give a fair conspectus of the total range of books published. The annual purchase should be at least 250 volumes per 1000 of population, of which 90 should be adult non-fiction. A viable unit of about 30,000 population was contemplated.

The standard for staff was that of one non-manual staff member per 2,500 population, with a percentage of 25 to 40 per cent qualified, according to the size of the unit.[6]

The new Libraries Act, 'The Public Libraries and Museums Act of 1964, based on these reports, was introduced into the House of Commons in 1964 and came into operation on 1st April 1965. This statute for England and Wales embodies the establishment of Advisory Councils, the promulgation of standards, the size of the library authority and powers in case of default, and the designation of Regional Councils.[7]

The local Government Act of 1972 of England and Wales created an entirely new public library map and new terms of reference for library co-operation in the future.

The formation of the Association of West Midland Metropolitan Chief Librarians in 1974 was with the object of discussing matters of common interest and to coordinate policy among a restricted membership of the seven metropolitan districts. Co-operation with allied services, co-operative binding, inter-availability of tickets and the possibility of forming a National Liaison Committee of Metropolitan District Chief Librarians are the points under purview.

The co-operative role of the public library is also enhanced by schemes that have been evolved within the special and the academic libraries.[8]

National Libraries

By an Act of Parliament of 1753 the establishment of the British Museum was made. The Act provided for bringing together in a single repository the collections of libraries which were under the possession of the Crown and the Harleian manuscripts. Before the museum was opened to the public in 1759, it was augmented by a gift of the Royal Library, which was transferred to the trustees by George II in 1757.

It embraced, from the beginning, both printed books and manuscripts. As we have seen, the Royal Library was transferred in 1757 to the newly founded British Museum and its right to free copies of published works was afterwards adjudged to have been transferred at the same time. In 1971 a White Paper on working of all the constituents of the British National Library was presented to Parliament by which it got the collective title "the British Library" and British Library Act was passed in 1972.

The structure of the British Library comprises three divisions plus a central administrative unit. The Reference Division comprises the former British Museum Library and the Science Reference Library, the Newspaper Library, and the Library of the Library Association. There is a Central Administration and a Research and Development Department, incorporating the office for Scientific and Technical Information.[9]

Its main functions according to legislation adopted in 1972 are storing and providing for use in the reading rooms a complete set of national publications and as complete as possible collection of foreign literature for use in reading rooms; organizing effective central loan as well as photocopy services; and maintaining centralized cataloguing, collaboration, and cooperation with national and foreign research libraries.[10]

Academic Libraries

School Libraries

European culture is based upon a tradition of book reading. The association of a school with a library is common. The first reference to school library is lost in antiquity. The tradition of English school at Canterbury was begun in A.D. 298. The concept of the library as a place where other reference material besides books, may be kept is illustrated by Ashton's Ordinances at Shrewsbury in 1578, which prescribed buildings to include "a library and gallery for the said schools, furnished with all manner of books, maps, spheres, instruments of astronomy and all other things appertaining to learning which may be either given to the school or procured with the school money".[11]

The report of the Cross Commission in 1888 included among its recomendations the establishment of school libraries. "Unless the scholars ... acquire a taste for reading, their schools learning will not be followed up in later life and accordingly the establishment of school libraries is strongly recommended." It took some years for the suggestion to bear fruit. In 1906 the Board of Education in its Building Regulations for Secondary Schools stated that a room furnished for use as a library was desirable. In 1915 the English Association published its pamphlet (No. 33) on school libraries, drawing attention to the fact that certain well-known schools were making use of their libraries.

After the First World War, state-aided secondary education began to grow apace, there was an increasing interest in the provision of libraries. In 1928 the Board of Education published a memorandum on the subject. In 1937 the School Library Association was founded. The Spens Report on Secondary Education (1938) noted, in dealing with the teaching of English, that "there is often more real education going on in a good school's library than in any of its classrooms", and the Norwood Report of Curriculum and Examinations in Secondary Schools (1943) devoted a considerable amount of attention to libraries.

The passage of the New Education Act in 1944, making secondary education universal, created a new situation fraught with immense opportunity. In 1961, Sir John Hasom, while gathering evidence for his report "Half our future", said "only a quarter of the schools in our survey had an adequate library room which they were able to keep for its proper use and more than another quarter had no library room at all."[12] The report points out that 'It is now a common place that the school library is as essential for work in the humanities as the laboratory is in science".

By then, the primary and junior schools of the country had caught an idea that books, as a library collection, were an excellent and indeed necessary adjunct to the bringing up of the young. By the time of the Plowden report, it could be confidently asserted that junior schools' libraries of 4,000 to 5,000 books were quite common.[13]

Aims of the School Library

(i) To introduce boys and girls to books of all kinds;
(ii) To encourage reading for pleasure;
(iii) To teach pupils to use books and to learn from them without the presence or help of a teacher;
(iv) To teach them to understand the library's management (the use of the catalogue and classification scheme), so that they may be able to use public or university library without difficulty;
(v) To teach respect for books and to remove bad habits such as the turning down of page corners to mark a place.

There is a provision of class libraries in the primary schools and subject-libraries in secondary and grammar schools.

College Libraries

Technical and Further Educaiton Colleges

In the early years of organized further education in England and Wales very few technical colleges possessed identifiable libraries. For the most part books were kept in classrooms and laboratories and used for teaching or ready reference. The first official recognition of a need for some kind of a library can be found in the Thomson Report on natural science in education (1918), which recommended that libraries of technical books should be available to senior students. In 1926 the Board of Education found an almost universal lack of adequate libraries in colleges. A survey in 1927 for the Association of Technical Institutions, revealed that where a library did exist, on average its stock was three hundred volumes, with an annual expenditure of £ 20.

The next ten years brought only marginal improvement. Even by 1938, much of technical education was still almost not associated with reading. Only 13 libraries had collections of over 5,000 volumes, only 15 had a book fund of £ 200, and there were in all just 21 full time college librarians.

The Second World War prevented any action to improve matters, and it is not until the post-war period of reorganisation and expansion in technical eduation that the start of significant library development, could be seen.

After recognising the importance of college libraries, in 1956, a White Paper on technical education was issued recommending that every technical college should have a library with an adequate book fund. It also encourages the provision of information service to industry and cooperation with other libraries.[14]

To classify their bookstock, most colleges at this time favoured DDC or UDC or modified versions of these schemes; nearly all libraries did their own cataloguing. The only group to have a co-operative scheme was in Hamfordshire, where county Library headquarters supplied books with UDC classification. In library technology Hatfield was again a leader, creating the basis of the National Reprographic Centre for Documentation; but the provision of microforms spread slowly. Photocopying was becoming a common service, but Telex was used experimentally by only one college library by 1960.[15]

User instruction services were, however, more advanced. Many libraries had issued introductory guides and other publications such as reading lists, accession lists and bulletins. The formal teaching of library and literature use by lectures and project work had become and established part of many colleges' library service.

By 1974, there were 552 technical and further education colleges in England and Wales, including the thirty polytechnics. 94 per cent of them had a libarary. The average college library by 1974 had a total staff of 3.4 of whom 1.5 were professional librarians, while stocks averaged 16,500 volumes and 162 current serials, with additions of nearly 1500 volumes per annum.[16]

Colleges of Educaion

The history of libraries in colleges of education is sketchy until 1938. In the years upto the Second World War library development in training colleges for teachers was slow and insignificant. The Education Act of 1944 resulted in a need for more teachers, many of whom were recruited from returning ex-servicemen. There was also a rise in the birth rate, which affected primary and secondary education in the late 1940s and 1950s and higher education in the later 1950 and early 1960s. To cope with these developments many new colleges were established under local government control, their numbers grew to 113 by 1967. The impact on college libraries was considerable. In 1960 the original two-year course of training was lengthened to three years and the Robbins Report of 1963 resulted in the introduction of degree courses (B.Ed) from the mid-1960s. Training colleges were known from 1964 as colleges of education–more advanced courses produced a different kind of pressure on college libraries: there was a need for more advanced material, more reference works and bibliographies and more bibliographical advice and assistance to readers.

The 1972 James Report on teacher education and training gave recommendations on the restructuring of courses for teachers, involving a new diploma (Dip.HE) and degree, and on the role of colleges in relation to universities, polytechnics and other colleges. This gave rise to a White Paper in late 1972, entitled 'Education: A framework for expansion'. This produced a new round of college mergers and expansion and upgrading of existing single colleges. The products of these changes are the new colleges of higher education, which local education authorities began to create in 1975. Many college authorities have appointed librarians with the salary and status of a head of academic department, to ensure proper coordination and improvement of services.[17]

Co-operation and Coordination

As early as 1652, Dr. Laingbaine, the Provost of Queen's College, Oxford, suggested that libraries should have a common catalogue of resources to help students to locate any items they needed.[18]

By 1955 the pattern of college development had become clearer, and so had the possible requirement for a local regional information service. Coordination was successful because full financial control remained with the country technical librarian.

The outstanding development in the field of co-operative activity had been the Council of Polytechnic Librarians (COPOL) which paves the way of Chief Librarians in dealing with the directors of polytechnics, local authorities, the DES and other interested parties. COPOL has regular meetings, its sub-committees report on topics of current interest, it organises seminars for polytechnic library staff development, and it exchanges statistical and other data for use by chief librarians in planning. There is a COPOL vacation reading scheme to enable students to use the polytechnic or university library nearest to their homes, during vacations. Local cooperation between libraries has become a major concern for several polytechnics, such as Newcastle-upon-Tyne and Sheffield, and Hatfield.

In 1976 eleven polytechnic libraries had operational systems, ranging from on-line circulation control with Telepen Data-Capture equipment at Sheffield's new Eric Mensforth Library to the full British Library Bibliographic Services Division (BIBSD) cataloguing service to which city of London Polytechnic has subscribed to since 1974. Kingston is a full member of Birmingham Libraries Co-operative Mechanisation Project (BICMSP), while Sunderland has been producing a machine-readable catalogue since late 1973.[19]

University Libraries

It is a truism that, by and large, libraries reflect the communities they are designed to serve. Nowhere is this more true than in relation to the libraries of academic institutions. A proper understanding of the British University library can follow only from a clear appreciation of the British University.[20]

Oxford University

Although Oxford was recognised as a studium generale before 1200, it was not until 1214 that recognition by the Pope gave it full standing as a university. Robert Grorseteste, Bishop of Lincoln, gave a small library to the Oxford in 1253, and there was a small library for the general use of the scholars in St. Mary's Church, but most of the college libraries at Oxford were not begun until the fourteenth century or later.

The general university library at Oxford had a complicated early history and did not emerge as an effective collection until the fifteenth century. In fifteenth-century Oxford, only graduates and people in religious orders who had studied philosophy eight years were allowed to study in the library of the university.[21]

The religious troubles of the sixteenth century severely crippled it. When Henry VIII ordered the dissolution of the monasteries and religious orders in 1537, it marked the beginning of one of the most tragic episodes in the history of libraries. The valuable libraries of the monasteries suffered destruction simply because they were housed in an institution under attack. Consequently, thousands of invaluable and irreplaceable books and manuscripts were destroyed. In the 1550s Edward VI's Royal Commissioners almost completely destroyed the remainder of the libraries of Combridge and Oxford.

The Central Library at Oxford was reborn between 1598 and 1602 when the indefatigable Thomas Bodley refurnished it with two library necessities: stacks and books. Thomas James was selected as the first librarian of the new library that was to become known as the "Bodleian". James issued the first printed catalogues to the library, numbering about two thousand titles, in 1605. Its growth since that date has been continuous. The Bodleian library moved into a new, sparate library building in 1612. By 1620 the Bodleian claimed 16,000 volumes and by 1770, nearly 30,000 and by 1900 the Oxford University libraries contained over 8,00,000 volumes and 41,000 manuscripts.[22]

English higher education, once the monopoly of Oxford and Cambridge, has expanded with increasing rapidity in the twentieth century. Oxford and Cambridge continue their leadership in academic library areas, although the libraries at both institutions are characterized by extreme decentralization. Both libraries contain in aggregate very substantial research collections, and are counted among the finest university libraries in the world.

Cambridge University

The earliest specific reference to a library of the University of Cambridge is to be found in the wills of William Hunden and William Loring (March 1416). There are, of course, earlier references to books in the possession of the university, but make no mention either of a library or of a librarian. The available evidence suggests that from the middle of the fourteenth century at least, the university owned and kept in its treasury a small collection of books which began to be expanded and was formally established as the common library of the university during the second decade of the fifteenth century. In 1440 there were 99 books and in 1473 the collection was increased to 330 volumes. They were, however, primarily medieval in content.[23]

Down to the nineteenth century there were really only two universities in England, Cambridge and Oxford; The libraries of these two universities were already centuries old by 1500, but the religious troubles of the following century severely crippled them.

Although the Cambridge University libraries fared better in the sixteenth century than those at Oxford, the Central Library there still had only 300 printed books and 150 manuscripts in 1582. Moreover, Cambridge had no benefactor such as Sir Thomas Bodley. After the Restoration of Charles II in 1660, Cambridge received some royal attention and the library received several notable gifts and bequests from the King's friends. Henry Lucas left a collection of four thousand volumes to Cambridge in 1666, and Bishop Tobias Rustat gave £ 1,000 for the purchase of books. It contained nearly a million volumes by 1900.

University Libraries in Scotland and Ireland

Although Oxford and Cambridge were for centuries the only universities in England, other universities were established in Scotland and Ireland. The University of Glasgow, founded in 1453, had a notable library almost from the beginning, while St. Andrews University, founded about the same time, dates its Central Library from 1610. The library at the University of Edinburgh was founded in 1583. A fourth Scottish University, at Aberdeen, was founded before 1500, but its earliest library records date from the 1630 and its collection never equalled the others in size or importance.

In Ireland the Library of Trinity College in Dublin began in 1601. By 1604 this collection contained four thousand volumes, and it grew steadily to become in time the most important library in Ireland. By 1900 it contained over 3,00,000 volumes and two thousand manuscripts.

English higher education, once the monopoly of Oxford and Cambridge, has expanded with increasing rapidity in the twentieth century. These new libraries were generally spared any serious difficulty in First World War, but placed a severe test in the Second World War. Today a number of major universities exist across England, and they are served by large and modern libraries. The University of London is typical, with its impressive library numbering over four million volumes.[24]

Universities of United Kingdom

There are forty-four universities in England, Scotland and Wales, while two universities are in Northern Ireland. They are:

1.	University of Aberdeen	(1495)
2.	Aston University	(1966)
3.	University of Bath	(1966)
4.	University of Birmingham	(1900)
5.	University of Bradford	(1966)
6.	University of Bristol	(1909)
7.	Brunel University	(1966)
8.	University of Buckingham	(1983)
9.	University of Cambridge	13th Century
10.	City University	(1966)
11.	University of Dundee	(1967)
12.	University of Durham	(1832)
13.	University of East Anglia	(1964)
14.	University of Edinburgh	(1583)
15.	University of Essex	(1961)
16.	University of Exeter	(1955)
17.	University of Glasgow	(1451, 1577)
18.	Heriot-Watt University	(1966)
19.	University of Hull	(1954)
20.	University of Keele	(1962)
21.	University of Kent at Canterbury	(1965)
22.	University of Lancaster	(1964)
23.	University of Leeds	(1904)
24.	University of Leicester	(1957)
25.	University of Liverpool	(1903)
26.	University of London	(1836)
27.	Loughborough University of Technology	(1966)
28.	Victoria University of Manchester	(1903)
29.	University of Newcastle Upon Tyne	(1851, 1963)
30.	University of Nottingham	(1948)

31. Open University (1969)
32. University of Oxford 13th Century
33. University of Reading (1926)
34. University of St. Andrews (1411)
35. University of Salford (1967)
36. University of Sheffield (1905)
37. University of Southampton (1952)
38. University of Stirling (1967)
39. University of Strathclyde (1964)
40. University of Surrey (1966)
41. University of Sussex (1961)
42. University of Wales (1893)
43. University of Warwick (1965)
44. University of York (1963)
45. University of Ulster (1984)
46. Queen's University of Belfast (1908, 1982)[25]

Collection

The University Library is a repository for a great variety of material, in manuscript, type-written, printed, photographed and recorded-speech form, which it is important to preserve irrespective of whether or not it is being put to current use. The Policy document of a university library will consider all subject fields which are to be developed in relation to the needs of the students and staff of the university, all special collections and all types of material–whether printed or not. Some examples of the material are given below:

(a) Students' tests; (b) Books currently published; (c) Serials; (d) Currently published periodicals; (e) Rare books and manuscripts; (f) Back sets of periodicals; (g) Maps; (h) Music; microforms, recorded sound on tapes or records; Cine films and other visual aids; and cards and tapes for computers.

The value of the holdings of a university library is determined not only by their usefulness as instructional tools, but also by their research potential–a factor which it is not by any means easy to assess. The prime obligation of a university library is to the members of the institution of which it forms a part. It has to satisfy the needs of the undergraduate, and also to meet the requirements of the graduate student who is embarking on research, and the much more complex and exacting demands of the mature scholar. The University library runs an extensive loan service, and has to undertake all the administrative tasks entailed in such a service.

Library Staff

British University libraries normally have four or five grades of staff, the graduate grade, the professionally qualified non-graduate grade, the professionally unqualified non-graduate grade, secretarial and clerical grade and the technicians' grade. Cleaners, porters and maintenance staff are not included in these categories.

The graduate grade is divided into several sections by salary scales-librarian, deputy librarian and assistant librarians. In universities these scales are on par with the academic staff salary scales. The qualifications of the staff are comparable with those of their academic colleagues.[26]

University Library Co-operation

Among the university libraries, the co-operative links exist through the scheme of Regional Library Co-operation, which was established between 1930 and 1940, mainly on the initiative of the Carnegie United Kingdom Trust. Under this scheme a union catalogue is maintained in each of the regions (with one exception) into which England and Wales are divided, with the aim of making known the contents of each library in the region. Any library which is unable to satisfy a request from its own stock forwards it to the regional bureau, and if the item is available in the region the holding library is asked to send it to the library making the request. If the item is not available in the region, the request is in most cases sent to the National Central Library–to which university libraries also apply direct–which may supply it from its own stock, or trace it to a special or academic library co-operating directly, or to another region by means of its own catalogue, or by circulating the request. A similar scheme is in operation is Scotland through the Scottish Central Library in Edinburgh. In this inter-lending scheme the university libraries play a prominent part.

The libraries of British universities do not regard their obligations as being confined to students and teachers in their own institutions. They are an integral and important part of the general pattern of library services in Great Britain, and any assessment of their usefulness should take this fact into consideration. Together with the public libraries of the big cities and of certain larger counties, they constitute a rich accumulation of the records of mankind's experience and achievement.

Educational Research Institutions

Department of Education and Science (DES)

The main areas of responsibility of DES are: (1) general promotion of education, (2) the Government's relations with universities (GB), and (3) fostering Civil sense in Britain. The main concerns of the department are formulating national education policies, allocating resources and co-ordinating with the other partners in the education service (the local education authorities, governing bodies of educational institutions, the teaching profession, the Churches and voluntary organisations). The Department of Education and Science discharges its responsibilities through research Councils and University Grants Committee. The Department is also responsible for the training and supply of all teachers.

National Foundation for Educational Research (NFER)

The major research institute outside the universities is the autonomous National Foundation for Educational Research in England and Wales, with income mainly from funds received from research projects and from corporate members, including local education authorities, teachers' organisations and universities. It also receives a small government grant.[27]

The NFER was founded in 1946 and has the legal status of an independent research foundation. Its main area of work is the national monitoring of students' achievement within the basic areas of the curriculum. It also focuses on teaching styles and pupils performance at the primary level, the development of assessment materials in Welsh language, the evaluation of technical education programmes, and assessment in special education. It carries research work in the primary school and method of learning reading.[28]

Research into the theory and practice of education and the organisation of educational services is supported financially by central and local governments. Universities and other higher educational institutions, teachers' associations and certain independent bodies shoulder this responsibility.

Libraries Cooperation and Networking

National Central Library (NCL)

Library cooperation in England started at the beginning of the twentieth century. Both inside and outside the library profession it was felt that book stocks of individual libraries should be coordinated and their use should be maximized. In the early days some public libraries exchanged their printed catalogues and made personal arrangements for lending books to each other.

Today, compared with other countries, a high standard of voluntary co-operation exists with the various libraries of the U.K. national network; public library membership is free and the tickets of one authority are accepted by other authorities. Public reference libraries are open and free of charge to all. Public university and special libraries co-operate and a more responsible national library service with a unified control is prevalent.

The co-operation started with the Adams' report submitted to the Carnegie United Kingdom Trustees (CUKT) in 1915 with a recommendation to establish a Central Library of Students (CLS). The CLS came into being in March 1916. In the early days, only some eight public libraries participated in the scheme of co-operation. In 1919 the University Extension Book Union was started and the CLS further extended its services to soldiers. In 1923-24, co-operation with special libraries was established.

In 1924-25, the Scottish Central Library for Students and in 1926, the Irish Central Library for Students also joined and more special libraries were added to the list.

The work of the CLS was given further impetus by the publication in 1927 of the Departmental Committee Report on Public Libraries in England and Wales (Kenyan Committee Report). In March 1930 the CLS became the National Central Library (NCL). Royal Charter was granted to the NCL in 1931 and its functions were:

(i) to supply on loan to libraries, or in exceptional cases to individuals, books for study which cannot conveniently be obtained by any other way;
(ii) to supply such books on loan to groups and to adult students;
(iii) to act as an exchange or clearing house for mutual loans of such books among the libraries; and
(iv) to act as a centre of bibliographical information, both for national and international purposes.

Regional Library Systems

The early 1930s also saw the establishment of regional library systems.

The Kenyan Committee had recommended the setting up of a system of library regions covering the whole country and linked by the CLS. In 1931 the CLS became the NCL.

The Northern Regional Library System had come into existence in 1930; while inter-library lending began in 1931; a union catalogue of stock of participant libraries was started, a duplicate copy being sent to the NCL. The pattern was so successful that it was adopted by other areas, and the 1930s saw the creation of regional library bureaus in the West Midlands (1930), Wales and Monmouthshire (1931), the South-East (1933), the East Midlands (1934) the North-West (1935), Yorkshire (1935), and the South-West (1936). Scotland and Ireland were served by their own central libraries and these formed part of the country-wide regional libraries network. These regional libraries provided a united regional front coordinating with the NCL.

The war and post-war years caused arrears in Union catalogues and other work undertaken by both the NCL and the regional library bureaus. These arrears, together with the inadequate financial resources and continuing debate on the general principles of library cooperation led to the appointment of a Joint Working Party to investigate the national network.

Development in library co-operation, particularly in the field of special libraries resulted in the publication of many works of co-operative effort, some of which include the British National Bibliograph–the superb example of co-operative cataloguing, the National Foundation of Educational Research's Technical Education Abstracts, British Technology Index and British Humanities Index etc.

The NCL—the national centre of the regional library systems had begun to build up its central loan stock in the field of humanities and social sciences, since it was assumed that scientific needs would be satisfactorily dealt with by the National Lending Library for Science and Technology (NLLST). Today, the NCL is providing almost all loan services in the humanities and, to a great extent in the social sciences. It is estimated that some 2500 libraries of all kinds of benefit from its services.

Co-operation by negotiation has been established with foreign libraries; redistribution and exchange has been conducted through the British National Book Centre; and the National Central Library had undertaken the publication of the British Union Catalogue of Periodicals (BUCOP), the publication of which has made possible the identification of periodicals in all fields of knowledge.

University Library Systems

Although some university libraries have participated in regional schemes, the arrangements for the loan of books among university libraries were made exclusively through the Association of University Teachers (upto 1931) and by the NCL (after 1931). In 1950, Standing Conference of National and University libraries (SCONUL) was inaugurated to get University Library Co-operation and examination of the problems of university libraries. The emphasis on university libraries co-operation was laid on by the Robins Report on Higher Education (1961-63) and Parry Report (June 1967).

Integrated National Library Service

The Parry Committee recommended inter alia that the library departments of the British Museum should be reconstituted as a national library. In December 1967, the Secretary of State for Education and Science set up the National Libraries Committee under Dr. F.S. Dainton, Vice-Chancellor of Nottingham University for the purpose. The report of this Committee was presented to Parliament in June 1969.

The Dainton Committee clearly stated that, except in sharing a common aim, the many different libraries and information services do not at present form a well-ordered pattern of complementary or co-operating parts and that, with such diversity of aims and services, unified administration is not possible. The Committee recommended that the future administrative structure of a national library service should be so designed as to ensure that the necessary degree of co-operation between the various library units could be established and maintained and that these conditions could only be satisfied by the creation of a strong Central administration.

In a government White Paper published on January 13,1971, it was announced to establish a National Libraries Organization to be called the British Library.[29]

The passing of the British Library Act marks the recasting of the whole structure of national libraries and agencies. The new structure brought together the National Central Library and National Lending Library to form the British Library Lending Division.

Library Networks

Interlending Networks

Most countries operate an interlending systems of some kind or other.

Upto 1962 the only nationally organised loan facilities in UK, regardless of subject were those centred on the National Central Library. In the area of science and technology the Science Museum Library, in 1925, made its resources available to research institutions, universities and societies by means of postal loans: a service that was further extended in 1926. The National Central Library began to concentrate on the acquisition of British monographs in the humanities and social sciences, complementing the National Lending Library's policy of acquiring serial publications in these subjects areas.

In 1973, the National Lending Library for Science and Technology was amalgamated with the National Central Library to become the British Library Lending Division. Since then it has systematically built up its collections of periodicals, books, conference proceedings, translation, reports and theses covering all subjects. Its declared purpose is to supplement internal library resources of existing organisations working primarily through a system of approved libraries serving as local agents for individual enquirers. The number of approved libraries is now more than 5300 with and additional 3800 overseas users in 120 different countries. The number of home requests per annum is nearly 2.4 million and that for overseas exceeds 5.44 million with heavy use from Scandinavian countries, France and Germany. Approximately 84 per cent of the requests are satisfied from Lending Division stocks, 5 per cent from back-up and special support libraries and nearly 5 per cent through locations found in the union catalogues.[30]

Comprehensive coverage of monographs is aimed at including texts at undergraduate, graduate, and practitioner level but excluding fiction. For languages other than English the aim is comprehensive coverage for Slavonic scientific texts. The Division also collects reports, dissertations, and translations and publishers guides to these collections.

For monographs not held at Boston Spa, locations are sought through the Union Catalogue of books which is an amalgam of the National Central Library's (NCL) Outlier Union Catalogue and part of the National Union Catalogue, a collection of six regional catalogues excluding the London Union Catalogue, the South East Regional Catalogue and that of the Welsh region. From 1977 a combined International Standard Book Number list of all regional holdings has been produced in microform with and update every two months.

Regional Library Networks

The regional systems is basically one of voluntary involvement relying mainly on union catalogues and the ability of member libraries to meet their various obligations. Their achievements include regional self-sufficiency for current British material, permanent retention of at least one copy of every non-fiction book, comprehensive regional coverage of sections of the Dewey Decimal Classification and the maintenance of joint fiction reserves.

The regions started the production of Computer Output on Microfilm (COM) catalogue arranged by ISBN, available to member libraries, other regions and the Lending Division itself in order to improve its own referral service for unsatisfied requests. The Lending Division regularly produces an updated combined regional ISBN list thereby allowing users to find location for monographs in libraries throughout the country.

Local Co-operative Schemes

Inspite of the continuing expansion of the British Library Lending Division and the relative ease of access to its comprehensive range of documents, local area schemes play an important role in the nation's total library and information network. Important for the success of local co-operative schemes has been the formation of the Standing Conference of Co-operative Library and Information Service (SCOCLIS).

Some of the organisations and services for the networking are given below:

The London and South Eastern Library Region (LASER);
Machine Readable Catalogue (MARC);
British Library Automated Information Service (BLAISE);
Cataloguing-in-Publication (CIP);
UKMARC Current;
UKMARC Retrospective;
Research in British Universities, Polytechnics and Colleges;
British Education Index;
Conference Index;
International Serials Data Service;
Local Catalogue (LOCAS);
Birmingham Libraries Cooperative Mechanization Project (BLCMP);
South-West Academic Libraries Co-operative Automation Projects (SWALCAP); and
Scottish Libraries Co-operative Automation Project (SCOLCAP)

Subject Based Network: Education

Education Information Network in the European Community (EURYDICE):

Sponsored by the European Community is a new information network

EURYDICE, launched in September 1980 and designed to supply policy makers with quick and complete answers on a wide range of educational matters. The Central Unit, which operates formally in Brussels, is responsible for the creation of a union catalogue. Each of the National Information Centres, working informally, coordinates the activities of specialized subject information centres within its national boundaries. Topics so far delineated include the education of migrants and their families, policies of admission to higher education, teaching and learning foreign languages, and transmission from school to work. The UK Centre—Educational Policy Information Centre (EPIC) is situated at the National Foundation for Educational Research in Slough, Bedfordshire.

Educational Policy Information Centre (EPIC)

The Educational Policy Information Centre (EPIC) at the National Foundation for Educational Research in Slough, Bedfordshire is the National Centre for UK. Out of EPIC has grown the project for the Education Management Information Exchange (EMIE). It was established in 1981 to provide information service for all local authority education departments in England and Wales, the emphasis being on evaluated information. Sponsored by the Society of Education Officers, the DES and the NFER, the EMIE service has been funded for four years. During 1982 the service was offered to all local educational authorities in England and Wales and it was intended to be computerised, ultimately to become accessible on line. The computerized data base uses IBM Stairs and consists of two files: one of abstracts of documents received from local educational authorities and other sources; the other directory type file of LEA contacts and descriptions of interesting programmes and initiatives. The intention was to make the service self-supporting by the end of 1984. Topic areas for the present are:

Transition from school to work;
Falling schools rolls;
Induction and in-service training of teachers;
Micro-technology and educational implications;
Assessment of performance;
Special education; and
Education in the 16-19 age range.

EPIC, the UK's National Units, is a link to EURYDICE. The concept of setting up a network for the rapid exchange of information for the benefit of those in policy-making position was adopted by the Council of the European Community and the Ministers of Education in 1976. To participate in the network each member State has designated one or two national units linked to a central unit established in Brussels. The aim of the system is to serve educational policy-makers.

US EDUCATIONAL INFORMATION SYSTEM

Libraries

Historical Perspectives

Among the valued possessions which all the early settlers brought to America were books and literary tastes. Puritans brought with them and later imported more religious works. Among the collections, theological and moral works were most numerous, but there were also textbooks for self-instruction; handbooks on medicine, law, and farming; dictionaries and encyclopaedias; and some historical, political, scientific and classical works. These books, constituted the collections of the first libraries in America, and although they were the private libraries of individuals, they were often shared with friends and neighbours. John Harvard had more than three hundred, Elder William Brewster, four hundred and John Winthrop, Jr., Governor of Connecticut, had the largest scientific library in the colonies–over one thousand volumes.[31]

In 1636 Harvard College was the first college to be opened at Cambridge in the Massachusetts Bay Colony after the name of John Harvard who not only willed half of his property but all his library of more than three hundred volumes to this college. This college library can be called as the first academic library of America. In 1693 the Virginia colonists successfully established the second colonial college, the college of William and Mary; and in 1701 Yale College was founded in Connecticut.

Public Libraries

Provisions for what may be called the first public library (here the term "public library" is used in the sense that it was open to the public; it was not supported by taxes levied for that purpose) in the colonies were made in the will of Captain Robert Keayne of Boston (March 23, 1655/56), who gave £ 300 for a public building in Boston which was to include a room for a library.[32]

Towards the end of the seventeenth century Rev. Thomas Bray was appointed as Commissary for the Colony of Maryland to work toward the establishment of the Anglican Church there; he immediately proposed a system of parochial libraries for the colonies for the Anglican clergy. He established libraries in the English Colonies from Massachusetts to South Carolina. His society is said to have been responsible for founding thirty-nine libraries in the colonies with more than thirty-four thousand volumes.[33]

The desire of self-improvement—always a characteristic of the American Colonists—found a new expression in the social library. This interest in learning was not confined to the wealthy alone but was imbibed in workers working at lowly jobs. In 1731 Benjamin Franklin started a Subscription Library. Once begun, social libraries spread rapidly. In 1733, the Book Company of Durham, Connecticut, was established, and in 1747 the Redwood Library was founded in Newport, Rhode Island, by Abraham Redwood. In 1754 the New York Society Library was established.

After the Revolution, the growth of the social library was greatly accelerated and new forms appeared. Some were organized for a particular purpose, such as althenaeum; others were designed to meet the special needs or reading interests of a particular clientele, such as the mechanics' apprentices, Mercantile clerks, factory and mill workers, and members of Young Men's Christian Association.

An increasing interest in magazines, newspapers and pamphlets led to a movement to establish and maintain by subscription, reading rooms where members could have access at all times to periodical publications. In 1807, the Boston Althenaeum opened as the Anthology Reading Room and Library. On April 5, 1815 the Philadelphia Althenaeum was started and within a decade Althenaeums were established in Brunswick, Salem, and Portland, Maine, in the New York Society Library, and in Frankfort, Kentucky.

William Wood, a Boston merchant, believed that much could be done for the welfare of apprentices through libraries and consequently in 1820, the Mechanicas' Apprentices' Library was established in Boston through his philanthropy. Apprentices libraries were organized in other cities, including some libraries for girls, and some of them offered courses, sponsored debates and engaged in other activities.

As a consequence of America becoming an industrial nation in the early nineteenth century and with the increasing trade and commerce, the mercantile community became very important. Unfortunately, however, the mercantile class did not have the educational background which their growing social importance demanded.

William Wood began a companion movement to provide libraries for the "Young gentlemen employed by the merchants" and in 1820 the Boston Mercantile library was established. Similar libraries were organized in New York (1820) and in Philadelphia (1821).[34] By 1875 there were fifteen mercantile libraries located in eleven states.

Factory or mill libraries were established by some of the larger manufacturers in New England and the Middle states for the use of employees and their families. One of the best-known mill libraries was the Pacific Mills Library in Lawrence, Massachusetts.

In the Young Men's Christian Association Libraries, which were organized as a means of self-improvement for the members, the emphasis at first was placed on books of a religious and moral nature; later, however, history, travel, and biography were added to the collections. This type of social library developed only in the middle of the nineteenth century after the first one was opened in Boston in 1851.

The second quarter of the nineteenth century was a period of scholarly and literary activity and accomplishment. The period brought many of the changes in education that eventually led to free, universal, secular elementary and secondary schools. In this climate the free public library came into being. In 1852 the Boston Public Library was organized. In 1854 the free public tax-supported library became a part of American life.

The public library developed where there was a concentrated population with more than average education and where there was adequate taxable wealth to support it. Before the Civil War, public libraries flourished in the North Eastern Region of the country; after the Civil War, they had their greatest growth in the West and North.

The Library of Congress

The period following the Revolution was a time of extraordinary political, economic, and social change, characterised by a developing sense of nationalism; widespread interest in formal education and in self-education and self-improvement etc. All these developments were accompanied by the establishment of libraries—their size and importance depending upon the needs they were to serve.

The new capital city, Washington, did not have any library facilities, and therefore, a library had to be organised to provide for the needs of the National Congress for books and information. For the purpose of serving the Congress, the Library of Congress was authorised in 1800. The library is supported by Congressional appropriations and by the gifts of individuals and foundations. The Librarian of Congress Library is appointed by the President with the consent of the Senate.

In size, the collections today are perhaps the largest in the world; in scope they are definitely universal. As David Mearns has said, "From every region of the earth, from every age, by every means of transportation they have been brought together; and although statistics may suggest their magnitude, enunciation cannot elucidate their lively resourcefulness. To be understood, they must be experienced, they must be used, they must be tested and tried."[35]

Similarly states also began to establish libraries to serve the State Governments and by 1876, every state and territory had a governmental library whose purposes were (i) to collect and preserve complete sets of all publications of the state or territory and, as far as possible, of the several states and territories; and (ii) to collect works in America history, especially of the state or territory.

Academic Libraries

School Libraries

The school library, like all other kinds of libraries, came into being when there was a need for its resources and services. In the nineteenth century and the early part of the twentieth, when the mastery of subject matter was the primary goal and the textbook and the recitation were the methods used to achieve it, there was not much need for library materials.

In the 1920s and 1930s the emphasis in education shifted from the subject matter to the learner and in these child-centred schools students were provided an opportunity to develop all their potentialities. To cater to this demand, some high school libraries were organised and in some elementary schools a room was set aside as the library with a teacher serving as part-time librarian.

In 1925, a Joint Committee of the Department of Elementary School Principals of the National Education Association and the school libraries section of the ALA made a study of the conditions of elementary school libraries and drew up standards for them. Inspite of the efforts of many educators, libraries and professional organizations, there were many elementary schools where children did not have the services of centralized libraries.

In the late thirties, the U.S. Office of education reported a total of 278,000 centralized school libraries with a total of 2,88,00,000 volumes, but more than 33,000 schools were still served by classroom collections which were usually supplied by the public library.[36]

During 1940s came the concept of education for life adjustment, enrichment of the Curriculum and the project method of teaching called for a greater number and diversity of library materials than were then available. In 1937 the library services Branch of US Office of Education was established with a school library specialist on its staff.

There were 5705 separate junior high schools in 1960-61, out of which 86.4 per cent had centralized libraries, but 27.4 per cent of these libraries were not served by a school librarian.[37]

The situation improved progressively and presently almost all the elementary and junior high schools have libraries with trained librarians.

Secondary School Libraries

Several important factors contributed to the development of the high school library. Among the factors which have contributed strongly to the development of high school libraries are: (i) college admission requirements; (ii) the insistence on higher standard of secondary school library services by regional accrediting association, national professional organizations and state departments of education; and (iii) several studies which have underscored the necessity for quality library service in the secondary school programme.[38]

In 1901 the North Central Association established a Commission on Accredited Schools to recommend standards for secondary schools. The standards, agreed upon in 1902, included the statement that library facilities should be adequate to meet the needs of instruction.[39]

Other educational agencies also became interested in high school libraries, and in 1915 the Library Committee of the Department of Secondary Education of the National Education Association was formed to investigate actual conditions of high school libraries. The Committee emphasized that the library should be an education centre, not just a collection of books; that it should provide the reading and reference facilities needed for an effective library programme; and that books and other materials should be chosen in the light of the specific aims and purposes of the school.

As a consequence thereof the modern high school library of USA enjoys all facilities that are needed to meet the requirement of teachers and students. Collection includes reference materials, a wide selection of paper backs, news papers on microfilm, micro-readers, programmed materials, teaching machines, individual projectors for viewing slides and film strips, television equipment and equipment for the production and reproduction of materials.

New organizational patterns, such as multiple libraries divided by grade level, a multiple library system departmentalized by subjects, or library resource centres for each area of the curriculum such as the social sciences, the arts or the sciences have been introduced.

Training for staff and new library positions for school librarians, the increasing number of conferences, the establishment of a school library system etc, have given to the library the most prominent place in the programme of school education.

Junior College Library

In 1984 there were 1261 Junior College Libraries which make 3.5 per cent of the total libraries in United States.[40] The Junior College Library exists to serve the needs of this multipurpose institution and because these needs are many and varied, the responsibilities of the library are also in tune. It tries to provide the materials and services to support each of the programmes offered—general education, vocational, technical, semi-professional and adult education—and serves the needs of widely different students who enroll in these courses and the demands and needs of the faculty who teach them.

The development of an appropriate collections of materials to serve these purposes becomes very wide. The collection should be as broad in coverage as the course offerings, providing books, periodicals, pamphlets, audio-visual and other educational resources and materials in each area of emphasis in the several curricula. It includes professional and other materials for faculty use and it also covers recreational materials for reading, viewing, or listening for both students and faculty.

A broad educational background, an acquaintance with the literature of the subject fields, and an ability to identify and appraise resources for the diversity of course offerings are desirable qualifications of staff members.

The executive director of the American Association of Junior Colleges has said that, "of all aspects of Junior College development, low attention has been given to Junior College Library than to any other part of the instructional programme."[41] The explanation for this state of affairs can be found in the following: (i) the rapid growth of junior colleges, (ii) insufficient funds, (iii) non-mandatory nature of the accreditation by the state accrediting agency for opening a two-year college. However, some improvement has been brought about by the creation of a national committee on Junior College Libraries which is composed of representatives from the American Association of Junior Colleges and the American

Library Association.

College Library

Before describing the working of College library it is necessary to understand the term 'college' in American context. In general, the name "college" is given to an institution of higher learning which offers a four-years curriculum leading to a bachelor's degree in arts and sciences which requires for admission graduation from an accredited secondary school or its equivalent, and which is not divided into separate schools and faculties. There are liberal arts colleges, many of which emphasize specialization in given fields rather than liberal education; these are colleges for the preparation of teachers, technical colleges and agricultural colleges. Some colleges offer a five-year course leading to the master's degree. Some call themselves universities before they have developed a sufficient number of professional schools or faculties to justify the title. Colleges may be under state, municipal or denominational control; or they may be privately endowed and controlled. Enrolments range from less than five hundred students to more than ten thousands.

At the turn of the present century, college libraries entered upon a period of growth and after First World War expanded rapidly. In the beginning their major concern was to acquire and to preserve materials rather than to encourage and facilitate their use, for at that time, the textbook was the chief method of instructions. In the thirties the college library began to concern itself with selecting and evaluating learning materials to support the teaching programme and with aiding students in their use.

In the forties and fifties, educational emphases on education for democratic living; education for world affairs, specialization; the teaching of science and mathematics, foreign languages and the importance of using a variety of materials called for new courses and new methods of instruction. The Library endeavoured to support the new curricular and instructional programmes by longer hours of service, larger collections, open stacks, flexible circulation policies, new attention to instruction in library use, acquisition of various kinds of print and non-print materials, and the provision of carrels, listening and viewing facilities.[42]

Collection

The College Library is to provide a live and growing collection of books, periodicals, pamphlets, newspapers, audio-visual materials and microforms in both English and foreign languages. A minimum of 50,000 carefully chosen volumes is considered to give effective support to the instructional programme of a college having an enrolment of 600 students.

The collection supports not only the traditional programmes but such new programmes as independent study, tutorial and seminar type experiences, programmes of study abroad and education for world affairs, residence-hall libraries, year-round study, and off-campus course.

Staff

The staff of professional librarians are broadly educated and have some subject specialization as well as some language proficiency. They keep up with trends in higher education, curriculum development, methods of teaching, and new materials and new sources of materials in order to be able to participate actively in the instructional programme of the college.

The college library is organized and administered by the Director or Chief Librarian. The size of the professional staff is determined by the type of organization within the library, the college enrolments, the size and character of the collection, the teaching methods in use, the number of hours the library is open, the arrangement of the building, and the range of service.

Organization

The college libraries participate in inter-institutional co-operative systems to strengthen and improve library resources and services by dividing responsibility for the acquisition of materials; sharing resources, maintaining location records of important materials or titles; preparing union lists of periodicals, reference works or special collections and exchanging cataloguing and other bibliographical information. The following examples of inter-institutional library co-operation among colleges within a state can be mentioned:(i) the co-operative library system developed by seven liberal arts colleges which comprise the Arkansas Foundation of Associated Colleges; (ii) the Area College Library Co-operative Programme formed by nine colleges in Pennsylvania; and (iii) Libras, an organization formed by the libraries of eight Chicago-area private colleges for the purpose of inter-library sharing.

It has also brought about the mechanization of certain library operations in technical processes, circulation routines and acquisition procedures which have improved library services for the college community and more efficient use of time on the part of the professional staff.

Inspite of the changes and improvement in the organization of college library and its services, the common problems, as in the case of India, in U.S. College library are: (i) lack of fund to meet all the expected services and materials from the library; (ii) shortage of better qualified staff for want of attractive salaries; and (iii) shortage of efficient equipment etc.

There were 1986 university, college libraries in 1984 which make 6.0 per cent of the total libraries in U.S.A.[43]

University Library

"A University is an institution of higher education which has a liberal arts college; offers a programme of graduate study; has usually two or more professional schools or faculties; and is empowered to confer degrees in various fields of study."[44]

Earlier all institutions of higher learning in America were called colleges. Later, new state institutions called universities were organised and some of the private colleges were reorganized in order to assume the broadened university functions. The University of Virginia established by Thomas Jefferson in 1825, has been called America's first real State University.[45] By the time of Civil War, 21 state universities and several municipal universities had been founded. There were 3728 (11.3%) universities, colleges and departmental libraries in 1984.[46]

One of the major influences on American higher education in the nineteenth century was the German university. The first American university to be founded in the true German tradition was Johns Hopkins University in 1876. Following the example of Johns Hopkins, some of the firmly established private colleges like Harvard, Yale, Columbia and Princeton were reorganized and expanded into universities along the lines of the German tradition.

The German educated scholars of the latter half of the nineteenth century brought back such instructional techniques as the seminar, the laboratory method, and the lecture. These new methods influenced the development and use of the university libraries.

Functions

The purpose of the university library programme is to support the university's total programme. The University library serves from the freshman to the doctoral candidate engaged in scholarly research. For undergraduate students, the library programme provides materials and services specially designed to meet their requirements. For the students pursuing advanced study, the faculty members involved in that level of study, and resident or visiting research specialists, it provides resources and the services to support each of the graduate programmes and materials of sufficient quantity and diversity to support research of whatever kind in every subject field. It also participates in the publishing programme of the university and serves both as a repository and a generating source of knowledge and ideas.

Collection

The collection of the university library is diverse and embraces all subjects and provides:

(i) A general collection of materials of common interest to several fields and including the most recent editions as well as those which have historical value;
(ii) General and specialized reference, circular, and research materials in both English and foreign languages;
(iii) Rare materials, such as incunabula, first editions, manuscripts, papers, letters, museum objects and historical maps;
(iv) Newspapers and periodicals in English and foreign languages;
(v) Publications of federal, state, local and foreign governments as well as those of the United Nations;
(vi) Special materials, such as monographs studies, results of research, theses, dissertations, archives, clippings, visual and audio-visual materials, and microforms; and
(vii) Diverse forms of materials and equipment, such as disk and tape recordings, films, soundtracks, language laboratories, video tapes, listening and viewing apparatus, photocopiers, and—increasingly computers and auxiliary machines.

Organization

Until about the middle of this century, the university library usually was a central library. Today, a number of patterns are in use. Some universities provide a library for undergraduates in a separate building, with all the materials, facilities and services necessary to meet their basic needs. In some universities the undergraduate library is not housed in a separate building but occupies one or more floors of the central library. In other instances, the central library contains all collections, but special provisions are made for undergraduates.

Services and Staff

The University Library serves the academic community by:

(i) Introducing the student to the techniques, and possibilities of investigations and giving him the opportunity and resources to pursue it;
(ii) Acquainting student with bibliographies in their subject fields and giving instructions in their use;
(iii) Giving assistance in bibliographical methods;
(iv) Assisting faculty members in developing their own bibliographical knowledge and keeping abreast of developments in their fields; and
(v) Providing ready access to materials, facilities for uninterrupted individual study, and such aids as translation assistance, typing facilities and photocopying services.

In an effort to provide more efficient service to the academic community, the university library participates in co-operative undertakings in bibliographical service, such as:

(i) Inter Library Lending;
(ii) Cooperative and centralized cataloguing;
(iii) Compilation of bibliographies and union lists;
(iv) Development of the National Union Catalogue at the Library of Congress and of regional and local union catalogues and bibliographical centres;
(v) Specialization in collecting materials (Farmington Plan);
(vi) Centralized storage centres for little-used materials (Centre for Research Libraries);
(vii) Cooperative photographic projects (Library of Congress Microfilm Project).

The director of the University Library is expected to have the training, ability and skill to carry out this highly complex function.[47] The members of staff are professional librarians who have a broad general education and the specialization which are required in each area of service offered by the library.

Research Libraries

The common basic function of all research libraries is to provide the resources and services to meet the research requirements of their users in the form in which they are needed and at the time when they are required. This includes not only the areas of immediate concern, but also the areas of emerging and developing importance within the scope of a particular library's mission. The two-specific functions of all research libraries are:

(i) Providing factual information responsive to specific inquiries, including the selection and synthesis of information from various resources and directing the inquirers' attention to related information beyond the immediate scope of the query;
(ii) Providing professional guidance to readers in the use of library collection and bibliographic resources, and acquainting them with other information sources such as individual subject specialists, information centres, and research organisations.

Services

By the very nature of its purpose for being the research library it offers many types of specialized services such as:

(i) Acquiring, organising and preparing for use needed and pertinent materials without delay;
(ii) Preparing and circulating lists of new acquisitions;
(iii) Examining new materials and providing to appropriate users information about them in the form of reviews, abstracts, table of contents, and photocopies of excerpts;
(iv) Maintaining highly specialized reference files and indexes;
(v) Conducting Literature searches;
(vi) Providing accurate, relevant information to inquirers;
(vii) Preparing bibliographies;
(viii) Translating publications wholly or in part;
(ix) Providing quick reference and referral service, person to person and by telephone;
(x) Providing cheap and rapid means of photo copying;
(xi) Operating a delivery service, on occasion; and

(xii) Extending the limits of its own resources by inter-library loan and through such methods of bibliographical cooperation as union lists and catalogues and the exchanging of catalogues and bibliographies.

Co-operative Activities

Among the most notable examples of the co-operative undertakings of research libraries are:

Farmington Plan Centre for Research Libraries; Federal National Foundation on the Arts and the Humanities Act of 1965 and Higher Education Act of 1965.

Co-operative Acquisition Project (CAP)
National Programme of Acquisition and Cataloguing (NPAC)
Research Libraries Group (RIG)
On-line Computer Library Centre (OCLC)
Research Libraries Information Network (RLIN) etc.

United States Department of Education

The Act to establish a "Department of Education" was passed in 1867. It states as is given under Sec.1. "There shall be established, at the city of Washington, a department of education, for the purpose of collecting such statistics and facts as shall show the conditions and progress of education in the several states and territories, and of diffusing such information respecting the organization and management of schools and school systems and methods of teaching, as shall aid the people of the United States in the establishment and maintenance of efficient school system, and otherwise promote the cause of education throughout the country."[48]

The Congress, after a year changed the name to "Office of Education" and transferred it to the Jurisdiction of the Interior Department. Two years later the name was changed to "Bureau of Education".

In 1930, the designation, Office of Education was restored and in 1939, it was transferred to the Federal Security Agency, which was reorganised in 1953 as the Department of Health, Education and Welfare. In 1979, the 'Office of Education' was separated from the Department of Health, Education and Welfare and was converted to a full-fledged Department of Education by the Department of Education Organisation Act in 1979.[49]

Basic Functions

The basic function of the Department of Education has remained unchanged since its creation to collect and disseminate information and statistics on education. But under its mandate to promote the course of education and under specific legislation, the Department now has five other essential functions.

(i) Administering grants to the States according to the regulations and procedures established by the Office of Education.
(ii) Contracting with colleges, universities, States and private agencies for studies and research on educational problems;
(iii) Providing consultative services, largely to State Departments of Education, professional societies, colleges and universities, and other Federal departments, including international organisations;
(iv) Operating educational programme under agreement and in co-operation with other Federal agencies, and helping the State Departments to locate and qualify teachers for State Departments' Educational Programmes in under-developed nations and for international exchange projects; and
(v) Collecting educational information and disseminating in three broad categories: (a) vital statistics, sometimes tabular, without comment or analysis, (b) reports containing statistics, and (c) publications not printed but otherwise duplicated.

Statistics of the Office identify the nation's educational needs, strengths, weaknesses and potential problems. Office of Education statistics are valued by teachers, administrators, planners, school builders and architects, specialists in pupil transportation, educational publishers, manufacturers of educational equipment and persons engaged in plant maintenance and feeding.[50]

Publications

Apart from other adhoc publications, the Department brings out every year publications on almost all the aspects of American education. Some of the regular ones are:

1. American Education;

2. Education Directory of Education Association;
3. Education Directory of Higher Education;
4. Education Directory, Public School System;
5. Digest of Educational Statistics; and
6. Projections of Education Statistics.[51]

Library Co-operation and Networking

The beginning of library networks would coincide with the beginning of library co-operation – a movement that is said to have started in 1853, when Charles Jewett suggested the use of stereotype plates to produce a national union catalogue. Other landmarks on the long and difficult road to library co-operation include the initiation of the Library of Congress' Catalogue card production and distribution service in 1901, and the development of LC book catalogue and the National Union Catalogue.

Library networks are a product of the times. They are the natural consequences of political, economic and technological trends that affect all aspects of our society. More specifically, library networks are the result of economic constraints, technological imperatives and the need of access to vast and growing body of print and non-print materials.

There was a time when scholarly libraries attempted to acquire all published materials in specific subject areas. Those days are gone now. In the United States alone, approximately 40,000 books are published each year, and the world-wide publication of periodicals is estimated to be around 120,000 titles per year. Libraries must select from among numerous serials, foreign publications and also government documents. Faced with this explosion of information, libraries can no longer hope to meet the needs of their clients through the materials from their own collections.

The economic picture in recent years has been gloomy. For most libraries, inflation and declining fiscal capacity at all levels of government have resulted in a double problem.

Increased cost and reduced budgets. Libraries have struggled to do more with less, and most have scrambled to find new ways to increase their productivity. Significantly, while labour and materials cost have risen sharply, the costs of computer and communications capabilities have decreased. As a result, many library administrators have turned to information technology to help reduce costs, increase productivity and improve access to materials owned by other institutions.

In tracing the history of on-line networking, one might begin in the mid-1960s with such projects as shared cataloguing between the Columbia,

Harvard, and Yale medical libraries. Then in April 1968 came the creation of the Weekly Machine-readable cataloguing (MARC) tape service at the Library of Congress. In 1971 Ohio College Library Centre (OCLC) now the On-line Computer Library Centre went on line, followed by Bibliographic Automation of Large Libraries using on-line Time sharing system (BALLOTS), later Research Libraries information Network (RLIN) in 1972, and the Washington Library Network in 1975. Emphasis during these years was on encouraging libraries to join the networks.[52]

The OCLIC initiative sparked changes in a number of regional network activities. The New England Library Information Network (NELINET) abandoned its efforts to develop an independent data base and contracted for services with OCLC, as did the Pittsburgh Regional Library Centre and the Five Associated University Libraries group. South Eastern Library Network (SOLINET) and Mid West Regional Library Network (MIDLNET) have also joined.

This system of distributing OCLC services through state and regional networks worked so well that, in the period from 1971 to 1982, OCLC grew from a system providing on-line service to a single library through one terminal linked to a sole computer to a system serving 4490 terminals in more than 3,000 libraries and requiring more than 30 mainframe and mini-computers.[53]

Other Major Networks

Although the vast majority of state and multi-state networks was designed to broker the services of OCLC, a few chose to develop independent data bases and offer additional services. Included in this later group are the Washington Library Network (WLN) the Research Libraries Information Network (RLIN) and Research Libraries Group (RLG).

Regional Service Centres

South-Eastern Library Network, Inc (SOLINET) and NELINET have already been working. While some regional networks appear to be floundering, library agencies in West Virginia and other states have started to explore the possibility of providing automated state-wide networks. In addition to providing access to the major utilities, these networks have been able to incorporate a much higher degree of resource-sharing through document delivery.

State Library Networks

The state-wide library networks appear to be in a strong position at this point for a number of reasons:

(i) Current technology favours distributed systems;
(ii) State Library agencies have grown in strength both politically and economically; and
(iii) Networking is ready to move into a new phase in which document delivery becomes more significant.

Categories of Networks

The networks in America can be divided into four categories:

(i) Data-base Vendors—The first category of search service network which provides data bases for bibliographic and numerical searches;
(ii) Bibliographic utilities–These are referred to as 'Library Processing Facility'. The services include remote cataloguing access, circulation control and inter library loan;
(iii) National Library network; and
(iv) Regional, state and local networks. These are called 'user network' or affiliated network.[54]

Subject-Base Networks: Education

Educational Resources Information Centre (ERIC)

ERIC is a nation-wide, decentralised, on-line information network for acquiring, selecting, abstracting, indexing, storing, retrieving and disseminating the most significant and timely educational information and related reports. It consists of a coordinating staff in Washington, DC and 16 clearing houses operated in conjunction with professional organisations across the country. The abstracting journal is available by subscription from the Government Printing Office. Most of the documents may be purchased either in microfiche or paper form.[55] It offers a wide coverage of material in almost any education-related field. Many libraries have microforms copy for report literature readily at hand and so searching for documents is made easier. Most importantly, ERIC tends to be the data base which beginners learn first; it is most often used as a training device for searchers.[56] ERIC has been designed to accomplish three main objectives:

(i) To guarantee ready access to the World's English language literature relevant to education;
(ii) To generate new information products by reviewing, summarizing and interpreting current information products on priority topics. Products include bibliographies, state-of-knowledge papers, critical reviews and interpretative summaries; and
(iii) To infuse information about educational development and research findings.

ERIC takes the following steps to achieve ready local access to educational literature:

(i) Comprehensive, systematic acquisition of the separate reports from the thousands of sources in the United States and from selected English language sources overseas;
(ii) Selection of any current significant reports for dissemination;
(iii) Preparation of abstract of the reports;
(iv) Informing users through resources in education (RIE);
(v) References and delivering reporting through ERIC Documentation Reproduction Service (EDRS);
(vi) Supporting a guide to periodical literature—Current Index to journals in education (CIJE).

A flow chart showing the major steps taken to disseminate reports is shown in the figure 3.1.[57]

The ERIC system was begun in 1966 with the production and dissemination of the catalogue of selected documents on the disadvantaged. Development of ERIC programme began in earnest with the establishment of the first clearing house between March and June 1966.[58]

Organisation

ERIC has built upon the strength of universities and professional organisations in disseminating information. ERIC consists of four interrelated components:

(i) Central ERIC—with head quarter in the U.S. Department of

Fig. 3.1

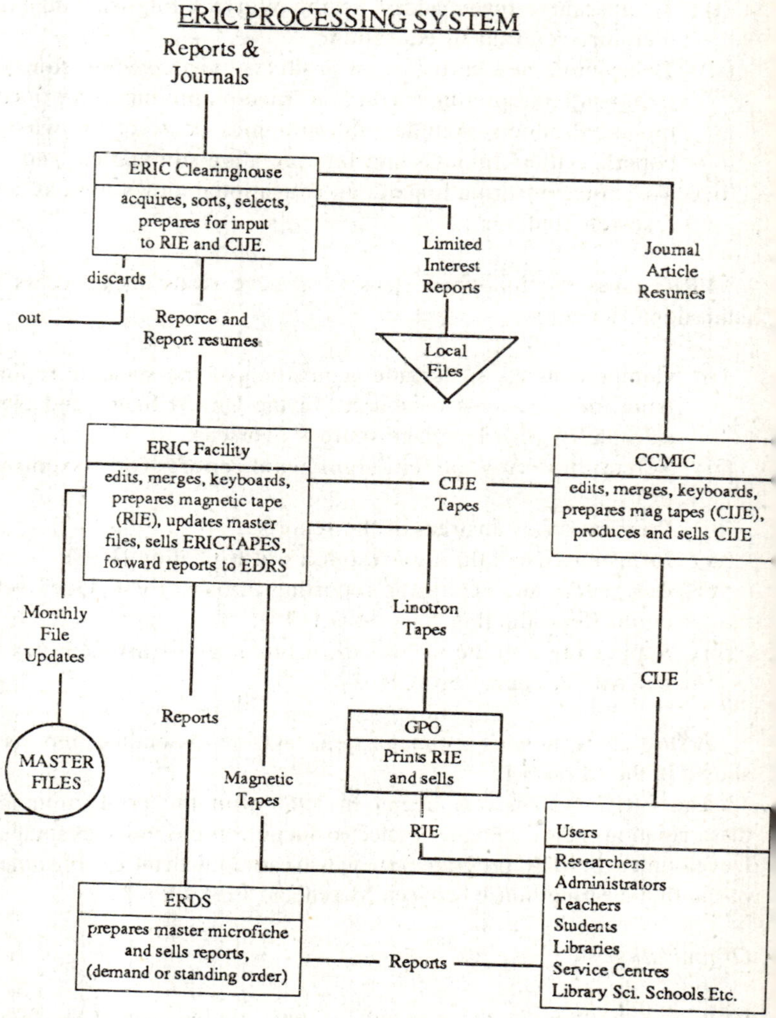

Source: Encyclopedia of Library and Information Science edited by Allen Kent and others. Vol. 7, p550

Education—it is responsible primarily for coordinating and developing the system;

(ii) The network of 16 clearing houses, each responsible for the collection, processing and dissemination of documents in a specific topic or field;

(iii) The ERIC facility, operated under contract to provide centralized computer and technical services; and

(iv) The ERIC Documentation Reproduction Service (EDRS) operated under contract to provide copies of documents made available through ERIC to users.

Central ERIC is responsible for collection of reports received from all projects or programmes supported by the U.S. Department of Education and from other federal agencies etc.[59]

The major clearing houses working under ERIC system are mentioned below:

Adult Education, Early Childhood Education, Educational Administration, Educational Facilities, Counselling and Personnel Services, Education Media and Technology, Exceptional Children, Vocational and Technical Education, Junior College Information, Higher Education, Library and Information Science, Rural Education, Science Education and Teacher Education etc.[60]

Inter-University Educational Information–Processing Network (EDUNET)

In 1966 the Inter University Communications Council (EDUCOM), a consortium of colleges and universities, proposed the establishment of a nationwide inter-university educational information-processing network, EDUNET. This pilot network was designed to evaluate how much network can assist education, particularly higher education. It was started with the following justification:

(i) Could make possible the sharing of informational resources among institutions;

(ii) Equalise excess to information, facilitate long distance interpersonal interactions;

(iii) Provide better bibliographical services;

(iv) Make life-saving information instantaneously available;

(v) Decrease production of unused copies of a wide range of

information materials;

(vi) Improve continuing education; and

(viii) Decrease administrative delays in higher education.

By such a network, universities could share library materials, data banks, computing facilities, instructional programmes and laboratory know-how.[61] Today, through EDUNET, faculty, staff, and students at 150 colleges and universities in the United States and several foreign countries can gain access to about two-dozen computers on campuses other than their own.

EDUNET is a facilitating network established to enhance the quality of instructional and research computing and to expand the opportunities for computer based resource exchange among institutions of higher education and research. It is a membership organization of colleges, universities and other non-profit-organizations that brings out resource sharing to its members and substantially increases the computing options available to them. By using remote facilities, member institutions can respond to unusual demands for computing while paying only for what is needed.

EDUNET does not own or operate computers for member-use. It arranges for the supply of computer resources from some of the finest university computing centres in the United States and provides the services that enable users on other campuses to identify, access and apply these resources. EDUNET relies on commercial data communications networks. Electronic mail is used to handle many user inquiries and to provide a common forum for discussion among members.

Network Services

Information Services

As an information clearing house, EDUNET helps clients and member schools learn what network opportunities exist and how they can best be pursued: EDUNET News, a quarterly publication distributed to individuals at member institutions and to other interested persons, and on on-line EDUNET resources data base.

Each member institution receives a copy of the EDUNET Member's guide, containing information necessary for effective use of the EDUNET system, which is updated frequently. It includes operational aids as well as detailed information on EDUNET suppliers and resources.

Other information services include access to electronic mail and conferencing facilities, regional faculty training workshop and disciplinary seminars, and user-need searches.

These include initiation of accounts with EDUNET suppliers central billing and accounting, vendor discounts on computing hardware, software etc. Technical services include faculty training seminars and workshop.[62]

INDIAN EDUCATIONAL INFORMATION SYSTEM

Libraries

Historical Perspectives

The history of learning in India stretches into the prehistoric past, but that of libraries in India is much shorter. Most of the ancient Indian literature passed from mouth to mouth and was preserved in the form of oral record. Literature and learning passed from one generation to another by the aid of the wonderful memory that the ancients possessed. So long as there was reliance on memory alone, there was no library, indeed, there could be none.

In India, though literature and learning flourished undoubtedly since the remote past and the history of our cultural heritage extends far back, there is no evidence of any libraries in ancient India. There was, of course, some collections of MSS at a few centres. The prevalent conditions at the time were not favourable to the development of libraries. At the time, learning was primarily religious in character and it was the monopoly of the priestly class which was averse to sharing it with others.[63]

Libraries in ancient India, such as they were, can be grouped broadly into three categories: (i) royal court collections, (ii) collections at places of learning, and (iii) collections of religious centres like the Brahmanical temples or maths, Buddhist Viharas or monasteries, and the Jain upasrayas.[64]

Learning was valued and scholars were respected. The references from the works of Hiuen Tsang indicate that rulers patronised scholarship and promoted the libraries.

The Kashmir ruler was having a very good collection in his palace library. The other noted instances of royal patronage are those of Harsha, Vikramaditya, Bhoja or Vishaldev Chalukya. Raja Bhoja (1018-60) founded a library at Dhar along with his Sanskrit College. There is also a reference to the library of the Chalukya King, Vishaldeva, which was known as Bharati Bhandagara. This tradition of royal libraries or court libraries continued and in the mediaeval period, there is evidence of court libraries of Kashmir, Bikaner, Mysore, Tanjore and some other Indian states.[65]

In ancient and mediaeval India, there were libraries attached to centres of learning where higher education was imparted. Amongst such centres, Takshashila (or Taxila as it is more familiarly known) is the oldest. It flourished over a range of more than a thousand years in the north-west corner of the Indian sub-continent, very near modern Rawalpindi. It drew scholars from far and wide. This centre of learning is referred to in the Jatakas, the famous Buddhist work. Some of its distinguished students are, Panini, the famous grammarian; Chanakya or Kautilya, the famous minister of Chandra Gupta Maurya; and Divaker, the famous physician.

Nalanda was another famous university centre. It was a religious centre where Buddhist and Jain luminaries met and discussed their practiçes and problems. Hiuen Tsang has left an interesting account of this centre but the library is described more fully in Tibetan sources. The library complex was styled as the Dharmaganja (piety mart) and comprised three grand buildings called Ratnasagar, Ratnadadhi and Ratnaganjaka.

There was another famous seat of learning near Nalanda, called Vikramshila. This was founded in the 8th Century A.D. by Dharmapala. The library attached to this university contained a great number of books on the Hindu religion. In the same region, another centre of learning which attained fame was at Odantapuri built in A.D. 749. Pala kings took interest in the development of this university and endowed a library of Buddhist and Brahmanical works. There were similar centres of learning with attached libraries at Somnapuri (North Bengal), at Varendra (North Bengal), at Mithila (Bihar) and Vallabhi (in Western India on the coast of Saurashtra). In the south, interesting details are available of a library attached to a Ghatikashala, an educational institution, at Nagai near the present railway junction of Wadi on the Bombay-Madras main route. It is dated A.D. 1092.

There were temple libraries but in number they were very few. The Jwalamukhi temple at Nagarhit (North India) had a valuable collection of 1300 ancient Hindu works. There were limited collections constituting temple libraries at some other places as well.

As regards the organisation and management of libraries in ancient and mediaeval India, Bhaskara Samhita tells us that a library should be located in a stone building, finely built. In shelving, each MSS was to be covered with a piece of cloth tied up and placed alongside others on iron stacks. The librarian, incharge of the materials had not only to look after the materials but also to guide readers in their studies and enquiries. The librarians got the same emoluments as the teachers and the librarians were reckoned on par with scholars or teachers.

During the mediaeval period it is a well-known fact that religious institutions of all denominations: Saiva, Vaishnava, Jaina and Buddhist flourished in the country either under royal patronage or with the support of private benefactions.

Besides public and state libraries—the existence of private collections of manuscripts during mediaeval times was evidenced both in the south and in the north of India. Mahmud of Ghazni is said to have maintained a large library at the capital of his Kingdom which had more than 30,000 volumes. Mahmud Ghazni, a minister of the Bahmani Sultan, owned a library of 3000 volumes and made frequent use of it. Akbar, the great had a splendid library of his own. Though himself an illiterate, he collected more than 24000 volumes of rare manuscripts. In the south, the library of Tipoo Sultan was famous for its rich contents of manuscripts, books and art objects.

As the British emerged from a trading company into the position of the ruling power, efficiency in administration demanded a regular supply of people who could act as agents in the service of the company. To arrange for this continuous supply of people, Warren Hastings, the then Governor General of India founded the Calcutta Madrassah in 1781. The Banaras Sanskrit College was established in 1972. In 1784, the Asiatic Society at Calcutta was founded. All these institutions were having libraries also. The government realised the importance of English education which would solve much of their administrative and clerical problems of administration at all levels. In 1817, the Hindu College was set-up in Calcutta for giving English education to Indian boys. As a consequence, schools and colleges began to be founded not only in the metropolis and other presidency towns but also in mofussil towns as well. Every school and college had a library of its own.

A scheme was drafted for the establishment of public library at Calcutta in 1835. The library at first housed in the apartment of Dr. F.P. Strong's house at Esplanade, Calcutta, later in July 1841 moved to the Metcalfe Hall. In 1902, the government secured full official control over the affairs of the Calcutta Public Library and the then Imperial Library was founded at Calcutta in 1903. Lord Curzon vitalized the dying institution by buying off the rights of the Calcutta Public Library. It was made imperative that all official publications were to be deposited in the Imperial Library, the National Library of today.

Special libraries forming valuable adjuncts to learned associations came into existence for meeting the demands of learned and scientific brains. The Asiatic Society was the first and the foremost of such libraries followed by various other libraries under the Government of India. The Indian Museums Act was passed in 1866 and the Museum Library another important special library, came into existence.

The library movement in the 19th century was not confined only to the cities and towns but also spread to the distant mofussil towns. Political consciousness dawned with the founding of the Indian National Congress in 1885 and love for the Vernacular language also became manifest by the establishment of libraries for Marathi and other regional languages. Such libraries which had books exclusively in local languages made a name and were very popular, e.g. Marathi language libraries were established at Thana, Bombay and Pune in 1893, 1898 and 1911 respectively. The influence and effect of these libraries were gradually felt in other states also.

Baroda under the enlightened rule of Sir Sayaji Rao Gaekwad III played a leading role in the development of libraries. All Gaekwad territory was covered by a network of libraries which were regularly fed from the headquarters library and the service provided was free and confined to the books in the native tongues. There were the district headquarters libraries and the state central library catering to the needs of the public. There were children's libraries as well. Under the guidance of the American Library expert Mr. W.A. Borden, the first systematic training classes for librarians and library workers were started. Library journals and Mitra Mandals or friends of libraries were also new features which created healthy enthusiasm all through the length and breadth of the country.

Punjab also developed an excellent library service through the efforts of a handful of youngmen under the guidance of the distinguished foreign library expert Mr. Asa Dan Dickinson who was the pioneer in writing the first book on library science in India (1926). The Punjab University started their first library training class in 1915. The first All-India Library Conference sponsored by the Government of India met at Lahore in 1918. The Indian Librarian, the first Library Journal of the country was started here.

Uttar Pradesh and Rajasthan did not make much progress in public library movement. There were many research and academic libraries in U.P. In Bihar and Orissa library development was not very striking but the Sinha Library and the Khuda Bux Library—played an important part in catering to the needs of research workers and are still important centres for serious students. Assam, in the British days, was considered to be a backward province in the development of libraries. Similar was the case with Madhya Pradesh.

In the south there was a tradition of library development. The first All India Public Library Conference met at Madras in 1927. Immediately thereafter Madras Library Association was formed. The Connemara Public Library offered increased library facilities to readers and open-access system was introduced. Much of the development of organised libraries in the country and particularly in Madras is due to the indefatigable enthusiasm of Dr. S.R. Ranganathan—who by his genius and sincere work has made a place for India in the International Library World. In Karnataka, Kerala and other areas of South India, both the efforts of the ruling class as also of the public and Christian missionaries helped the progress of literacy and the development of library habit in these areas.

Public Libraries

In Ancient and Mediaeval period, libraries, functioned almost as private libraries and entry to these was strictly restricted. As a result of this, the common masses of the country remained deprived of library service until the advent of the British rule.

First public libraries were set-up by Britishers in Bombay, Calcutta and Madras. Subsequently, in the provinces of Maharashtra, Gujarat and West Bengal, a number of libraries were opened by or with the encouragement received from the Britishers in the second half of 19th century. The Calcutta Public Library was established in the year 1836. Other important libraries set-up in the nineteenth century were Andrews Library (1850) at Surat, Gaya Public Library Gaya (1855), Connemara Public Library (1860) at Madras, Government Library (1867) at Junnagarh, Adyar Library (1886) at Madras, Dahi Laxmi Library (1892) at Nadiad etc. Even the libraries of this period, due to many factors were used mostly by the members of the upper class and the lower strata of the society could not make use of these libraries, though these libraries, opened their portals to the common masses.

The first three decades of the twentieth century will be remembered as golden period in the history of public library movement in India. In 1903 the reading room of Calcutta Public Library was opened by the British for the common man. This library developed later into Imperial Library and still later into the National Library. Library movement in Baroda is also a landmark of this period. On the invitation of Maharaja Sayaji Rao Gaikwad III, the then ruler of the erstwhile Baroda State, William Attenson

Borden came to Baroda and organised a free public library service. By the year 1910 Borden was able to establish a network of public libraries which included conventional libraries, mobile libraries, cinema libraries and manuscript libraries. His work was later continued by T.D. Wakins and N.M. Datt. In the Eastern part of the country the great lover of libraries, Munindradev Rai 'Mahashay' of Bengal, who formed Bengal Library Association, also did a lot for promoting and supporting library movement in the country in general and in Bengal in particular. The Committee appointed by the state Government under the Chairmanship of A.A.A. Fyzee in the year 1939 in Bombay which submitted its report in 1940, recommended building up a strong network of public library system in the State with State Central Library, district libraries, taluk libraries, block libraries etc. linked with each other in the form of chain.

With the appearance of Dr. S.R. Ranganathan on the scene, the public library got a great fillip. Ranganathan prepared 'Model Library Bill' and Development Plan. He also prepared draft library bills for almost all the Indian states. The governments of Madras (Tamil Nadu), Andhra Pradesh, Mysore (Karnataka) and Mahrashtra passed and enacted Library legislation in their states in 1948, 1960, 1965 and 1967 respectively, whereas West Bengal Library Act was adopted in 1979.

The Government of India took keen interest after Independence in providing public Library service to the masses. During the First Five Year Plan (1951-56) the Government included the scheme of improvement of public library services along with the community development programme. It was proposed under this Plan to set-up a National Central Library and one State Central Library in each state. The Central Government also entered into international organisations such as UNESCO for setting-up public libraries and Delhi Public Library (1952) was one such library set-up during this Plan Period. The Delivery of Books (Public Libraries) Act was passed in 1954 and later amended in 1956. The three libraries in Calcutta (National Library), in Madras (Connemara Public Library) and in Bombay (Asiatic Society Library) were declared copyright libraries. Delhi Public Library was included in 1982. Government of India set-up an Advisory Committee for Libraries (1957) under the Chairmanship of Shri K.P. Sinha.

Sinha Committee submitted its report in 1958-59 (Second Five Year Plan-Period) which was published in 1961. It recommended an integrated library system in the states linking the State Central Libraries with the National Library at one end and linking it with district, block and village panchayat libraries on the other. During this Plan, a sum of rupees 140 lacs was allotted by the Central Government for public library development.

During the Third Plan (1962-67/69) the Government felt that an adequate library system is an essential part of any well organised system of education. During this Plan-period the Planning Commission set-up a Working Group on Libraries (1964). The Working Group on development of libraries formulated a programme of public library development with an allocation of Rs.30.99 crores during the Fourth Five Year Plan.[66]

The development of public libraries has always been a state subject. The Central contribution to the development of public libraries has been channeled through the Raja Ram Mohan Roy Library Foundation which was set-up in 1972 by the Government of India. The Foundation has rendered assistance to about 16 thousand public libraries of various categories and nature.

National Library

The history of the National Library of India dates back to the establishment of Calcutta Public Library in the first half of the last century. Dr. F.P. Strong, Civil Surgeon of the 24-Parganas, generously allowed the use of his residence at 13 Esplanade Road, Calcutta for the Public Library. It was opened for public use on March 21, 1836.[67] After a temporary shift to Fort William in July 1841, the Library was finally shifted in June 1844 to Metcalfe Hall. The Calcutta Public Library fell on bad days in the last quarter of the nineteenth century. Viceroy Lord Curzon visited the library in 1899. He was very disappointed at the miserable condition of the extremely rich and rare book collection. He also noticed that for the want of necessary facilities the Library was very much under-used by the scholars and students. Earlier, he had also visited the Imperial Library, formed in 1891 by amalgamating several government departmental libraries. Its use was restricted to the superior officers of the Government. Lord Curzon ordered the amalgamation of the book collections of both these libraries for the benefit of the reading public. The Imperial Library Act was passed in 1902 and the Imperial Library was opened to the public on January 30, 1903 at Metcalfe Hall.

The new library was intended to be a library of reference, a working place for students, and a repository of material for the future historians of India, where so far as possible, every work written about India at any time could be obtained and read.

There was a phenomenal growth of the Library in the post-independence years. Indian publications in English and Indian languages registered a very steep rise and it resulted into an equally accelerated arrival of these books to the National library. Consequently, the 3.5 hundred thousand volumes library in the book collection of the National Library in 1947 shot upto 1 million volumes in 1960, 1.7 million in 1977 and as today it is on the threshold of touching the 2.4 million mark.[68]

The National Library of India Act, 1976 was passed by the Parliament and it was enacted on June 11, 1976. Under the new dispensation, the National Library was given the status of an autonomous institution to be managed by a Board and an Executive Council. The Library was to be headed by a Director and the Librarian was to work under the Director. Under the reorganised plan, the functional set-up of the National Library is as follows:

Director
Librarian
Deputy Librarians
Assistant Librarians
Administrative Officers
(Each Division is headed by an Assistant Librarian).

Library Book Collections

The current holdings of the National Library are in the vicinity of 2.4 million volumes, out of which over six hundred thousand are Indian and foreign official documents; seventy-two thousand are maps; thirty-thousand manuscripts and several thousand periodicals. A number of rare publications are also among the prized possessions of the National Library. This huge library book collection is housed in the main building at Belvedere, the Annexe, the New Stack Room (created by converting a series of residential quarters and by redesigning of interiors in 1957) and the Esplanade Reading Room.

Since 1904, the National Library has entered into book exchange agreements with foreign governments and institutions and as today about 140 main agreements are in operations from about fifty countries or so. Several international institutions and organizations have given the National Library a status of their depository library and under this privilege the Library receives all publications of United Nations, UNESCO, International Civil Aviation Organisation, International Court of Justice, International Labour Organization, Food and Agricultural Organisation and International Monetary Fund.

The Delivery of Books (Public Libraries) Act passed on May 29, 1954 and amended on December 29, 1956, stipulates that the National Library is to receive free of cost a copy of the printed material produced in India. Under these statutory provisions, a copy each of all the books published in India should reach the National Library directly from the publishers. This has made the compilation of the *Indian National Bibliography*, possible. It has been reported that this Act is not very effective and because of this the number of books reaching the Library is much below the expectation and the National Library has no control on this factor.[69]

Library Services

National Library has more than 12,000 holders of Reading Room Tickets and 27,000 holders of Lending Tickets. Reading room facilities are freely available to anyone above the age of 18 years subject to an introduction by a responsible person. The activity ranges from merely handing over a book to a reader to systematic retrieval of documents for a research scholar.

The Bibliography Divisions from the very beginning undertook an on-going project of compilation of a comprehensive annotated bibliography in 56 volumes, covering all aspects of Indology. The National Library compiles lists for reading or select bibliographies for scholars on request. The Reference Division provides reference service to the public. Microfilm facilities and photocopying services are available to readers on request at a very nominal cost.

Conservation and Preservation

Realizing the importance of preservation of books, especially rare reading materials in a tropical climate today the National Library has a fine team to run a successful preservation programme jointly shared by its Laboratory Division, Preservation Division, Rare Books Division and Reprography Division. The processes and methods used include disinfection, fumigation, testing of papers, de-acidification, special treatment with preservative mixtures, lamination, mending, binding, microfilming and photo-reproduction, and air-conditioned storage of rare books.[70]

The National Library also offers a regular short-term course to professional librarians in these techniques.

Academic Libraries

Schools Libraries

Very few school libraries in our country are worth the name and can ever stand any comparison with their Western counterparts. This state of affairs has been continuing for quite a long time. Considerable advancement has been made in several other allied areas. However, no such creditable progress is perceptible in the sphere of school libraries in general.[71]

Various commission and committees on education were appointed in pre-Independence days by the Government of India; but it was the Mudaliar Commission on Secondary Education in India which has, for the first time, focussed the pointed attention of the public and the State towards the need for a co-ordinated school library service. The Commission said that a well-thought out syllabus of studies may be rendered fruitless without the right techniques of teaching. The dynamic methods of teaching shift the emphasis from the quantum of knowledge imparted by the teacher or learnt by the student in the class-room to the right methods of acquiring it. So it is essential that every student should learn the art of studying. The art of studying implies several mental processes and variety of approaches. One of those approaches should aim at the "training in the use of reference material such as the list of contents and index in books, the dictionary, the atlas and reference books like the encyclopaedia or the book of knowledge."[72] The regular and increasing use of the school library is almost indispensable. While describing the present condition of our school libraries the Report regrets to note that, "In a majority of schools, there are at present no libraries worth the name. The books are usually old, outdated, unsuitable, usually selected without reference to students' taste and interests. They are stocked in a few book-shelves which are housed in an inadequate and unattractive room. The person in charge is often a clerk or an indifferent teacher, who does this work on a part-time basis and has neither a lover for books nor knowledge of library techniques. Naturally, therefore, there is nothing like an imaginative and well-planned library service which could inspire students to read and cultivate in them a sincere love of books. What makes this situation particularly difficult is the fact that most teachers and headmasters and even the educational administrators and authorities do not realize how unsatisfactory this position is and therefore, they have no sense of urgency in the matter."[73]

The present situation of the school library is not much different. The school code insists that unless a school has made a provision for a library with at least a fair stock of books and has a teacher to look after it, the school cannot have the necessary recognition or affiliation from the Board of Secondary Education. Even in the matter of receiving aid from the Government the compulsory provision of a library for the school is obligatory. Inspite of all of this, the conditions in the school library are unsatisfactory. The authorities do not insist upon a proper provision of a librarian to look after the school library with a whole time duty and a regular curriculum for library periods in the school routine. Even provision for regular book purchase is not very clearly made. All these ambiguous rules for the necessary provision of libraries in schools of all stages—primary, secondary and higher secondary—have resulted in the most unsatisfactory condition results.

The Assessment Committee on Basic Education in India has also recommended that no school may be considered a Basic School or assessed as such, unless it also fulfils the requisite that "a library with suitable books is available."[74]

The importance of having a good library in a school or college was emphasised as early as in 1935 by late Dr. A.C. Woolner, Vice-Chancellor, Panjab University, Lahore, in the following words:– "The ability to use a library is an acid test of the reality of the education. A good library is quite as important as laboratories and in fact the most important part of the equipment of a school or college".

It seems to be hardly understood at all by many educational authorities. It is much better to maintain two institutions with good libraries than six with inadequate libraries or ten with hardly any libraries at all.[75]

Primary School Libraries

Out of 4,74,636 primary schools only 1,39,986 (29.49%) have got library in them. The percentage of primary schools with library in rural and urban areas is 28.02 and 44.25 respectively. This clearly indicates the superiority of urban schools over rural ones in terms of availability of library facilities in primary schools.

Among the states, Haryana (87.39%) and Tamil Nadu (81.76%) have libraries in substantial majority of the schools. Whereas Assam (3.98%), Madhya Pradesh (6.6%), Manipur (8.50%), Meghalaya (1.51%), Orissa (9.08%) and West Bengal (6.02%) have a library in less than 10 per cent of the schools. Among the Union Territories, Chandigarh (92.31%), has the highest percentage of schools having library followed by Delhi (90.37%), A. and N. Islands (88.75%) and

Goa, Daman and Diu (87.91%), Dadra and Nagar Haveli (14.93%) has the lowest percentage.

Only 15.69 per cent of the schools are with more than 200 books in the library while 64.63 per cent of schools have less than 100 books and (41.43%) schools have only upto 50 books.

Middle School Libraries

In middle schools 83743 (74.50%), out of 1,12,404 have reported having a library in them. The percentage of middle schools with library is much higher than that in primary schools. Of the middle schools having library 68,897 are located in rural areas and the remaining 14,846 in urban areas. The percentage of schools having library in the rural areas is 73.15 per cent as against 81.46 per cent in urban areas.

Among the states, Sikkim has the library facility in all its 40 middle schools. Haryana (98.13%), Himachal Pradesh (94.70%), Karnataka (90.36%), Rajasthan (90.4%) and Tamil Nadu (93.39%) are the other states which have libraries in more than 90 per cent schools. Nagaland (33.94%) has the lowest percentage. Among Union Territories, Lakshadweep (80.00%) and Mizoram (67.35%) and all others have libraries in more than 95 per cent of the middle schools.

Of the 83743 middle schools having library 18.4 per cent have books upto 100. The proportion of middle schools having more than 500 books in their libraries is 27.29 per cent. The government schools have the highest percentage (33.46%) of libraries with more than 500 books while the lowest percentage (20.87%) under this category is of schools under local bodies.

Secondary School Libraries

Every secondary school is expected to have a library but the Fourth All-India Educational Survey conducted by NCERT has revealed that 19111 (5.21%) schools are without library. Contrary to the findings about primary and middle schools, secondary schools in rural areas are better placed so far as the availability of library is concerned. Out of the total 94.79 per cent schools having the libraries, rural based schools have 96.10 per cent and urban based have 91.37 per cent.

Among the states, Nagaland (73.14%) and among the union territories, Mizoram (74.56%) have the lowest percentage of secondary schools with library facility in them. Again, as in the middle schools, Sikkim has this facility in all its secondary schools followed by Haryana (99.18%).

Among the Union Territories, Arunachal Pradesh, Chandigarh have library in all the secondary schools. Delhi has in 96.53 per cent and Goa, Daman and Diu 96.69 per cent of the schools.

Considering the books available in the library, it is observed that nearly 26 per cent schools have more than 2000 books and 23.61 per cent schools upto 500 books in the library.

Higher Secondary School Libraries

Majority of higher secondary schools both in rural and urban areas have the library facility in them. Schools in rural areas have a slight edge over urban schools. The percentage of schools in rural areas with library is 97.45 as against 95.38 in urban areas.

Among the states, Haryana, Kerala, Manipur, Nagaland, Orissa, Sikkim and Tripura have library in all their higher secondary schools. The position of other states is as follows: Andhra Pradesh (98.72%)[76], Karnataka (99.74%), Punjab (98.39%), Rajasthan (98.36%), Tamil Nadu (99.04%) and Uttar Pradesh (98.03%). Gujarat (90.01%) has the lowest percentage. All higher secondary schools in Union Territories have got the library facility except two schools in Delhi.

In higher secondary schools 6106 (60.80%) of them have more than 2000 books in the library. Schools in urban areas have more books than their counterparts in rural areas. In urban areas 71.44 per cent of the schools have above 2000 books in the library as compared to 47.54 per cent of the schools in rural areas.

On the working of school libraries, the Report of the Secondary Education Commission (1952-53).[77] Unesco–Public Libraries in Asia (1956)[78] and Report of the Survey of Secondary School Libraries in UP (1957)[79] have emphasized that school libraries should co-operate among themselves as well as with the public libraries in resource sharing and technical aspects. This co-operation is essential for meeting the shortage of resources.

College Libraries

In 1823 the East India Company set up a committee known as 'the General Committee of Public Instruction' for the development of colleges. Calcutta Madrassah and Benaras Sanskrit College were recognised and other oriental colleges were established at Calcutta, Agra and Delhi. The Hindu College (Mahavidyalaya in Calcutta) had already been opened in 1817. In

1818 the Baptists founded the Serampore College and in 1820 the Bishop's College was founded at Sibpur, Howrah.

The growth of educational institutions and the concomitant growth of printed books, gave rise to institutional libraries. In 1830 the Hindu College Library had developed into "an excellent library of standard works of literature and science for the use of students."[80]

Most of the colleges at that time had libraries. Lord Auckland's Minute of 1839 reads "Lastly, in order to make the greatest use of the advantages of the colleges, I would attentively watch the degree to which the students profit by their access to the considerable libraries which are now attached to many of our institutions. Important deficiencies in those libraries should be promptly supplied."[81]

College libraries in India are still in an early stage of their development, though there is a growing awareness of their importance in college. Education Commission (1964-66) recommended that, "No new university or college or department should be set-up, without taking into account the needs of its library in terms of staff, books, journals, space etc. Nothing could be more damaging to a growing department than to neglect its library or give it a low priority".

Functions

The functions of the college library can be divided into two: (i) work behind the scene; and (ii) work with the readers. The first includes acquiring, preparing and preserving the reading materials, and the second involves the reference and readers' advisory service, circulation process and techniques.

Finance

Finance has always been a problem for any library and it is particularly so with an Indian college library. Higher education is being financed by Central Government through University Grants Commission (UGC) and State Governments. College library does not get regular and definite budget for its development and maintenance. The UGC grant is in the shape of an adhoc grant while the State Governments do not provide a separate budget for library. It is just a part of the total budget and the library gets the least priority from the management.

The other minor sources of income to library are like library fee, fines, sale of waste papers etc. It can be said that Indian college library is to face the shortage of funds. The average library expenditure to the total college expenditure is noted to be less than 2 per cent. This is far below the proportion recommended by the Education Commission (1964), which is 6.5 to 10 per cent depending on the stage of development of the library.

Collections

The College librarians have very little voice in the selection of subject books. In a few colleges, they participate in the process of selecting general books. The college libraries in general are ill equipped to meet the reading requirements of students, particularly post-graduate students and teachers with respect to both quantity and quality. It is surprising to note that there are colleges in the country offering post-graduate courses where the students do not have access even to a selective few of the most important journals in their respective areas of specialisation and are, therefore, not even aware of them.

The college library collection is limited mainly to books and periodicals. The modern media such as tapes, slides, films etc. are not available in a large majority of the colleges.

Library Services

The library hours of most of the colleges are the same as their office hours. This prevents the students from making use of libraries, as they would be attending the classes during the library working hours. The only library service universally rendered to the clientele in a college library is book lending. Even open access facility is not available in most of the college libraries References service is not provided due to lack of basic reference books and sufficient professional staff. Most of the libraries do not provide any documentation or bibliographical service to their clientele.

Library Staff

The staff position in a college library is inadequate from the point of view of both quality and quantity. The academic qualifications possessed by many librarians are not adequate to perform the specialized professional responsibilities. It is found that the authorities have not gone beyond providing the post of librarian and the necessity and sufficiency of other professional, semi-professional and non-professional staff in a college library have been completely ignored. The library staff are treated as ministerial staff. In many colleges, librarians are made to pay for the lost books.

As yet the college library plays no significant role in the academic preparation, and education does not involve the students in anything more than listening to lectures and reading the lecture notes dictated by teachers. In the interest of proper development of higher education, it is important to make a college library the intellectual hub of the institution serving equally to both the students and the teachers. Education, especially at higher levels, has been described more as a process for learning than of teaching, signifying the self-efforts required to be put in by the students. Well-equipped libraries with proper staff to meet the needs of the students is essential for this purpose.

Building up the general and reference collection, providing efficient and well-trained staff and proper status and salary to them, keeping the libraries open for longer hours, provision of sufficient funds, introduction of open access system, co-operation among college libraries, provision of documentation and bibliographical services are some of the aspects which need to be attended to immediately.[82]

University Library

Learning and teaching have been traditions in India since ancient times, Dr. S. Radhakrishnan, former President of India, once said, "In the old days teachers of India were themselves librarians and they were held in the highest esteem." Newton Mohun Dutt says "They were mobile libraries" and Richardson called them "Memory Libraries".[83]

Unfortunately, only privileged people such as Brahmins and a few Kshatriyas were able to take advantage of formal education in schools and colleges in ancient and mediaeval India. Even women were generally excluded. Therefore, academic libraries were used by only a few people. Most of the collections consisted of manuscripts only. However, the number of academic libraries in ancient India were very few.

Taxila University

Taxila University was founded in 414 A.D. in the city of Gandhara in North-West India. It is considered to be the first university in the world.[84] The university had an excellent library. The system of classification used in the library was devised by Panini, a great Sanskrit grammarian. But no one knows what that classification system was or how it worked. The library collection included works of Hinduism, political science, literature, medicine and philosophy. The city of Gandhara, including the university and the library was destroyed during the invasion of Hunas in the middle of the fifth century.

Nalanda University

Similarly, the Buddhist monastic institutions at Nalanda, Vallabhi, Odanta Puri, and Vikramsila became important centres of higher learning. All of these institutions maintained good working libraries to help their students and faculty. Nalanda University, which was located about 55 miles south-east of Patna in Bihar, occupied a unique place and played a dynamic role in the development of education in ancient India.[85] The university had a splendid library with a collection of invaluable manuscripts[86] and served over 10,000 students, many from China, Tibet, Korea, etc.

Thus, it can be said that in ancient India there were many good academic libraries. The accounts of these and many other libraries can be found in the writings of the famous Chinese travellers Fa-Hien, Hiuen-Tsang and I-Tsing. In the words of the Hiuen-Tsang, "The libraries were richly furnished, not only with orthodox literature but also with Vedic and other non-Buddhist works and with treatises on the arts and sciences taught in India at that time."[87]

In South India, the Chalukya Dynasty was very active in promoting higher education. One of its Kings, founded a residential college named Chatikasala in Nagai near Wadi in the 11th century, which had a good library. The Bahamani Kings did an excellent job by founding many colleges with libraries in their kingdom during the 14th century. It is evident from the above that academic libraries were not unknown in India in ancient and mediaeval period.

Libraries in the British Period 1800-1947

The development of academic libraries continued during the British period, but at a slower pace. Lord Wellesley, opened the first college, Fort William College during British rule in November 1800 at Calcutta. The library of the college had material in Arabic, Persian and Hindustani. The collection included 11,718 printed oriental books, 5224 European books and 4253 oriental manuscripts. The library provided a centre for the encouragement and development of scholarship among local students.[88] However, it gradually decayed and the institution was ultimately closed on January 24, 1854.

Calcutta University

Calcutta University was founded on the 24th January 1857. The model it was built upon was predominantly the British-based on the model of the University of London and was affiliating type at the start–conducting examination only. Initially then, there was no provision for teaching at the University and hence no need of a library of the present day type was felt.

The library attached to the Calcutta University was founded in 1873 which was used then mostly by the university officers, members of the Senate, examiners and paper setters, though the library attached to the university might have been helping the teachers and students in the different affiliated colleges occasionally. Sir Asutosh Mookerjee organized the teaching of post-graduate studies in the various branches of the subjects in Arts and Science under the University. This had a far-reaching effect as the centralised teaching for higher studies and research helped the growth of the University library. By 1876-1877 the Calcutta University Library had a good working collection, which included English works of reference, Indian antiquities, Arabic, French, Latin and Sanskrit classics.[89]

The average expenditure on books purchased during these early years was Rs.12,000 per year. In 1912 the Maharaja of Darbhanga contributed 2,50,000 rupees for a new university library building, and the library moved to its new quarters in the same year. A new library wing was added to the library in 1934 and the library became much more functional. Dr. Nihar Runjan Ray was the first professional librarian to be appointed as the University librarian, taking up that post in 1937.

Bombay University

Bombay University was established in 1857, but no official gave any thought to the question of attaching a library until a Bombay businessman, Premchand Ray Chund, donated 400,000 rupees in two equal instalments in 1864 for the construction of the University of Bombay Library building. The library building was completed in 1879 and was opened to students and faculty in February 1880. During the period 1930-1939 many special grants were given to the university library for collection development. The collection which stood at 4504 in 1900, rose to 70,000 in 1939 and in 1981-82 was 454,622 volumes. The library has one of the richest collections in the country.[90]

Madras University

The Madras University founded in 1857, did not have a library until 1904. It was only in 1905 that the library was opened on the premises of the Connemara Public Library. The University of Madras was lucky to have as its first professional librarian S.R. Ranganathan who was appointed in 1924. He introduced open access, reference service, inter-library loan, and the Colon Classification, and extended the library hours for the benefit of the users. In 1928 library was moved to the Senate House and in 1936 the library was shifted to its own building. The library had 370,000 volumes in its collection during 1981-82.

The universities had been in existence for 25 years when the first official word on developing academic libraries came in the form of a recommendation from the Hunter Education Commission in 1882. This Commission recommended special grants for academic libraries, but no grants were approved by the British Indian Government. In 1902 Sir Thomas Raleigh Commission evaluated the Indian higher education system and reported that either the collections of university libraries were poor or the universities did not have libraries.

The Commission recommended to provide good reference service to users. The affiliation of a college without library with the university would not be approved. In spite of these strong recommendations no proper attention was given to the improvement of academic libraries. In 1904, the Indian University Act was passed. This Act empowered universities to impose on colleges, applying for affiliation, maintenance of a library and lending of appropriate books (not text books) for the use of pupils.[91] The syndicate had authority to inspect libraries of all affiliated colleges. It was only after this Act that universities and colleges thought of maintaining libraries.

Calcutta University Commission 1917-1919

The British Indian Government appointed an Education Commission in 1917 to look into the affairs of Calcutta University. In its report the Calcutta University Commission (also known as the Sadler Commission after its Chairman) found that "one of the greatest weakneses of the existing system is the extraordinarily unimportant part which is played by the library."[92]

The Commission also recommended that libraries be strengthened and that training be given to the students and occasionally to the teachers in the use of the library. Though the Commission looked into the affairs of

Calcutta University only, its recommendations for libraries were very practical; they were recommended and applied to many other academic institutions in India. In fact, after publication of the report in August 1919, every academic institution paid attention to research and towards the growth of libraries. It was only after the recommendations of the Commission that professional librarians were appointed in the University libraries of Madras and Calcutta in 1924 and 1937, respectively.

It was only in 1924, with the joining of Dr. S.R. Ranganathan in the library profession as the Librarian of Madras University, that a revolution in librarianship came. Ranganathan reorganised the library; introduced an open-shelf system in 1926; provided reference service for 13 hours a day, 365 days a year; and even opened the University Library to public.

Due to Ranganathan's efforts, hard work, and guidance, the library became an important and busy centre of the campus. It had its impact on the other academic libraries in the country.

In a survey conducted by the University Commission (also known as the Wood and Abbot Committee) appointed in 1938 by the Government to study the financial situation of academic libraries, the Committee was shocked to find the poor allocation of funds to University libraries and recommended that larger grants should be made for libraries.

The other problems with the academic libraries in the pre-independence period, were (i) there were only a few trained librarians in the country; (ii) the librarians had not common voice or backing from any strong professional organisation to bring to the notice of controlling authorities the importance of libraries and librarianship as a support to education and research; and (iii) the pre-independence academic library had no significant part in the academic life of institutions of higher education, and had only a secondary position in the system.

University Libraries in Independent India

University Education Commission 1948-1949: The University Education Commission was appointed in 1948 by the Government of India, under the Chairmanship of Dr. S. Radhakrishnan, to survey institutions of higher learning and recommend reforms. The Commission (also known as the Radhakrishnan Commission, after its Chairman) looked very closely into conditions in college and university libraries. In its findings the Commission reported that library facilities in most colleges and universities were very poor. In its report the Commission wrote that "the library is the heart of all university work. Both for humanistic and scientific studies, a first class library is essential in a University... There is no doubt that in most of our universities the annual grants for libraries are very inadequate. We recommend that universities and colleges should work upto an optimum of 6.25 per cent of the total budget or Rupees 40.00 per student as the annual grant for their libraries....."[93]

The Commission also recommended a special grant every year to buy more important books and journals. Other recommendations include (i) open access to the general collection, (ii) training for library use, (iii) a well-qualified and trained staff, (iv) opening of libraries for a minimum of 12 hours a day, 7 days a week, (v) special grants for the acquisition of manuscripts, and (vi) provision of proper reference and bibliographic services.[94]

The Commission also recommended strongly the creation of an autonomous body on the model of the University Grants Committee of England to develop higher education in India. The Government of India accepted this recommendation, and the University Grants Commission (UGC) was instituted in 1953. The Commission was given a statutory form in 1956 by an Act of Parliament.

Role of the University Grants Commission (UGC)

The University Grants Commission of India soon after its establishment was seized with the programme of development of the libraries of the colleges and universities by constituting a Library Committee under the Chairmanship of Dr. S.R. Ranganathan in 1957 and by convening one seminar on the problems of University libraries. This Committee made certain recommendations for improvement of library services. The Committee's recommendations included (i) open access for readers, (ii) more professional staff, (iii) encouragement of inter-library loan, (iv) purchase of reproduction equipment, (v) quality collection development and reference service, (vi) better library buildings, and (vii) appointing of full-time teaching faculty in library schools.

The Committee also recommended that the qualifications of professional librarians be equal to those of the teaching faculty and that librarians should be recognized as equals of the teaching faculty in status and pay scales.

The UGC after approving some of the recommendations chiefly relating to staff, their qualifications, and emoluments, and expenditure on books and periodicals, communicated its view to universities and colleges for adoption. But, many institutions could not and did not adopt these recommendations and standards, as they were not binding on them, and education being a state subject (then) in the Indian Constitution, no State Government could be compelled to comply with.[95]

Education Commission: 1964-1966

In 1964 the Government of India decided to make a survey of Indian education system. The Education Commission was set-up under the Chairmanship of Dr. D.S. Kothari. The Commission reported its findings in 1966. The Education Commission also looked into the condition of academic libraries. Acknowledging the importance of the library, the Commission states, "As one goes higher up, the contact hours could be less, and self-study period even longer.....the most urgent reforms needed, therefore, is not to lengthen the working day in terms of the lecture delivered-these need to be cut down—but to increase the self-study facilities for students and to ensure that they work adequately. To make it possible, several additional facilities, now lacking in most of our educational institutions, will have to be provided. A well-kept and commodious library with an adequate number of reading seats is necessary, teachers must have rooms or lacking this, separate desks of their own in the library.[96]

Other Recommendations of the Commission include

(i) No university college or department be set-up without taking into account its library needs in terms of staff, books, journals, space etc. and

(ii) Libraries be given financial grants at the rate of 25 rupees per student enrolled and 300 rupees per faculty member with the provision that these figures be revised periodically.

The birth of U.G.C. was a turning point in the history of the development of academic libraries in India. There is no doubt that there has been substantial progress in many aspects of India librarianship since 1958. The University Grants Commission gave "a new lease of life to the university and college libraries. It gave librarians status, prestige and a better deal in life."[97]

Problems

(i) After the death of Dr. S.R. Ranganathan in 1972, there is no leader to guide the profession;
(ii) There is no union catalogue of books or union list of serials. Indian Council of Social Sciences Research (ICSSR) and Indian

National Scientific Documentation Centre (INSDOC) have prepared a few union catalogues of social science and science serials respectively, but they have not been kept uptodate;

(iii) There is no or a very limited Inter Library Loan activity in the country;

(iv) There is no plan for cooperative acquisition in academic libraries;

(v) Shared cataloguing and co-operative processing are also non-existent;[98] and

(vi) Though the Indian government has an extensive publications programmes, there are few depositories for Federal or State government documents. Therefore, it becomes very difficult for researchers to locate these government materials.

Ministry of Human Resources Development Department of Education

The Department of Education, one of the constituents of the Ministry of Human Resource Development, is under the charge of Minister of State with overall charge of Minister for Human Resource Development. The Secretariat of the Department is headed by the Secretary who is assisted by two Special Secretaries, Additional Secretary and Educational Adviser (Technical). The Department is organised into Bureaux, Divisions, Desks, Sections and Units. Each Bureau is under the charge of a Joint Secretary/ Joint Educational Adviser assisted by Divisional Heads.

The Department performs its functions with the help of number of offices, organizations and institutes. Some of the more important ones are mentioned below:–

(i) University Grants Commission (UGC)—For coordination and determination of standards in higher education. All universities and many other institutions in the field of higher education are looked after by UGC;

(ii) National Council of Educational Research and Training (NCERT)—Strives to promote qualitative aspects of school education throughout the country;

(iii) National Institute of Educational Planning and Administration (NIEPA)—takes care of the aspects of educational planning and administration and training of educational planners and administrators;

(iv) Resource Councils—viz. Indian Council of Social Science Research, Indian Council of Historical Research and Indian Council of Philosophical Research—promote and coordinate the research activities in humanities and social science;

(v) Libraries—The Public Libraries are under the purview of Department of Culture, another constituent of the Ministry of Human Resource Development. Since Independence both the activities of education and culture have been looked after by the Ministry of Education and Culture. Only recently the canvas of the Ministry of Human Resources Development has been increased and education and culture have been put in two separate departments but under the same Ministry. The academic libraries, belonging to schools, colleges, universities and research institutes/organisations in the field of education, all come under the purview of Department of Education; and

(vi) The other organizations belong to Management Education, Technical and Engineering Education, Physical and Teacher Education etc.

Functions

Important functions of the Department of Education are:

(i) to evolve educational policy in all aspects and to coordinate and determine the standards of higher education and technical education;

(ii) to administer copyright Act;

(iii) to improve the quality of text-books;

(iv) to administer scholarships and other schemes;

(v) to coordinate programmes of assistance and other activities with the UNESCO;

(vi) to develop and coordinate research in social sciences;

(vii) to foster and encourage studies and research in Sanskrit and other classical languages;

(viii) to develop activities in the field of non-formal education; and

(ix) to improve adult education.

Libraries' Co-operation and Networking

Academic libraries include school libraries, college libraries, university libraries and research organization information centres/libraries. It is already pointed out that the condition of school and college libraries in our country is not a happy one and co-operation, documentation services and resource sharing is not possible though it is very much necessary for these libraries with the existing material and manpower resources. However, these services can be expected from university and research organizations libraries and information centres. But here again the position is not satisfactory.

The special libraries pertaining to science field have accepted the challenge to provide timely, reliable and precise information but university libraries are slow in coming out of their inertia. The Ranganathan Committee[99] had suggested that in a university library, there should be a documentation section and a reference section charged with the responsibility of preparing documentation lists, and abstracts of the relevant articles in current periodicals having a bearing on the research work in the university and with the responsibility of helping the students, the teachers and the research workers in the choice of the books and articles in periodicals, appropriate to their interest.

There had been no systematic attempt to make a comprehensive survey of documentation services being provided by university libraries in India. From the account given by Srivastava,[100] it appears that university libraries in India have mostly concentrated on collection development, organization of the reading materials, development of manpower and very little attention has been paid to both reference service and documentation.

A study on documentation activities, in Indian universities was attempted by Goyal and Anand[101] and their findings have been published. The authors revealed that none of the 32 universities, out of the 100 addressed, provided the facilities of the documentation services to its users. Whatever services are provided, they are limited to 'new arrivals' type of lists compiled by librarians under the titles 'new arrivals', recent additions', 'just added' etc.

Co-operation has been mostly due to the initiative of professional people. It is informal and has no official support. Co-operation is more talked about than practised. And even it is limited only to inter-library loan. Due to the vastness of the country, high postal charges, and absence of automation programme and lack of communication facility, the inter-library loan is limited to the city only. Co-operative action in acquisition, technical processing etc. is still in the idea plane only.

The major research/special libraries in the field of education are NCERT, NIEPA, UGC and Association of Indian Universities (AIU), all located in Delhi. NASSDOC and Centre for Advanced Studies in Education and Psychology at Baroda are doing some work in documentation in education. The services provided by the first four are generally limited to house consumption while the services being provided by NASSDOC, pertaining to education are of very small magnitude because NASSDOC is mainly concerned with other subjects of social sciences like Economics, Political Science and Psychology etc. Education is not its thrust subject. Dr. Buch is responsible for three surveys of research in Education—containing dissertations and theses on education. The first and second have been published by the Centre at Baroda while the third has been published by NCERT.

Now UGC[102] has accepted the recommendations made by an expert Committee with regard to the setting up of two information centres in the fields of humanities and social sciences. The objectives of these centres would be to make available to research scholars and teachers the latest documents available in their field of specialization. Accordingly, two Information Centres, one at the SNDT Women's University (Bombay) and the other at the M.S. University of Baroda have been set up. The Centre of Baroda has been given the responsibility of education.

Indian Council of Social Science Research (ICSSR) was set-up in 1969 with the objective of supporting social science research, by sponsoring, promoting , coordinating , publishing and utilising research in the social sciences. The Council established the Social Science Documentation Centre (SSDOC), now National Science Documentation Centre (NASSDOC), on the lines of the Indian National Scientific and Documentation Center(INSDOC). The SSDOC was established in 1970. It has undertaken the following program and activities.[103]

- collection of reference material ;
- collection of unpublished doctoral theses approved by Indian Universities and research reports of projects sponsored/Undertaken by the ICSSR and other research institutions ;
- establishment of reprographic and microfilming unit ;
- preparation of select bibliographies;
- striving for bibliographical control over social sciences material; and
- award of study grants to research scholars for visiting libraries.

Projects undertaken by SSDOC are :

(i) Union catalogue of Social Science Serials ;

(ii) Union List of Social Science Periodicals ;
(iii) Union Catalogue of Newspapers;
(iv) Inter-library Resources Centre.

As it has already been pointed out that ICSSR has included education as one of the fields of its programme. But since it is not the field of its thrust, the services being provided by ICSSR or NASSDOC are not adequate for planners, administrators, teachers and researchers in the field of education These categories of users can be taken care of by a system or networking and not by a Centre to which education is a minor subject.

Keeping in view the present situation it can be said that in the field of education there is no centre or system worth the name for catering to co-operation, resource sharing, documentation and information services, and networking in India.

Library Networks

National Informatics Centre (NIC)

The concept of the formation of National Informatics Centre (NIC) was first conceptualised in 1973 and the concept was fructified in 1975. The Centre, set-up by the Government of India to play a promotional role in creating appropriate Information System, began its work with the following objectives.

(i) to design, develop and implement advanced computer based methodologies;
(ii) to promote adoption of computer-based data management techniques;
(iii) to generate specialised manpower in the field of informatics;
(iv) to build intra-city and inter-city computer networks in the country for inter-connecting various ministries/departments of the Central Government with those of the States and associated semi-Government and autonomous organisations for setting-up of a distributed governmental information system. In 1977, NIC commissioned the NICNET system for providing quick, and accurate data to the users.

The first phase of NIC drew to a close when the IX Asian Games (Asiad-82) Computer networks with its 34 terminals of NICNET spanning the 17 stadia in Delhi started functioning, NIC reached the second phase of extending NICNET services to State governments, thereby improving the information exchange between the Centre and the States. In the third phase NIC would have a connection with INSAT and bring all the districts of India within the ambit of NICNET.

Normally, dissemination of information processed in the NICNET is the responsibility of the user department. However, NIC has a central computer aided document preparation facility. Computer /output photo offset master , microfilm, microfiche reader/printer, etc. are some of the central facilities available for increasing the productivity of dissemination facilities.

National Information Centre training wing helps to plan the training programmes of various departments identifying the commonalities and differences in the requirements of the courses.

Pooling of the experience will make NIC more and more competent to handle the problems that may be faced by the ministries/departments in the future.

The Centre has been set-up as a catalyst for improvisation of governmental productivity through appropriate applications of computers, computer networks, data base methods, decision optimisation techniques and other informatics methodologies. It is in the purview of NIC to streamline information base, system analysis of the organisational structure, to make the quantitative studies for feeding to the planning process and in general to evolve an effective management information system for each ministry/department with exchange of information between ministries/ departments.[104]

No doubt NIC has a very comprehensive programme but its collection and dissemination will be useful more to socio-economic processes and not to academics. It is more of Data base, rather than Information Centre. Education requires a separate system for its own though it could be integrated into National Informatics Centre (NIC).

National Policy on Libary and Information System

In the following lines the main recommendations of Education Commissions, Education Policies, Library Associations and National Government after the Independence of the country are given.

Education Commissions

India achieved independence in 1947 and thereafter the Government of India appointed (a) University Education Commission, 1948, (b) Secondary

Education Commision, 1952, and (c) Education Commission, 1964-66. These Education Commissions investigated into the then educational system and spelled out aims and objectives of education for a new India, and suggested a model structure for the development of a proper educational system which would suit the needs and requirements of a new and free India.

The University Education Commission described libraries as the "heart of the Institution". Secondary Education Commission described them as the "hub of all the intellectual activities of the school." Kothari Commission acknowledging the importance of the library, states that the need is to increase the self-study facilities for students and to ensure that they work efficiently by providing adequate library facilities. To make it possible, several additional facilities, now lacking in most of our educational institutions, will have to be provided. It further states that no university college or department be set-up without taking into account its library needs in terms of staff, books, journals, space etc.[105]

National Policies on Education

National Policy on Education, (NPE) 1968; Draft National Policy on Education 1979 and National Policy on Education 1986.

All the three policy documents treat library and information system as adjunct to the system of education and do not lay any clear and vivid emphasis on their role in the development of national educational programme or to the national development as a whole. The New Education Policy document does not take into consideration the role of libraries altogether and makes a passing reference to libraries in para 3.2.1 and 4.67. In 3.2.1 it states, "norms have to be laid down regarding minimum facilities to be provided to every secondary school in terms of laboratories, libraries, playground etc". In 4.67 it states, "it has, however, to be recognised these will not bear any fruit unless educational institutions attain a minimum threshold of essential facilities in terms of buildings; blackboards; charts and posters; drinking water and bathroom facilities; laboratories; science kits and libraries; and minimum contingencies for organising socially useful productive work, nature studies, games and sports and cultural activities."[106]

On the other hand, the document lays stress on provision and employment of new technology with the expectation that the application of new technologies can convert educational institutions into 'learning' rather than 'teaching' institutions.

Library Association

The need for the formulation of a National Policy on Library and Information Systems, has been engaging the attention of the Indian Library profession since 1950's as emphasised particularly in the writings of Dr. S.R. Ranganathan and in the recommendations of the Library Advisory Committee 1958.

Prof. A. Das Gupta, Director, National Library, Calcutta and Prof. D.P. Chattopadhyaya, Chairman, Raja Rammohun Roy Library Foundation urged upon the Government the necessity of enunciating a National Policy for Library and Information Systems.

The Foundation submitted a draft National Policy on Library and Information Systems to the Government of India in July 1984.

In 1979, the Indian Association of Special Libraries and Information Centres (IASLIC) discussed the subject at its 12th Conference held at Roorkee. The Indian Library Association considered the matter at its 30th Conference at Jaipur in 1984. The Association submitted a draft policy statement to the Government of India in early 1985. The need for this policy was also emphasised by the Planning Commission Working Group in its report 'Modernisation of Library Services and Informatics for the seventh Five Year Plan 1985-90'.[107]

Central Government

The Government of India set-up a Committee under the Chairmanship of Professor D.P. Chattopadhyaya for the formulation of a National Policy on Library and Information Systems. The Committee submitted its final findings to the Government on May 30, 1986.

Chapter IV of the report deals with the Academic Library System. Emphasising upon the role of libraries, the Committee points out that libraries are central to education and the only way that our education system can be freed from cramming is to build teaching round the library resources of the educational institutions. The librarian should be regarded as a full member of the academic community.

No school or college should be established without a library and a properly qualified librarian. School library and community library should help each other and in the absence of one, other should serve the needs of both the institutions. There should be an agency at the State level for the development of school libraries.

The university and college libraries must be given adequate facilities in staffing, buildings, furniture, books etc. The UGC should devise and impose norms for the proper functioning of college and university libraries in the country.

Universities, colleges and research institutes in a particular area, should establish linkages among themselves and share their resources.

Universities and college libraries should emphasise on reference, bibliographical, SDI and CAS services rather than issuing and returning of the books.

Empowered Committee on National Policy on Library and Information System (1987)

The Empowered Committee which was also headed by Prof. D.P. Chattopadhyaya has submitted its report to the Government of India in April 1988. The review of this Committee can be considered the first comprehensive Government sponsored review of the library system in India. The report suggested a series of steps and some of these suggestions are understood to have been accepted by the Government. Important features of the report are:

- to ensure that every school and college has a library;
- to establish more effective linkages among academic libraries;
- to see that every State and Union Territory has a Public Library Act to improve the working of public libraries and extend their reach;
- to establish and maintain a network of public libraries funded by both the Central and State Governments;
- the annual allocation of funds may be 6 to 10 per cent of that allocated for education in the Central and State budgets;
- the Public Library will play a key role and work as the main agency of distance education; and
- to establish a National Library System with the National Library, Calcutta forming the appex.

For the implementation of its recommendations, the Committee has proposed that a National Commission on Libraries and Information Systems or a National Commission on Informatics and Documentation be constituted by an Act of Parliament as part of the Ministry of Human Resource Development. The Commission consisting of representatives of appropriate Central and State agencies will have the overall responsibility for implementing the proposed national policy. The Government has accepted the recommendation and asked the Department of Culture to prepare a draft bill on the National Commission on Libraries.[108]

Edunet

One of the recommendation of the Empowered Committee is to establish a network of university libraries and have centres in different regions of the country for the proper utilization and sharing of resources.

National Educational Documentation Centre

In 1987 Government of India, Ministry of Human Resource Development, Department of Education set-up a Committee under the Chairmanship of Dr. Amrik Singh for the establishment of the National Educational Documentation Centre. Report is yet to be submitted.

Though the matter has been discussed in seminars and conferences and we have recommendations of high power bodies for the establishment of a national information network, a clear policy or concrete programme for its emergence is yet to come.

REFERENCES

1. James, M.R. ed. Catalogue of the Library of the Leicester Abbey. In *Early Public Libraries* by Thomas Kelly; 1966;. London: Library Association, p.20
2. Kelly,Thomas. (1966). *Early Public Libraries*. London: Library Association, p.21-22
3. *ibid.* p.75
4. Luckham, Bryan, (1971). Library in Society. London: Library Association, p.4
5. Gardner, Frank M. (1971). *Public Library Legislation : A Comparative Study.* Paris: Unesco, p.108-109
6. *ibid.*, p.110
7. Jafferson, George (1977). *Library Cooperation*. London: Andre Deutsch, p.97
8. *ibid.*, p.98-99
9. Kent, Allen and others. eds. (1976). *Encyclopaedia of Library and Information Science*. New York: Marcel Dekker, Inc., Vol. 19, p.92
10. *ibid.*, p.108
11. Great Britain. Department of Education and Science. (1967) School Library. London: HMSO, p.2-3
12. Great Britain. Department of Education and Science Central Advisory Council of Education (1968). Half our Future (Newsom Report). London, HMSO, para 45
13. Great Britain. Department of Education and Science Central Advisory Council for Education (1967). Children and their Primary Schools (Plowden Report). London: HMSO para 591
14. Wright, G.H. (1958). Technical College Libraries In *Five Years' work in Librarianship.* 1951-55 edited by P.H. Sewell London: Library Association, p.40-50.

15. Yescombe, E.R. (1963). Libraries of Colleges of Technology and Further Education In *Five years' Work in Librarianship*. 1956-60 edited by P.H.Sewell. London: Library Association, p.79-98
16. Jafferson, George and Smith-Burnett, G.C.K.(1978). *The College Library*. London: Clive Bingley, p.25-26
17. Saunders, W.L. ed.(1976). *British Librarianship*. London: Library Association, p.251-271
18. Wright, Gordon H. (1978). Cooperation and Coordination In *College Library* edited by Jafferson and Smith Burnett. *op. cit.*, p.180.
19. Wilson, C.W.J. ed. (1977). *Directory of Operational Computer Applications in UK Libraries and Information Units*. 2nd edn London: Aslib.
20. Brayan, Harrison. (1976). *University Libraries in Britain*. London: Clive Bingley, p.12
21. Johnson, Elmer D. and Harris, Michael H. (1976). *History of Libraries in the Western World*. 3rd edn. New Jersey: Scarec, p.122-123
22. *ibid.*, p.155
23. Kent, Allen and others. eds. (1970). *Encyclopaedia of Library and Information Science. op. cit.*, Vol.4, p.50-51
24. Johnson, Elmer D. and Harris, Michael H. (1976). *History of Libraries in the Western World. op. cit.*, p.229
25. World of Learning 1986 (1985). London: Europe Publications, p.1336-1396
26. Great Britain University Grants Committee. (1967). Report of the Committee on Libraries. London: HMSO, Table 1, p.172
27. Great Britain, Central Office of Information (1988). Britain 1988–an official handbook. London: Central Office of Information, p. 53
28. Husen and Postlethwaite. eds. (1985). *International Encyclopaedia of Education, op. cit.*, Vol.7, p.4326
29. Kent, Allen and others. eds. (1970). *Encyclopaedia of Library and Information Science, op. cit.*, Vol. 5, p. 655-675
30. British Library Lending Division. (1980). BLLD, 1979-80: *Interlending Review* (3), p.79-80
31. Gates, Jean Key. (1968). *Introduction to Librarianship*. New York: McGraw-Hill.
32. Shera, Jesse H. (1949). *Foundation of the Public Library: The Origins of the Public Library Movement in New England 1629-1855*. Chicago: University of Chicago Press, p.19-24
33. Gates, Jean Key (1969). *Introduction to Librarianship, op. cit.*, p.63
34. U.S. Bureau of Education. (1976). Public Libraries in the United States of America, their history, condition and management, special report, part 1. Washington, DC: U.S. Government Printing Office. In Gates, Jean Key (1968). *Introduction to Librarianship*, p.21
35. Mearus, David C. (1965). The Answer: A Fog-laden Panorama of LC's Collections. *Library Journal*, 90, April 1965, p.1601
36. Joeckel, Carleton Bruns (1938). *Library Service Staff Study Number* (1). Washington, D.C: U.S. Government Printing Office, p.21 quoted in Gates, J.K.: *Introduction to Librarianship*
37. Mahar, M.D. and Halladay, D.C. eds, (1964). Statistics of Public School Libraries, 1960-61 Part 1: Basic Tables. Washington, D.C: U.S. Printing Office, p.3,32,43
38. Brubacher, John S. and Rudy, Willies (1958). *Higher Education in transition, an American history 1635-1656*. New York: Harper and Row, p.359
39. Gates, Jean Key (1968). *Introduction to Librarianship. op. cit.*, p.225

40. U.S. Department of Commerce-Bureau of Census (1985). Statistical abstracts of the United States 1986. 106th edn. Washington, D.C: Superintendent of Documents, p.160 Table 274
41. Gleazer, Edmund J. Jr., (1966). The Stake of the Junior College in its Libraries. *College and Research Libraries* 27; July, p.266
42. "Standards for College Libraries" (1959). *College and Research Libraries* 20; July, p.278
43. U.S. Department of Commerce–Bureau of Census (1985). *Statistical Abstracts of the United States* 1986. 106th edn. *Op. cit.*, p.160 Table 274
44. Good, Carter V. ed.(1959). *Dictionary of Education.* 2nd edn. New York McGraw-Hill, p.590
45. Brubacher, John S, and Rudy, Willis (1958) Higher Education in Transition an American History 1635-1956. *Op.cit.*, p.144
46. U.S. Department of Commerce–Bureau of Census (1985). *Statistical Abstracts of the United States* 1986. 106th edn. *Op. cit.*, 160 Table 274
47. Quoted *In* Gates: *Introduction to Librarianship. Op. cit.*, p.294
48. Kursh, Harry (1965). *The United States Office of Education: A Century of Service.* New York: Chilton Books, p. 11-12
49. U.S. Office of the Federal Register, National Archives and Records Administration. (1987). *Government Mannual 1987/88.* Washington, D.C: Superintendent of Documents, p.263
50. Kursh, Harry (1965). The United States Office of Education:A Century of Service. *op. cit.*, p.41-42
51. U.S. Superintendent of Documents. (1986). *Monthly Catalogue of United States Government Publications–Cumulative Index.* Vol.II-Subject Index. p. 1-1108 to 1-1113
52. Katz, William A. (1982) *Introduction to Reference Work.* 4th edn. New York: McGraw-Hill, Vol.II, p.208
53. Mathews, Joseph R. and Williams, Joan Fryer (1982). Bibliographic Utilities Progress and Problems. *Library Technology Reports* 18; November-December, p.653
54. Katz, William A. (1982) *Introduction to Reference Work* 4th edn. *Op. cit.*, Vol.II p.209
55. Mason, Marilyn Gell (1983). *Federal Role in Library and Information Service.* New York: Knowledge Industry Publications, p.42
56. Katz, William A. (1982). *Introduction to Reference Work. Op.cit.*, Vol.II, p.178-79
57. Kent, Allen and others. eds. (1972), Encyclopaedia of Library and Information Science. New York: Marcel Dekker, Vol.7, p. 550
58. Marron, Harvey (1972). Educational Resources Information Centre (ERIC). In *Encyclopaedia of Library and Information Science* edited by Kent and Lancour. *Op. cit.*, Vol.7 p.546-556
59. Deighton, Lee C. ed. '1971'. *Encyclopaedia of Education.* London, Macmillan, Vol.3, p.204
60. Burchinal, Lee, C. (n.d.). *Educational Resources Information Centre.* Washington, D.C: ERIC, p.203-206
61. Miller, James G. (1972). EDUNET In *Encyclopaedia of Library and Information Science,* edited by Kent and Lancour. *op. cit.*, Vol.7, p.564-565
62. *ibid.*
63. Marshal, D.N. (1983). *History of Libraries–Ancient and mediaeval.* New

Delhi: Oxford and IBH Pub. Co., p.111
64. *ibid.*, p.112-113
65. *ibid.*, p.114
66. Sharma, Pandey S.K. (1985). *Public Libraries in India*. New Delhi: Ess. Ess Publications, -p.12-13
67. Choudhary, S. (1972). National Library of India. *IASLIC Bulletin* 17(3) September, p.171
68. Jain, V.K. (1985). National Library in India. In *Handbook of Libraries, Archives and Information Centres in India* edited by B.M. Gupta and others. New Delhi: Information Industry Publication, p.10
69. Panwar, B.S. (1971). Story of a National Library. *Herald Library Science*. 10(3) July, p.372
70. Kaula, P.N. (1981). National Library of India: Functions and Activities. *Herald of Library Science* 20(3-4) July-October, p.195
71. Mookerjee, Subodh Kumar (1969). *Development of Libraries and Library Science in India*. Calcutta: World Press, p.137
72. India. Ministry of Education (1953). Report of Secondary Education Commission (Chairman: R.S. Mudaliar). New Delhi: Ministry of Education, p.23
73. *ibid* , p.110
74. India. Ministry of Education (1957). Report of the Assessment Committee on Basic Education. In *Administration and Organisation of school libraries in India* by G.L. Trehan (1965). Delhi: Streling, p.6
75. Trehan, G.L. (1965). *Administration and Organisation of School Libraries in India*. Delhi: Sterling, p.7
76. National Council of Educational Research and Training (NCERT).(1982). fourth All India Educational Survey, New Delhi: NCERT, p.164-168
77. India. Ministry of Education (1953). Report of Secondary Education Commission. *op. cit.*, p.113-114
78. Unesco (1956). Public Libraries in Asia—Delhi: (Seminar Libraries manual No.7.) Paris: Unesco, p.132
79. India. Ministry of Education. (1957). Report of the Survey of Secondary School Libraries in U.P. New Delhi: Ministry of Education, p.81
80. Sengupta, Benoyendra and Chakraborty, Bhubaneswar (1981). Library, Library science and librarianship. Calcutta: World Press, p.36
81. *ibid.*, p.56
82. Bavakuthy, M. (1983). Libraries in India: Some observations In *fifty years of librarianship in India, past, present and future*–Twenty-ninth All India Library Conference (Seminar papers). Delhi: ILA, p.11-18
83. Kaula, P.N. ed. (1958). *Library Movement in India*. Delhi; Delhi Library Association, p.58
84. Trehan, G.L. (1975). *Learning and libraries in ancient India*. Chandigarh: Library Literature House, p.33
85. Dattas, Bimal Kumar (1970). *Libraries and Librarianship of Ancient and Mediaval India*. Delhi: Atma Ram, p.26
86. Banerjee, S.R, (1960). Development of libraries in India. *IASLIC Bulletin*. Vol.1, p.39-62
87. Sharma, Ravindra N. (1985). India, academic libraries In *Encyclopaedia of Library and Information Science*, Edited by Allen Kent and others. New York: Marcel Dekker, Inc., vol. 39, Supplement 4, p.204
88. Fazle Kabir, Abalfazal M. (1979). English libraries in Eighteenth Century

Bengal. *Journal of Library History*. Vol. 14, p.436-456

89. Subramanyan, Mani (1985). History and development of University libraries in India. In *Encyclopaedia of library and information science*, edited by Kent and others. *Op. cit.*, Vol. 39, p.207
90. Sharma, Ravindra N. (1985). *India, academic libraries. Op. cit.*, p.207
91. Khurshid, Anis. (1972). Growth of libraries in India. *International Library Review*. Vol.4, p.21-65
92. Bose, P.Chandra. (1957). An account of the origin and development of the Calcutta University Library. *India Librarian* Vol.12, p.19-26
93. University and College Libraries: A survey and recommendations, December 1948-August 1949 Vol. 1, (1950). *Indian Librarian*. Vol.4, p.132-134
94. *ibid.*, p.133
95. Viswanathan, C.G. (1972). *University libraries of India: Principles and Policy*. New Delhi: Author, p.8-9
96. India. Ministry of Education (1970). Report of the Education Commission, 1964-66-Education and National Development. New Delhi: NCERT, Vol.1, p.71
97. Sharma, Jagdish S. (1965). *The Substance of Library Science*. New Delhi: Asia Publishing House, p.28
98. Rajagopalan, T.S. (1978). An overview of problems and prospects of resource sharing among libraries in India. *ILA Bulletin* Vol.14, p.1-16
99. University Grants Commission New Delhi (1965). Committee on University and College Libraries. New Delhi: U.G.C., p.72
100. Kesarwani, S.K. and Bhat, S.G. (1986), Documentation services in university libraries. *ILA Bulletin*, Vol.22, (1-2), April-Sept., p.30-39
101. Goyal, P.K. and Anand, A.K. (1982). Status of documentation activities in India universities, *Annals of Library Science and Documentation*, Vol.29, p.159-169
102. University Grants Commission, New Delhi (1986). Report for the year 1985-86. New Delhi: U.G.C., p.53-54
103. Jambekar, Ashok. (1985). Country paper–India In *Sharing of Information: South Asian Initiatives* edited by M. Silva and M. Nansyakkara. New Delhi: McGraw-Hill, p.97-123.
104. Seshagiri, N. (1986). Government Data Network. In *Handbook of libraries, archives and information centres in India* edited by B.M. Gupta and others. New Delhi: *Information Industry*, Vol.3, p.37-57
105. Verma, S.C. (1986). New Education Policy and Libraries. *ILA Bulletin*. Vol.21, p.101-102
106. India. Ministry of Human Resource Development–Department of Education (1985). Challenges of Education: A Policy Perspective. New Delhi: Department of Education, Sections 3.2.1 and 4.67
107. India. Ministry of Human Resource Development–Department of Culture (1986). National Policy on Library and Information System: A presentation (Chairman–D.P. Chattopadhyaya. New Delhi: Department of Culture, p.1
108. Empowered Committee on National Policy on Library and Information System (1987). (Chairman: D.P. Chattopadhyaya). *Hindu* (Delhi Edition). April 27, 1988, p.8, Columns 3-6

4

METHODOLOGY

The preceding two chapters presented a review of the Educational Systems and Educational Information Systems in UK, USA and India. This chapter discusses details of the method used for 'A Comparative Study of National Information Systems for Education in UK, USA and India with a view to developing a model for India', its design for research, choice of the instruments and procedure of data collection. Survey method of research is used for the purpose of analytic and descriptive study of the problem.

Method

The present study uses Literature Survey method to describe the present status of Educational Systems and Educational Information Systems of UK and USA. The method used in so far as India is concerned is both literature survey and the questionnaire method. The literature survey has been used for educational system and questionnaire for educational information system. The advantages of the survey methods are:

(i) Intelligent decisions can be made concerning the planning, development, and organisation services;

(ii) Library surveys are systematic, in-depth examinations of libraries, library systems, or networks of libraries. Comparisons are made in these surveys among various libraries, or units thereof, in accordance with the established professional standards;

(iii) The Information collected through surveys allows generalizations to be made about characteristics, opinions, beliefs, attitudes, and so on, of the entire population being studied;

(iv) This can save time and money, without sacrificing efficiency, accuracy, and information adequacy in the research process; and

(v) Allows investigators to gather information about target populations without undertaking a complete enumeration.[1]

In view of these merits and the specific objectives of the study, it was considered desirable to use survey method of research.

Users of Educational Information

First of all, the expected users of the information and those who are responsible for generation of information were identified. These are classified as under:

(i) Educational Planners;
(ii) Educational Administrators;
(iii) Teachers at School Level;
(iv) Teachers at Higher Level;
(v) Teacher Educators;
(vi) Researchers in Education; and
(vii) Librarians/Documentalists in the libraries of educational institutions.

The above categories constituted the sampling frame. The categories of students and general public have been excluded because the amount of educational information used by them is very negligible and their inclusion in the study would not have affected the results of the study but would have enlarged the scope and made it unwieldy. However, the category of researchers in education does include research students through whom students' needs can be known. General public, as parents is partly represented by the first five categories.

In order to make the above categories of personnel specific, it was considered desirable to specify their authenticated definitions. These are given below.

Educational Planner

Educational planning attempts systematically to forecast numbers of pupils, students and teachers as well as the level of educational expenditure, and to allocate resources efficiently between different levels of education.[2] However, educational planner is one who deals with educational planning or/ policy. Educational Policy: a judgement, derived from some system of values and some assessment of situational factors, operating within institutionalized education as a general plan for guiding decisions regarding means of attaining desired educational objectives.[3]

Educational Administrator

Any educational official responsible for the management or direction of an educatioal establishment or system or an administrative unit of it, typically includes such officers as college principals, deans, school inspectors and presidents of institutions.[4]

Teacher

(1) a person employed in an official capacity for the purpose of guiding and directing the learning experiences of pupils or students in an educational institution, whether public or private;
(2) a person who because of rich or unusual experience or education or both in a given field is able to contribute to the growth and development of other persons who come in contact with him;
(3) a person who has completed a professional curriculum in a teacher education institution and whose training has been officially recognized by the award of an appropriate teaching certificate; and
(4) a person who instructs others.[5]

Teacher Educator

A member of a college faculty who is primarily concerned with the professional preparation of teachers.[6]

Researcher in Education

The problem for a researcher in education deals with any significant, perplexing, and challenging situation, real or artificial, the solution of which requires reflective thinking. A perplexing situation after it has been translated into a question or a series of questions that help to determine the direction of subsequent inquiry.[7] The researcher in education is one who studies or investigates in the field of education or educational problems. Research in education involves the process of careful, critical, disciplined inquiry, varying in technique and method according to the nature and conditions of the problem identified, directed toward the clarification or resolution (or both) of a problem.[8]

Librarian

One who has charge of the contents of a library, making the stock and library services available to those who need them or are entitled to them.[9]

A class of library personnel with professional responsibilities, including those of management, which require independent judgement, interpretation of rules or procedure, analysis of library problems, and formulation of original and creative solutions, normally utilizing knowledge of library and information science.[10]

Documentalists (Information Scientist)

One who is highly competent or knowledgeable in the creation, use, and management of information, usually with an emphasis on the process of acquiring, organizing, storing, and retrieving information rather than on its content.[11]

One who practizes documentation. An information officer or intelligence officer who is concerned with the collection and dissemination of knowledge, rather than the librarian who is concerned with the techniques of handling records of knowledge, making them available and possibly exploiting them. He is concerned with assembling information contained within documents together with data from other sources to form a new compilation.[12]

Nature and Scope of Data

To achieve the formulated objectives of the study the following data about the users needs, demands and preferences were collected. The data about the general characteristics of the respondents like designations, official address, academic and professional qualifications, field of working and experience gained, type of institution they work in, their study habits, possessing of personal library, use of library, study of journals, having knowledge of educational information system of UK or/and USA etc.

To know the needs of respondents, the data gathered are about the library of the institute, duration of time they spend in the library, the reasons for not using the library regularly, the purpose of visiting the library, the type of information they require, etc.

In addition to this, information was gathered about demands and preferences of the respondents and what they expect from an ideal information system for education in India.

Sample Frame

The data required for the study were to be gathered from the seven aforesaid categories of subjects. Before selecting the actual sample of the survey, a sampling frame was specified. It consists of the users of educational information specified earlier and the institution/organization where they are working.

The educational institutions and organizations from where the respondents were selected included: (i) Education Division of the Planning Commission; (ii) Planning Division of the Department of Education of the Ministry of Human Resource Development; (iii) National Council of Educational Research and Training (NCERT); (iv) National Institute of Educational Planning and Administration (NIEPA); (v) State Councils of Educational Research and Training (SCERT)/State Institutes of Education (SIE) of all States and Union Territories; (vi) University Grants Commission (UGC); (vii) Association of Indian Universities (AIU); (viii) Field Advisers of the NCERT in all the States and Union Territories; (ix) very often the users were not available in the above institutions during the period of the survey. Therefore, in order to complete the survey the users of information participating in seminars, workshops and training programmes held at NCERT and NIEPA during the months of January-March 1987 were contacted and information in the questionnaire was elicited from them; (x) Schools (include Government/Public, Central and recognized by the Government); (xi) Universities–Department of Education; (xii) Teacher Training Colleges; and (xiii) libraries and documentation centres relating to educational institutions like universities, colleges, schools, teacher training colleges, research institutes and associations.

Sampling Procedure

The objectives of the study are directed towards the views of a select group of experts who in their discharge of day to day work have to depend on the information system in education. These experts may be working in different institutions. So the selection of the respondents is made in two stages. In the first stage the institutions were selected and after their selection, the respondents selected at random from among the lists of the staff working in them.

The purposive approach to sampling was necessitated by the fact that various types of respondents are not available everywhere. This approach is recommended in such situations especially when the choice of selected units, which in our case are institutions/organizations is very limited. The method may be biased but this fact can be ignored in view of the nature of the study. Since the selection of respondents within an institution is random, the biases can reasonably be taken to have been removed to a large extent. This is the case with the selection of Planners, Administrators and Librarians/Documentalists.

Secondly in the selection of researchers, teachers at various levels where the number of institutions is very large, this method was considered to be the most appropriate. This is usually done in case of rural socio-economic surveys that are continually carried out by National Sample Survey Organization (NSSO) in India. There are half a million villages in India. No sampling frame of rural households (70 million) is available. Purposive selections are resorted to for selection of village from which households are selected at random.[13] Similar process was adopted in selection of institutions and respondents from among the selected institutions.

Size of Sample

Planners/Administrators

The institutions identified for the planners and administrators working in the field of education are the Education Division of the Planning Commission, Planning Division of the Department of Education, Ministry of Human Resource Development, National Council of Educational Research and Training (NCERT), National Institute of Educational Planning and Administration (NIEPA) University Grants Commission (UGC) and Association of Indian Universities (AIU), State Council for Educational Research and Training (SCERTS), States Institutes of Education (SIE) and State Departments of Education, State Directorates of Education. In addition to this heads of departments of education in the universities, principals of teacher training colleges etc. were also identified as planners/administrators.

Teachers at School level

In this category only senior secondary schools were taken into consideration. Primary and middle schools have been excluded assuming that there would be very few library facilities and teachers might not be very well-versed with the use of library and using educational information.

Teachers at higher level

This category includes the academic persons of the colleges, departments of universities including departments of library and information science.

Teacher Educators

Respondents were drawn from the teachers of the training colleges of primary as well as secondary level i.e. JBT/BT, B.Ed. and M.Ed., Ph.D. etc. The respondents were also drawn from the departments of education of universities where teacher training programme is available.

Researchers

Respondents of this type were drawn only from researchers doing Ph.D. in education or library science. Some members have also been included who have kept themselves in this category and are working in educational research institutions. The addresses were taken from Central Institute of Education (CIE), Jamia Millia Islamia and Banaras Hindu University personally while in case of researchers belonging to other universities, their names and addresses where drawn from Association of Indian Universities (AIU).

Librarians/Documentalists

The respondents were restricted only to universities and institutions related to education disciplines. The addresses were taken from Handbook of Indian Universities published every year by AIU. The addresses for this category of respondents belonging to teacher training colleges, research institutes, Central and State ministries were taken from the directories and other sources for the purpose.

The Sample

The sample consisted of 1000 users of educational information. The details of the sample have been tabulated in Table 4.1.

TABLE 4.1: Classification of Target Group of Respondents

Users	Questionnaire mailed	Responded	% of response
(1)	(2)	(3)	(4)
Planners	100	36	36.00
Administrators	100	46	46.00
Teachers Sec.	200	64	32.00
Teahers Hr.	150	54	36.00
Teacher Educators	150	56	37.33
Researchers	150	44	29.33
Lib./Doc.	150	55	36.66
Total	1000	355	35.5

Trends of Response

The total response was not received at a time. Several reminders were to be sent to the respondents to get their views. Table 4.2 shows the trends in response.

TABLE 4.2: Trends in Responses at Different Stages

User's Category	Questionnaire sent	Trends of receipt of the filled questionnaire					Total
		0	1st	2nd	3rd	4th+	
(1)	(2)	(3)	(4)	(5)	(6)	(7)	(8)
Planners	100	4	10	14	6	2	36
Administrators	100	7	12	19	6	2	46
Teachers Sec.	200	12	22	16	10	4	64
Teachers Hr.	150	6	14	22	9	3	54
Teacher Educators	150	10	15	20	8	3	56
Researchers	150	3	13	18	9	1	44
Lib./Doc.	150	15	16	12	9	3	55
Total	1000	57	102	121	57	18	355
Percentage		16.1	28.7	34.0	16.1	5.1	100.0

Tools of Data Collection

Information Schedule

In many ways, the task of analysing a library's user population is like M.P. area or market analysis which attempts to discover the composition of the population which needs to be served. The emphasis should be on factors of an area analysis which helps to identify institutions, communities, groupings of users, etc, enumerates the people in the institutions and groupings and characterizes or describes them in terms of factors or variables which are related to utilization of the library or information resources. Variables can be like:.

(i) work related information
(ii) work activity–teaching, research, administration etc.
(iii) distance from library. [14]

For constructing the information schedule library records were consulted in the libraries listed below:

Libraries visited

(i) Department of Library, Documentation and Information, National Council of Educational Research and Training, New Delhi.
(ii) Library, National Institute of Educational Planning and Administration, New Delhi.
(iii) Library, Department of Education (CIE) University of Delhi, Delhi.
(iv) Library, State Institute of Education, Delhi Administrtion, Delhi.
(v) Government Senior Secondary School Library, Yamuna Vihar, Delhi-110053.

Records consulted

(i) Membership records for name, designation, address;
(ii) Borrowing records, types of documents got issued;
(iii) Catalogues–for study interest;
(iv) Rules and regulations for library hours;
(v) Inter-Library Loan records for books issued to other libraries and got from other libraries.

Sources of Literature Review

It is critical for a researcher to know in what areas other researchers have worked and the nature of their work. The identification of problems, refinement of ideas, specification of research procedures, measurement clarity, and understanding of results can all be facilitated by comprehensive review of previous work. The resources for reviewing the literature–indexes, abstracts, reference works, journals and reviews–are essential to the researcher.[15]

The important sources of the literature review for the present study were:

(i) Dissertation Abstracts International–Series A;
(ii) Education Index;
(iii) British Education Index;
(iv) Index India;
(v) Library Literature;

(vi) Library and Information Science Abstracts;

(vii) Catalogues of: American Information Centre, New Delhi, British Library, New Delhi, NCERT, NIEPA and Central Secretariat libraries, Department of Culture, Ministry of Human Resource Development, New Delhi;

(viii) Theses available in National Documentation Centre for Social Sciences (ICSSR) on the topics of Education and Library and Information Science; and

(ix) Dissertations available in the library of the National Science Library (NSL) and Department of Library and Information Science, University of Delhi.

Informal Discussion with Experts

In addition to this, the investigator discussed the problems of literature review for the purpose with the academic staff of NCERT, NIEPA, INSDOC and Department of Library, and Information Science of University of Delhi. The investigator also got the opportunity of discussing the subject with the academic staff of Jamia Millia Islamia and Central Institute of Education (Department of Education), University of Delhi, who often visit NCERT library.

Keeping in view the data to be collected through the information schedule, following items were included in information schedule by the investigator:

(i) Name;

(ii) Designation;

(iii) Academic qualifications;

(iv) Professional qualifications;

(v) Official address;

(vi) Nature of work;

(vii) Type of organization working in;

(viii) What groups borrow which kinds of library materials;

(ix) Subject interests;

(x) Why do people use or not use libraries;

(xi) What influences libraries and librarians exert on reading habits and tastes of library clientele;

(xii) To what extent are clientele satisfied or dissatisfied with library materials, services, personnel, physical resources, etc.;

(xiii) What groups use various kinds of library services; and

(xiv) What are significant factors related to use or non-use of libraries by various individuals and groups.

Questionnaire

The purpose of the research is to obtain valid and reliable information so that research questions can be answered. A thorough search and review of possible available literature related to the topic under study was made. To get the firsthand insights, authorities in the area of research were consulted and information was obtained. For proper conceptualization, understanding of the research problem, clarity of the questions, and brevity and economy of participant efforts were taken care of. With the help of the information schedule a questionnaire was prepared and distributed for try-out among the potential respondents. Five potential respondents among each of the seven identified categories of users were picked up. The respondents were selected from amongst the Delhi-based so that if need be, a discussion can be held for amending the sequence, language, logic, deletion and addition of the questions. Care was taken to select the respondents from different managements of the institutions viz. government departments, research institutions, universities, teacher training colleges, colleges and schools, etc.

The respondents were contacted personally and questions were discussed to remove the ambiguity or irrelevance.

After getting the suggestions, the questionnaire was finalised (appended at Appendix D) and distributed through mail as well as personally as it was necessitated. As sufficient number of responses were not received, after a month a reminder was sent. It was followed by four reminders after an interval of a fortnight each time. These reminders were accompanied with a spare copy of the questionnaire for use in the event of earlier one being misplaced in the transit.

Personal Interview

In survey research, the search for new information is by no means limited to the use of questionnaire. As the purpose of the survey is to acquire current information about the experiences and opinions of people, the interview serves as a useful survey tool. In some fields the superiority of the interview technique over mail questionnaire has been acknowledged, establishing that verbal communications in research subjects elicit significantly more complete answers to questions than the printed survey instrument. Verbal responses of the interview are often valuable original evidence and research data.

Having this in mind, an interview schedule was prepared. (Appended at Appendix-E) The interviewee was selected from Delhi-based potential users of the information system. The sample included planners, administrators and teacher educators, teachers at the higher level and librarians/documentalists. The interview was planned to elicit their opinions about the structure, financial, operational and allied aspects of the information system; teachers at secondary level and researchers were kept out from this because they seemed to be more concerned with services and environment of the system rather than organization, administration and finance of an information system.

For further indepth study, supplementaries were prepared after going through the responses from the respondents to whom questionnaires were already sent.

Procedure of Data Collection

Following steps were used for collection of relevant data from the target groups using the tools described earlier.

As a first step of collection of data information schedule was constructed by the investigator. The purpose of information schedule being to find out the various aspects on which the information was needed to develop the questionnaire and interview schedule. Thus with the help of the information schedule a questionnaire was designed which is given at Appendix-D.

The questionnaire was distributed and tested among the Delhi-based potential respondents. Five potential respondents among each of the seven identified categories of users were picked up. The respondents were contacted personally and questions were discussed to remove the ambiguity and irrelevance.

After getting the suggestions, the questionnaire was modified and finalised and distributed through mail as well as personally as it was necessitated. In case of the personal distribution, efforts were made to collect the same and it took 45 to 60 minutes to get the information through the questionnaire from the individual respondent.

After receiving the filled in questionnaires, they were analysed, and on the anlaysis the investigator found that some aspects of the proposed model of National Information System for Education in India required further clarifications. Keeping this in view, an interview schedule was constructed for Delhi-based planners, administrators, teachers at higher level, teacher educators, and librarians/documentalists. The teachers at school level and researchers were left out because the points to be clarified related to the administrative, organizational and financial aspects of the proposed system.

The interviewees were identified and a letter along with the interview schedule was sent for getting the appointment from the concerned interviewee. In many cases the respondents were to be reminded through telephone or personal visits for getting the time and data for interview. To get the required number of interviews it took two months.

In the actual interview not only their views on the points mentioned in the interview schedule were recorded, but for having to the insights of their opinions supplementaries were asked.

The whole process for data collection took 15 months.

REFERENCES

1. Busha, Charles H. and Harter, Stephen P (1980). *Research Methods in Librarianship: Techniques and interpretation*. New York: Academic Press, p.53-54
2. Hilis, P.J. ed. (1982) *Dictionary of Education*. London: Routledge and Kegan Paul, p.142
3. Good, Carter V. ed. (1959). *Dictionary of Education*. New York: Mcgraw-Hill, p.193
4. *ibid.*, p.15
5. *ibid.*, p.550
6. *ibid.*, p.194
7. ibid., p.414
8. *ibid.*, p.464
9. Harrod, Leonard Montague (1971). *The Librarians' Glossary*, 3rd edn. London: Andre Deutsch, p.377
10. *ALA Glossary of Library and Information Science*. (1983). Chicago: American Library Association, p.130
11. *ibid.*, p.118
12. Harrod, Leonard Montague (1971) *The Librarians' Glossary. Op. cit.*, p.223
13. Namboodiri, N. Krishnan, (1978) *Survey Sampling and Measurement*. New York: Academic Press, p.278
14. Olson, Edwin E. (1972). User population characteristics related to library utilization In *Quantitative methods in librarianship, standards, research, management* edited by Irene Braden Hoadley and Alice S. Clark. West Port, Greenwood, p.108-112
15. Adams, Gerald R. and Schvaneveldt, lay D. (1985) *Understanding Research Methods*. New York, Longman, p. 50

5

ANALYSIS AND INTERPRETATION OF DATA

A questionnaire with mostly structured responses was distributed among different categories of users to know their qualifications, field of work, needs, demands and preferences for educational information system in India. Besides this an interview schedule was canvassed among selected respondents. The findings based on responses to this questionnaire and interview have been reported, analysed and interpreted in the subsequent pages.

The details of content and structure of these two tools have been described in detail under Methodology in Chapter 4.

Sample

In all 1000 questionnaires were distributed among planners, administrators, teachers at school level, teachers at higher level, teachers in teacher training colleges, researchers doing research on different aspects of education, and librarians/documentalists working in educational institutions. Filled in questionnaires were received from 355 respondents to whom these were issued. The details have already been shown earlier in Table 4.1.

The low response (32%) from teachers at school level may be that they are not conscious about library services due to the poor library services in school, and thus become apathetic in their attitude. The reason for low response (29.3%) from researchers may be due to the change in their addresses because of either employment or transfer during the period. The reason for high response (46.0%) from administrators is due to the location of their offices in big cities and other facilities for communication at their disposal. It may be misleading if one infers that the administrators are more conscious of the use of library/information system. Looking at the problem from practical point of view one finds that other categories, though equally conscious about the usefulness of the system cannot utilise these to their maximum benefit because they do not have resources for communication at their command.

Trends in Responses

Not only the responses of different categories of users are different, their trends of responses also vary which have already been indicated earlier in the Table 4.2.

A little less than one-sixth (16.1%) did not require any reminder as they voluntarily responded to the questionnaire while as another about three-tenths (28.7%) required one reminder. Thus we find that more than half of the respondents required more than one reminders. About one third (34.0%) responded after 2nd reminder. Therefore, in all (78.8%) responses were received on maximum of upto two reminders. This may be partly due to unfamiliarity with the type of questionnaire on information system ever administered.

The trends in responses show that attitude towards responding the questionnaire is almost the same among different categories of users.

Qualifications

The academic and professional qualifications of the respondents have an important bearing on the problems of use of information system that the researcher has set before him to be investigated in the present study. Therefore, it was thought prudent to investigate this aspect of the respondents.

Academic

The academic qualifications of the respondents have been recorded in the Table given below :

TABLE 5.1 (a) : Academic Qualifications

Sl.No.	User categories	Graduate	Post-Graduate	M.Phil/ Ph.D	Not Mentioned	Total
(1)	(2)	(3)	(4)	(5)	(6)	(7)
1.	Planner	3	21	8	4	36
2.	Administrator	6	28	9	3	46
3.	Teacher (S)	7	53	1	3	64
4.	Teacher (H)	0	26	28	0	54
5.	Teacher (E)	10	31	14	1	56
6.	Researcher	2	22	20	0	44
7.	Lib./Doc.	11	41	3	0	55
	Total	39	222	83	11	355
	Percentage	11.0	62.5	23.5	3.0	100.0

About there-fourths (73.5%) of the respondent are graduate or post-graduate including 62.5 per cent or a little less than two-thirds as postgraduate. Thus, we observe that a large majority of the respondents are post-graduates. About one-fourth (23.5%) have either Ph.D. or M.Phil. degree whereas the remaining 3 per cent have not reported their academic qualifications. The respondents being in possession of high academic qualifications is presumed to ensure a faithful response to the problem in hand.

A look on the Table 5.1 (a) reveals that only about one-tenth (9.4%) of the planners are graduates whereas the remaining nine-tenths are post-graduates and above. It is heartening to note that one-fourth (25%) have Ph.D. or M.Phil degrees.

Professional

TABLE 5.1 (b): Professional Qualifications

Sl. No.	User Categories	Below Graduate	Graduate	Post-graduate	M.Phil/ Ph.D	Not mentioned	Total
(1)	(2)	(3)	(4)	(5)	(6)	(7)	(8)
1.	Planner	4	9	11	3	9	36
2.	Administrator	2	16	12	1	15	46
3.	Teacher (S)	2	35	16	3	8	64
4.	Teacher (H)	0	5	21	7	21	54
5.	Teacher (E)	0	15	25	14	2	56
6.	Researcher	0	6	18	2	18	44
7.	Lib./Doc.	0	31	21	3	0	55
	Total	8	117	124	33	73	355
	Percentage	2.2	33.0	35.0	9.3	20.5	100.0

A little more than two-thirds of the respondents have either graduate (33.0%) or post-graduate (35.0%) professional qualifications whereas less than 10 per cent (9.3) are M.Phil/Ph.D. Only a small fraction of about one in forty (2.2%) are less than graduate.

Percentage of post-graduates among various categories range from (25.0%) in case of teachers at school level to (44.6%) in case of teacher educators. Graduates are found mostly among teachers at school level (54.7%) and Lib./Doc. (54.6%). The three categories of respondents i.e., planners, administrators and teachers (S) by their very nature of work do not require very high professional qualifications. Therefore, we find that percentage among them with M.Phil/Ph.D. is lesser than that of other categories. Generally it is found that higher the level of professional work, higher is the qualification.

A comparison of Tables 5.1 (a) and 5.1 (b) shows that whereas about three-fourths (74.5%) of the librarians/documentalists are post-graduates while only about two-fifths (38.2%) have post-graduate professional qualifications. Similar trend is observed in other groups also resulting in a situation where comparatively lesser percentages among post-graduates have professional qualifications. The reasons are not far to seek.

Nature of Work

TABLE 5.2: Nature of Work

Sl.No.	Respondents	Nature of work							Total
		School Edun.	College Edun.	University Edun.	Non-formal Edun.	Adult Edun.	Lib Sc.	Others	
(1)	(2)	(3)	(4)	(5)	(6)	(7)	(8)	(9)	(10)
1.	Planner	29	15	13	19	17	0	5	98
2.	Administrator	21	14	4	3	5	3	2	52
3.	Teacher (S)	55	0	0	6	3	0	0	64
4.	Teacher (H)	21	12	13	9	4	12	2	73
5.	Teacher (E)	35	19	13	8	4	0	1	80
6.	Researcher	20	4	5	4	4	6	5	48
7.	Lib./Doc.	13	13	27	10	8	55	4	130
	Total	194	77	75	59	45	76	19	545
	Percentage	35.6	14.2	13.7	10.8	8.3	13.9	3.5	100.0

Since some of respondents work in more than one area, the total 355 does not tally with 545 responses above. Planners and administrators in Department of Education of Ministry of Human Resource Development, Planning Commission, National Institute of Educational Planning and Administration, National Council of Educational Research and Training, States Council of Educational Research and Training, etc. work on many aspects of education because working on policy matters relating to education, one is expected to deal with different fields of education like women's education, teacher education, etc.

Out of 355 respondents 19 are involved in other activities than the specified fields of education in the questionnaire. They are handling topics like Sanskrit education, education for Scheduled Castes and Scheduled

Tribes, editing of journals and their distribution, guidance of students with mental or physical handicaps, extension and development of education and training and vocationalizaiton of education etc.

The significant point is that no person at the level of planner and teacher training college is dealing with library education i.e., the aspect of library and information education is being neglected and does not enjoy the accepted position in our educational system.

More than one-third (35.6%) of respondents deal with school education. The relative proportional respondents working for college education (14.2%) university education (13.7%), library and documentation (13.9%) do not show much of difference. Same is the case with respondents dealing with non-formal education (10.8%) and adult education (8.3%).

The weakest link in the information system appears to be at school and college level as only one-tenth each of the Lib./Doc. work at that levels. This percentage is more than double at the university level (20.8%) and is more than four times (42.2%) when it comes to work in the field of library and documentation. Comparatively all categories of respondents show higher percentages among them working at school level. These percentages decline as we go upto college education, university education and other fields shown in the Table 5.2.

Experience

The experienced opinion of an experienced person carries much weight in formulating any policy or developing a model system. To find out how much our target groups are experienced an enquiry was made. The replies are presented in Table 5.3.

TABLE : 5.3: Experience of Respondents

Sl.No.	Respondents	Experience in years			Total
		0-10	11-20	21 and above	
(1)	(2)	(3)	(4)	(5)	(6)
1.	Planner	20	9	7	36
2.	Administrator	20	17	9	46
3.	Teacher (S)	13	31	20	64
4.	Teacher (H)	28	17	9	54
5.	Teacher (E)	22	26	8	56
6.	Researcher	28	7	9	44
7.	Lib./Doc.	8	22	25	55
	Total	139	129	87	355
	Percentage	39.2	36.3	24.5	100.0

From the Table we get that (39.2%) are of experience between 0-10 years; (36.3%) are of 11-20 years; and (24.5%) are of more than 20 years. So we have (60.8%) from our target population who have more than 11 years of experience.

Respondents and their Working Institutions

The need of different types of information depends not only upon the work one is doing but it also depends upon the nature of the institution in which one is working. In order tc know the institutional affiliation of the respondents they were asked to identity the nature of the institutions in which they are working. The replies have been analyzed in the Table 5.4.

TABLE : 5.4Relation of Respondents to Nature of Institution

Sl. No.	Respondents	Nature of Institution							Total
		Govt. Dept.	Research Inst.	Univ.	Teachers Training College	Coll-ege	School	Others	
(1)	(2)	(3)	(4)	(5)	(6)	(7)	(8)	(9)	(10)
1.	Planner	21	12	1	0	2	0	0	36
2.	Administrator	12	4	5	5	12	8	0	46
3.	Teacher (S)	5	2	0	5	0	52	0	64
4.	Teacher (H)	5	13	19	10	7	0	0	54
5.	Teacher (E)	8	10	8	30	0	0	0	56
6.	Researcher	4	18	9	1	3	1	8*	44
7.	Lib/Doc.	7	14	19	4	8	3	0	55
	Total	62	73	61	55	32	64	8	355
	Percentage	17.5	20.5	17.2	15.5	9.0	18.0	2.3	100.0

*Engaged in research for full time and are not employed anywhere.

The proportion of respondents working in government departments (17.5%), universities (17.2%) and in schools (18.0%) is almost the same. About one in five (20.5%) works in research institutions while the remaining work in teacher training colleges (15.5%), colleges of general education (9.0%) and other institutions (2.3%).

One in three of those working in government departments is charged with duties of planning and about one-fifth in administration. Thus we find a little more than half are mainly concerned with planning and administration. One-fourth of those working in research institutions are engaged in research while a little less than one-third each of those in universities are working in higher education are teachers in higher education or librarian/documentalists.

A large majority of school teachers, as is obvious, work at school stage. The order of number of respondents working in different institutions is research institutions, schools, government departments, universities, teacher training colleges, colleges and independent researchers. If we club the categories into two i.e. government departments + research institutes and independent researchers and teaching community i.e. universities+teacher training colleges+colleges+schools, it would be 40:60. It means that almost all the categories are equally important and we will have to develop the system in such a way that it may give equal importance to all the users.

Time Devoted by Respondents to their Subjects

To know the respondents' interest in the field of their work and use of the library and information services, it would be in the fitness of things to study how much time each of the category devotes to its subject field. The analysis of the responses is given in the Table 5.5 as is under. Here we have clubbed the planners and administrators together and teachers at higher level i.e. (in universities, colleges and teachers of training colleges) assuming that their nature of work and needs are similar.

TABLE : 5.5: Time Devoted by the Respondents to Their Subject

Sl.No.	Users	Number of clock hours spent in library per week				Total
		1 - 4	5-10	11-15	More than 15	
(1)	(2)	(3)	(4)	(5)	(6)	(7)
1.	Planner+ Administrator	9	29	20	12	70
2.	Teacher (S)	12	22	12	13	59
3.	Teacher (H)	13	22	21	51	107
4.	Researcher	2	14	3	23	42
5.	Lib./Doc.	19	20	7	6	52
	Total	55	107	63	105	330
	Percentage	16.7	32.4	19.1	31.8	100.0

Out of 355 respondents 25 did not mention the time devoted per week to the study of their subjects. One-third of the respondents i.e. 32.4 per cent devote 5 to 10 hours per week to their subject field. While almost equal number of respondents, i.e. 31.8 per cent devote more than 15 hours per week. This is due to the fact that the latter group comprises most of teachers and researchers. From the table it is clear that researchers come first with 76 per cent and teachers at higher level come second with 47.66 per cent in the category of time between 15 hours and more per week.

Possession of Personal Libraries

It is assumed that the persons who are in the habit of study and have developed interests they should own their personal libraries/collections, however, small it may be. This is corroborated by the fact that more than half (54.6%) of respondents do own their personal collections.

TABLE : 5.6: Ownership of Personal Libraries

Sl.	Users	Having	Not having	Total
(1)	(2)	(3)	(4)	(5)
1.	Planner	33	3	36
2.	Administrator	24	22	46
3.	Teacher (S)	31	33	64
4.	Teacher (H)	34	20	54
5.	Teacher (E)	28	28	56
6.	Researcher	24	20	44
7.	Lib./Doc.	20	35	55
	Total	194	161	355
	Percentage	54.6	45.4	100.0

The respondents who have libraries rank in the following order: (i) Planner, 91.7 per cent, (ii) Teacher at Higher level, 63.0 per cent, (iii) Researcher, 54.5per cent, (iv) Administrator, 52.2 per cent, (v) Teacher Educator, 50.0 per cent, (vi) Teacher at School level, 48.4 per cent and (vii) Librarian/Documentalist, 36.4 per cent. It is possible that some may wonder that planners hold that 1st rank while researchers hold 3rd and librarians/documentalists hold the 7th, the last rank. The plausible explanation seems to be is that planner in this survey are working in Department of Education Ministry of Human Resource Development), Planning Commission, NIEPA, NCERT and State Council of Educational Research and Training (SCERTs) in the states. It is also possible that they may be having top level posts. By virtue of their position they would be getting publications and reports in their personal names and they must be having many reports and occasional papers on state policy or national policy in their own name or must have brought out publications on behalf of their institutions. This way they may have developed their personal libraries.

About low percentage of libraries with researchers, we may find the explanation that as the needs of the researcher are varied and short lived, he would like to have a large and varied topics collection which may not be possible for an individual due to the shortage of financial resources and scarcity of space at his disposal. He has to depend upon the resources of the institutional libraries for his need.

About the librarians having low percentage of owning libraries, the reason may be that he is in a position to meet his needs from his own library or from other libraries and thus need not have his personal library.

After knowing the possession of library, it would be useful to know the size of collection of the library having a fair idea of the interest and study habits of a particular user category. The Table 5.7 presents the position in respect of various user categories.

Number of Books in Personal Libraries

Out of 194 respondents possessing libraries, 12 have not mentioned the number of books in their libraries.

TABLE 5.7: Number of Books in Respondents Personal Libraries

		Number of books in personal libraries					
Sl.No.	Users	Upto 50	51-100	101-200	201-500	More than 500	Total
(1)	(2)	(3)	(4)	(5)	(6)	(7)	(8)
1.	Planner	5	2	7	5	4	23
2.	Administrator	3	4	5	4	8	24
3.	Teacher (S)	13	5	5	3	3	29
4.	Teacher (H)	6	6	8	14	0	34
5.	Teacher (E)	3	2	7	10	6	28
6.	Researcher	8	2	4	6	4	24
7.	Lib./Doc.	2	3	3	7	5	20
	Total	40	24	39	49	30	182
	Percentage	22.0	13.2	21.4	26.9	16.5	100.0

From the table we see that 22.0 per cent having libraries with the collection of upto 50 books; 13.2 per cent from 51 to 100; 21.4 per cent from 101-200 books; 26.9 per cent have a collection of books 201 to 500 and 16.5 per cent have more than 500 books.

If we consider that a collection of more than 100 books is sufficient for an individual to keep himself up to date then we find that about two-thirds of respondents have a good personal collection judged by this standard.

Some other observations have been made while analyzing the individual questionnaire of the planners and administrators:

(i) The planners and administrators working in research institutions have their personal libraries;
(ii) Persons working in government departments generally have less libraries. It seems that for their requirements they take the help of their juniors; and
(iii) As we have seen in Table 5.6 that only 54.6 per cent of our respondents have libraries and 45.4 per cent do not have.

It can be concluded that information services in the field of education will have to be strengthened.

Reading of Journals

Book may become obsolete with the passage of time while journals keep pace with the time and hence with the new knowledge. In order to keep abreast with new developments and trends in the theory and policy of a particular field and the technological applications in it, it is necessary to keep oneself informed of the journals and periodical publications in that field. The Table 5.8 indicates the respondents' reading habit of Journals.

A very significant point emerging from analyzing data is that about four-fifths (78.6%) of our respondents make use of the journals regularly. It is, therefore, necessary that we should provide information services to the persons dealing in education to have access to new developments, ideas, theories, policies and trends in the field of education.

We see that all teahers at higher level read journals, while the percentage of researchers is 86.4 per cent, teacher educators 84.0 per cent, administrators 78.3 per cent, planners 77.8 per cent, teachers at school level 64.0 per cent and librarians/documentalists 63.6 per cent respectively. It is surprising to note that proportion among researchers studying the journals is less than that of among the teachers at higher education level.

TABLE 5.8: Respondents Classified into the Reading Habits of Journals

Sl.No.	Respondents	Use journals	Do not Use journals	Total
(1)	(2)	(3)	(4)	(5)
1.	Planner	28	8	36
2.	Administrator	36	10	46
3.	Teacher (S)	41	23	64
4.	Teacher (H)	54	0	54
5.	Teacher (E)	47	9	56
6.	Researcher	38	6	44
7.	Lib./Doc.	35	20	55
	Total	279	76	355
	Percentage	78.6	21.4	100.0

Methods of Meeting Needs for Journals

To supplement the above information it would be essential for us to know what modes they use for meeting their needs for journals.

TABLE : 5.9: Methods of Meeting Needs of Journals

Sl. No.	Users	Modes				
		Through subscription	Loan from library	Studying in library	Loan from friends	By gift
(1)	(2)	(3)	(4)	(5)	(6)	(7)
1.	Planner	13	18	21	5	7
2.	Administrator	16	13	19	3	8
3.	Teacher (S)	23	15	29	8	0
4.	Teacher (H)	17	24	39	7	10
5.	Teacher (E)	22	20	35	6	6
6.	Researcher	16	13	34	8	10
7.	Lib./Doc.	13	15	25	7	2
	Total	120	118	202	44	43
	Percentage	43.0	42.3	72.4	15.8	15.4

The 279 respondents who regularly consult periodicals and journals employ different methods to have access to them. It may not be possible for one to subscribe all the journals of his interest or get all the journals from one source. Therefore, it becomes necessary for the reader to tap different sources. Respondents may simultaneously get journals through more than one source. Therefore, the figures in different rows of Table 5.9 cannot be added.

In addition to these five modes of using of journals there are some 'others' mentioned by the respondents, like the libraries of other institutions, review copies, reprints, through professional bodies of which they may be members, etc. Such readers make a small fraction. Therefore, these have been ignored.

Form the Table 5.9 we find that study in the library ranks first (72.4%) and is followed by loan from libraries (42.3%), loan from friends (15.8%) and by gift (15.4%).

If use at libraries for meeting the need of journals is considered we find that maximum of respondents depend upon them. This emphasises the need for the development of library services for the users in the field of education.

One more significant point revealed is that the planners and administrators do not make much use of these modes. The plausible reasons may be that they have shortage of time at their disposal and may be taking help of their juniors as pointed out earlier.

Use of Library Services

The need for strengthening of library services is further increased when we find that a vast majority (86.2%) of respondents make use of different services provided by libraries.

TABLE : 5.10: Use of Library Services

Sl. No.	Respondents	Use	Do not use	Total
(1)	(2)	(3)	(4)	(5)
1.	Planner	30	6	36
2.	Administrator	32	14	46
3.	Teacher (S)	49	15	64
4.	Teacher (H)	54	0	54
5.	Teacher (E)	47	9	56
6.	Researcher	44	0	44
7.	Lib/Doc.	50	5	55
	Total	306	49	355
	Percentage	86.2	13.8	100.0

All the teachers at higher level and researchers use the library services while librarians/documentalist (90.9%), teacher educators (83.9%), planners (83.3%), teachers at school level (76.6%), and administrators (69.6%) follow in the order in which their names are noted.

Time Spent in the Library

TABLE : 5.11: Time Spent in the Library

Sl. No.	User	Time spent per week (in clock hours)					Total
		1 - 4	5 - 10	11 - 15	16 - 20	More than 20	
(1)	(2)	(3)	(4)	(5)	(6)	(7)	(8)
1.	Planner	15	11	2	1	1	30
2.	Administrator	19	10	2	0	1	32
3.	Teacher (S)	25	19	2	2	1	49
4.	Teacher (H)	16	29	3	2	4	54
5.	Teacher (E)	15	26	3	1	2	47
6.	Researcher	12	13	10	4	5	44
7.	Lib./Doc.	4	7	0	0	39	50
	Total	106	115	22	10	53	306
	Percentage	34.6	37.6	7.2	3.3	17.3	100.0

Out of 355 resondents 49 do not make use of the library. About one-third (34.6%) use the library for 1-4 hours per week, 115 (37.6%) for 5-10 hours per week, 22(7.2%) for 11- 15 hours, 10 (3.3%) for 16 - 20 hours and 53 (7.3%) for more than 20 hours per week. The respondents making the maximum use of library belong to the category of librarians/ documentalists, thus becoming first in this category. May be that they have mentioned all the hours working in the library as the time for making use of the library. If it is so (which seems to be a fact), then we can ignore it and can safely say that researchers come first and teachers at higher level come next in making use of library for the maximum hours.

Reasons for not using Library

We find that 49 (13.8%) out of 355 respondents do not make use of their organisation library. There can be various reasons for it viz. (i) they need not use it for their work or duty, (ii) they do not have time at their disposal for the library because they are busy on their jobs, and (iii) there may be deficiencies in functioning of the library and they do not get satisfactory services from the library and hence they do not make use of it.

TABLE : 5.12: Reasons for Not Using Library

Sl. No.	User	Reasons for not using the library				
		Under stocked	Disorga-nised	Atmosphere not conductive	Location not ideal	Timings not convenient
(1)	(2)	(3)	(4)	(5)	(6)	(7)
1.	Planner (6)	5	4	4	2	2
2.	Administrator (14)	5	1	4	4	11
3.	Teacher (S) (15)	15	5	6	4	12
4.	Teacher (E) (9)	9	7	6	4	8
5.	Lib./Doc. (5)	1	1	1	1	1
	Total(49)	40	18	21	15	34
	Percentage	81.6	36.7	42.9	30.6	69.4

Reasons for not using the library rank in the order of understocked 40(81.6%), timings are not convenient 34 (69.4%), atmosphere not conducive 21 (42.9%), disorganized 18 (36.7%) and location not ideal 15 (30.6%).

The remedial measures suggested in this regard are given below:

(i) Libraries should be provided sufficient funds for collections of the reading materials, inter-library loan (ILL) and resource sharing should be arranged and strengthened;

(ii) Timings of libraries should be extended so that it is convenient to users;

(iii) To have reading material in disorganised state is not good in the fair name of the profession. Librarians should take every pain to organise the material in proper way so that all the five laws of library science can be fulfilled. For this training-in-service, refresher courses, workshops, seminars etc. should be organised to make the librarians conscious of the proper organisation of the reading materials;

(iv) Efforts should also be made to provide a very healthy and pleasant atmosphere to the readers. There should be proper arrangement of cooling and heating to keep the temperature normal;

(v) A quiet atmosphere should be provided;

(vi) Stacks, furniture, books should be properly arranged and kept clean and neat;

(vii) There should be proper lay out of guides, charts and curtains on the walls. In shot reader should feel homely and cheerful while making use of the library;

(viii) So far as location of the library is concerned, the reason seems to be a bit out of control of the librarian, yet a calm atmosphere or an easy approach can be provided to the readers for making the library more useful and functioning.

In brief, for making the library more useful and attractive a proper and comprehensive policy at the national, state, district and local level should be formulated.

The reasons advanced by the respondents for not using the library are more than one. Hence the raw totals become irrelevant. The reason advanced by them are not only those that have been mentioned above. Among 'other' reasons the most common is the reason like paucity of time. The reason 'paucity of time' is advanced by a small fraction of planners, administrators, teachers at school level and teacher educators is understandable.

Some of the respondents who are regular users of their departmental libraries have also complained about understocked and disorganised libraries with inconvenient location and timings, besides incongenial atmosphere.

Purpose of Visit to Library

TABLE : 5.13: Purpose of Visiting the Library

Sl. No.	Users	Not commented	commented	Obtaining New information	Verification of Information	Others
(1)	(2)	(3)	(4)	(5)	(6)	(7)
1.	Planner (36)	0	36	33	17	6
2.	Administrator (46)	1	45	36	22	8
3.	Teacher (S) (64)	0	64	57	29	5
4.	Teacher (H) (54)	2	52	52	32	4
5.	Teacher (E) (56)	0	56	52	27	4
6.	Researcher (44)	2	42	41	24	2
7.	Lib/Doc (55)	3	52	50	35	16
	Total(355)	8	347	321	186	45
	Percentage (100.0)	(2.3)	97.7	92.5	53.6	13.0

Only 8 (2.3%) out of 355 have not offered their comments. The comments of remaining 347 respondents are analyzed above. The purpose for using the library can be categorised viz. (i) obtaining new information (ii) for the verification of information and (iii) others.

A large majority of respondents 321 (92.5%) visit the library for obtaining new information while 186 (53.6%) visit it for verification purpose. In this there is overlapping because the respondents may visit the library for both the purposes. Planners and administrators, while preparing reports and pilot studies, may ask their junior colleagues to verify the figures on statements while teaching and research communities make visits generally for new information.

So for as other purposes are concerned, the teachers (S) visit the library to borrow the newspapers and popular magazines, and to get books issued for further distribution among the students. The comments from teachers (H) and teacher educators are like that they go to the library to prepare the lecture, to prepare for guiding the researchers, and to know what new information has been added to the subject, etc. Again such purposes can be expected from these categories. The comments from planners and administrators are such as, for decision taking, motivation of staff, for up-dating of knowledge, for supplementing of knowledge and up-dating of data base etc. Researchers visit the library to see the abstracts and indexes etc. Librarians use the library to disseminate services, provide references to readers, for professional growth, etc. Such replies are expected from these categories of respondents.

The other category of purposes also includes recreational purposes like स्वत: सुखाय 'Svath Sukhaaya'. So we can say that other purposes mentioned are related to subject fields of the user categories and are also in general for recreation and pasttime.

Basic Information Sought by Respondents

It is not possible to properly plan and develop the library and documentation services unless we know the requirements of the users. What types of information different categories of readers seek from the library will help us in developing the information system in tune with the clientele requirement. Information regarding this was collected and is summarised in Table 5.14.

From the Table 5.14 we observe that the order of the most sought after type of information are research findings (18.0%), teaching and training methodologies (16.0%), curriculum materials (14.8%) case studies on education (14.4%) recent trend in theories, principles, definitions and approaches in education (14.3%) policy making and management of education (12.5%), and basic statistics (10.0%).

TABLE : 5.14: Types of Information Sought

Sl. No.	Types of Information	Users							Total
		Planer (36)	Administrator (46)	Teacher (S) (64)	Teacher (H) (54)	Teacher (E) (56)	Researcher (44)	Lib./Doc. (55)	355 (100.0)
(1)	(2)	(3)	(4)	(5)	(6)	(7)	(8)	(9)	(10)
1.	B.S.	21	10	14	12	12	21	23	113 (10.0)
2.	C.M.	19	18	40	30	30	12	19	168 (14.8)
3.	TTM	20	19	42	28	38	17	18	182 (16.0)
4.	R.F.	24	17	18	32	36	40	37	204 (18.0)
5.	P.M. & M.E	25	19	22	20	24	23	9	142 (12.5)
6.	C.S.	23	8	12	39	31	29	21	163 (14.4)
	1st world	9	2	2	13	11	11	7	55 (4.9)
	2nd world	2	2	3	14	8	4	5	38 (3.3)
	3rd world	12	4	7	12	12	14	9	70 (6.2)
7.	R.T.T.P.D.A.	24	18	26	13	34	23	22	160 (14.3)
	Total	156	109	174	174	205	165	149	1132
	Average	(4.3)	(2.4)	(2.7)	(3.2)	(3.7)	(3.8)	(2.7)	

Note : Percentages to the row total are given in parenthesis.

B.S. – Basic statistics; C.M. – Curriculum materials; T.T.M..- Teaching & Training Methodologies;

R.F. – Research findings; P.M. & M.E. – Policy making & management of education; C.S. – Case Studies on education;

R.T.T.P.D.A. – Recent trends in theories, principles, definitions and approaches;

1st world – U.S.A, Canada and European countries, etc.; 2nd world-USSR and other communist countries; 3rd world–Developing countries.

Another phenomenon revealed by the analysis is that in addition to the type of information mentioned in the table some categories of the users mentioned that they are interested in some additional information, viz. teachers are interested in education and development, child development philosophical treatises etc; researchers are interested in information about science and technological policies, political news and national progress; librarians showed their interest in recreation, political events and economic developments, professional knowledge and bibliographical references. The planners make the most (58.3%) use of the basic statistics while teacher educators are the least (21.4%) users. Curriculum materials are mostly (62.5%) used by teachers at schools level whereas the researchers are the least (27.2%) users. Information regarding teaching and training methodologies is mostly (67.8%) used by the teacher educators, while the lowest interest (32.7%) in it is shown by the category in librarians/documentalists. Teachers at higher level make the most (72.2%) use of case studies while least (17.3%) use is made by the administrators. The case studies in education relating to 3rd world are most (42.9%) used while the least (23.3%) use is made of the case studies relating to 2nd world. Information in respect of trends in theories, principles, definitions and approaches is mostly (66.7%) used by planners while teachers at higher level make the least (24.1%) use of this aspect of information.

From the Table 5.14 we see that the average use of different types of information is made in the order: planners (4.3%), researchers (3.8%), teacher educators (37%), teachers at higher level (3.2%) teachers at school level (2.7%), librarians/documentalists (2.7%) and administrators (2.4%).

Locating in Reading Material

TABLE : 5.15: Methods of Locating Reading Materrial

Sl.No.	Users	Consult library staff	Other methods	Not mentioned	Total
(1)	(2)	(3)	(4)	(5)	(6)
1.	Planner	32	3	1	36
2.	Administrator	35	4	7	46
3.	Teacher (S)	52	3	9	64
4.	Teacher (H)	47	7	–	54
5.	Teacher (E)	49	2	5	56
6.	Researcher	42	–	2	44
7.	Lib./Doc.	33	18	4	55
	Total	290	37	28	355
	Percentage	(81.7)	(10.4)	(7.9)	(100.0)

A large proportion among users (81.7%) consult the library staff to get their information or documents. From this it is very evident that for rendering good, quick and efficient service we need co-operative and knowledgeable library staff so that they can meet out the demands of the users.

About one-tenth (10.4%) mentioned that they use other means for finding out the information. Among such means are visits to other libraries and to consult the knowledgeable persons or friends. School teachers make a complaint that books are generally locked in almirahas and thus they consult friends. The teachers at higher level mention that they use different sources and tools like indexes, abstracts etc. Most of the teaching community, researchers and librarians know how to find out the information themselves with the help of various tools available in the library.

Out of 355 respondents 28 (7.9%) do not mention how they find information in the library. The probable reasons for it can be either they get information from their juniors or they know how to consult the catalogue and find the documents on the shelves or they do not visit library. The other reason can be that to consult the library staff in finding out an information or a document, is so evident that they did not bother about mentioning this.

Arrangement for Inter Library Loan (ILL)

No library, howsoever, big or small it may be rich or poor in its collection, is self-sufficient and can fulfil all the demands of its clientele with its own resources. The librarian will have to take recourse to inter library loan (ILL) by establishing report with other libraries for getting the demands of his clientele fulfilled. Similarly, users may have take the help of his library to get documents on ILL from other libraries or will go to other library for the documents/information not available in his own library. An enquiry was made to know whether users are conscious of the services like 'ILL' and 'visiting of other libraries' for the documents/information not available in their own libraries. The responses are analysed and presented in the table 5.16 given below:-

TABLE : 5.16: Use of ILL and Other Libraries

Sl. No.	Users	Total number of respondents	ILL	Consulting of other libraries
(1)	(2)	(3)	(4)	(5)
1.	Planner	36	18	28
2.	Administrator	46	21	28
3.	Teacher (S)	64	34	40
4.	Teacher (H)	54	30	37
5.	Teacher (E)	56	21	42
6.	Researcher	44	24	23
7.	Lib./Doc.	55	55	39
	Total	355	203	237
	Percentage	100.0	57.2	66.8

Out of 355 respondents, 14 (3 planners, 1 administrator and 10 teachers at school level) did not mention whether they are availing of the services of ILL or consulting the other libraries.

Comparison of the two services shows that ILL service (57.2%) and consultation of other libraries (66.8%) is almost equal. The librarians should develop relation among one another in such a manner that rese-archers of one library can use the resources of other libraries fully either by ILL or through personal visits. In this way we would be observing 1st, 2nd and 3rd laws of library science, thus saving lot of national resources and avoid unnecessary duplication. This also necessitates the network of the information centres and their resource sharing.

As we have seen from the table all the user categories have multiple choices, hence row totals are redundant. The responses show that half among planners make use of ILL and (77.8%) consult other libraries while the corresponding figures for administrators are (45.6% and 60.9%); for teachers at school level (53.1% and 62.5%); for teachers at higher level (55.5% and 68.5%); for teacher educators (37.5% and 75.0%); for researchers (54.5% and 52.3%)) and for librarians/documentalists (100.0% and 70.9%).

In addition to these services some respondents mention some other alternatives for meeting their needs, if documents/information is/are not available in their own library. Among these other services, planners, administrators and teachers at school level mentioned services such as purchase of the required material or its acquisition from friends. Some even feel that they have to forget and be satisfied with whatever is available in their own library. The teahers at higher level and teacher educators consult other sources, purchase and, the material get photocopies or reprints. Researchers try to explore in their own way or try to get copies from authors. The librarian try to get the information on telephone, to consult the library accession list, indexes and abstracts etc. to fulfil the needs. Taking all these together makes only a fraction of the whole requirement to be met with the resources available in other libraries. So this can be ignored keeping in view the demand met by ILL and visiting of other libraries for consultation.

Some of the respondents make a comment which is not healthy from library point of view i.e., 'satisfied whatever is available in own library'. It is, therefore, necessary to orient the users about different types of services including ILL available in the library. This role can be assumed by librarians themselves.

Therefore, it becomes imperative that librarians undergo refresher courses and training-inservice so that their professional skill is upgraded to enable them to do full justice to their profession.

Time Availability of Reading Material

Dr. Ranganathan's laws of library science expect that every reader gets his/her document in the shortest possible time or right document to the right reader at the right time. This means that libraries should develop its services in such a manner that readers should get their required material without any delay. To know the present position of working of the libraries in the field of education, respondents were required to give their comments about the service conditions of their libraries. The views of the respondents are enlisted below in the Table 5.17.

TABLE : 5.17: Extent of Delay in Getting Reading Material

Sl. No.	Users	In time	Extent of Delay				Total
			Total	Slight delay	Moderate delay	Considerable delay	Respon.
(1)	(2)	(3)	(4)	(5)	(6)	(7)	(8)
1.	Planners	16	20	6	9	5	36
2.	Administrator	24	22	6	9	7	46
3.	Teacher (S)	29	35	3	19	13	64
4.	Teacher (H)	32	22	2	12	8	54
5.	Teacher (E)	26	30	3	14	13	56
6.	Researcher	23	21	3	12	6	44
7.	Lib./Doc.	20	35	11	18	6	55
	Total	170	185	34	93	58	355
	Percentage	47.9	52.1	18.4	50.3	31.3	

From the Table 5.17 we observe that 170 (47.9%) respondents get the information in time while 185 (52.1%) do not get it in time. It means that almost 50 per cent of the users are not satisfied with the library services. Further we find that 34 (18.4%) get the document/information with slight delay; 93 (50.3%) get the reading materials with moderately delay and 58 (31.3%) respondents get them with considerable delay.

From the above analysis, it is a matter of great concern to know that materials are not being provided to readers in time. Processing tools like classification, cataloguing, indexing and shelf arrangement should be strengthened. The card preparation specially for micro documents may be done more appropriately. Subject headings and thesaurus or subject headings lists should be complete and up-to-date.

One more revealing fact is that even librarians who are responsible for providing reading materials in time are conscious of the delay in providing the material. The need is that they should be trained in storing and retrieving of the materials to avoid the delay in providing the required material to the reader.

Helpfulness of Library Staff

Any information system is made of three ingredients i.e., user, information personnel and reading material. The information personnel is a link between the user and information. If the library staff is helpful and trained in locating the information and intelligent enough to understand the need of the user, services to the users could be of high quality and rendered speedily. But, if the staff is not of helping nature, the service will be badly affected and the purpose for which the information system is established, is lost. To know the respondents' reactions about the helpful attitude of the staff towards the users, the respondents were requested to give their impression about the attitude of the library staff. The responses have been analysed in table 5.18.

TABLE : 5.18: Library Staff-Opinion About

Sl. No.	Users	Attitude of the Professional Library Staff			Total
		Helpful	Not helpful	No comments	
(1)	(2)	(3)	(4)	(5)	(6)
1.	Planner	31	2	3	36
2.	Administrator	41	5	0	46
3.	Teacher (S)	48	16	0	64
4.	Teacher (H)	45	9	0	54
5.	Teacher (E)	40	14	2	56
6.	Researcher	37	5	2	44
7.	Lib./Doc.	42	12	1	55
	Total	284	63	8	355
	Percentage	80.4	17.7	2.3	100.0

Eight (2.3%) respondents, 3 among planners, 2 from teacher educators, 2 from researchers and 1 from librarians give no comments about the attitude of the librarians towards users. Even though 80 per cent of the respondents feel that the library staff is helpful we find that 63 (17.7%) are of the view that librarians are not of helpful attitude towards the users. This is not an insignificant percentage and hence it is to be taken note of. Taken together negative and indifferent attitude of the respondents, about one-fifth among the users feel that the librarian is not of helpful attitude. This is an indication that full and proper care should be given while selection is made for the profession. This is personality facet and should be taken proper care in the syllabus and training for the library personnel. Refresher courses, seminars, workshops should be arranged and organized to develop the helpful attitude among the professional staff working in libraries.

Further, it reveals contrary to the expectation, that librarians working with planners and administrators i.e., in the government departments are of more helpful nature than those working in educational and research institutes/organisations. The reason may be that in educational organisations the disciplinary powers are not directly in the hands of the academicians with whom librarians are to work while in the government departments the disciplinary powers are with the persons with whom they are working. But it should not be the case because to render help to the readers under the element of fear or punishment is not a healthy sign of the profession. It should be a trait of the profession.

One more significant point revealed in the analysis is that, the librarians themselves are conscious of the fact that their attitude towards users is not helpful. 12 (22.2%) out of 54, express the opinion that the attitude of the librarians is not helpful towards the users. Self-consciousness is a great boon to learn and develop one's personality. Hence, it is clear that the workshops and short-term training courses are required to be arranged for the development of helpful attitude of the librarians towards the readers.

Professional Qualities of Library Staff

Certain qualities are necessary pre-requisites for professional staff. Therefore, it was further thought necessary to ascertain the basic qualities of the professional staff viz. understanding of the need of the user, to know the contents of the material, the processing, collection and dissemination of information and cooperation extended to the users for meeting their needs. The respondents' views on this are analysed in the table 5.19 given below:

TABLE : 5.19: Views About The Professional Staff

Sl.No.	Users	Total Respond.	Respondents' views about library staff		
			Capable to understand	Trained in handling information work	Co-operative
(1)	(2)	(3)	(4)	(5)	(6)
1.	Planner	31	19	16	22
2.	Administrator	41	20	20	29
3.	Teacher (S)	48	27	13	43
4.	Teacher (H)	45	22	24	37
5.	Teacher (E)	40	22	21	38
6.	Researcher	37	19	21	32
7.	Lib./Doc.	42	24	22	32
	Total	284	153	137	233

Out of 355 respondent 284 expressed positive views about the professional staff of the library. As the respondents expressed views about more than one aspect of the professional staff, the figures in rows are not additive. The largest number (95.0%) of teacher educators consider that professional staff is co-operative while only 70.7% (least) fo administrators consider them co-operative. The highest number (62.5%) goes to teachers at school level who consider that librarians are trained in handling of information while the lowest (48.8%) to administrators who opine that the librarians are trained in handling of the information; 61.3% (highest) of the planners are of the view that librarians are capable to understand the information need while (48.8%) (lowest) administrators are of the view that librarians are capable of understanding the information needs of the users.

The reason for co-operative attitude of librarians expressed by the largest number of teacher educators may be that in teacher training colleges library working in one of the optional papers in the syllabus of B.Ed. and M.Ed. This paper is generally taught by the librarian of the college. Due to partnership in teaching the attitude of librarian towards the teacher becomes more co-operative or teachers may be having based opinions about the attitude of the librarian. The opinions of teachers at school level about the training for handling of the information needs are due to the fact that in school the information needs are very simple and straight forward i.e., a particular book by an author or under a specific title or on a particular subject, which can be found out easily and thus largest number of teachers at school level expressed that librarians can handle the information. Again 48.8 per cent of administrators are of the view that librarians do have training for handling of the information need. So far understanding capacity of the information need by the librarian, the 1st number goes to the planners (61.3%) and the last goes to administrators (48.8%). The librarians who are working continuously with planners know their parameters and thus collect and process the information in such a manner so that at the time of need by planners, information is provided without much delay. The reason for appreciating the qualities of librarians by a fewer number of administrators are likely to be that the needs of administrators are not much varied and mostly are of routine nature. They do fulfil their needs without much help of the librarians and that is why only a few appreciate the qualities of the librarians or professional staff of the library.

Deficiencies of Library Staff

The redeeming feature of the study is that a large majority of the users have positive attitude towards the library staff, but it would be necessary to probe further in this direction. It is heartening to note that many respondents have pointed out a large number of deficiencies among the library staff as is evident from the Table 5.20.

TABLE : 5.20: Deficiencies of the Library Staff

Sl.No.	Users	Deficiencies of Library Staff				
		Inadequate staff	Unable to understand information	Lock of training	Non-Coop.	Specific duties are not assigned
(1)	(2)	(3)	(4)	(5)	(6)	(7)
1.	Planner (36)	4	2	3	0	1
2.	Administrator (46)	0	2	2	2	2
3.	Teacher (S) (64)	4	3	2	3	4
4.	Teacher (H) (54)	2	3	0	4	0
5.	Teacher (E) (56)	8	5	7	12	7
6.	Researcher (44)	4	3	3	1	3
7.	Lib./Doc. (55)	4	3	3	1	1
	Total (355)	26	21	20	23	18
	Percentage	7.3	5.9	5.6	6.5	5.1

It is clear that only a very small percentage of respondents pointed out the deficiencies of the library staff. Never the less, it is an indication that for rendering an excellent service and for maximum utilization of the library resources we should have adequate staff with good academic qualifications and proper training to understand and handling of the information needs of the users. Their personality should be developed in such a way that the staff should always adopt co-operative attitude and duties should be assigned according to the knowledge, training, taste and interest of the individual to get maximum out of him. However, if at any time it is not possible to have the proper person for a specific job, he should be trained and given incentives to make himself suitable for the job assigned to him.

Adequacy, Coherence and Promptness of Information

TABLE : 5.21: Adequacy Coherence and Promptness

Sl. No.	User	Supply of Information											
		Adequate				Prompt				Coherent			
		Always	Sometimes	Never	Total	Always	Sometimes	Never	Total	Always	Sometimes	Never	Total
(1)	(2)	(3)	(4)	(5)	(6)	(7)	(8)	(9)	(10)	(11)	(12)	(13)	(14)
1.	Planner (36)	10	20	0	30	12	17	0	29	6	17	1	24
2.	Administrator (46)	13	19	3	35	14	12	2	28	8	14	1	23
3.	Teacher (S) (64)	19	33	4	56	17	24	2	43	8	19	4	31
4.	Teacher (H) (54)	14	29	3	46	11	18	4	33	11	17	2	30
5.	Teacher (E) (56)	9	29	9	47	9	24	5	38	7	19	6	32
6.	Researcher (44)	15	23	2	40	6	22	4	32	5	17	4	26
7.	Lib./Doc. (55)	24	23	4	51	16	29	6	51	16	24	11	51
	Total (355)	104	176	25	305	85	146	23	254	61	127	29	217
Percentage (100.0)		34.1	57.7	8.2	85.9	33.5	57.5	9.0	71.5	28.1	58.5	13.4	61.1

Adequacy – What is required is fully sufficient and suitable for use.
Coherence – Logically connected information.
Promptness – In time.

We find that 305 (85.9%) out of 355 respondents expressed their opinions about the adequacy of information, 254 (71.5%) for promptness, and 217 (61.1%) for coherence of information. Further it is seen that 34.1% always get adequate information, while 57.7 per cent get sometimes and 8.2% never get adequate information. In other words about two-third of the respondents do not get adequate information. It clearly indicates that resources of the library in itself are not sufficient. Resources of different libraries and information centres are to be shared to provide adequate information to the users. Further, we see that information is got in-time by 254 (71.5%) out of 355 respondents. About one-third (33.5%) opine that they always get information in time; while 146 (57.5%) get information in time sometimes only; and 23 (9.0%) never get information in time. Again we find that about two-thirds (66.5%) of the respondents never get information in time. Now the reasons for this can be looked into wrong processing, badly managed and poor tools for arranging the reading materials in the information centre. About the state of getting 'coherent information' the table reveals that 217 (61.1%) advanced their views. Out of these 28.1 per cent are getting coherent information always while 58.5 per cent get sometimes only and 13.4 per cent never get coherent information. As a result it can be said that about three-fourths of the respondents are not getting coherent information. It makes necessary for the information system to prepare digests and literature review for giving the coherent information to the users.

Sources of Information

For meeting most of the needs of the users of the information centre/systems, the centre should have comprehensive and representative collection pertaining to all aspects of the subjects or disciplines. The respondents were asked to give the sources they used for getting the information. The replies analysed have been presented in the following table.

TABLE : 5.22: Information Sources

Sl. No.	Sources of information	USERS						
		Planner (36)	Administrator (46)	Teacher (S) (64)	Teacher (H) (54)	Teacher (E) (56)	Researcher (44)	Lib./ Doc. (55)
(1)	(2)	(3)	(4)	(5)	(6)	(7)	(8)	(9)
1.	Books	34	42	56	47	53	38	50
2.	Journals	33	33	49	47	48	41	50
3.	Newspapers	21	36	57	28	36	19	35
4.	Govt. Documents	26	28	22	23	30	28	30
5.	Monographs	17	6	7	20	32	26	15
6.	Ref. works	21	25	30	30	37	31	42
7.	Survey Reports	23	12	18	20	33	28	20
8.	A.V. Material	3	9	16	5	19	4	5
9.	Museum Objects	0	0	2	0	0	0	6
10.	Abstracts	8	6	2	21	24	31	28
11.	Index	10	8	2	20	18	15	33
12.	State of Art	0	4	0	4	4	3	18
13.	Lit. Review	11	11	12	16	18	23	14
14.	Digest	13	11	11	14	17	8	19
15.	Biliography	12	14	11	22	20	26	32
16.	Dissertation/ thesis	11	12	7	19	31	25	20

The order of preference of sources of information is likely to change from one type of user to another. For example so far planners are concerned the order of information is books, journals and government documents. As against this the order of preference for administrators is books, newspapers and journals. It may sound paradoxical so far as teachers at school level are concerned as they report that newspapers are the main source of information followed by books and journals. The reasons are not far to seek. They by their very vocation have to refer to books and journals and may have construed 'sources of information' as sources of information about world events. In case of teachers at higher level and teacher educators the order is books, journals and reference books. Researchers have mostly to refer to journals followed by reading of books and abstracts. In case of librarians/documentalists the preference order is books, journals and reference works.

In addition to the above mentioned sources respondents suggested some other sources like textbooks, maps, yearbooks etc. The greatest number of books are used by the teacher educators (94.6%) while the least number is used by the researchers (86.3%). As for journals the highest and lowest categories of users are researchers (93.8%) and administrators (71.7%) respectively. In case of newspapers the teachers at school level are at the top (89.1%) and researchers at the bottom (43.2%).

The first and the last category of users in other areas are described below:

(i) Planner (72.2%) and teachers at school level (34.3%) for government documents;
(ii) Researchers (59.1%) and teachers at school level (10.9%) for monographs;
(iii) Librarians/documentalists (76.4%) and teachers at school level (46.9%) for reference books.
(iv) Planners (63.9%) and administrators (26.1%) for survey reports;
(v) Teacher educators (33.9%) and planners (8.3%) for audio-visual materials;
(vi) Librarians/documentalists (10.9%) and teachers at school level (3.1%) used museum objects while all other categories are not making use of this source;
(vii) Researchers (70.4%) and teachers at school level (3.1%) for abstracts;
(viii) Librarians/documentalists (60.9%) and teachers at school level (3.1%) indexes;

(ix) Librarians/documentalists (32.7%) and teachers at school level (0.0%) for state of art;

(x) Researchers (52.3%) and teachers at school level (18.7%) for literature review;

(xi) Planners (36.1%) and teachers at school level (17.2%) for digest;

(xii) Researchers (59.1%) and teachers at school level (17.2%) for bibliographies; and

(xiii) Researchers (56.8%) and teachers at school level (10.9%) for dissertations and theses.

From the above analysis the behaviour of users categories seem to be correct according to the experience in the actual field. This analysis also makes the library staff clear that not only collection should be developed according to the need to the users category but their processing should also be made according to users category so that exhaustive and efficient service can be provided to the users.

Use of Literature by the Respondents

It has been said that the policy for library collection is based upon 'best selection' at the least cost for the maximum use'. Having this principle in mind, the respondents were asked about extent of their requirement of current and retrospect Indian and foreign literature so that library should be equipped with the material for meeting maximum of their needs. As there are always constraints of financial resources, no library or information centre can afford to keep all the published literature in the centre. Users needs can be met through the library services like ILL etc. Their requirements have been discussed under the following four heads:

(i) Current Indian literature;

(ii) Retrospect Indian literature;

(iii) Current foreign literature;

(iv) Retrospect foreign literature.

Besides these four dimensions of origin of literature following three dimensions were also considered in order to know the interest of respondents according to the source of literature in terms of relative development of the regions of the world:

- First World literature;
- Second World literature; and
- Third World literature.

TABLE : 5.23: Current Indian Literature

Sl. No.	Users	Indian Current Literature				Total
		No comments	Completely	Substantially	Marginally	
(1)	(2)	(3)	(4)	(5)	(6)	(7)
1.	Planner	2	11	19	4	36
2.	Administrator	3	21	15	7	46
3.	Teacher (S)	4	29	21	10	64
4.	Teacher (H)	7	20	22	5	54
5.	Teacher (E)	4	22	23	7	56
6.	Researcher	3	16	23	2	44
7.	Lib./Doc.	3	26	20	6	55
	Total	26	145	143	41	355
	Percentage	7.3	40.8	40.3	11.6	100.0

About one in fourteen, 26 (7.3%) respondent do not give their comments for the requirement of current Indian literature. 145 (40.8%) are interested in studying the current Indian literature completely; 143 (40.3%) read the literature substantially while 41 (11.6%) are using it marginally only. Librarians/documentalists is the user category who uses the literature mostly (50.0%) while the percentage of planners for using the literature completely is the least (32.3%), researchers are the largest (56.1%) community who makes substantial use of it while administrators are the least (34.9%) users of it substantially. The teachers at school level is the only biggest (16.7%) group who makes marginal use of it while smallest (4.9%) percentage of making marginal use of it is that of researchers. Taking the total use of the current Indian literature we find that librarians rank first (94.5%) and teachers at higher level hold the last rank (87.0%) for making use of it.

The percentage of making complete use of the current Indian literature and using it substantially is almost the same i.e. (40.8%) and (40.3%). Keeping this in view, an information centre should have a substantial portion of printed literature on educational aspects though it would not be possible to have all the printed literature in any centre.

Coming to retrospect literature we find that a quite significant number 120 (33.8%) out of 355 do not express their opinion. Only 11.5 per cent are in favour of complete use, while 35.2 per cent are for substantial use and 19.5 per cent make marginal use of it.

TABLE : 5.24: Use of Retrospect Indian Literature

Sl. No.	Users	Use of Indian retrospect literature				Total
		No comments	Completely	Substantially	Marginally	
(1)	(2)	(3)	(4)	(5)	(6)	(7)
1.	Planner	10	6	13	7	36
2.	Administrator	20	6	15	5	46
3.	Teacher (S)	30	3	12	19	64
4.	Teacher (H)	15	6	21	12	54
5.	Teacher (E)	21	6	18	11	56
6.	Researcher	5	5	28	6	44
7.	Lib./Doc.	19	9	18	9	55
	Total	120	41	125	69	355
	Percentage	33.8	11.5	35.2	19.5	100.0

From this it is very clear that we would be very selective in selecting the retrospect literature. It will solve our problem of storage space as well as of financial resources.

Here again we find that librarians rank 1st (25%) in complete use of the retrospect literature while researchers group stands first (71.8%) in making substantial use of retrospect literature. Teachers at school level are the largest (55.9%) group making the marginal use of the literature.

Taking total use of literature researchers are the first (88.6%) while teachers at school level are the last (53.1%)

TABLE : 5.25: Use of Current Foreign Literature

Sl. No.	Users	Use of foreign current literature				Total
		No comments	Completely	Substantially	Marginally	
(1)	(2)	(3)	(4)	(5)	(6)	(7)
1.	Planner	19	5	7	5	36
2.	Administrator	19	7	10	10	46
3.	Teacher (S)	28	10	13	13	64
4.	Teacher (H)	13	11	23	7	54
5.	Teacher (E)	18	7	18	13	56
6.	Researcher	10	7	21	6	44
7.	Lib./Doc.	15	13	20	7	55
	Total	122	60	112	61	355
	Percentage	34.4	16.9	31.5	17.2	100.0

It is evident that respondents are uninterested in foreign current literature in comparison to Indian current literature. 122 (34.4%) respondents did not comment in this case while in Indian current literature the percentage of non-response was (7.3%) only. The corresponding figures for complete study are also quite less i.e., 16.9% in comparison to 40.8 per cent.

In both the cases the librarians are the largest group in making complete study i.e., (32.5%) and (50.0%) while in totality, in Indian case it was librarians (94.5%) where as in foreign the largest group is the researchers (77.3).

From the above analysis we can conclude that so far as foreign current literature is concerned we should be more selective.

TABLE : 5.26: Use of Foreign Retrospect Literature

Sl. No.	Users	Use of foreign retrospect literature				Total
		No comments	Completely	Substantially	Marginally	
(1)	(2)	(3)	(4)	(5)	(6)	(7)
1.	Planner	12	5	15	4	36
2.	Administrator	23	3	10	10	46
3.	Teacher (S)	38	3	8	15	64
4.	Teacher (H)	16	5	15	18	54
5.	Teacher (E)	34	4	11	7	56
6.	Researcher	15	2	18	9	44
7.	Lib./Doc.	29	4	14	8	55
	Total	167	26	91	71	355
	Percentage	47.0	7.4	25.6	20.0	100.0

Only about half 188 (53.0%) of the respondents have given their views. 167 (47.0%) do not show any interest in replying to the study of retrospect foreign literature and only 26 (7.4%) are interested in the complete study of the retrospect foreign literature.

So in collection of the material foreign retrospect literature should gets the fourth priority.

Literature Relating to the Regions of the World

In order the know interest of he respondents according to source of literature in terms of relative development of the 1st, 2nd and 3rd worlds, analysis has been made in the following Tables.

TABLE : 5.27: Literature Relating to First World

Sl.No.	Users	Use of First World Literature				Total
		No comments	Completely	Substantially	Marginally	
(1)	(2)	(3)	(4)	(5)	(6)	(7)
1.	Planner	23	3	5	5	36
2.	Administrator	26	2	11	7	46
3.	Teacher (S)	45	5	7	7	64
4.	Teacher (H)	22	11	16	5	54
5.	Teacher (E)	21	6	19	10	56
6.	Researcher	14	7	16	7	44
7.	Lib./Doc.	22	7	17	9	55
	Total	173	41	91	50	355
	Percentage	48.7	11.5	25.6	14.2	100.0

TABLE 5.28: Literature Relating to Second World

Sl.No.	Users	Use of Second World Literature				Total
		No comments	Completely	Substantially	Marginally	
(1)	(2)	(3)	(4)	(5)	(6)	(7)
1.	Planner	23	4	3	6	36
2.	Administrator	27	2	6	11	46
3.	Teacher (S)	45	4	4	11	64
4.	Teacher (H)	31	3	10	10	54
5.	Teacher (E)	24	4	6	12	56
6.	Researcher	19	2	11	12	44
7.	Lib./Doc.	27	4	10	14	55
	Total	206	23	50	76	355
	Percentage	58.0	6.5	14.1	21.4	100.0

TABLE : 5.29: Literature Relating to Third World

Sl.No.	Users	Use of Third World Literature				Total
		No comments	Completely	Substantially	Marginally	
(1)	(2)	(3)	(4)	(5)	(6)	(7)
1.	Planner	18	3	6	9	36
2.	Administrators	25	7	8	6	46
3.	Teacher (S)	43	4	6	11	64
4.	Teacher (H)	21	10	8	15	54
5.	Teacher (E)	27	12	11	6	56
6.	Researcher	10	8	13	13	44
7.	Lib./Doc.	26	4	15	10	55
	Total	170	48	67	70	355
	Percentage	47.9	13.5	18.9	19.7	100.0

We see that respondents incline towards Third World more in comparison to First World and Second World. The positive response is (48.7%), (42.0%) and (52.1%) from First World, Second World and Third World respectively. Another phenomenon from the study of users behaviour is evidently clear that the category of 'Researchers' is the largest group interested in the study and their percentage is (68.2%), (56.8%) and (77.3%) in the First World, Second World and Third World respectively. Form this it can be concluded that in collection priority goes to Third, First and Second World respectively.

Language of Material used by the Respondents

After knowing the contents of the collection, it is very essential to know in which language material should be kept in the information centres/libraries. In this connection the respondents were asked to specify in which language they would like to read the material. The responses have been analysed and the results are presented in Table 5.30.

TABLE : 5.30: Language of Material Used by The Respondents

Sl.No.	Users	Language			
		English	Hindi	Regional	Foreign (other than Eng.)
(1)	(2)	(3)	(4)	(5)	(6)
1.	Planner (36)	36	19	8	1
2.	Administrator (46)	42	26	12	–
3.	Teacher (S) (64)	60	50	14	–
4.	Teacher (H) (54)	52	21	14	1
5.	Teacher (E) (56)	50	36	18	–
6.	Researcher (44)	41	16	4	2
7.	Lib./Doc. (55)	50	29	8	2
	Total (355)	331	197	78	6
	Percentage (100.0)	93.2	55.5	22.5	1.7

We observe that most of the readers (93.2%) are in favour of material in English language followed by Hindi (55.5%), regional languages (22.5%) and foreign languages other than English (1.7%) in this order.

The largest group, in favour of reading material in English language is of planners (100.0%). In Hindi it is of teachers at school level and in regional languages is that of teacher educators. This means that while building the collection at national level priority should be given to English Hindi and regional languages respectively. So far as material in foreign languages other than English is concerned 5 respondents are interested in French while only one is in favour of German language. It means that reading material on education need not be built up in foreign languages (other than English). However, the important and popular works in foreign languages can be had in English translations.

As the respondents are interested in reading material in more than one language, row totals are meaningless. Majority of the respondents excepting teachers at school level expressed their views in favour of English Hindi and regional language of their respective states. However, majority of researchers are in favour of English only.

The highest percentage (78.1%) of teachers at school level for Hindi seems to be due to the fact that most of the respondents of this category are from Hindi belt and it can safely be assumed that the respondents of this category from other states would have shown their preferences for their respective regional languages.

The Most Used Language

To fortify the views expressed above another supplementary query was made about the language most used.

TABLE : 5.31: The Most Used Languages by The Respondents

Sl. No.	Users	Language			Total
		English	Hindi	Regional	
(1)	(2)	(3)	(4)	(5)	(6)
1.	Planner	33	3	0	36
2.	Administrator	35	4	7	46
3.	Teacher (S)	32	25	7	64
4.	Teacher (H)	49	2	3	54
5.	Teacher (E)	42	11	3	56
6.	Researcher	43	1	0	44
7.	Lib./Doc.	52	3	0	55
	Total	286	49	20	355
	Percentage	80.6	13.8	5.6	100.0

The responses confirm it again that most of the respondents 80.6 per cent work in English and 13.8 per cent are using Hindi as their working language while 5.6 percent are working in regional languages. The analysis again indicates that not only bulk of the collection should be in English but the working language of the system should also be English. Hindi and regional languages should be represented in the working of the system in a way of translation arrangement. Whenever an enquiry is received in Hindi or in a regional language that should be replied in Hindi or in the regional language as the case may be.

We see that in case of planners, researchers and librarians there is no need of regional language. In case of administrators, teachers at school level, teachers at higher level and teacher educators the need for regional language is felt by 15.2 per cent, 10.9 per cent, 5.6 per cent and 5.4 per cent respectively. This need can easily be met with translation arrangement.

In the case of Hindi we see that only the category of teachers at school level (39.0%) are using Hindi as their working language, but as stated earlier it is due to the fact that most of the respondents of this category belong to Hindi belt as adequate responses have not been received in this category from southern, eastern and western parts of India. It is, therefore, easily assumed that this response may be a biased one and thus it should not be taken in reaching the conclusion.

Analyses show that English should be the working language of the system and Hindi and regional languages can be taken care of through translation arrangements.

Fulfilments of Local and Non-Local Needs by Individual Information Centre

To find out the effectiveness of the present libraries/information centres working in the educational institutions respondents were asked to observe the effectiveness of their libraries information centres to the extent that they are meeting only local needs, or they are being used by other users belonging to other institutions for their needs.

The responses are analysed in Table 5.32 below:

TABLE 5.32: Local And Non-Local Users' Needs Met by Information Centres

Sl. No.	Users	Meet local needs	Meet outsiders needs	No comments	Total
(1)	(2)	(3)	(4)	(5)	(6)
1.	Planner	17	15	4	36
2.	Administrator	28	14	4	46
3.	Teacher (S)	38	20	6	64
4.	Teacher (H)	24	20	10	54
5.	Teacher (E)	32	21	3	56
6.	Researcher	18	21	5	44
7.	Lib./Doc.	38	16	1	55
	Total	195	127	33	355
	Percentage	54.9	35.8	9.3	100.0

The table indicates that 33 (9.3%) out of 355 have not indicated any view about the effectiveness of the information centres to meet the need of the local and non-local users. Out of the remaining 322 respondents 195 (60.6%) opine that they fulfil only the needs of the local users while 127 (39.4%) do not agree to this view and say that the information centres are capable of fulfilling the need of outsiders also. One significant point to note is that (53.8%) researchers are of the view that they do meet the needs of outsiders while on the contrary (70.4%) librarians think that these libraries are capable of meeting the needs of the local users only.

Opinions are almost equally divided about the effectiveness of the information centres on meeting the needs of the local users only and serving the outsiders also, if 'no response' is considered along with the respondents who opine for meeting the needs of outsiders also. But there is no denying of the fact that in the present situation information centres are needed to be strengthened to make them capable of meeting the needs of others in addition to local users. Hence there is the need for co-operation and resource sharing among the institutions to make them more effective. The truth is that the existing information institutions do offer services to others in addition to local members but their resources are not adequate enough to serve other users to a great extent.

Functional Freedom of an Information Centre

To find out the views of the respondents as to what extent it is true that an information institution which is in a subordinate position cannot provide an effective service until and unless it is given some amount of functional freedom.

TABLE : 5.33: Views on Whether Subordinated Role Can Improve Services

Sl. No.	Users	Views of Respondents			Total
		Cannot improve	Can improve	No comments	
(1)	(2)	(3)	(4)	(5)	(6)
1.	Planner	20	11	5	36
2.	Administrator	25	10	11	46
3.	Teacher (S)	36	17	11	64
4.	Teacher (H)	23	20	11	54
5.	Teacher (E)	26	26	4	56
6.	Researcher	23	17	4	44
7.	Lib./Doc.	43	9	3	55
	Total	196	110	49	355
	Percentage	55.2	31.0	13.8	100.0

The Table 5.33 indicates that 49 (13.8%) respondents are silent on the statement i.e., information institution cannot make improvement being in a subordinate position nor they express their views otherwise.

Out of the remaining 306, 196 (64.0%) state 'yes' to the statement while 110 (31.0%) do not agree to the statement and their opinions are that though being in a subordinate position, and information centre can make improvement in its services.

82.7 per cent librarians, the persons at the helm of affairs of the information centres, are of the view that it is not possible for the information centres, being in a subordinate position, to make improvement. The same view is supported by planners (64.5%), administrators (71.4%) teachers at school level (67.9%) teachers at higher level (53.5%), teacher educators (50.0%) and researchers (57.5%).

Notwithstanding 36.0 per cent of the respondents do not favour this view. The conclusion can be drawn that information unit not only be supported by the parent institution but it should also participate in a bigger network and standardize its working procedure and other working conditions.

Views on National Information System for Education

Respondents were asked to express their views about the desirability of having a National Information System for Education in India. The responses are analysed in the Table 5.34 given below.

TABLE : 5.34: Views on National Information system For Education

Sl. No.	Users	Should have	Should not have	No comments	Total
(1)	(2)	(3)	(4)	(5)	(6)
1.	Planner	34	0	2	36
2.	Administrator	43	3	0	46
3.	Teacher (S)	60	2	2	64
4.	Teacher (H)	49	1	4	54
5.	Teacher (E)	50	0	6	56
6.	Researcher	41	0	3	44
7.	Lib./Doc.	55	0	0	55
	Total	332	6	17	355
	Percentage	93.5	1.7	4.8	100.0

Seventeen (4.8%) out of 355 respondents do not give their comments on the desirability of having the National Information System for Education in India (NISE). Out of the remaining 338 respondents (1.7%) are not in favour of the NISE. They feel that there is no need of NISE while (93.5%) desire that there should be an NISE. The respondents who have not opted for NISE are 3 of administrators, two of teachers at school level while one is from teacher at higher level.

Since an overwhelming majority of the respondents are in favour of establishing NISE, it becomes necessary to have one for our country. Hence there is a need to define the objectives and examine the structure and activities of the proposed NISE.

Objectives of NISE

A query was made from respondents as to what should be the objectives of the proposed NISE. The responses have been analysed in Table 5.35.

TABLE 5.35: Objectives of Nise

Sl. No.	Users	Objectives					
		To provide the information with easy access	To ensure a reliable and needed information	To generate and maintain adequate media	To have linkage within country	To have linkage within the EIS of world	Trg. of inform person.
(1)	(2)	(3)	(4)	(5)	(6)	(7)	(8)
1.	Planner (36)	36	36	36	36	35	36
2.	Administrator (46)	41	40	38	38	40	35
3.	Teacher (S) (64)	52	53	53	52	57	52
4.	Teacher (H) (54)	46	46	47	46	46	46
5.	Teacher (E) (56)	50	44	44	45	45	44
6.	Researcher (44)	42	40	42	42	42	40
7.	Lib./Doc. (55)	55	54	54	51	50	52
	Total (355)	322	313	314	310	315	305
Percentage (100.)		90.7	88.2	88.5	87.3	88.7	85.9

As there are many choices the row totals are redundant. The first rank positive response of (90.7%) goes to the objective to 'provide the information with easy access'; the 2nd rank positive response of (88.7%) goes to the objective 'To have linkage with other educational information systems of the world'. The 3rd rank positive response of (88.5%) goes to the objective 'to generate and maintain adequate media'; the 4th rank positive response of (88.2%) goes to objective 'to ensure all reliable and needed information'; the fifth rank positive response of (87.3%) goes to objective 'to have linkage with the sisterly information systems within the country'; and the sixth rank positive response of (85.9%) goes to the objective 'training of information personnel in the field of education'. The last objective of training needs some clarification. Here the respondents limit the training only to 'training in service and that is only for persons working in the education field for standardization for the procedure, products and services of the system. This caution is given mostly by the respondents belonging to 'librarians/documentalists category'.

In addition to the above mentioned objectives of the system respondents have suggested some more objectives of the system viz.

(i) To provide information on policy, planning, management, monitoring and evaluation;
(ii) To build cooperation between academicians and professionals for promoting the use of library and documentation services i.e., users education;
(iii) To achieve economy by the maximum utilization of the existing resources and networking of the existing institutions;
(iv) To act as repository for audiovisual films etc. and such other material from U.N. agencies;
(v) To provide effective document back-up service;
(vi) To have an effective resource sharing programme;
(vii) To provide ready-made information on research studies;
(viii) The national centre should act as a clearing house for educational information; and
(ix) To disseminate the knowledge about the information system itself.

Many of the objectives mentioned above indicate toward the services of the system which have been taken care of in the services of the system

Evolution of the System

As is evident from the above that there was an overwhelming suggestion for setting up of NISE with clear-cut objectives some of which have been enumerated above. Obviously, the next question is how this systems should be evolved. The replies have been analysed in the undermentioned Table 5.36.

TABLE : 5.36: Evolution of Nise

Sl. No.	Users	Respondents' Response				Total
		New set up	Networking of existing Insts.	Others	No comments	
(1)	(2)	(3)	(4)	(5)	(6)	(7)
1.	Planner	8	23	3	2	36
2.	Administrator	14	30	1	1	46
3.	Teacher (S)	35	24	2	3	64
4.	Teacher (H)	24	26	2	2	54
5.	Teacher (E)	26	30	0	0	56
6.	Researcher	14	28	1	1	44
7.	Lib./Doc.	13	40	1	1	55
	Total	134	201	10	10	355
	Percentage	37.8	56.6	2.8	2.8	100.0

Ten (2.8%) respondents have not made any comment on the type of its set-up. However, one suggestion is that it should be a part of NISSAT.

So far as Regional libraries are concerned, they are required and would be a link between the chain of the system. Special Subject Libraries are not possible in Indian context because that means our model should be like ERIC of U.S.A., where different clearing houses are developed for different aspects of education. In USA Education is decentralised and is in private hands while in India education is in the concurrent list and almost whole of it is in government hand. The same authority is looking after all aspects of education. Then language problem also stands in the way. Keeping in view all these difficulties and differences, Special Subject Libraries and then linking in between them would not be possible. So far as part of NISSAT is concerned, it would not be possible, because NISSAT is for a special field and education cannot be fitted in that system. Secondly, NISSAT is a mission oriented educational set-up, while keeping in view the structure and nature of set-up, it is a discipline-oriented one and to make it a part of NISAT would be just a round peg in a square hole. Let us now examine the two alternatives i.e., new set-up or networking of the existing institutions.

134 (37.8%) respondents are in favour of new set-up and 201(56.6%) favour the networking of the existing institutions. Even these (37.8%)

suggest that there would be a networking of the new set-up units. They are not against the networking, what they want is that there should be totally a new set-up. Taking stock of the existing resources of men and material in educational institutional libraries and the finance that would be involved in setting up the new system, the new set-up is not desirable. Not only that our present economy cannot afford the required resources, it would be wastage if the existing resources are not utilized fully. Therefore, it is desirable to have the networking of the existing institutions in the field of education. However, their procedures, practices and activities are to be standardized and they should be helped financially so that they can play the part of an active participant.

Status of NISE

There is a lot of controversy in our public life about the status of a number of organizations. Therefore, it would be in the fitness of things to know what the status of NISE, the respondents think should be.

TABLE : 5.37: Status of NISE

Sl. No.	Users	Govt. Deptt.	Autonomous Body	Others	No comments	Total
(1)	(2)	(3)	(4)	(5)	(6)	(7)
1.	Planner	6	28	0	2	36
2.	Administrator	8	38	0	0	46
3.	Teacher (S)	24	38	1	1	64
4.	Teacher (H)	2	49	1	2	54
5.	Teacher (E)	12	42	1	1	56
6.	Researcher	11	30	1	2	44
7.	Lib./Doc.	9	45	0	1	55
	Total	72	270	4	9	355
	Percentage	20.3	76.1	1.1	2.5	100.0

The total definite responses are (97.5%). 9 (2.5%) do not give their comments on the status of NISE. The option of 72 (20.3%) is for government department while 270 (76.1%) are in favour of an autonomous body and the remaining 4 (1.2%) want other arrangement. The 'other category' suggests that it should be a private organization maintained by subscription through interested users. One is of the view that it should be a constituent of NCERT.

Taking 'private organization' into consideration it can be said that it is not possible Firstly, it requires a big organisation and lot of funds. The subscription fee would be very high for researchers and students. Secondly, information is needed by planners and administrators who are working in government organizations and thus the subscription may not be possible. Thirdly, the cost benefit analysis of investment in education is never 1:1. Then investment in education has a very long gestation period, which, in private organisation, cannot be tolerated. Last though not the least, the greatest problem is to procure the information from government agencies, education being the state subject. Therefore, it can be safely concluded that NISE as a private venture is neither possible nor desirable.

So far as 'constituent of NCERT' is concerned that is also not possible. The reasons can be that the venture is for all levels of educations while NCERT looks after only school education. Higher education is not in its purview. For smooth and effective functioning it requires the help of Central and State Governments which are the generators and consumers of information related to education in a big way. In view of this it can either complete be a government department or an independent autonomous body. Since there is an overwhelming support for an autonomous status, it would be better to have an autonomous body for this venture rather than a government department. Government department does not enjoy autonomy in its functioning while autonomous body under the stewardship of academicians, system analysts and information personnel can give better results. Hence the status of NISE should be an autonomous body.

Finance for NISE

Finance for an institution is what blood is for a human body. As human body cannot function without the requisite quantity of blood, similarly an institution cannot function properly without the sufficient quantity of finance. Finance should flow regularly, permanently and in a sufficient quantity. Keeping in view the importance of finance for an institution, the respondents were asked to point out the source of finance for NISE. The responses are analysed in the undermentioned Table 5.38.

Table : 5.38: Source of Finance For Nise

Sl. No.	Users	Source of Finance				Total
		Central Govts.	Central Govt. and State Govts.	Others	No comment	
(1)	(2)	(3)	(4)	(5)	(6)	(7)
1.	Planner	13	20	3	0	36
2.	Administrator	18	28	0	0	46
3.	Teacher (S)	35	24	5	0	64
4.	Teacher (H)	29	21	2	2	54
5.	Teacher (E)	27	25	4	0	56
6.	Researcher	20	18	5	1	44
7.	Lib./Doc.	26	28	1	0	55
	Total	168	164	20	3	355
	Percentage	47.3	46.2	5.6	0.9	100

Three respondents (0.9%) did not give their comments on the source of finance, 168 (47.3%) are in favour of that the whole amount should come from Central Government; 164 (46.2%) suggest that both Central and State Governments should contribute while 20 (5.6%) are of the view that finance should come from other sources. These other sources are viz. private initiative, international organisations like Unesco and IBE, public corporation endowments, from R and D funds, private industrialists, NCERT, UGC etc.

The practical aspects of the proposal are not easy to determine Private investment neither would be regular nor would be sufficient. International organizations like Unesco and IBE can give adhoc grant for initial set-up or machines or other equipment but that cannot be a regular flow. It is always for short term project or for the initial year of a long term project. From R&D, the funds would not be sufficient as the cost benefit analysis of education is not 1:1. It is always less than one and gestation period is very long. It is a very long term investment.

Funds from NCERT and UGC are not possible, because they are working under Central Government and their programmes are to be approved by the Government. As in table 5.37 it has already been explained that it cannot become a part of either NCERT or UGC. It is to work as an independent autonomous body. So there are only two sources i.e., Central Government alone, or Central Government and State Governments together contribute towards its functioning. The respondents are almost equally divided for the two major alternatives. It seems logical that as the organization is to serve both the State and Central Governments, so both should contribute towards its functioning. Now the question comes in which ratio State and Central Government should contribute in this venture. The simple and straight answer would be that 50 per cent of its expenditure it should be met by the Central Government and 50 per cent by the States. Even if it is agreed to the question arises in which proportion States should contribute towards its expenditure. Without going in argumentative interpretation it should be based in the well established rules i.e., on population base. Education is for masses so information on education is also for the masses.

As the Finance Commission divides the central taxes among the States on the basis of population, similarly States can contribute the required portion of its share on the basis of population to the common funds. The finance can be provided to the requirement of the information units situated in the States and Centre for the purpose. One thing more in this respect i.e., as it has been decided that the system is to be developed from the existing institutions the funds from the common budget would be only the additional expenditure of the institution for meeting the new responsibility given to it as the participative unit of the system.

Organisational Set-up of the System

Now the next important thing is to find out what its organizational set-up should be. Respondents were asked to suggest the alternative they prefer among the following three:

(i) Centralization in administration and decentralization in activities of processing and disseminations;

(ii) Centralization in organization, policy and control while decentralization for dissemination at geographical levels; and

(iii) Centralization should be limited to co-ordination and advisory functions only.

The responses have been analysed in the Table 5.39.

TABLE : 5.39: Organisational Set-Up of the System

Sl. No.	Users	Centralization in Admn.	Centralization in organ.	Centralization in coordn.	No comments	Total
(1)	(2)	(3)	(4)	(5)	(6)	(7)
1.	Planner	7	21	5	3	36
2.	Administrator	21	13	11	1	46
3.	Teacher (S)	32	12	14	6	64
4.	Teacher (H)	23	13	16	2	54
5.	Teacher (E)	24	17	14	1	56
6.	Researcher	16	15	9	4	44
7.	Lib./Doc.	23	20	11	1	55
	Total	146	111	80	18	355
	Percentage	41.1	31.1	22.5	5.1	100.0

Out of 355 respondent 337 (94.9%) expressed their views clearly while 18 (5.1%) did not make any comment. Among the respondents 146 (41.1%) are in favour of centralisation in administration, whereas 111(31.3%) are for centralization in organization and 80 (22.5%) favouring centralization in coordination only. The largest number in favour of centralisation in organisation is that of planners (63.6%), while the smallest is of teachers at school (20.7%), while the larger number in favour of centralization coordination and policy only is 30.8% teachers at higher levels, the smallest in this category is of planners 15.2 per cent. Keeping in view the set-up, status and source of finance as stated earlier and education being a State earlier subject, one may incline to agree with the determined view of the planners group for centralisation in organization, policy and control while decentralisation in dissemination at geographical levels.

Levels of Collection of Information

A further probe was made to ascertain the levels of operation of collection of the information system. For knowing the level of collection of information 5-point scale was given to the respondents. They were required to choose one out of them. The responses have been analysed in Table 5.40.

TABLE : 5.40: Levels of Operation For Collection of Information

Sl.No.	Users	All levels	Levels National	State	District	Institute	Total
(1)	(2)	(3)	(4)	(5)	(6)	(7)	(8)
1.	Planner	19	3	4	7	3	36
2.	Administrator	26	8	4	6	2	46
3.	Teacher (S)	20	27	8	4	5	64
4.	Teacher (H)	25	13	4	6	6	54
5.	Teacher (E)	26	14	7	4	5	56
6.	Researcher	23	9	4	5	3	44
7.	Lib./Doc.	24	16	3	6	6	55
	Total	163	90	34	38	30	355
	Percentage	45.9	25.4	9.6	10.7	8.4	100.0

One hundred sixty-three (45.9%) respondents are of the view that information should be collected at all the levels i.e. at national, state, district and institutional level; 90 (25.4%) want that collection should be made only on national level; 34 (9.6%) at state level and; 38 (10.7%) are in favour of at district level and 30 (8.4%) are in favour of institutional level. Keeping the nature of data/information connected with education in view, we will have to collect data/information at all levels. All the institutes will collect their data individually and pass on to the district authority. The district will collect and arrange the data of the whole district and will pass it on to the State level information centre. The States will collect the data and pass it on to national level centre, where it would be processed and disseminated according to the need .

Levels of Dissemination of Information

After determining the levels for collection of information Respondents were requested to give their views about the dissemination levels. The responses are analysed in the Table 5.41.

TABLE : 5.41: Levels For Dissemination of Information

Sl.No.	Users	All levels	Levels National	 State	 District	 Institute	Total
(1)	(2)	(3)	(4)	(5)	(6)	(7)	(8)
1.	Planner	23	1	2	7	3	36
2.	Administrator	23	7	4	6	6	46
3.	Teacher (S)	32	12	7	4	9	64
4.	Teacher (H)	27	12	5	4	6	54
5.	Teacher (E)	30	12	5	5	4	56
6.	Researcher	27	11	1	3	2	44
7.	Lib./Doc	24	16	3	6	6	55
	Total	186	71	27	35	36	355
	Percentage	52.4	20.0	7.6	9.9	10.1	100.0

186 (52.4%) out of 355 opine that dissemination should be at all the four levels; 71 (20.0%) are in favour of national level only; 27(7.6%) are in favour of only at state level; 35(9.9%) are in favour of district level while the remaining 36(10.1%) say that dissemination should be at the institutional level. From the above analyses, it can be concluded that dissemination should be at all the levels, but processing for dissemination should be at national and state level. Since dissemination requires a lot of processing, printing, binding and other process like comparing (with the previous years or state-to-state) etc., it should be done only at national and state levels. Yes, till it gets final shape in printed form data can be disseminated for research and planning purpose in raw form at district and even at institutional level.

Levels of Cooperation of the System

No library or system can meet the needs of users independently. It has to share with other national, regional and international systems concerning with education. To find out what levels are to co-operate, respondents were asked to give their opinions about the levels of co-operation. The responses have been analysed in the Table 5.42.

TABLE : 5.42: Levels of Co-operation of the System

		Levels					
Sl.No.	Users	IRNS	RNS	NS	National	State	Total
(1)	(2)	(3)	(4)	(5)	(6)	(7)	(8)
1.	Planner	14	6	6	3	7	36
2.	Administrator	8	9	11	8	10	46
3.	Teacher (S)	5	5	7	40	7	64
4.	Teacher (H)	16	14	8	9	7	54
5.	Teacher (E)	14	13	9	11	9	56
6.	Researcher	19	10	3	6	6	44
7.	Lib./Doc	16	7	11	14	7	55
	Total	92	64	55	91	53	355
	Percentage	25.9	18.0	15.5	25.6	15.0	100.0

IRNS-International Regional National State Levels, RNS-Regional National State Levels, NS-National State Levels.

92 (25.9%) are of the view that the system should co-operate at all the four levels i.e. International, Regional, National and State levels; 64 (18.0%) are in favour of co-operation at Regional, National and State levels; 55 (15.5%) favour State and National levels only; 91 (25.6%) are in favour of co-operation limited only to National level while 53 (15.0%) want that co-operation should be limited to State level only.

From the analysis it is clear that we should have co-operation with Educational Information Systems of International and Regional levels; while we should have co-operation with other information systems at the National level and with educational institutions at the State level.

Nodal Points for Co-operation

(i) International and Regional levels

After deciding cooperation at International, Regional, National, and State levels, an enquiry was made from the respondents as to what should be the nodal points at different levels of co-operation.

The responses have been analysed in the Table 5.43.

TABLE : 5.43: Nodal Points at International and Regional Levels

		Nodal Points					
		International level			Regional level		
Sl.No.	Users	UNESCO Paris	IBE Geneva	Total	UNESCO ESCAP	SAARC	Total
(1)	(2)	(3)	(4)	(5)	(6)	(7)	(8)
1.	Planner	30	6	36	26	10	36
2.	Administrator	38	8	46	31	15	46
3.	Teacher (S)	60	4	64	42	22	64
4.	Teacher (H)	42	12	54	34	20	54
5.	Teacher (E)	50	6	56	39	17	56
6.	Researcher	35	9	44	31	13	44
7.	Lib./Doc.	41	14	55	40	15	55
	Total	296	59	355	243	112	355
	Percentage	83.4	16.6	100.0	68.5	31.5	100.0

In the opinion of 296 (83.4%) respondents UNESCO (Paris) should be the nodal point for international co-operation while 59 (16.6%) are in favour of International Bureau of Education (IBE) as the nodal point for international co-operation.

No doubt respondents are in favour of UNESCO (Paris) Office for international nodal point but keeping in view the magnitude and nature of information relating to educational field we will have to have some relations with IBE and also with other Educational systems of individual nations like ERIC for USA and Educational information systems for West European countries. Some respondents suggest that in addition to UNESCO (Paris), IBE (Geneva), IIEP (Paris) should also be taken as nodal points at the international level.

So far as nodal point at Regional level is concerned 243 (68.5%) favour Unesco Regional office (at Bangkok) and 112(31.5%) for SAARC (at Kathmandu). So far as Unesco Regional Office (Bangkok) is concerned, it is alright but in the case of SAARC, it would not be advisable to make it as regional nodal point as it is still in the embroynic stage. However, the recommendation in this regard can not be brushed aside as of no significance. The proposed system will have to take special care of the exchange of educational information relating to SAARC countries.

(ii) National level

Five nodal points were identified at the national level. These are Ministry of Human Resource Development (Department of Education) NIEPA, NCERT, UGC and National Library.

The respondents have suggested more that one institution as a nodal point at the national level. Some respondents have included many possibilities of nodal points in 'other category'. These include a suggestion for a new set-up with different clearing houses for different aspects, such as INSDOC, IGNOU, ICSSR etc.

The responses have been analysed in the Table 5.44.

TABLE : 5.44: Nodal Point at The National Level

Sl.No.	Users	Nodal Point at the National Level					Total
		M/HRD (D.E)	NIEPA	NCERT	UGC	National Library	
(1)	(2)	(3)	(4)	(5)	(6)	(7)	(8)
1.	Planner (36)	19	16	18	10	11	74
2.	Administrator (46)	16	12	21	11	14	74
3.	Teacher (S) (64)	21	12	33	8	11	85
4.	Teacher (H) (54)	17	17	29	15	14	92
5.	Teacher (E) (56)	20	14	36	17	15	102
6.	Researcher (44)	21	25	17	15	14	92
7.	Lib./Doc. (55)	26	5	19	10	13	73
	Total	140	101	173	86	92	592
	Percentage	23.6	17.1	29.2	14.5	15.6	100.0

As the respondents have suggested more than one choice for nodal point at national level, the total 592 (355) does not tally. 140(23.6%) suggest that Ministry of Human Resources Development (Department of Education) should be nodal point at national level while 10 (17.1%)

opt for National Institute of Educational Planning and Administration (NIEPA). 173 (29.2%), 86 (14.5%) and 92 (15.6%) are in favour of NCERT, UGC and National Library respectively. Rankwise the institutions stand as NCERT, M/HRD, NIEPA, National Library and UGC.

Planner (52.8%) is the largest group in favour of M/HRD while the least (31.5%) is of teachers at higher level; for NIEPA the largest group is of Researchers (56.8%) and least (9.1%) is of Librarians/Documentalists. For NCERT the largest (64.3%) group is of Teacher Educators and least (34.5%) is of Librarians/Documentalists. For U.G.C. the largest group is of researchers (34.2%) and least group is of Teachers at School level (12.5%); the National Library to be nodal point gets the largest number from researchers (31.8%) and least from teachers at school level (17.2%).

From the above analyses two noteworthy points emerge i.e., users are not in favour of any existing institution to be as a nodal point. They want a new organisation to be set up for the purpose and then this organisation should have close co-operation with the existing institutions. Another point seems to be that users' views are biased ones. For examples teacher educators 64.3 per cent and Teachers at school level 51.6 per cent are in favour of NCERT. This is because both these categories come under the direct purview of NCERT.

Planners and Librarians/Documentalists favour M/HRD because they think that whatever is to emerge will emerge from M/HRD.

Researchers prefer NIEPA because literature on planning and administration problems would be available with this institute.

The investigator infers from above that a special autonomous organisation under the administrative control of M/HRD should be set up for the purpose. The institution should have close contact with these institutions for special aspects fo education with which they are dealing at the present. The other suggested institutes like INSDOC, ICSSR and IGNOU to be the nodal points of the system are not feasible because INSDOC is for science, ICSSR is for social sciences and IGNOU is a general university not having specialisation in education.

(iii) State, District and Institute

For all States the SCERTs and SIEs are considered to fall under one category because all SIEs are to be converted into SCERTs to have a uniform pattern. All except a few SIEs have been converted into SCERTs and the remaining a few will be converted soon. Similarly principals and headmasters have been put in one category because they perform the same or similar functions.

The responses are analysed in the Table 5.45.

TABLE 5.45: Nodal Point For State, District and Institute level

Sl.No.	Users	Nodal Points										
		State				District				Institute		
		SCERT	DE	SL	TOTAL	DPO	DEO	DL	TOTAL	PRINCIPAL	LIBRARIAN	TOTAL
(1)	(2)	(3)	(4)	(5)	(6)	(7)	(8)	(9)	(10)	(11)	(12)	(13)
1.	Planner (36)	32	12	5	49	7	23	10	40	16	20	36
2.	Administrator (46)	28	12	8	48	6	29	15	50	22	24	46
3.	Teacher (S) (64)	39	24	4	67	6	31	33	70	25	39	64
4.	Teacher(H) (54)	29	14	13	56	8	16	30	54	20	34	54
5.	Teacher(E) (56)	31	13	14	58	3	32	21	56	24	32	56
6.	Researcher (44)	35	14	10	59	14	15	18	47	14	30	44
7.	Lib./Doc.(55)	24	18	13	55	2	20	33	55	11	44	55
	Total (355)	218	107	67	392	46	166	160	372	132	223	355
	Percentage	55.6	27.6	17.1	100.0	12.4	44.6	43.0	100.0	37.2	62.8	100.0

SCERT – State Council of Educational Research and Training
DE – Directorate of Education
SL – State Central Library
DPO – District Planning Officer
DEO – District Education Officer
DL – District Library

Nodal Point at State Level

It is clear from the analyses that 218 (55.6%) are in favour of SCERT as a nodal point of the system at state level. Not only all the user categories support it with majority but individually they support the case with more than 50 per cent except Librarian/Documentalist category. This category also supports it with largest number in view of any other alternative. Planners support it strongly (88.9%). The present State educational set-up also supports this case because SCERT plays a very pivotal role in the educational structure of the State.

Nodal Point at the District Level

166 (44.6%) respondents support the case of district Education Officer as a nodal point at the district level. Though it is not the absolute majority of the respondents, yet it is the largest group in comparison to the supporters of other alternatives i.e. District Planning Officer and District Library. The supporters 160 (43.0%) of District Library as a nodal point at the district level is very close to that of the supporters of DEO as a nodal point. But the financial and administrative powers of DEO in getting the information from other sources are more than that of District Librarian in the present set-up of state education. So DEO should be a better alternative for the nodal point at the district level. The case is being supported by the new pattern which is going to be adopted in the near future. An office of Chief District Education Officer is planned in the new set-up for the district education administration.

Nodal Point at Institutional Level

223 (62.8%) respondents support the case of librarian as a nodal point at the institution level. Not only the absolute majority of the total respondents but absolute majority of the individual group of users also support the librarian. This would be an ideal point because it would be difficult for a principal to be regular in maintaining the up-to-date record of his institution. Librarian can seek the advice of the principal in formulating the policy and procedure of collecting the data/information about the institution.

Individual Library Participation in NISE

The library of an institution is the nerve centre of any information system. Therefore, it is worthwhile to know whether institutional library should participate in the proposed NISE.

Respondents views are analysed in the Table 5.46.

TABLE : 5.46: Participation of Individual Library to the System

Sl.No.	Users	Participation of the Library		
		Yes	No	Total
(1)	(2)	(3)	(4)	(5)
1.	Planner	31	5	36
2.	Administrator	38	8	46
3.	Teacher (S)	59	5	64
4.	Teacher (H)	48	6	54
5.	Teacher (E)	50	6	56
6.	Researcher	39	5	44
7.	Lib./Doc.	46	9	55
	Total	311	44	355
	Percentage	87.6	12.4	100.0

A large majority 311 (87.6%) of respondents felt that their institute library should participate in the system while only 44 (12.4%) did not favour such a participation. The percentage of respondents in favour of participation is as follows: planners (86.1%); administrators (82.6%); teachers at school level (92.2%); teachers at higher level (88.9%); teacher educators (89.3%); researchers (88.6%) and Librarians/documentalists (83.6%) respectively. The largest number (92.2%) in favour of participation is of teachers at school level while the least number (82.6%) is of administrators.

Operational Mechanism of the System

Respondents were asked what operational mechanism should be adopted by the information system to collect, process, store, retrieve and disseminate information. The responses have been analysed in Table 5.47.

TABLE : 5.47: Operational Mechanism of The System

Sl.No.	Users	Mechanism			Total
		Manually	SM - SC	Computerized	
1.	Planner	2	24	10	36
2.	Administrator	15	18	13	46
3.	Teacher (S)	15	34	15	64
4.	Teacher (H)	1	25	28	54
5.	Teacher (E)	12	24	20	56
6.	Researcher	4	23	17	44
7.	Lib./Doc.	5	29	21	55
	Total	54 (15.2)	177(49.9)	124(34.9)	355(100.0)

54 (15.2%) are in favour of manually operated system while 177(49.9%) favour Semi-manual and Semi-computerized system, the remaining 124 (39.9%) support the fully computerized system. The highest number (32.6%) in favour of manual operation is of administrators, while the least number (1.9%) is of teachers at higher level. For SM-SC the highest number (66.2%) is of planners and the least number (39.1%) in this category is of administrators. For fully computerized the highest number (51.8%) is of teachers at higher level and the least number (23.4%) is of teachers at school level in this category. Keeping in view the standard of technology and economic conditions of the country the respondents are right in favouring SM-SC operational mechanism of the system.

Services to be Rendered by the Proposed System

The respondents were asked as to what services they expect from the system. The responses have been analysed in the Table 5.48.

TABLE : 5.48: Services to be Rendered by the Proposed System

Sl. No.	Services	Users							Total
		Planner (36)	Admn. (46)	TS (64)	TH (54)	TE (56)	Researcher (44)	Lib/Doc (55)	
(1)	(2)	(3)	(4)	(5)	(6)	(7)	(8)	(9)	(10)
1.	Bib. Services	19	19	24	39	33	34	46	214
2.	Doc. Services	28	27	27	46	38	38	49	253
3.	State of Art	11	5	9	18	8	16	15	82
4.	Data services	28	17	23	40	21	32	39	200
5.	Reprography	12	9	8	23	16	25	41	134
6.	Translation	20	14	26	33	27	31	44	195
7.	Un. catalogue	14	10	14	20	19	22	44	143
8.	ILL	22	6	21	36	25	27	41	178
9.	Newsletter	23	21	35	32	35	25	29	200
	Total	177	128	187	287	222	250.	348	1599
	Percentage	49.8	36.1	52.7	80.8	62.5	20.4	98.0	

Since the respondents have more than one choice, column totals are redundant. Among services rendered the documentation gets the first pirority 253(71.3%); bibliographical service the second rank i.e., 214(60.3%); data service the third rank i.e., 200(56.3%); newsletter, bulletin etc. gets the same preference i.e., 200(56.3%) translation the fifth rank with 195(54.9%) and Inter library loan (ILL) the sixth preference with 178(50.1%); Union catalogue the seventh rank with 143(40.5%) while reprographic services the eighth rank with 134 (37.7%) and state of art the ninth rank with 82(23.1%). All these are important services and we find that there is a fair amount of demand for them commensurate with their importance.

Language of Information System

India is a multi-language country. States have different languages as media of instruction even upto post-graduate level. Keeping this in view, respondents were asked what language/languages should be the media of communication of the system. Their replies are tabulated in Table 5.49.

TABLE : 5.49: Languages for Information System

Sl.No.	Users	English	Hindi	English+Hindi	Eng+Hi+Regl.	Total
(1)	(2)	(3)	(4)	(5)	(6)	(7)
1.	Planner	11	0	10	15	36
2.	Administrator	11	0	13	22	46
3.	Teacher (S)	10	0	36	18	64
4.	Teacher (H)	17	0	15	22	54
5.	Teacher (E)	10	0	21	25	56
6.	Researcher	11	0	18	15	44
7.	Lib./Doc.	15	0	18	22	55
	Total	85	0	131	139	355
	Percentage	24.0	0.0	37.0	39.0	100.0

From the above responses, we see that 39 per cent of the total respondents are in favour of English+Hindi+Regional Languages. Thirty-Seven per cent of the total respondents favour English+Hindi as the languages of the system. Only 24 per cent of the respondents would like to have English as the language of the system. The highest number (31.5%) of teachers at higher level are in favour of English language, the highest number (56.3%) for both English+Hindi as the languages of the system is from teachers at school level. The reason may be the fact that among the target groups the majority of the respondents are from Hindi belt and that is why the majority is in favour of English and Hindi as the language of the system. From the group which favours English+Hindi+Regional language as the media of communication of the system, the highest number is of administrators (47.8%). The administrators are more practical in this respect in comparison to other target groups.

Since the clientele of the system will be of diverse background and from different language groups, it seems to be reasonable to expect emphasis on bi-lingual or trilingual system of communication.

The problem was solved in the subsequent interview where it was clarified that in the initial stages English should be the only language at the national level, while English and regional languages should be at the state level and afterwards Hindi can also be introduced at the national level. The regional languages can be taken care of with the help of translation at the national level and state levels wherever it is necessary.

Tenure of Translators for the System

Translation being an important service, it was thought proper to get the views of the respondents to know what arrangement should be made for the translators i.e., whether there should be a panel of translators or permanent translators should be appointed for the system. The responses have been analysed in the Table 5.50.

TABLE : 5.50: Tenure of Translators

Sl.No.	Users	Mode of Translators		Total
		Panel	Permanent	
(1)	(2)	(3)	(4)	(5)
1.	Planner	28	8	36
2.	Administrator	29	17	46
3.	Teacher (S)	33	31	64
4.	Teacher (H)	41	13	54
5.	Teacher (E)	31	25	56
6.	Researcher	25	19	44
7.	Lib./Doc.	32	23	55
	Total	219	136	355
	Percentage	61.7	38.3	100.0

219 (61.7%) respondents are in favour of panel of translators while 131 (38.6%) favour the permanent translators. The highest (77.8%) group is that of planners in the first case while the least (51.6%) group in this case is that of the teachers at school level. The highest (48.4%) group of teachers at school level and (22.2%) of planners, the least group, support the idea of permanent translators. The solution seems to be that some translators are to be kept permanently and major portion of the requirement is to be met by panel of translators.

Presentation of Regional Language Material

India is a multi-languages country. All languages cannot be made the languages of the system for obvious difficulties. Respondents were requested to advance their views regarding the presentation of education material in regional languages for dissemination by the system. The views of the respondents are analysed in the Table 5.51.

TABLE : 5.51: Presentation of Educational Material In Regional Languages

		Mode of Dissemination				
Sl.No.	Users	Abstracts in English	Abstracts in Hindi	Abstracts in Regl. Languages	Indexing Only	Total
(1)	(2)	(3)	(4)	(5)	(6)	(7)
1.	Planner (36)	30	14	10	5	59
2.	Administrator (46)	29	16	16	0	61
3.	Teacher (S) (64)	32	36	20	7	95
4.	Teacher (H) (54)	45	13	20	8	86
5.	Teacher (E) (56)	33	14	21	6	74
6.	Researcher (44)	31	9	16	5	61
7.	Lib./Doc. (55)	36	15	20	6	77
	Total (355)	236	117	123	37	513
	Percentage	66.5	32.9	34.6	10.4	

236 (66.5%) want that regional language material should be presented in abstract form in English; 117 (32.9%) want material in regional languages to be abstracted in Hindi while 123 (34.6%) would like abstract to be in the regional language itself. 37 (10.4%) of the respondents are of

the view that the material in regional languages should be presented in indexing only. The solution seems to be that some selection method will have to be adopted i.e., at the international, regional and national levels the material is to be presented in English. While at the state, district and institute level, it is to be presented in regional language abstract, the literature of wider importance can be presented in English and Regional languages.

CONCLUSION

Views of the users of the libraries and the information systems (run by the libraries) were elicited through a questionnaire as already stated. The questionnaire covered a wide range that included needs, demands and preferences. The predominant view that emerges is that the country should have a National Information System for Education (NISE). The following aspects which have a bearing on the system have been discussed in this chapter besides other connected issues:

(i) objectives;
(ii) functions;
(iii) Organisational system: (a) structure, (b) nodal at various levels, (c) levels of co-operation, (d) levels of collection and dissemination;
(iv) operation of the system—computerized, semi-computerized or manual;
(v) financing; and
(vi) views about an ideal National Information System for Education in India.

This has clearly indicated the broad bases for the development of the model for the system which will be discussed in the next chapter.

6

AN INFORMATION SYSTEM – CONCEPT, DESIGN AND FUNCTIONS

An Information System

A network is a form of arrangement or an administrative structure that links a group of individuals or organisations who have agreed to work together for any purpose such as in the acquisition programmes, technical processing, and resource sharing etc. Information networking generally entails the sharing of resources so that the information needs of both actual and the potential users of information–from the local to national level are met. This helps in meeting the information needs of all network participants. The concept of network and networking is applicable within an information system and amongst various information systems. In this study the concept has been used to include the networking in the system. As such subsequent sections deal with this in detail.

National Information System

According to Atherton, "a national information system is basically a network of existing information resources together with new services for identified gaps, so co-ordinated as to reinforce and enhance the activities of the individual units and thus enable specific categories of users to receive the information relevant to their needs and abilities".[1] Intergovernmental Conference of Scientific and Technical Information for Development defines it as "a set of interrelated information systems associated with communication facilities, which are co-operating through more or less formal agreements and institutional arrangements, in order to jointly implement information handling operation, with a view to pooling their resources and to offer better services to the users. They generally follow identical or compatible rules and procedures. In modern practice, many information systems are in fact based upon networks and the two terms are often used interchangeably".[2]

There are two types of information systems—Mission-oriented, and Discipline-oriented. These can be managed from one and the same centre. 'Education' is a blend of the two types. However, it is more of a kind of 'Mission-oriented system'.

Need of an Information System

One single library or information resource base cannot handle the voluminous amount and range of information currently available and expected to be generated in the future.

Education programmes which pay only a lip service to information building, as is evident from New Education Policy, Five Year Plans, Library Legislation, social status of library personnel and importance given to the profession by the central and state governments, face the risk of isolating themselves and becoming inadequate and ineffective in fulfilling their mission. Regardless of the stage of development of their information collection, education libraries/information centres are now compelled because of various reasons given below, to participate in resource sharing and in networking:

(i) Growth of literature on education;
(ii) New thrust in education programmes;
(iii) Multiplicity of institutions engaged in education information activities;
(iv) Rising costs of input and their optimum utilization;
(v) Improvement in the mobility of data/information;
(vi) Professional contact among education specialists; and
(vii) Improved flow of education information.

Growth of Literature on Education

The rapid growth of education programmes, in number and in scope i.e., extending from in-school to out-of-school, alongside changes in government policies and intensified activities in education have brought about new dimensions to education information. The current education literature includes curriculum materials, training manuals, syllabi, research studies, audio-visual materials and policies and management, case studies and reports.

The development supports the assumption in the world of information in general that information is increasing at an exponential rate of 13 per cent per year, meaning that the total volume of recorded information is doubling every seven or eight years.[3] This so-called 'information explosion' is clearly being felt in the field of education. The phenomenal growth in information calls for improved access to education information, a need which networks can easily fulfil.

New Thrusts in Education Programmes

Networks in education information can backstop the development of new thrust in education programmes. By providing up-to-date information to education planners and decision-makers, networks facilitate the planning and implementation of education policies and activities.

The value of information as a support to more efficient implementation of education programmes in the country has been stressed to meet new programme thrusts like universalisation of primary education, vocationalization of education, distance and non-formal education, adult education and educational technology etc.

The Committee on National Policy on Library and Information Systems in 1986 and the Empowered Committee on the same subject in 1987 as well as the Working Group 1985 on Libraries in the Seventh Plan have all emphasised emphatically on the need of Networking of academic and research libraries in the field of education.

Multiplicity of Institutions Engaged in Education Information Activities

The multiplicity of data gathering and disseminating institutions working at many levels and independently of one another underlines the need for networks capable of co-ordinating their activities. In education, information users and producers come from Administrative-education sector (e.g. ministries of education, health, agriculture, social welfare) and from the formal education sector (e.g. colleges, universities, teacher training colleges, secondary and primary schools).

Within the broad field of education, networks have been established in USA, UK and many other countries.

To be sure, institutions engaged in various aspects of education services cannot persist in a parochial approach to the collection and utilization of education information. By organising themselves into a network, these institutions, besides co-ordinating and expediting the flow of information between information producers and users, can also reduce the duplication of information generation and dissemination activities. If user's needs are to be met adequately and expeditiously they must be reached wherever they are. Users' access to information can be widely improved if isolated education information centres join a network, thus saving users' time and effort in data collection and search.

A problem related to the multiplicity of organisations engaged in education activities is their geographical isolation from one another. This situation handicaps the collection, retrieval and dissemination of education data. In countries like India, where education programmes have been divided into central, state and local governments and national programmes have been spread over to state and regional levels there is an urgent need to link these levels, if they are to be kept updated of one another's most recently produced information/material.

National level networks serve domestic needs as well as systematically link other education related agencies within the country. They also provide a link with other education information programmes being operated in different countries of the region.

Rising Costs of Input and their Optimum Utilisation

The costs of library services have been on the upswing in recent years. The high rates of books, journals and audio-visual material hinder libraries from maintaining comprehensive collections. As to be expected almost every library has a limited budget for acquisitions. Libraries, therefore, tend to limit their purchases to cover materials which comprise the core collection in education, which are in constant demand by local users. Budgetary constraints amidst rising costs call attention to the usefulness of co-operative arrangements in sustaining regular services and acquisition activities, and providing new ones as costs are spread over many co-operating institutions.

Various institutions engaged in education can adopt a co-operative acquisition scheme such as one centre concentrating on acquiring all periodicals in one branch of the subject, the other on reference books, third on government documents, literature of conferences, seminars and other reports, etc., fourth on international material and so on and so forth.

In addition to assigning specialisations in materials in a particular branch of the subject acquisitions, there are many other co-operative ventures which libraries can go into. These include co-operative cataloguing, joint bibliography development, compilation of directories, manpower training programme, and information dissemination service. Information needs which are beyond the capacity of small information centres can be met using the experience and resources of other network members. Projects which are beyond the resources of any single unit can be undertaken jointly (e.g. research, training, information repackaging etc.).

A library which does not resort to some kind of resource sharing will eventually not be in a position to handle the increasing volume of published information resulting into dissatisfaction and frustration of its users.

Improvment in the Mobility of Data/Information

Although more and more education data and information are being collected, dissemination is largely limited to programme elites, scholars and policy-makers and comparatively speaking they are already receiving an over-supply of information while local users (e.g. teachers and trainers) are practically starving for such data and information.

For examples many education libraries in the country are located in the offices of the Ministry of Human Resource Development of Central Government and Departments of Education of state governments and other research institutions in different capital cities of various Indian States and often cater to a select clientele. Major resources within such libraries are used to meet the needs of this relatively small sector of population, to the disadvantage of large groups of population of education professionals at places far away from such cities and who may be directly involved in the actual teaching at the local level. Mobility of data/ information through networks helps in satisfying needs of such users.

Mobility of data is also hampered by other factors. For examples, findings of research studies are not always circulated to people who should know them, for two reasons, the findings are not formally published, or they are reproduced in a limited number only. Another aspect of the problem is that while an organised body of information is available, it may be in media forms not suited to user needs. As a result, available resources are under-utilised and considerable efforts and lengthy searches are needed to locate and obtain information. More importantly, time consuming data and information search has, in many cases, influenced a great many to undertake their own data gathering efforts, thus duplicating a work that may have long been completed but whose results may not have been sufficiently disseminated.[4]

Professional Contacts among Education Specialists

A network encourages professional contacts among educationists, users of information, education documentalists, librarians, information and communication specialists. Experiences and expertise are shared through meetings and training programmes. Effective solutions to common problems can also be shared and discussed. In so far as library and information professionals are concerned it fosters opportunities for their continuing education and professional development of effective documentation and information systems in the field of education.

Improved Flow of Education Information

The establishment of education information networks in the developing countries can help improve the flow of information to and from the developing or information-poor countries. At present, information resources in education are located primarily in the developed or information-rich countries.[5] National level networks do improve the administrative efficiency and can help in acquiring such information. The networking also helps exchange of data and later the mobility of data for national level.

We may conclude about with the well stated words by James E. Allen, Jr "We must press our efforts to ensure that all types of libraries are brought into a total service which can make real the potential inherent in the separate parts. The time is indeed passed when we can think compartmentally of a 'public library programme', 'school library programme', a 'college library programme', or even the programme of a highly specialised private library. We need to acknowledge the interrelation of these resources and services; we need to plan from the vantage point of a library user, who cares little about the type of library, but a great deal about the ability of that library or that library system to supply his needs."

Basic Characteristics and Objectives

Basic Characteristics of Networks

Information networks usually have the following basic characteristics:

(i) the members are located at different places (e.g. regions, states, and districts).
(ii) the pre-requisite of networking is that they are to have standard

ways of organising and transmitting information or data e.g. in the collection of data, storage, and dissemination of information);

(iii) there is two-way communication and transfer of information among the members; and

(iv) they have information resources and disseminate information through products and publications to their members.[6]

Objectives

Objectives can be divided into broad, overall objectives and specific objectives or requirements that are needed to achieve the overall objectives.[7]

Broad objectives of the system are: to support the general policy of the Government concerning educational research and development of the field, that is, to provide all types of information necessary for the development of educational research (fundamental and applied) and for the introduction of up-dates technology (in case of educational information system).

The overall objectives of an information system are: (i) to render, as best as possible, library and information services in the field of an information system in general to all those who are interested and might be interested; (ii) to make sure that the educationists and persons interested in the research and development of education have information conducive to the development of high quality education; (iii) to allow for better use of the existing research and development in the country; (iv) to improve the practical utilisation of the results of indigenous research; and (v) to facilitate the evaluation and utilisation of foreign methodology and contents.

Usually the broad objectives cannot be used by themselves as guides for design of a system or for its analysis. They must be translated into specific objectives and requirements, which should be quantified whenever possible.

Specific objectives of an information system might be:

(i) to study user needs as a basis for information system evaluation and design;

(ii) to select and acquire those information resources needed to support research priorities;

(iii) to provide access to recorded material;

(iv) to provide retrospective search service;
(v) to respond to requests for data;
(vi) to provide literature analysis;
(vii) to identify and establish better ways of improving the flow of educational information among member institutions;
(viii) to provide fast inter/library loan; and
(ix) to provide an SDI service covering journal articles and reports.[8]

Membership and Components of Information System

Membership

The members may comprise individuals or organizations located in different places and bound by an agreement to pursue common goals with certain parameters: What does the network exists for? Who are qualified to join it? What costs are to be shared? The negotiations of mutually acceptable agreements and policies, is central to an information network.[9]

These questions would help in drawing membership and also determining as to who is qualified to become its member.

The effectiveness of network operations is determined to a great extent by the members' level of commitment to the networks' goals, the extent by which members are made aware of one another's activities, the compatibility of the information systems and services of members, the design of co-operative working arrangements to develop and strengthen information flow among members.

Components

The most efficient and effective functioning of the information system is dependent upon the various aspects of the functioning of different components of the network. They have been identified and the most essential ones for an orderly, planned development of a network have been given below:

(i) provision of organisational structure that provides for fiscal and legal responsibility, planning and policy formulation. It must require commitment, operational agreement and common purpose;

(ii) identification of nodes that provide for designation of role specialization as well as for geographic configuration;

(iii) identification of primary patron groups and provision for assignment of responsibility for information service to all within the network;

(iv) establishment of a communication system that provides 'conversational mode' format and is designed to carry the desired message/document load at each level of operation;

(v) provision of facility that provides for interfacing with other networks and determines the optimum communication path within the network;[10]

(vi) identification of categories of user-groups and their needs and delegating responsibilities to the respective nodes for providing services to specific user-groups and answering their special needs;

(vii) development of common standards that foster understanding among the nodes;

(viii) formulation of guidelines in the selection of the network's materials/literature collection such as books, microfilm etc;

(ix) collaborative development of resources. This can include provision for cooperative acquisition and the strengthening of local resources for frequently used materials. The development of multi-media resources is considered essential;

(x) development of a central bibliographic record to facilitate location of items within the network;

(xi) formulation of evaluation criteria and procedure to enable the nodes to receive feedback from users on ways to improve their services and network operations; and

(xii) provision of training programmes for users and operators concerning the network's policies and procedures.[11]

Types of Information Network

A network may be described based on one or more of the following criteria:

(i) organisational function;
(ii) contents or specialised purposes; and
(iii) structure of configuration.

Organisational Function

Some networks consist primarily of libraries, while others are mainly composed of information or data centres. Networks can also consist of a combination of functions, like those of a documentation centre-cum-library an integrated data, information and library network under the same authority or under different but co-operating authorities.[12]

Contents or Specialized Purposes

In addition to a network in general, networks can also be established to focus on specific subject and serve specific groups e.g. An education network can be supported by 'Higher education network, women education network educational planning and administration network, etc. One single information network can not be expected to effectively meet the vast and varied information requirements of multi-disciplinary user groups.[13] There can also be sub-network to meet the information requirements of the larger user group. ERIC which is supported by 16 clearing houses is an example of this kind of networking based on contents and specialised purposes.

By Structure of Configuration

Network structure can be discussed in terms of elements, configurations and levels. The elements of a library network consist of nodes (i.e. a participatory library or an information centre) and arcs (i.e. possible communication links). The pattern that results when nodes and arcs are connected is the network configuration. The levels of a network may be indicated by different stages in processing activities. Network configuration is an important specification because it affects the communication channels and the flow pattern of messages.[14]

Four common network configurations applied in library and information field include the star (Directed/Centralised Network); distributed (Non-Directed/Decentralised Network) hierarchical; and composite network (Combination of Directed and Non-Directed Network).[15]

Star (Directed/Centralised) Network

The star network is one in which one member of the network holds the majority of the resources while, at the same time, all the members of the network act as resources.[16]

A totally centralised network is described by the star configuration. Activities or services provided by the network are controlled by the Central node. A common example of the star configuration is the inter-library network of a large metropolitan library with multiple branches. Services are administered from decentralised locations throughout the city, but management of the network is centralised.[17] This type of network is illustrated in fig. 6.1 below:

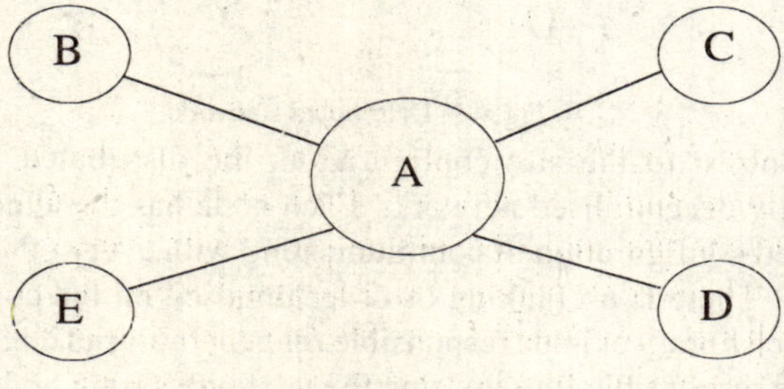

Fig. 6.1: Star Network

The Delhi Public Library is a network that illustrates the star configuration. The main library acts as the central node. The decentralized nodes are represented by the branch libraries. Members/users are interconnected through a coordinating centre.[18]

Communication routes do not exist between the outer nodes of the purely centralized network. All communications are controlled by the Central node. From a management perspective, the star configuration may appear attractive because record keeping and major processing are centralised with one staff instead of duplicated at the multiple processing centres. From a user's perspective, the star configuration may appear very inefficient because the time delay experienced by the user always involves the centre mode processing as well as the time required by each additional library from the outer nodes.[19]

Distributed (Non-Directed/Decentralised) Network

The distributed network includes members who have equal, but different resources; each member having direct access to the resources of the other network members.[20] The basic rationale of the distributed network is the network members' sharing of the different resources of each other. The distributed network configuration is given in fig. 6.2.

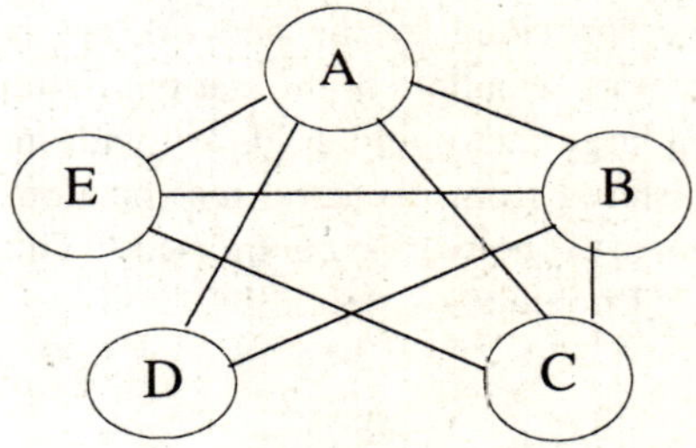

Fig. 6.2: Distributed Network

In contrast to the star configuration, the distributed network is a completely decentralised network. Each node has the alternative in the distributed configuration of communicating with every other node in the network. There is no ranking or order imposed on the communication links. Each library or node responsible for generating an inter-library loan request is responsible for choosing the next processing node for unfilled requests.[21] Each member user is connected with every other users, without any member acting as overall network coordinator.[22]

Hierarchical Network

Hierarchical network exists in an environment in which network members share resources locally, without sending the request for needs on to the next higher level in the system or, in effect, the next greater resource centre.[23] This type of topology is illustrated in Fig. 6.3.

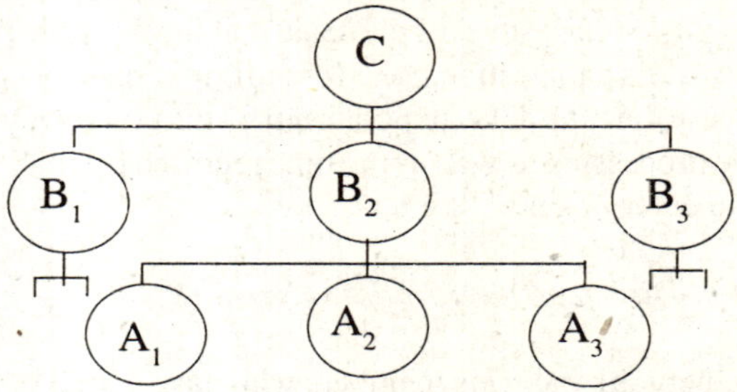

Fig. 6.3: Hierarchical Network

From fig. 6.3 the hierarchical network can be seen as one in which network members A_1, A_2, and A_3 are involved in resource sharing, finding that their resource needs can usually be met as a result of resources sharing activity. When necessary these three units refer their requests to the next higher level or to the next greater resource centre -B_2. Should the occasion arise that these units do not have the requested materials, unit C is then contracted, other members of the network are aware that Unit C can be relied upon as a location of requested materials not found at the other locations. In a sense, member C is the hand maiden of the hierarchical network, even though it is necessary, from time to time, to call on members B_1 and B_3 as possible locations of requested materials.[24]

The hierarchical network enables one to cluster activities based on some criterion such as organisational priorities or processing activity. The collections of libraries in a hierarchical network tend to have more comprehensive collections in the upper level of hierarchy.[25] Members are grouped in a hierarchical order of greater resources and expertise.

Composite Network

In fact, most library and information networks do not conform strictly to one type of configuration. Network structure usually consists of a combination of configurations. Its structure is a composite of the star, distributed and hierarchical configurations. The network incorporates various configurations to facilitate information flows within and between each level of the network.

The Illinois Library and Information Network (ILINET) can be used as an example of a composite network. The ILINET is a statewide service managed by the Illinois State Library. It provides a range of library-related services, the most extensive of which is inter-library loan, and reference services. The network is hierarchical and has the following four levels:

(i) Local libraries;
(ii) Co-operative Library Systems;
(iii) Research and Reference Centre Libraries; and
(iv) Special Resource Centres.

Figure 6.4 is a block diagram representing the general flow of requests among the different levels of the network.

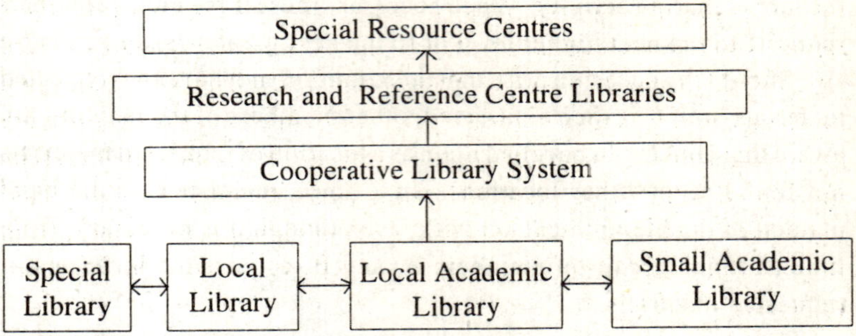

Fig. 6.4 : ILINET: Overall Flow of Requests

Communication between the local libraries and the library system in ILINET can be viewed as a star configuration. Each library system has centralised control over the processing of inter library loan requests received from their constituent libraries. The local libraries are represented by the multiple nodes.

We see from fig. 6.4 that requests referred to the Special Resource Centres must first be processed by the Centre level, Communication among the four Research and Reference Centre Libraries does not occur in a predetermined order and every centre can communicate with every other centre. Thus we have an example of a distributed network.

At present there are three Special Resource Centres. Requests received by these libraries from ILINET must be forwarded by one of the Centre libraries. Further, requests received at North Western or the University of Chicago must be referred by the Illinois State Library or the University of Illinois. Communication between the centre level and the Special Resource Libraries may be viewed as a star configuration with two possible central nodes, i.e. the Illinois State Library and the University of Illionois. Each 'Central' node is connected to every Special Resource Library.

In summary, the structure of ILINET is a composite network consisting of star, distributed and hierarchical configurations.

Directed Network with a Specialised Centre

In this type, network configurations is linked to another specialised centre only through the co-ordinating unit, which in turn passes on the information to its members. Thus, the national education programmes clearing house interfaces with the Indian National Commission for Co-operation with UNESCO.

A directed network can interface with a specialised centre as illustrated in fig. 6.5.[27]

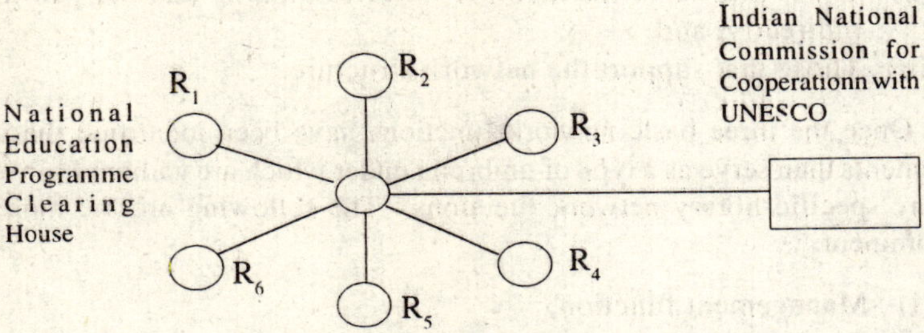

Fig. 6.5 : Directed Network with a Specialised Centre

A directed network interfaces with a specialised centre for the benefit of the network members.

Interface of Two Directed Networks

In this type, Network configuration is linked to a related worldwide/ Nationwide unit. As national or regional networks begin to develop, there may be need to link up related international or national units.

For example, the education network can interface with the IBE or UNESCO network or National Social Sciences network.

Two Directed networks interfacing have been shown in figure 6.6 below:[28]

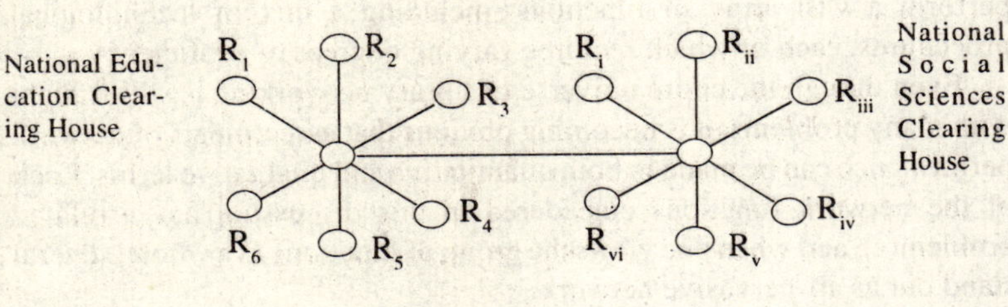

Fig. 6.6 : Interface of Two Directed Networks

Functions of an Information System

The knowledge that the primary raison d'etre of a network is to ultimately provide member library users more extensive access to a universe of library materials, also make it possible to identify three primary classes into which network functions can be categorized:

(i) Those that serve the patron;
(ii) Those that serve the member libraries directly and the patron indirectly; and
(iii) Those that support the network structure.[29]

Once the three basic network functions have been identified these elements then serve as a type of umbrella under which are gathered some more specific library network functions. The following are the more prominent:

(i) Management function;
(ii) Developing of standards;
(iii) Co-operative acquisition;
(iv) Processing;
(v) Information storage and retrieval function;
(vi) Control of Serials and Periodicals;
(vii) Inter-Library loan function;
(viii) Documents delivery function;
(ix) Co-operative storage function;
(x) Referral function;
(xi) Communications function;
(xii) Education function; and
(xiii) Marketing function.[30]

If one judges by the above list, it is apparent that library networks perform a vast array of functions, including a mix of technological procedures, each of which requires varying degrees of proficiency.

Even though the entire universe of library networking is still fraught with many problems, it is becoming obvious that assessments of network performance can be made in both quantitative and qualitative terms. Each of the network functions considered in this discussion has a related problem(s), and when one views the group of functions as a whole, several stand out as all-pervasive network.

Management Function

The area of administration and management touches virtually all aspects of the operation of the library network, their combined function must be seen as having paramount importance.[31] This is especially true since the planning and policy/making functions that normally fall within their purview are activities that have an effect on the structure and direction of the network. Another element that makes the administration and management function so vital is the fact that it includes funding. In view of the economic facts of life, especially, keen and perceptive network administration is needed today. The ill–administered networks fall by the wayside.

Development of Standards

Following closely behind the administration and management function in importance is development of standards and particularly bibliographic standards.[32] The two terms used often in this context are standardization and standards. It would be interesting to define the two terms.

The term standardization is defined as: The mediated process of formulating and applying rules for an orderly and consistent approach to a specific activity for the benefit of all concerned and, in particular, for the promotion of overall economy taking due account of functional conditions.[33]

Standard – The result of a particular standardization efforts which, after approval by a recognised authority, takes the form of a document containing a set of conditions to be fulfilled.[34] Bibliographic standards, then, can be seen as dictating statements which state the composition of bibliographic data.

The provision of standardized bibliographic records is of fundamental importance to the beginning of any library network.

Co-operative Acquisitions

Next in the order of importance is the co-operative acquisitions component of the acquisitions function.[35] This area affords tremendous possibilities for cost reduction, especially as other network functions such as inter-library loan and inter-library reference service force networking costs to rise. A cooperative acquisitions programme poorly planned can yield, if not disastrous, extremely expensive results.

Processing

There is little doubt that cataloguing is well suited to a network operation. A manually based cataloguing operation in a small or medium sized library may work but for large libraries or collections, manual cataloguing is time–consuming as it involves much checking, typing, filing and other routine clerical work.[36] On the other hand, substantial savings in effort and time are made if the national focal point, which undertakes the acquisitions of documents also processes and catalogues them and mails them to the members along with catalogue cards.

Co-operative cataloguing can be done even if the book ordering is not centralized. It is of course, assumed here that a standard method of classification and cataloguing has been established among the network members.

These schemes make effective use of professional staff time, expensive mechanical equipment and bibliographical tools used in cataloguing. This will further enhance the standards of processing and cataloguing when a union catalogue of the holdings of member libraries is prepared.

The chief problem is to secure sufficient speed of operation so that individual centres experience no delays in receiving processed books and reconciling differing procedures among participants to arrive at one uniform method.[37]

Information Storage and Retrieval Function

A collection of information items may take many forms in a library, an abstract journal or even a handbook. Retrieval is the operation by which information is selected from a document, a collection, not only a library catalogue, but also from an index or from a bibliography. The process of retrieval involves repeated search for information.

The information retrieval process includes a complex series of operations:

(a) the potential user must formulate a query or express some interest;
(b) to express its query in terms of the characteristics of the recorded information;
(c) to search the reformulated query in terms of the existing variables in the system;
(d) this user profile must be compared with profiles in the system and the location of matching materials identified; and
(e) the materials themselves must be located and presented to the user.

The need for profiles is fairly obvious. Since both authors and users employ subject words inconsistently, it would seem that user and document profiles would be more successfully matched if the keys in both were standardized.[38]

Control of Serials and Periodicals

Serials control is another area of high transaction level. The local data about serials has to be standardized.[39] An effort is to be made to build a core data base on bibliographic information on serials and periodicals titles to be available for use on the international, regional, national, state and local levels.[40]

Listing of serials and periodicals in a union catalogue is an essential network feature, requiring each member to take responsibility for forwarding information about these documents to national focal point. Union catalogue or the listing of periodicals is conducted on a national basis and most often the central compiler is the national focal point. The information required for speedy compilation of the union catalogue will have to be sent promptly to the national focal point.

Inter-Library Loan Function

Inter-Library loan is one of the most frequently and enthusiastically cited network benefits as it provides mechanisms for efficient document delivery at a much lower cost than actually purchasing the said document. This activity is especially useful in the case of rare and important documents and also those in limited circulation. Mechanisms for the safe/speedy delivery of documents to and from network members are vital and may involve the use of drop-off and pick-up points.

The concept of the library as a resource is changing, because of continuing high rates of publication and the fact that fewer libraries can afford to maintain comprehensive collections. The inter-library or network data base is gradually being regarded by some as a shared resource on a regional or even national basis. Again, quid pro quo arrangements must be developed, and certain group rules established. The computerized network provides the tool with which libraries can implement hitherto unmanageable projects.[41]

For a smooth inter-library loan, network members have to work out mechanisms by which to identify the content of their respective collections.

Documents Delivery Function

The document delivery function of a library network is next in importance.[42] As library networking develops, various types of document delivery systems are to be employed and system planners now feel that the time has come to make a hard/nosed assessment of this function.

Co-operative Storage Function

Co-operative storage provides a means by which libraries may, with minimal expenditures, retain and even acquire infrequently used but potentially valuable research materials.

A central storage should have a comprehensive collection of all publications developed in the regions that it covers. The importance lies in storing the index file and documents in such a way as to make them easy to use.

Williams has identified several types and approaches to storage. These are:[43] (i) Fixed storage, (ii) Flexible storage, (iii) Variable storage, (iv) In variable format, fixed storage, (v) Manual storage, (vi) Semi-automatic storage, (vii) Automatic storage, (viii) Master image storage, and (ix) Random access storage.

There are certain problems associated with the storage:

(i) Space for storage is always ultimately short;
(ii) Control procedures need to be instituted for classified and proprietary information;
(iii) Misplaced documents cause irksome and costly problems;
(iv) Multiple copies after problems in control and updating of information;
(v) Duplication and processing of the original document require care in the processing;
(vi) Document wear. Excessive use and wear cause deterioration; and
(vii) Conversion changes in equipment or systems (from manual to automatic or semi-automatic) may require conversion from one form to another. Retaining the clarity, accuracy and integrity of the information requires planning and care.[44]

Referral Function

The functions of a referral service include the following:

(a) to collect, on a world-wide basis, information about data and information sources within the subject or mission;
(b) to prepare a comprehensive inventory of the kinds of data/ information/services available from these sources with a detailed subject index for access;
(c) to guide users to the appropriate sources of the required data or information.[45]

Appropriate information can be supplied from such a referral service to other dissemination centres, including those in other countries.

Communications Function

The significance of the communication function cannot be underplayed.[46] The use of telecommunications is becoming increasingly important. One facet of the communication function is the union of library materials with users - equal opportunity of access to information. This notion must be regarded as the sine qua non of a national library network.

Education Function

This function involves two aspects, education of information users i.e., user education and in-service training for the personnel handling information.

The reason for educating the users are two-fold. First, the sheer bulk of printed matter being produced today causes considerable problems for users and acquaintance with techniques for the selection and distillation of this material is important to avoid narrowing of the users' appreciation of relevance. Second, the ability of intelligent reading is not developed from an early age and the use of the printed word as a primary source of knowledge is not emphasised.

The need of an in-service training is to assist in the mastery of skills, techniques, procedures and other activities that are specific to a particular function or job. The orientation phase should emphasize on three types of content:

(i) Knowledge of the agency as the trainee needs for his particular job. This knowledge includes the philosophy, function, structure, and place of the agency in the larger governmental structure and in the community of which it is a part;

(ii) The place of the particular new job in the agency function and structure; and

(iii) The specific knowledge and skill needed for performing the initial task for which the trainee will be given responsibility.[47]

Marketing Function

With the support of network members, a network can undertake marketing strategies to offer its service to both individual/corporate clients.

Marketing is the very rational process of interacting with, and attuning to the user–finding out exactly what his needs are and how they can be served most conveniently.

Promotion of services can be by word-of-mouth, formal advertising, educational and orientation programmes etc. A successful means of reaching its clientele should be with the most effective messages via the best media.[48]

Organisational Units of an Information System

In the education field, potential network members are easily identifiable. At the national level are the libraries of various departments of the Ministry of Education which implements education programmes. These departments include those concerned with non-formal education, teacher training, higher education secondary education, primary and pre-primary education, vocational training, educational research, planning and administration etc.

At the local level (i.e. state/regional/district), potential members include the education cells or branches lodged in the regional offices of the Ministry of Education or in the state offices of the State Departments of Education.

At the lower level, potential members include non-formal education centres, teacher training colleges, universities, colleges and schools, Offices of the Ministries of Health, Labour, Agriculture and Social Welfare and other Ministries which are implementing education programmes.

The different kinds of institutional units that perform the functions and provide the services and products needed by users of education information are described below. Emphasis is placed on the description of the organization, functions and services of the units rather than the users served.

Library

Libraries are now associated with the largely passive functions of a depository for documents, organized and maintained for reference and study, with the emphasis on the collection and circulation of documents.

Library collects, processes, shelves or stacks and lends primary sources of scientific and technical information in the form of books, periodicals, and maps. Its collection and catalogues are accessible to users who locate information they need on their own initiative. A library also provides access to its collection of secondary sources, such as abstracts, indexes and bibliographies.

Documentation Centre

A specialized documentation centre scrutinizes and evalutes primary or secondary sources of educational information which includes publications and documents usually neglected by the librarians. The result of the documentation centre's retrieval is used either in answering very specific questions asked by the research workers or educationists, or by less pin-pointed dissemination of specialized information in a processed form such as publication of indexes, asbtracts, literature reports etc. In its role as an agent digesting the primary sources of education information into a form which is directly accessible for the user of the centre, a documentation centre provides even translations or reprographic facsimiles of the original literature.[49]

The organization of a documentation centre, apart from administrative services, can comprise three main divisions:

(i) Library division;
(ii) Documentation division; and
(iii) Publishing division.

The library division comprises the documentation centre's collection and performs functions concerning acquisition, processing, storage and conservation.

The documentation division handles information and thus processes information upon request from outside or on its own initiative, foreseeing the immediate and long-range national requirements for education documentation and information.

The functions of the publishing division is to compile, edit and reproduce by printing, photocopying, duplicating or other processes, copies of documents for delivery to educationists or for dissemination of information throughout the country and for exchange with foreign documentation centres.

Some of the services operated by a documentation centre are designed to respond to individual request from educationists and research workers or other authorised users. They are generally known as 'responsive services'. Those that are found most essential in developing countries are:

(i) Bibliography compilation service designed to help the educationist or researcher to find out what has been published anywhere in the world on his subject;
(ii) Document procurement service; and
(iii) Translation service.

Clearing House

This is a document handling system with the main function being to provide a switching operation which performs either of two functions or both. It allows access through referrals to appropriate resources, or serves as a central agency for the collection, classification and dissemination of specialised information.

A clearing house may have six functions: library, documentation, audio-visual production, publications, organizational communications, and data processing. Like documentation centres, clearing houses need to engage the services of subject specialists. However, its services are more extensive than those of a library or a documentation centre. Some of the important services are:

(a) to collect data, and conduct search as well as publish materials;
(b) to act as a link between groups engaged in research in the same field;
(c) to publish compilations of previously unpublished materials and seek out users instead of waiting to be approached by them; and
(d) to evaluate available information, adapt and process it to meet the requirements of potential users instead of merely producing lists of information sources.

Referral Centre

A referral centre generally performs the task of referring enquires to sources of information, in addition to the performance of other functions.

A referral centre may perform any or all of the following functions:

(a) To collect information about data and information resources within a special subject or mission;
(b) To prepare comprehensive inventories of the kinds of data/information/services available from various sources;
(c) To prepare detailed subject index to facilitate access; and
(d) To guide users to appropriate sources of information.[50]

To facilitate provisional referral service, data concerning information resources are compiled in a directory. Specialised index card index files maintained by referral centres cover information about research studies, bibliographies, surveys, projects sponsored by the government and private agencies, experts and consultants; conference, seminars, workshops and training programmes, and funding/aid authorities, organizations or agencies.

Information Centres

Information services units in organizations are frequently titled information centres or information departments. A precise definition of an information centre is difficult because the concept has been changing. The tremendous increase in research and development activities has stepped up the demands for more efficient personnel and better-integrated information services. The result has been a trend to unify library, patent, translation, report writing, archival, abstracting, literature search, editorial, communications, and publications activities within a single facility.[51] It at times publishes indexing bulletin, translations and research briefs.

The centralization of all, some, or only two or three of these activities has at times been included in the scope of activities of an information centre. Some information centres offer additional services, such as providing replies to queries, retrospective searches, selecetive dissemination of information.[52]

Information Analysis Centre

The term information analysis centre is very recent, but the concept is as old as human culture. Information analysis centres may seem costly but, at least in theory, are the most efficient systems for transferring to a user timely, authoritative, evaluated information in a convenient form. In an era marked by constant expansion of scientific and technical literature, it is apparent that users want the data and information contained in the literature and not the document. "......retrieval of documents is not the same as retrieval of information; a technical specialist really needs the information contained in the published literature, not the published literature itself. To retrieve information as contrasted to documents, the technical community has devised the specialized data and information (analysis) centre".[53]

The Committee on Scientific and Technical Information (COSATI) formulated the following definition: "An information analysis centre is a formally structured organizational unit specifically (but not necessarily exclusively) established for the purpose of acquiring, selection, storing, retrieving, evaluating, analysing, and synthesizing a body of information and/or data in a clearly defined specialised field or pertaining to a specific mission with the intent of compiling, digesting, repackaging, or otherwise organizing and presenting pertinent information and/or data in a form most authoritative, timely, and useful to a society of peers and management." [54]

The following are some of the significant activities and products of the Information Analysis Centre:

Activities

- selection and collection of documents;
- abstracting/indexing;
- extraction; and
- evaluation.

Products

- bibliographies, current awareness bulletins;
- indexes, bibliographies, customer searches;
- descriptive reviews, compilations;
- Critical review of area; and
- Critical compilation of data.[55]

Data Centres

An organization handling raw or partially processed data or results, including census-type data on population and commodities as well as data on pure science and the social sciences is known as a data centre.

The basic services of a data centre include data evaluation, compilation and dissemination, and referral service. A data centre may be attached to a university, a research institute, a data evaluation centre or a major information centre.

Comparison of Information Service Organizations

Information services can be classified by their major activity (function) or product. Weisman has compared functions, products and services of several types of information service organizations in the United States. His findings are reproduced in Table 6.1[56] and although they may not hold for services outside the US, they provide an interesting study.

Table 6.2 is reproduced from the UNISISI draft document "Using and improving National Information Systems for Development" (1974). This outlines the possible operations and responsible institutions in a national information systems.[57]

TABLE 6.1 : Comparison of functions, products, and service operations among types of U.S. information service organizations .

	Special Library	Documentations Centre	Referal Centre	Clearing-house	Information Services centre	Information Analysis centre
Functions						
Collection						
Document	M	M	O	M	M	m
Data/information	O	O	O	r	M	M
Processing						
Document	M	M	O	M	M	m
Data/information	r	O	O	r	M	M
Storage						
Document	M	M	O	M	M	m
Data/information	O	O	O	r	M	M
Retrieval						
Document	M	M	O	M	M	m
Data/information	O	O	O	r	M	M
Dissemination						
Document	M	M	O	M	M	O
Data/information	O	O	O	O	M	M

Publication or Reproduction						
Document	O	M	O	M	M	M
Data/information	O	O	O	O	M	M
Information Generation						
Document	O	O	O	O	m	M
Data/information	O	O	O	O	m	M
Archives	M	m	O	O	r	O
Services						
Consultation and advice	r	O	r	r	m	M
Replies to inquiries	m	r	r	r	M	M
Referral	r	r	M	M	m	r
Retrospective search	M	M	O	M	M	r
SDI	m	m	O	m	m	r
Serves visitors	M	O	O	r	m	r
Conducts seminars and conferences	O	O	O	O	m	r
Conducts research	O	O	O	O	O	m
Transalation services	m	O	O	r	m	r
State of art reports	O	O	O	O	m	M
Critical reviews	O	O	O	O	O	M
Critical compilations	O	O	O	O	O	M
Products						
Handbooks	O	O	O	O	m	M
Bibliographies	M	M	r	M	M	m
Data sheets	O	O	O	O	m	M
Current awareness bulletins	M	r	O	M	M	m
Periodicals	m	O	O	O	m	r
Abstracts	r	r	O	r	m	m
Indexes	m	r	O	r	m	r
Newsletters	m	m	m	m	m	m
Film	O	O	O	O	m	r
Directories	m	O	M	m	m	r
Translations	r	O	O	r	m	r
Thesauri	m	r	O	m	m	m
Recommondations	O	O	O	O	m	m
Correlations	O	O	O	O	O	M
Acquisitions lists	M	M	O	m	m	r
Conference proceedings	O	O	O	O	m	r

(M = major activity, m = minor activity, r = rare activity, O = no activity)

Source: Atherton, Pauline, (1977). *Handbook for Information Systems and Services*. Paris: Unesco, Table 4.1 p 87

TABLE 6.2: Flow of operations and responsible institution in a national information system

Operating in Chronological Order	Responsible Institutions (b)
1. Determining the needs of the users	Extension service (a), SDI service
2. Searching for all existing information	Referral centre, library, documentation centre
3. Acquiring missing information (mainly primary information in this case) (d)	Library, Documentation centre
4. Storing missing information (e)	Library, Documentation centre
5. Consolidating all information available	Information analysis centre
6. Storing consolidated information	Library, Documentation centre
7. Reproducing consolidated information available	Data dissemination centre, SDI service
8. Distributing consolidated information to extension service (c)	Data dissemination Centre. SDI service
9. Translating consolidated information	Translating centre
10. Storing translation	Library, Documentation centre
11. Repackaging translation	Extension service (c), SDI service
12. Reproducing repackaged information	Extension service, data dissemination centre
13. Storing repackaged information	Library, Documentation centre
14. Promoting repackaged information to the users	Extension service (c), SDI service
15. Distributing repackaged information to the users	Extension service (c), SDI service

(a) Case where the information product to be developed will probably cover the needs of a large range of users.
(b) Only the main representatives are cited here.
(c) Including consulting firm, professional association, education programmes, etc.
(d) In other words : (1) existing consolidated information was not sufficient in the examples considered here; (2) research results in their raw form (that is, primary information) were available .
(e) Including preparatory operations for retrieval (indexing, cataloguing, abstracting).

Source: Atherton, Pauline. (1977). *Handbook for Information Systems and Services.* Paris: Unesco, Table 4.1.1 p.88.

Design Consideration of an Information System

System designates an organization of interacting parts intended to accomplish a particular purpose. The performance variables of a system are properties descriptive of the results of operations of the system, with respect to its attainment of the goals set for it. It is said that a system is what the designer chooses to make it, and that a system can be judged as 'good' only if it accomplishes the purpose for which it is designed.

A system can achieve functional status in one of the two ways. It can be designed, or it can 'just grow', developing first in one direction and then another, in reaction to random variations of environment.

For designing of a system, the following factors arc to be considered:[58]

Know the Background

With the presumption that management, after study and due deliberation, has made the decision to institute an information system, the starting point for the system designer may indeed be the study of the fundamental background information which will influence and determine the parameters and components of the system.

Every organization has its unique character which must be understood before any meaningful and workable plans can be made. Thus, a first step for the system designer, is to obtain or develop background knowledge or a 'biography' of the organization and its activities. Background information can be obtained from the pre-inception study, from the publications of the organisation, descriptive literature, policy and administrative manuals, and from various records. The principal data source, however, is discussion with the organizational officials and operating personnel.

Developing this information requires examination of answers to questions like: mission and activities of the organization; its goals, field of activity and full scope or involvement; information needed in order to do the work; what are the sources of information; interest of the user community and other potential user groups; the goals, mission, and the scope of the system on a short term basis or on a long-term basis; constraint factors from the viewpoint of management, costs, state-of-the-art the field(s) of coverage, facilities and equipment and duplication or overlap with other services within the organization and outside it.[59]

Users and Their Needs

The wise system designer recognizes that the user of information must be an active participant in the system because the design of the system is directed towards the needs of the user.

The information service must anticipate, match, and be responsive to the requirement of its clientele.

Types of Users

The important groups of users of an education information system are distinguishable according to the kind of activity in which they are engaged:

(i) Planners and administrators in the field of education;
(ii) Teachers at school and higher education level;
(iii) Teacher educators;
(iv) Researchers; and
(v) Librarians/Documentalists; etc.

The user groups identified above are very broadly defined and are not exhaustive. They do not include, for example, such large user groups as students and general public interested in different educational fields.

First of all, information users themselves are identified in relation to various characteristics: type of users, information needs, the purposes for which they need information, their age, qualifications, professional position etc. Information about the occupation of the user and the kind of establishment he is employed in, helps in determining his information needs. Different aspects of his professional activities influence the time he spends on information retrieval, use of information sources, and frequency of use of libraries and information centres.

To determine the scope of the collection of materials and the kinds of information services to be offered, a system designer may seek the following information about the user:

- subject and associated interests;
- education, training and special expertise;
- functions, activities and responsibilities in the institution;
- professional bodies of which the user is a member;
- outside organisations with which the user has academic or professional contacts;

- kinds of information media preferred by the user periodicals, newspapers, audio visual etc;
- types of information services preferred by the user: current awareness service, SDI, abstracting, digest, data, state of art report, bibliographical and reprographic etc; and
- time most convenient to the user to receive library services.[60]

Types of Information Needs

Distinguishing the following concepts contributes much to the clarity of user studies:

Need: for information or entities as perceived by others (objective assessments based on problem analysis, commonly referred to as need).

Want: need as perceived by staff, commonly referred to as want.

Demand: Need as articulated by the (potential) user (demand) or by an information system (recognised need).

Not all needs are translated into wants; the user may not be aware that available information or entities could help to solve the problem at hand or may, perhaps sub–consciously, perceive the cost of obtaining such information or entities as so high as to suppress even the thought of getting the information or entities. Conversely, not all wants correspond to real needs.[61]

M. Voigt maintains that the users refer to information sources mainly in three circumstances:

(a) While getting current awareness of results both in their particular narrow field and the related disciplines;
(b) In their day-to-day work, when they need some factual information – figures, methods and designs; and
(c) When embarking on a new problem or a project, as well as when completing it and writing about it a retrospective search to identify as many published and unpublished sources on the subject as possible.

The following methods can be applied in collecting information about the user's needs:

- study of the organizational chart of the institution;
- study of the functions/activities of the institution;
- study of the annual reports, project reports and other publications;
- study of papers, books etc. published by users;

- observing user at his work place;
- personal informal contacts with users;
- feedback from information services rendered;
- providing suggestions from users, about their subject interest, institutional interest, etc;
- attending meetings within the institutions of which projects and problems may be discussed;
- study of documents used by the user;
- participation in institutional work orientation programmes; and
- study of reference queries received from users.[62]

Resources limitations usually preclude investigating every body's needs; management must set priorities as to whose needs are most urgent and should therefore be investigated. It is not to take the most convenient road and investigate the needs of present users.[63]

Coverage

A component inseparable from the user community in design considerations is that of scope of education. Since the mission of any information system is to facilitate the fulfilment of the education mission of the population it serves, the coverage, may be clearly circumscribed by the mission of the community. In a newly developed or developing field, coverage may have to be continuously monitored as the state-of-art evolves as also in order to be responsive to the changing needs of the contributors and users of the information of the field. Factors the designer needs to investigate and analyse can be indicated by the following questions:

(i) What are the principal fields that should be covered? Do these fields have subdivisions that need coverage?
(ii) What related fields should be covered?
(iii) What sources of information – printed and otherwise, formal and informal – provide the coverage?
(iv) What primary journals service the pertinent field(s)?
(v) What secondary publications (abstracting and indexing journals) service the field(s)?
(vi) What are the current research and development activities in the field(s)?
(vii) Which individuals and organisations are concerned with these activities?

(viii) The degree of coverage or overlap with another system and the practicability and desirability of cooperative work-sharing with it should also be considered.

(ix) The growth in holdings is directly related to the growth of the field of coverage. With the literature of any field, in general, doubling almost every 10-12 years, the system designer must plan for space expansion, for attendant modifications and augmentation and processing of the information. He should expect that the field(s) of coverage will remain dynamic.[64]

Centralization or Decentralization

The problem of centralization or decentralization is to be decided by the designer in relation to services. A network is not a rigid alliance, but is a system of linkages for information exchange and sharing, and members can undertake other activities in pursuit of their respective objectives. A designer has to develop an organizational structure and identify nodes and network relationships.

Conrad has observed that in practice there are many arrangements wherein some services are provided locally and others from a centralized point. He concludes that a completely decentralized operation is never justified where one is dealing with other than a highly specialised area.[65]

Centralization offers the advantages of greater efficiency, economy and availability of the full resources of a system to any and every component of users. Internally generated and proprietary information is sometimes an area of concern in centralised systems.

The advantages of decentralizati n are quicker, direct and personalized services. However, the main drawback of decentralization is fragmentation of resources to the detriment of the mission and goals of users.

Three questions provide a good basis for decision making with regard to structure. These are:

- How much centralization is appropriate?
- Who will co-ordinate the work?
- Will it be necessary to have sub-central nodes in the states.

Services

The important focus of the system is services. An information system exists to perform services. The services it performs are related directly to user needs. The designer recognizes that the user of information must be integrated into the system as an active participant whose needs direct the design. The information base must, therefore, match and be responsive to his requirements. Constant liaison with the community should be built up into the system.

Services may be grouped into four general categories: Documentation work; Dissemination; Enquiry; and Special activities.

Often it is advisable to try out individual services on a small sample group of users to determine interest and to test procedures before a decision is made to implement them permanently. However, all services cannot lend themselves to trial, especially if start-up costs are extensive.

The system designer has to decide what is optimum within this spectrum. Factors for his consideration are:

- (i) The goals of the community;
- (ii) The technical sophistication and degree of homogeneity of the community;
- (iii) The size of the community;
- (iv) The size, character and resources of the system; and
- (v) The priority of services to be offered.

In analysing the sequence, the consideration of the following variables would be appropriate:

- (a) nature and scope of task;
- (b) time schedule;
- (c) methods, techniques and procedures;
- (d) equipment and materials;
- (e) manpower;
- (f) facilities; and
- (g) benefits and requirements.[66]

Organisational Considerations

A. General Organisation : Organizationally, information services/centres vary in practice, often depending on the historical motivations of its involvement and institution. There are various ways in which it may be found: (i) at the corporate or headquarters level as an autonomous department or activity; (ii) as part of the department it mainly serves; and (iii) as part of the administration or service department.

Ideally, the system should be unencumbered of organizational loyalties that might deter its usefulness to the full community of users it has been designed to serve. So organisationally, it should be free to interact with its users and to present opportunities for them to participate in the system's planning, development, growth, and assessment. Close under-system interaction enhances services because the needs of the user can be more readily determined and met. If the majority of the users are homogeneous, the system could well be located within the department and if the user community is heterogenous, then an autonomous organizational structure might be advisable.

For the operational success of the system, Wasserman and Daniel identify some factors in the organizational placement of the system. They are:

(i) the significance of a sympathetic managerial attitude in the acceptance and full use of the centre;
(ii) the importance of sponsorship by an information conscious, high level officer;
(iii) the organisational perils involved in subordination of the centre to another department; and
(iv) the necessity of achieving the highest possible bureaucratic sanctuary within the organisation.[67]

B. Types of Organisational Structure: To make a choice for the organisational structure of an Education Information System, three types of networking structure may be considered for the purpose. These are: directed network, non-directed, and combination of these two.

The information structure in the field of education has not reached a sophisticated level in which a more decentralised type of networking can function effectively. In this case, the most functional arrangement is the third networking option, which provides a clearing house or focal point and allows free interaction on a bilateral/multilateral basis among members.

The library or information centre in the national education programme may serve as a focal point as in the case of directed network type.

C. Advisory Committee: Is an instrument that has been found to work successfully in meeting political considerations and produces serendipitous results in other areas. The advisory committee can and should help the system bridge the two masters it serves – the management and users. It relates the "information centre to the various components of its community of users, provides an internal political mechanism for gaining budgetary support, and help to delineate the scope of operation. An Advisory Committee is a means for aiding evaluation of activities and quality assurance of services and products, as well as providing an avenue for feedback. The Advisory Committee ideally offers policy counsel and guidance, but its advisory powers should not interfere with the administration and operation of the system. The system designer should guard, if he can, the operational integrity of the system. The membership of the advisory committee should come from appropriately qualified, respected persons within and without the organisation, the field(s) of interest, and the community of usters".[68]

D. Location: The overriding need in the organisational position of the information service is to do justice to the information requirements of the organisations of which it is part. The blend of service needs, personalities, data requirements and other factors of different organisations make it impossible to generalize about the most appropriate location for such a service in any given institutional setting. Perhaps the only guida-nce possible is that the original placement should be given considerable attention but that, once made, it need not fix the position inexorably.[69]

E. Governmental Support: In both policy and legalistic sense, an information network may require an official legal framework. Whenever possible, the mandate and responsibilities of the national education information network should be explicitly stated by the highest authority – the Minister of M/HRD. The policies and priorities of parent bodies should give adequate resources to information units and allow them sufficient flexibility in the performance of their duties.[70]

F. The Charter: Costallo has strongly advocated that every information system should develop a charter. The charter is a document which is both an instrument defining the constituted authority and obligations of the system and prescribing administrative methods to be followed routinely for the performance of designated operations, and also an instrument to monitor the effectiveness of the system.[71] The charter generally includes: (i) General Scope; (ii) Activities; (iii) Organisational structure Administrative and Working organisatinal structures; (iv) Possible future operations; (vi) Finances, (v) Services and Products; (vii) Privileges and Obligations of membership; (viii) and Relations with other organisations.[72]

G. Mechanisation: Before deciding on a machine system for any process or function in an information system, one should know how the present operation works. The objectives and costs of the present procedure should also be examined and compared with the objectives and costs of the new machine system. Several other factors which would help an information system to decide how and what to mechanise are:

(i) the quality of information needed;

(ii) access to the material;
(iii) the speed with which the information must be provided
(iv) the amount of manipulation and processing and control that the data must undergo; and
(v) the availability of mechanized equipment in the organisation-cost-benefit analysis are to be made in deciding whether the full-time use of a computer or its share is to be utilised.[73]

Manpower Requirement

It is probably unnecessary to say much about staff, it is important to so organise the work as to ensure that the maximum value is obtained from the energy expended, bearing in mind the few possible permutations in its make-up and the varied services it may be called upon to perform.

With greater number greater devolution is essential. Here two patterns are possible. Either a complete devolution to a deputy of all supervisory duties or, treating the chief and deputy as one, a partial devolution to each senior officer making him responsible for a series of duties and for the related work of junior staff. The second method is greatly to be preferred. It ensures unity of policy, gives a proper measure of responsibility to all senior officers, and does not seal off the head but enables him to know all his senior staff at least reasonably well.[74]

Qualitative Considerations

As a final element of the design of an information system, we might consider the qualitative criteria formulated by Thomas. Thomas has observed that an information system's performance properties determine the quality of the information it provides. The quality of information is judged by the system's ability to meet its users' needs and the way it helps them make more accurate decisions. The eight properties identified by Thomas are:[75]

(i) Capacity, (ii) Quality, (iii) Compatibility, (iv) Timeliness, (v) Coherence, (vi) Flexibility, (vii) Dependability, and (viii) Economy.

These eight qualitative factors can also serve as a basis for evaluating the system and as quality control measures.

The Evaluation of an Information System

In the social process of information transfer the ultimate evaluation must be from the viewpoint of the potential recipients: have they received the information needed, wanted, demanded, and are the costs of this information provision personally or socially acceptable? There is also the question of evaluation from the view point of the sources of information, who are concerned to know whether they have got their messages across, to whom and with what effect.

Criteria of Evaluation

With respect to any activity, evaluation puts the questions how well has it been performed? How much benefit is derived from it. There may be more than one criterion that appears relevant to a particular activity. Orr used two elements i.e. quality and value as criteria for evaluating an information system. According to him 'quality' is the criteria related to performance and 'value' is related to benefit. His evaluation can be explained with the help of following diagram.[76]

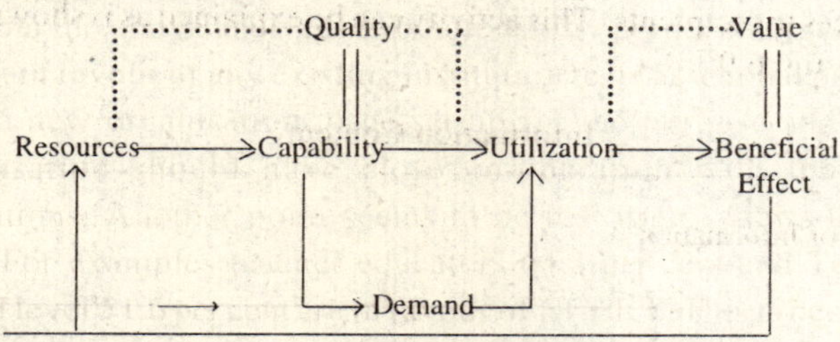

Fig. 6.8: Criteria of Evaluation

The provision of resources to an information system results in its having a capability to provide various services; the utilization (use) of these services takes place when demands are made on the system; and the recipients may derive benefit from this use.

The arrows represent the following propositions:

Other things being equal, (i) the capability of a system will tend to increase as resources devoted to it increase, (ii) the demand on a system will tend to increase as its capability increases, (iii) the utilization of a system will tend to increase as the demand on it increases, (iv) the utilization of a system will tend to increase as its capability increases, (v) the beneficial effects of a system will tend to increase as its utilization increases, and (vi) the resources available to a system will tend to increase as its beneficial effects increase.

The above propositions imply that there is always a limit to the extent that any factor in the sequence can be increased or improved. The other phrase, "other things being equal" implies that many factors may counteract each suggested relationship; extra resources may be misused, and fail to increase capability; new capabilities may be irrelevant or ill marketed, and fail to increase utilization; extra uses may be trivial or may divert recipients away from real needs, and thus fail to produce beneficial effects; benefits received by users may not be perceived by funders, and so not result in extra resources.

It is not always easy to develop direct measures of quality and value. The dashed lines in Orr's diagram suggest indirect measures that are often used as Orr pointed out that measure of increased value could be enlarged resources; if recipients pay for the service, it must be of value to them.

A Framework for Evaluation

Information systems process source messages for delivery via products and services to recipients. This activity can be explained as is shown in the following fig. 6.9[77]

Information Content

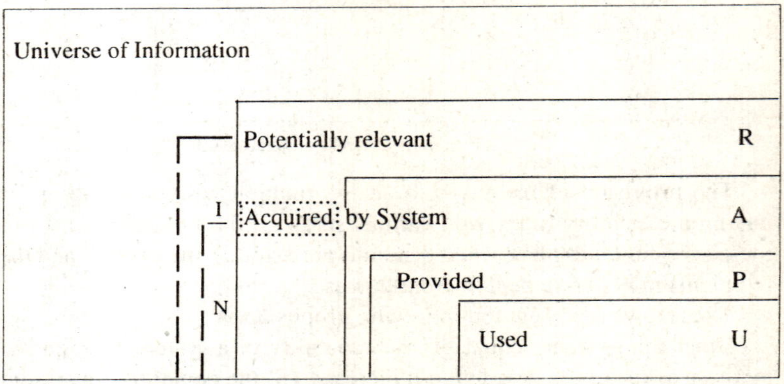

Fig. 6.9 : Information - Provision Model

Of the whole universe of information messages only some are relevant to potential users of a particular system. Of these potentially relevant messages, most information systems manage to acquire only a proportion of the potentially relevant material in a system (Out of these some must be irrelevant material, which has been shown by the outer dashed line in the figure). Only a proportion is provided to recipients on demand (output may well be mixed with irrelevant material). Of the messages provided, only a proportion may be actually used (those not used are suggested by the inter dashed line).

Comparison between various boxes in the figure suggests various measures of quality. For example, the ratio A/R is a measure of the system *coverage*: the ratio P/A (potentially relevant messages/potentially relevant messages acquired) is a measure of how comprehensive is *recall* from the stores; the ratio of N to P is a measure of how selectively the system extracts relevant material from its store, called the precision; the ratio I/A would be a measure of irrelevant material acquired, the ratio U/P would measure redundancy in *message provision.*

Recipient Viewpoint

Now let us consider the process from the viewpoint of recipient. But before that, let us define some related concepts.[78]

WANT – is an information need that is recognised as such by a potential recipient.

DEMAND – of all the existing needs/wants, only a proportion results, in positive action to acquire information, advancing beyond the wish. This proportion is the total demand.

Of this total, only some will be addressed to a particular information system, and only a fraction of these will be satisfactorily met. This can be explained with the help of a fig. 6.10[79] given below:

USER-SATISFACTION MODEL

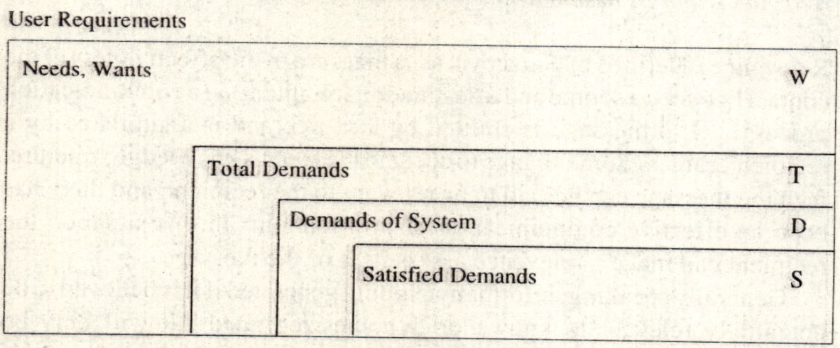

Fig. 6.10 : User-Satisfaction Model

The ratio S/D is a direct measure of the quality of a service, the ratio D/T measures the extent to which a system is attracting active users (the market penetration); and T/W would measure the extent to which the global information is reaching those who need/want information.

This analysis has identified criteria by which the quality of an information system may be assessed.

Quality of Services

(i) The first is the pervasive importance of time in information provision: (a) the time interval between initiation of a demand and delivery of output; (b) the currency and up-to-dateness of delivered information; and (c) the frequency of any regularly delivered output.

(ii) The second, there is the reliability of information provided – (a) its accuracy, (b) freedom from error; and (c) lack of bias.

(iii) Third, there is the appropriateness of the form in which information is presented -- (a) quantity, (b) format, (c) terminology, and (d) language.

(iv) Fourth, the cost to the system of providing information and the cost to the recipient of obtaining it.[80]

Aspects of Evaluation

For evaluation of an information system following aspects are to be considered:

Relevance and its assessment

Relevance is defined by Saracevic as 'a measure of the effectiveness of the contact between a source and a destination (recipient) in a communication process.[81] If a message is emitted by a source and is assimilated by a recipient, causing some change to occur in the latter's knowledge structure, then the message can be said to be relevant to the recipient, and there has been an effective communication of information. In this situation the recipient can make a relevance assessment of the message.

Generally speaking, information is only generated if it is believed to be potentially relevant to known or hypothesized needs; it will only be recorded if a use later in time is foreseen; messages are only replicated if a publisher believes that there is an audience for whom they are relevant; published messages are only acquired and stored by an information system if judged relevant to actual or potential users of the system; analysis (classification and indexing) of document is done to express the perceived relevance of each item to the hypothesized information needs of users; in retrieval, the search terms used are those judged to be relevant to the enquiry made. Only the ultimate recipient of an information message can make an unequivocal judgement: 'Yes, it is relevant to me'.

Evaluation is often concerned with the comparison of relevance assessment. A study of the coverage of a system is matching the relevance assessments made in the acquisition process against some more comprehensive assessment of the universe of information messages. A measurement of 'recall' in a subject search is matching the relevance assessments made by the search system with more comprehensive assessment of the stock of messages in the system. A measurement of 'precision' matches search system assessment against those of the recipient.

All relevance assessment is subjective and hence variable according to the assessor's understanding of the message content and understanding of the information need, his purpose in making the assessment, and the general context in which a particular assessment is made.

Service Qualities

Information systems provide services to potential recipients. The service qualities can be judged in relation to more 'ineffable' characteristics.

The fact that a range of different services is available from a system is often attractive to users. People have a wide spectrum of need. There is a possibility of providing beyond the standard services and giving a 'tailor-made' output is an evidence of good quality.

Simplicity of use of a system is a highly appreciated quality because users may not have the time, inclination, or even ability to learn a procedure that is complex. Technical assistance in using the system is appreciated; so also the provision of training facilities for those who do wish to learn; explanation to users what the system is doing; why there is an unavoidable delay; and why output takes the form that it does etc. The atmosphere of the system's attractiveness of the physical environment in which the users access the system, the 'courtesy' and 'enthusiasm' of information staff, the feeling of personal attention that they impart, is very important.[82]

All these 'ineffable' qualities can play a large part in affecting user reaction to an information system.

Performance

All measures of quality are concerned with comparing i.e., what has actually been done with what could have been done in some ideal or optimal circumstances. Since actuality usually falls short of the ideal or optimal, evaluation may also wish to identify reasons for the short-fall.

A performance measure is a relation between some value derived from normal system activity and some corresponding value derived from the real or hypothesized activity of an 'optimal system'. Often the relation used is a simple ratio (such as items received/items sought). There are situations when more than one measure can be used to characterise the performance of an activity.

It is essential that performance standards be established in conjunction with each procedure identified. Performance standards include four distinct aspects: (i) quantity, (ii) quality, (iii) time, and (iv) cost.[83]

To evaluate performance, identification of causes of less than ideal performance – 'failure analysis', as it is often called, is to be made. Such a study involves examining the reasons for retrieval failure as well as the reasons for retrieval success. It also involves studying queries for which performance was particularly poor or particularly good to find a reason that might explain the performance differential. Such detailed analysis provides insight into the effects of individual information system components as well as the effects of characteristics of entities and queries.[84]

System Efficiency: Cost Effectiveness

Cost has always been a major factor in the evaluation of information system, but it has assumed increasing importance because economic constraints justify discontinuation of some services.

The aim of every information system is to achieve maximum effectiveness in meeting the requirements of potential recipients. It can provide better or more wide–ranging services if it uses its resources wisely, and minimises the cost of its activities.

Costing is not a simple activity. Cost elements to be taken into account may, according to Vickery, include:

(i) labour;
(ii) Expenditure on information materials acquired;
(iii) Consumables (paper, storage media, etc.);

(iv) Use of equipment (depreciation, maintenance);
(v) External charges (for processing, telecommunications, postage, transport, travel, etc);
(vi) Service overheads (accommodation rent, rates, maintenance and insurance; water, power heat, cleaning costs; general office services);
(vii) Administrative overheads (the costs of supervision, accounting, personnel, etc); and
(viii) Development (cost associated with developing the system may have to be recovered).[85]

Coverage of Acquisition Search

Information system of every kind conducts a continual search for potential sources, and on locating them attempts to acquire their emitted messages. The coverage achieved is a measure of the success of this search process. In principle, coverage can be expressed as the simple ratio of source message acquired/source messages emitted.

Counting the acquired messages is usually straightforward. It is much more difficult to devise a way of identifying emitted messages not acquired. The ratio of messages acquired/messages identified is a measure of success in the acquisition process, but it is not a true measure of coverage.

An information system identifies a comprehension on collection that covers its interests, and by comparison of stock estimating a relative measure of coverage – and collection of a well-established system. In England, BLLD can be considered as the standard for the coverage for information system. An alternative strategy is to identify one or more collections, each limited in subject scope but having the appearance of being comprehensive within the scope, and to compare system stock with each. If sufficiently numerous and diverse comparisons can be made, some overall relative measure of the coverage of one's own collection can be estimated.

It has been expressed that if an information system is seeking individually emitted source messages, it is likely that the unit cost of actually acquiring each is approximately the same, but the unit cost of identification is likely to increase. The cost/coverage curve will be of the form of the well-known 'Law of diminishing returns'.[86]

If the system is looking for messages embedded in other source material – say, relevant articles in journals – then the Bradfor distribution of messages among publications also plays a role. The unit acquisition cost per publication may remain approximately constant, but the yield of relevant items per publication declines and overall cost/coverage is increased.

Retrieval from Store

The appropriateness of substantive data to the user's background depends on the approtriateness of the documents delivered, which, in turn, depends on the collection and on the ability of the information system to select documents by appropriateness. A collection developed for a specific use group may exclude documents clearly inappropriate to their background.

A user wants to obtain just the substantive data/information that are needed to solve the problem. He wants to obtain the data with a minimum of effort, avoiding repetition and wordiness.

The document delivery is influenced by four factors, namely concentration of relevant documents, evidence of duplicate relevant documents, uniqueness of substantive data contained in documents and conciseness of document.

The concentration of relevant documents as measured by precision depends on three factors: the collection composition (how many relevant documents are in the collection); the number of irrelevant documents correctly rejected as measured by discrimination; and the completeness of the set of relevant documents found as measured by recall.

Let us understand the problem by quantitative measures. The most basic measures are recall and discrimination. Inspite of the fact that relevance is a matter of degree, the most common formulas deal with the simplest cases: documents are considered either relevant or not relevant and either retrieved or not retrieved. In this case retrieval performance can be analysed based on the following table:

	Relevant	Not relevant
Retrieved	A Hits	B Noise or Waste
Not retrieved	C Misses	D Rejects

The above table represents the collection of stored documents. Each act of retrieval divides the store into two parts: items retrieved and those not retrieved.

Relevance assessment can then, in principle, divide each of these parts into relevant and non-relevant portions. We are left with four quantities: relevant items either hit or missed, irrelevant waste retrieved and items correct rejected.

The model clearly suggests two possible criteria of quality: to minimize the number of misses and to minimise the amount of waste retrieval. The ideal performance is one in which no relevant documents are missed and no irrelevant documents are retrieved.

Recall and discrimination are measures of system success, fall-out is a measure of system failure. Recall is a commonly used measure. Fall-out is used occasionally, discrimination rarely used and the measure used instead is precision.

$$\text{Recall (r)} = \frac{\text{relevant retrieved}}{\text{all relevant}} = \frac{A}{A + C}$$

(Recall measures the ability of the system to retrieve relevant documents)

$$\text{Discrimination (d)} = \frac{\text{Irrelevant rejected}}{\text{all irrelevant}} = \frac{D}{B + D}$$

(Discrimination measures the ability of the system to reject irrelevant documents)

$$\text{Fall out (f)} = \frac{\text{Irrelevant retrieved}}{\text{all irrelevant}} = \frac{B}{B + D}$$

(Fall out, the complement of discrimination, measures the same ability).

$$\text{Precision (p)} = \frac{\text{relevant retrieved}}{\text{all retrieved}} = \frac{A}{A + B}$$

(Precision measures the combined effect of three factors: (i) number of relevant documents in the collection, (ii) recall, and (iii) discrimination).

Precision is a useful measure from the point of view of user. However, precision does not measure a single ISAR system ability. It is not a good measure for analysing individual information storage and retrieval system abilities.[87]

REFERENCES

1. Atherton, Pauline. (1977). *Handbooks of Information Systems and Services.* Paris: Unesco, p.17
2. Unesco-UNISIST II. (1979). *International Conference on Scientific and Technical Information for Development-Main Working document.* Paris: Unesco, (P.G. 1-79/CONF 201/Col.5).
3. Unesco. Principal Regional Office for Asia and Pacific-Population Education Programme Service. (1985). Information networking in population education. Bangkok: Unesco, p.27
4. *ibid.*, p.13
5. Kalbe, Helen. (1978). Worldwide population information network: status and goals. *Special Libraries.* 69 (7). July, p.237-280
6. Mercadu, Cesar. (1982). Information networking: concepts and models. Quezon city: Institute of Mass Communication, University of the Philippines, p.12
7. Soergel, Dagobert (1985). *Organising Information.* New York: Academic, p.74
8. Atherton Pauline. (1977). *Handbook of Information Systems and Services. Op. cit.*, p.40
9. Marcadu, Cesar, (1982). Information networking: concepts and models. *Op. cit.*, p.12
10. Atherton, Pauline. (1977). *Handbook of information systems and services. Op. cit.*, p.110
11. Unesco. (1985). Information networking in population education. *Op. cit.*, p.14
12. Millard, William, (1975). Information network in biomedicine. *Journal of Biocommunications.* 11(3) November, p.7-14
13. *ibid.*
14. Rouse, S.H. (1975). A selected review of the literature on interlibrary loan networks. *Network* 2(1), p.17-25
15. *ibid.*
16. Maruskin, Albert F. (1980). OCLC; its governance, function, financing and technology. New York: Marcel Dekkar, p.20
17. Rouse, William B. and Rouse Sandra H. (1980) Management of Library networks: policy analysis, implementation and control. New York: John Wiley and Sons, p.20-21
18. Unesco. (1985). Information networking in population education. *op. cit.*, p.19
19. Rouse and Rouse. (1980). Management of Library networks..... *op. cit.*, p.20-21
20. Kent, Allen. (1980) Network anatomy and network objectives. In OCLC: its governance, function, financing and Technology by Albert F. Maruskin. *Op. cit.* p.22
21. Rouse and Rouse. (1980). Management of library networks..... *op. cit.* p.22
22. Unesco. (1985). Information networking in population education. *op. cit.*, p.22
23. Maruskin, Albert F. (1980). OCLC... *op. cit.*, p.20
24. *ibid.*, p.22
25. Davis, R.M. (1971). National biomedical communications network as a developing structure In *Conference on Inter-library Communications and Information Networks.* Chicago: American Library Association, p.294-309
26. Rouse and Rouse (1980). Management of library networks......*op. cit.*, p.25-27
27. Unesco. (1985). Information networking in population education. *op. cit.*, p.112
28. *ibid.*

29. Williams, James G. and Flynn, Roger (1978). Network topology: functions of existing networks. (Paper delivered at the Pittsburgh Conference November 6-8, 1978), p.2
30. *ibid.*, p.15
31. *ibid.*, p.45
32. *ibid.*
33. Schmierer, Helen B. (1975). Bibliographic standards. *Annual Review of Information Science and Technology*. Vol. 10, p. 107
34. *ibid.*
35. Williams and Flynn. (1978). Network topology....*op. cit.*, p. 45
36. Martin, Susan K. (1981). *Library networks*, 1981-82. New York: Knowledge Industry. p.11
37. Atherton, Pauline. (1977). *Handbook for information systems and services. op. cit;* p. 114
38. *ibid.*, p. 147-148
39. The Ohio College Library Centre. (1967). Code of Regulations. p.1
40. Maruskin, Albert F. (1980). OCLC......*op. cit.*, p. 35
41. Martin. Susan K. (1981). Library networks 1981-82. *op. cit.*, p. 13
42. Williams and Flynn. (1978). Network topology...*op. cit.*, p. 45
43. Williams, W.F. (1965). *Principles of automated information retrieval.* Illinois: Business Press, p. 439
44. Weisman, Herman M. (1972). *Information systems, services and centers.* New York: Decker and Hayes, p. 81-82
45. Atherton, Pauline. (1977). *Handbook for information systems and services. op. cit.*, p. 102
46. Williams and Flynn. (1978). Network topolog...*op. cit.*, p. 45
47. Atherton, Pauline. (1977). *Handbook of information systems and services. op. cit.*, p. 216
48. *ibid.*, p. 80-81
49. Unesco. Principal Regional Office for Asia and the Pacific-Population Education Programme Service. (1985). Information networking in population education. *op. cit.*, p. 32-39
50. Atherton, Pauline. (1977). *Handbook for information systems and services. op. cit.*, p. 93-103
51. Cohan, Leonard and Craven, Kehneth. (1961). Science Information Personnel. Washington, D.C.: U.S. Office of Education,p. 139
52. Weisman, Herman M. (1972). Information systems, services and centres. *op. cit.*, p. 1653.
53. *ibid.*, p. 140-141
54. *ibid.*, p. 142
55. Brady, Edward L. (1968). Status report on National Standard Reference Data System. Washington, D.C.: Government Printing Office, p. 168
56. Weisman, Herman M. (1972). Information Systems, services and centers. *op. cit.*, Table 1 p. 20-21
57. Unesco. (1974). Study on the problems of accessibility and dissemination of data for science and technology. Paris: Unesco, p. 102 (SC/74/WS/16
58. Kent, Allen. (1966). *Information analysis and retrieval.* New York: Jonh Wiley, p. 283
59. Weisman, Herman M. (1972). *Information systems, services* and centers. *op. cit.*, p. 34-35

60. Atherton, Pauline. (1977). *Handbook of information systems and services. op. cit.*, p. 125
61. Soergel, Degobert. (1985). Organising information-principles of data base and retrieval systems. Orlando: Academic, p. 98-99
62. Atherton, Pauline (1977). *Handbook of information systems and services. op. cit.*, p. 125-127
63. Soergel, Dagobert. (1985). Organising information ... *op.cit.*, p. 97-98
64. Weisman, Herman M. (1972). Information systems, services and centers. *op. cit.*, p. 37-38
65. Conard, Carleton C. (1967). Coordination and integration of technical information services. *Journal of chemical documentation*. Vol. 7 May, p.111-115
66. Weisman, Heerman M. (1972). Information systems, services and centers. *op. cit*, p. 38-40
67. Wasserman, Paul and Daniel, Evelyn. (1969). Library and information center management. *Annual Review of Information Science and Technology*. Vol. 4, p. 405-438
68. Weisman (1972). Information systems... *op. cit.*, p. 41
69. Atherton, Pauline. (1977). *Handbook of information systems... op. cit.*, p. 57-58.
70. Unesco. (1985). Information networking in population education *op. cit.*, p. 51
71. Costello, John C. (1964). The Charter: A 'must' for effective information system, planning and design. *Journal of Chemical Documentation*. Vol. 4, January,p. 120
72. Weisman, Herman M. (1972). *Information Systems. op. cit.*, Appendix-A p. 182-199
73. Atherton, Pauline. (1977). Handbook of Information systems,services, *op. cit.*, p. 193
74. *ibid.*, p. 60-61
75. Weisman, Herman M. (1972). Information systems, services and centers. *op. cit.*, p. 50-51
76. Orr, R.M. (1973). Measuring the goodness of library services. *Journal of Documentation*. Vol. 29, p.315-332
77. Vickery, Brien and Vickery, Alina. (1987). *Information science in theory and practice*. London: Butterworths, p. 263
78. Line, M.B. (1974). Draft Definitions. *Aslib Proceedings*. Vol. 26, p. 87
79. Orr. R.M. (1973). Measuring the goodness of library services. *op. cit.*, p. 315-332
80. Vickery and Vickery (1987). Information science..... *op. cit.*, p. 264
81. Saraceivic, T. (1970). The concept of relevance in information science *In introduction to information science* edited by T. Saraceivic and others. New York: Bowker, p.111-151
82. Vickery and Vickery (1987). *Information science, theory and practice. op. cit.*, p. 266
83. Burch, John G, Jr. And Strater, Felix R. Jr. (1974). *Information systems: theory and practice*. California: Hamilton, p.362
84. Soergel, Dagobert. (1985). Organising information: principles of data base and retrieval system, *op.cit.*, p. 390
85. Vickery and Vickery. (1987). Information science.... *op.cit.*, p. 268
86. *ibid.*, p. 270-271
87. Soergel, Dagobert. (1985). Organising information: principles of data base and retrieval system. *op. cit.*, p. 118-121

7

NATIONAL INFORMATION SYSTEM FOR EDUCATION IN INDIA A PROPOSED MODEL

Need

The educational system in a dynamic society cannot remain static and has to contribute to the process of social, economic and technological changes of a country. In such a situation educational reforms are needed continuously. Thus educational reform is not a matter of debate in India. What is, however, still debatable is the content and direction of the reform and the objectives to be achieved through the reformed educational system.

To make the educational policy able to provide answers to 'why education'; 'how education' and 'what type of education' and 'contents of the system', it is necessary to make the concerned–planners, administrators, teachers, researchers and documentalists–aware of the education prospectively and retrospectively.

The age-old idea that education is some kind of social service performed by a welfare state is no longer valid and today education is the most critical input into the entire processes of social, economic, political and cultural transformation of India.

When it is said that education is the most powerful tool for change, it follows that it must train the minds of the educated to cope with the change. Educational system throughout the length and breadth of India must actively promote that value system and outlook which is consistent with the kind of society we wish to establish. In the fast changing world of today no education system can be frozen into a mould. It would need periodic revision and change to enable the educated to grapple with social, economic and technological changes.[1]

India has an abundance of recorded information, not shortage, even in the field of education. However, this precious resource is concentrated in relatively few locations, often virtually inaccessible to millions of people and is lying largely untapped. Thus, the challenge is to find the means for making these resources available to more people through an effective identification of location and distribution system.

The rapid growth of research and development activities in the field of education has necessitated the building up of information facilities in India. In view of the increasing role of education in the economic and social development of the country, there is a pressing need to speed up the utilization of research results in education and to improve the transfer of new and adequate information methodology to assist further development of planning and management of education in government administration and research. Further steps must be taken in the development of information services which should be able to meet the information requirements; increasing them as regards the quantity and deepening them as regards the quality of information.

To achieve this objective isolated libraries would not be in a position to supply the desired information to the patrons. This can be achieved through an information system or a network.

The basic objective of a network is to provide better services to patrons of member libraries. 'Better' can be defined in quantitative terms, for example, lower cost, access to more materials, more rapid availability of materials; 'better' can also be defined in qualitative terms, such as convenience of access and hospitableness of the network environment, both for librarians and patrons. This basic objective of network entails a shift in the philosophy of member libraries from reliance on 'local holdings' to reliance on 'access' to materials held elsewhere.[2]

Creation of an effective national library and information network to serve all engaged in the field of education in India is a cornerstone of the proposed national programme.

Before undertaking this, it is necessary to understand the existing educational information system of India which needs to be ultimately transformed to the desired information system in education. For this purpose the existing educational information system is outlined in the next section.

Existing Educational Information System

The development of sound education policies, plans and programmes requires a variety of information. A constant flow of information, to and from all groups taking part in the educational enterprise, such as policy makers, administrators, researchers, teacher educators, teachers and members of the community at large, is required for awareness of innovation and improvement in our educational system.

In India the Central Government acts as the coordinating authority for dissemination of information at the national level. There is no single integrated system of educational information although there are several systems operating for the various administrative functions at the centre, state or district level. The six parallel educational information systems working in India are:[3]

(i) Statistical Information System;
(ii) Budget and Accounts Information System;
(iii) Administrative Information System;
(iv) Information System for Planning Purposes;
(v) Monitoring and Evaluation Information System; and
(vi) Information System of Research and Studies.

Out of all these systems, the statistical information system is well established with a large network at national, state and lower levels of administration. Budget and accounts information which needs to be standardized for all parts of the country is operating under the directions of the Union Ministry of Finance.

The system of information for administration varies from one administration unit to another and from one level of administration to another. It is not standardized.

The system of information for planning purposes owes its origin and utility to the formulation of Annual and Five Year Plans at various levels.

The system of information for monitoring and evaluation was developed as a part of Plan-information system. But now it is tending to emerge as an independent system. At the state level, there are quarterly progress reports on various Plan schemes for all sectors of education which form part of the system of monitoring in the planning process.

The information on research and studies is scattered and limited. Research and studies conducted or sponsored by the government are either in typed or cyclostyled form and are usually for limited circulation. Their findings are used for policy and planning purposes. As they are generally not in published form and also are unpriced, their dissemination is equal to naught. In the case of independent research, particularly by universities, the impact is almost negligible in governmental work because such research is not directed to assist any specific governmental activity.

Out of the above mentioned six information systems considered to be useful for education, the two systems, the Statistical and the Research and studies have special significance for our present study. The other four can be covered in the ambit of these two.

The Ministry of HRD, Department of Education plays a major role in ensuring a coordinated development of education all over the country. The States have the major responsibility in administering education, particularly at the school level.

For the coordination and determination of standards in higher education, the UGC has been established by an Act of Parliament. The NCERT is engaged in promoting the quality of school education throughout the country. The NIEPA provides technical support to the Ministry in educational planning and administration.

At the State level, by and large the State Education Department is vested with the policy, coordination and administration. The Directorates of Education are responsible for implementation through the region/ district and block levels organisations.[4]

Outline of the Educational Statistical System

Under the existing system of collection of educational statistics, the Ministry of HRD obtains certain basic data from the State Governments which is collected annually on census basis.

The responsibility for collection of statistics largely rests with the Ministry of HRD, Office of the Registrar General, the Institute of Applied Manpower Research, the National Sample Survey Organisation, NCERT, UGC, Planning Commission and other similar agencies.

Information System on Research and Studies

There is no formal system of dissemination like regular publication and it is used for only official purposes which is restricted to a few only.

There is no regular indexing and abstracting service system in the education field. At some places such services are given but they are irregular and for in house consumption only. The sources of information are also limited to those available in the institution library. But even these are either not regular or are very much behind schedule, or their coverage in education is not comprehensive.

Objectives of the Proposed System

Creation of an effective national library and information network to serve all in the field of education is a cornerstone of the national programme of educational activities.

The objectives of the information system are:

(i) to provide equal access to information. For this the variable type of users needs, type of member library and type of materials are to be taken into account;

(ii) to give a positive net effect to the library user in terms of access to more materials or services, to provide local and increased service at the least cost. The activities involved in realising this objective are (a) sharing the burden of purchasing of materials, (b) sharing the burden of processing of the material, (c) sharing of services, (d) sharing of human expertise, and (e) increasing use of modern technology i.e. computers and/or telecommunication;

(iii) to bring about a change in the attitude of member libraries. They are required to change from a 'local holdings' attitude to a 'shared access' orientation. Members should be completely responsive to the stated goals and needs of the network;

(iv) to improve services to patrons of member libraries by filling up the existing lacunae and establishing new services;

(v) to develop a nation–wide network of libraries and information centres for effective sharing of recorded information. It will require an integrated system encompassing institutions and organisations at the national, state, district and institutional levels;

(vi) to develop a linkages with other related information services within the country and other education information services existing in other parts of the world;

(vii) to develop the necessary infrastructure for the development of manpower to handle the information on education effectively;

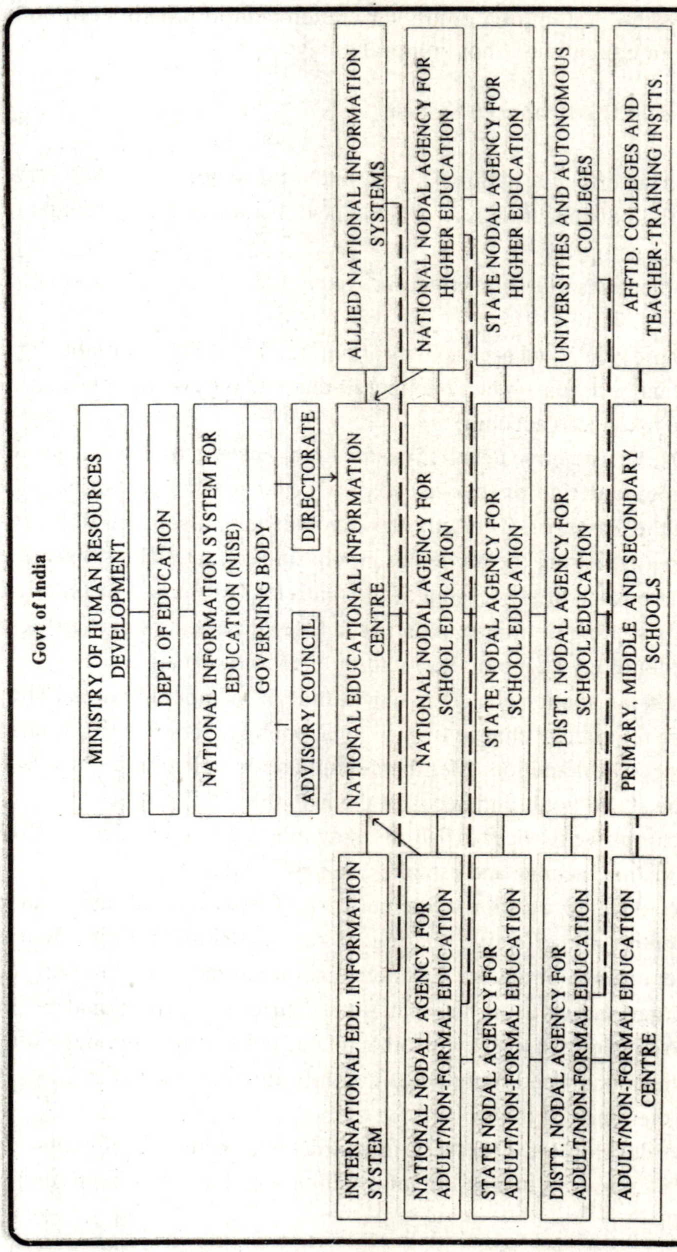

Fig. 7.1: National Information System for Education in India (NISE) – A Proposed Model

(viii) to develop internationally compatible national standards for information techniques and methods; and

(ix) to introduce and develop modern information technology and managerial methods in information work.

Planning and Coordination

The NISE is to be planned and coordinated taking into account both the goals to be achieved and the standardized methods to be used by the system, and knitting the units together as well as the various special characteristics of the information work.

The questionnaire and interview indicate that the National Information System for Education in India should be a centralised system in administration and organisation. The decentralisation does not suit the system taking into consideration the working and financing arrangement of the existing functional units in the field of education.

At present two main information systems are working in the country i.e. NISSAT in the field of Science and Technology and NASSDOC in the field of Social Sciences. NASSDOC has regional centres for Eastern zone, Western zone, Southern zone and Northern zone at geographical levels whereas NISSAT network comprises broadly the Sectoral System and the Local Information Units. The NISSAT sectoral centres are to cater to the information requirements concerning the particular discipline, mission or product. They are also expected to coordinate with all the remaining information centres (called Local Information Units (LIUs) in that particular area. Local information units provide more or less in-house information services in the concerned discipline or subject to its parent body, which may be research laboratory, R&D institution, industrial/establishment, government department or other similar institution. The LIU is to depend upon the sectoral centre for services which are not available with it and also to feedback to the sectoral centre, all the internally generated information.

Taking a clue from the working of NISSAT/NASSDOC the different stages or regions in education like higher education, secondary education, primary education and non–formal education cannot be organised into sectors or regions. Education is a unified discipline and it cannot be divided into regions for overall policy and result. For getting a unified system and overall development a well-knit system is to be developed. The pattern of Registrar General Office for census operation is more suitable for NISE.

The governing body of system will have full control over the National Centre, State Centres, District Centres. The District Centres will extend required support to the institutional centres in terms of equipment and financial assistance for collection and services. The staff, services and equipments upto district level will be fully financed and controlled by the system. The staff will have the hierarchical pattern for promotion etc.

Central, state and district authorities will provide the land, building and facilities for establishment of the system units/centres and issue necessary orders for collection of documents, information and data by the system units. The National nodal point should be a new set-up, whereas the existing SCERT and the Chief District Education Officer should be given the responsibilities of functioning as State nodal point and District nodal point respectively. Institutional library should take care of the institutional centre.

At the national level, Central Department of Education would co-operate, while at the state and district levels, the State Departments of Education would extend full co-operation. At institutional level the state, district and Principal/Headmaster and the system authorities would take care to develop the library and its proper functioning so that it could become an effective unit at the root level to the system.

The different authorities involved in the system should co-operate on various principles (legal framework, and other similar regulations, voluntary co-operation, financial and other contractual arrangements, etc.) which must be worked out in detail, taking into consideration the specific characteristics and the functioning of the units. A mechanism for co-ordination of the sub-units within the NISE should be planned and established, based upon decision to be taken in these respects by the governing body of the system.

Finance

Financing of the system should be shared both by the Central Government and State Governments. Their share would be 50 per cent or as the governing body of the system will decide. The share of each State may be determined either on the basis of the population of the State or the per capita income of the State. A very small fee can be charged from the users for the services, such as translation, reprographic services, inter-library loan facilities for individual use, preparation of bibliography or documentation list, literature survey or state-of-the art report for an individual use and other services which are required by an individual for his private use.

Translation Arrangement

The survey and interview expressed that there should be arrangement for both permanent translators as well as a panel of translators. Translation from English or Hindi to regional languages, and vice versa should be arranged on permanent basis while a panel of translators can be identified for foreign language and inter-regional language translations. The translation aspects should be dealt with at the national level centre and the state level centres only.

Language of the System

English would be the language of the system for all operations being undertaken at the national level. At state, district and institutional levels regional language would also be used for dissemination purposes.

Membership of the Information System

In the education field, potential network members are easily identifiable. At the national level are the libraries of various institutions/organisations working under the administrative control of the Department of Education, Ministry of HRD, UGC, Association of Indian Universities (AIU), NCERT, NIEPA, Directorate General of Adult Education and all other institutions dealing with educational activities at the national level.

At the State level, State Departments of Education, State Councils of Educational Research and Training (SCERTs)/State Institutes of Education (SIEs), Directorates of Education, Universities, Teacher Training Institutes, organizations dealing with adult/non-formal education and all other institutions/organisations dealing with educational activities at the State level.

At the district level, libraries of the Chief Education Officer, District Education Officer (DEO) for school sector and DEO for Adult/Non-formal Education sector, Resource Centre for open school, District Vocational Training Centre, District Institute of Education Training (DIET) and all other offices dealing with educational activities at the district level.

At the lower level, the membership of the network can be extended to

Village Education Committee, Adult Education Centres, NFE Centres, schools, colleges and teacher training colleges. In addition to this other institutions related to the activities of education would be the members of the proposed network. At the international level it would co-operate with the educational networks of foreign countries like ERIC or Euroedudoc and international organisations e.g. Unesco and International Bureau of Education (IBE).

At the national level, the network would cooperate with the other allied information systems of the country e.g. NASSDOC, NISSAT and NIC NET etc.

Governance

Libraries working together, sharing their services and materials, can meet the full needs of their users. It is true that inter-dependence among libraries is growing. But the question is whether the library network and inter-dependence grow in a logical and integrated manner. The answer lies in the planning and development of an efficient and effective national library and information services in education that seek to provide effective transmission from all educational information institutional sources to all educational information institutional receivers.

For this we require a good governance. Every organisational unit must be managed and at some level of organisational complexity a policy-setting body above operational management is required. We refer to this higher management as governance. Governance provides stability to making a network 'an organisation controlled by principles and not by persons.' The purpose of governance is to provide a mechanism for identifying goals and objectives of the library network; for the establishment of policies by which the library will operate; and for the resolution of conflict; governance is also the mechanism for overcoming the barriers to networking and development of appropriate environment for cooperation. Montgomery and Dawlin[5] state that "governance in the context of library networks is the sum of the relationships between participants (and their institutions) and the network organisation(s)."

"The purpose of the governing body can be stated as the exercise of authority to set policy and objectives that serve the needs of the network's constituency and to direct management to attain these objectives. (Constituency means all levels of the network hierarchy). In so doing, governance must ensure that the policies and objectives adopted and the actions taken are for the benefit of the network organisation per se which must have priority consideration over any individual organisation making up its constituency."[6]

According to Stevens, library network governance may be categorised into: (i) governance by government, (ii) governance by the membership under a legal charter and by-laws, and (iii) governance under a quasi-government body.[7]

The results of our questionnaire and interview favour the second type of governance i.e. under a legal charter and by laws.

A Statutory Body

As we have already recognised that NISE would be a new federal agency and keeping in view the role and functions to be performed by the NISE, statutory body is recommended.

The purpose of the statue is to create a basic legal structure to deal effectively with the problems that will accompany the development of an effective national system. Parliament should authorise the Executive Branch to proceed and appropriate central funds to carry out the work, and therefore, it should be under an Act of the Parliament. This ensures access to library and information services for all the nation's citizens.

Federal regulation in the public interest is considered vital for several reasons, such as the ultimate resolution of the copyright question in a manner that balances proprietary interests against the public interest in effecting access to recorded knowledge. The world knowledge record is one that requires the active participation of the federal government. Parliamentary action is required to provide an adequate statutory base for inter-state library networks.

Attention must also be given to the question of the future of that agency as a policy formulating, planning research and coordinating mechanism at the national level.

The governance should exert financial control, develop an organisation that would assist the network constituency in meeting their own service requirements, provide a management structure capable of achieving the stated objectives of the network organisation.

Composition of the Governing Council

It is proposed that governing council may consist of 15 members from government and user categories. Users must be included in this educational and marketing effort. They should understand the costs and benefits of resource sharing, the role of the technology, and the problems of funding and governance. The following membership of the Council is recommended:

(i) Chairman – Central Education Minister
(ii) 4 State representatives – from Departments of Education of States. One member each from the Eastern Zone, Western Zone, Northern Zone and Southern Zone. The representation should be for 2 years and should rotate alphabetically within the States of a Zone;
(iii) Member Secretary - Director, NISE
(iv) One Planner – Representative of Planning Commission;
(v) One Administrator – Representative of Central Department of Education;
(vi) One Financial Adviser – Representative of Ministry of Finance;
(vii) 3 Educationists – one from Higher Education sector one from School Education sector, one from Non-formal/Adult Education sector;
(viii) 2 Librarian/Information Scientists. One from University level and one from school level;
(ix) One Technology expert

The term of Director, NISE should be of 6 years and the other nominated members of the Governing Council of the NISE should be of 5 years so that both change and continuity can be achieved. The meeting of governing council may be held twice a year.

Functions of Governing Council

The role of the Governing Council is that of a planner, organiser, financier and evaluator, Principal functions envisaged are:

(i) to oversee the operation of a nation-wide service;
(ii) to encourage the extension of service to all possible areas and groups;
(iii) to ensure a comprehensive national collection;
(iv) to reduce barriers to the free flow of published materials, and to communication;
(v) to make available sufficient funds;
(vi) to facilitate the full development of information dissemination in India and abroad;
(vii) to assist in the establishment of a nationwide library and information service;

(viii) to assist states, districts and institutions in establishing systems of inter connection and information dissemination;

(ix) to increase equitable access to information by all citizens;

(x) to assist in conducting planning, research, demonstration, training and dissemination activities of value to a nationwide information and library interconnection service;

(xi) to encourage the creation of new libraries and information centres and the improvement of existing services so as to enhance local, state and regional developments;

(xii) to encourage the application of technology to library and information services for purposes of greater efficiency, increased and more equitable access to information;

(xiii) to find the ways that would assure maximum freedom of access and expression and act to protect libraries and information centres from interference with the content of materials in their care and from restrictions on circulation;

(xiv) to set a direction for action; and

(xv) to establish the standard by which library network effectiveness should be measured, etc.

It is the people who matter rather than the forms of governance. People who are sincere and dedicated to the cause can make a network function. Simplicity in governance is probably a key to successful operation. The network must contribute to the central activity – the main mission i.e. the service. If proper service is provided, the user community would not bother much about the system or its governance.

Executive Committe

As Governing Council cannot meet so often, another body, therefore, is needed to meet at short intervals for attending to the urgent matters. It can be called as 'executive committee'. The executive committee should consist of five members. The composition is proposed as shown below:

(i) Director, NISE–President

(ii) One Member–Representative of Ministry of Finance

(iii) One member–Representative of Ministry of HRD

(iv) One member–Representative of Planning Commission

(v) One member–A person of standing in the field of library and information science.

The meetings of Executive Committee may be called as frequently as warranted by the Director, NISE for any consultation or decision.

Organisational Units of Information System

Survey and interview made it very clear that the proposed National Information System for Education (NISE) should be of four levels i.e. national, state, district and institutional.

Nodal Point at National Level

Majority of the users are of the view that the institution to be the Nodal point at national level should be a new establishment. Quite a good number of respondents and interviewees suggested that one or the other of the existing organisations at the national level e.g. Ministry of HRD–Department of Education, NCERT, NIEPA, UGC and National Library can be developed as a Nodal point at the National level. Yet, none of the above mentioned organisations was considered by a majority to be able to fulfil the objectives of the proposed system. NCERT which was recommended by the largest number of respondents could be a possibility to a great extent but with the present constitution and set up, NCERT also probably cannot fulfil the obligations of the proposed NISE. The clear-cut verdict is that there should be a new set-up, though it can be established in the NIE (NCERT) Campus at New Delhi and NCERT headquarter's library can be developed as a National Library of Education to make full use of its existing resources.

Once it has been decided that there should be a new organisation to be the Nodal point for national level of NISE, its working and activities would be as mentioned under:

Divisions

It would have––

(i) National Education Library
(ii) Documentation Division
(iii) Translation Division
(iv) Publication Division
(v) Reprographic Division

(vi) Information Unit at Department of Education (Ministry of Human Resource Development)
(vii) Regional Centres Division; and
(viii) Administration Division

Activities

The activities of the national level Nodal point should be as given below:

(i) Relating to Library, including inter-library loan
(ii) Relating to documentation
(iii) Relating to information analysis
(iv) Relating to referral services
(iv) Relating to clearing house functions
(vi) Relating to extension and advisory services.

National Education Library

National Education Library should ensure that there exists within the country at least one accessible copy of each significant publication of worldwide educational literature. The library should perform the functions of acquisitions, cataloguing, storage and conservation.

- This library should have a cooperative acquisition programme with the material relevant to the various national research institutions in the field of education but integrated through a national union catalogue centrally situated and regionally distributed through reprographic techniques.
- It should act as dormitory for housing old periodicals
- It should also make a special effort to collect books by Indian authors and periodicals in Indian languages.
- It should handle all inter-library loan business
- It should help in fulfilling the NISE's national and international obligations and in supporting its documentation activities.
- The building up of the collection should be in stages.

Documentation Centre

The activities under the field of documentation centre include:

(a) to be a depository for reports of educational work of the nation, both published and unpublished;

(b) to publish bibliographies, abstracts, reviews, catalogues, reference works, serials and all other works brought out by information analyses centre/data centre of the NISE;

(c) to provide documentation services including translation and reprographic services; and

(d) to organise advanced training programmes in the fields of information, documentation, translation, reprography etc.

Information Analysis Centre/Data Centre

The activities of this unit should include:

(a) to collect, maintain, store and retrieve everything related to information and data about the educational field;

(b) to analyse, synthesize and evaluate information and data for providing critical compilations e.g. data sheets, literature searches, bibliographies, references, summaries, directories etc;

(c) to communicate the information to others through State of the art reports, current awareness services (CAS), selective dissemination information service (SDI), accession lists, bulletins, newsletters etc;

(d) to respond to enquiries.

Referral Centre

The Referral Centre unit of the system should undertake the following activities:

(a) to collect, on a world-wide basis, information about data and information sources in the field of education;

(b) to prepare a comprehensive inventory of the kinds of data/information/services available from these sources with a detailed subject index for access;

(c) to guide users to the appropriate sources of the required data or information.

To facilitate referral, specialized card index files have to be kept on:

(i) research studies, dissertations, expert reports, bibliographies, surveys, research evaluation and other documents of potential interest;

(ii) government sponsored, individual, institutional and international development projects;
(iii) experts available to serve as consultants, or help with projects;
(iv) authorities, organisations, institutions or agencies carrying out or giving assistance in the field of education;
(v) contacts in concerned countries; and
(vi) conferences, seminars, exhibitions which directly or indirectly concern the educational developments of the country; and (vii) data on training programmes for experts, professionals and users etc.

Clearing House

The clearing house activities of the system should include:

(i) to collect special types of documents in order to redistribute them upon request or voluntarily. Union catalogues and lists are compiled for this specific purpose;
(ii) to act as a link between groups engaged in research in the same field;
(iii) to publish compilations of previously unpublished materials and seek out users instead of waiting to be approached by them; and
(iv) to evaluate available information, adopt and process it to meet the requirements of potential users.

Extension and Advisory Services

The extension and advisory services of the system should include:

(i) personal visits by the experts of the system to the state educational information centres, conferences and courses on searching for handling and utilizing educational information;
(ii) to discuss problems, assist in the framing of enquiries and direct clients to the most relevant sources of information and assistance available.

For the above mentioned activities of the National Nodal point, the activities of different units can be combined and thus smaller number of units can operate the system successfully, if system authorities feel so.

Administrative Division

The administration division should take care of the administration, organization and coordination of the system as a whole so that there should be smooth functioning of all the four levels of the system and the system can serve the education community to their entire satisfaction.

State Level Nodal Point

The survey reveals it very clearly that at the State level, either State Council of Educational Research and Training (SCERT) or in its absence, State Institute of Education (SIE) should be the Nodal point at State level.

The State level centre of the system should perform its activities with the following units:

(i) State education library
(ii) Documentation unit
(iii) Translation and Reprographic facilities
(iv) Administrative unit.

The reference, referral and clearing house activities would be taken care by documentation unit and administrative unit of the State level centre. The centre would be dealing directly with the national level and other State level centres.

The administrative unit of the centre would control the working of district units of the system and provide all extension and advisory services to the district units.

The main activities of the State centre are;

(i) to survey the information sources of the State and organise their mobilsation for covering the information demand of the State;
(ii) to supplement the acquisition's of the district and institutional units of the State;
(iii) to establish, maintain, update and publish State union catalogues;
(iv) to establish a strong reprographic unit and to serve the state with reprographic copies of information services;
(v) to procure, on request, documents within and outside the State;
(vi) to prepare and publish current awareness services on unpublished literature;

(vii) to assist the development of information services at all levels (institution, district, State and national).
(viii) to provide translation facilities limited only from English and/ or Hindi to the State languge or vise versa.

District Units

District units of the system are proposed to be set up at the office of the Chief Education Officer. Its main activities should include:

(i) District education library
(ii) Documentation unit within the library for special collection of reports, information and data;
(iii) Reprographic facilities; and
(iv) Development of its own data bank;

The library along with its collection of reports and data should serve the users located at district levels. The centre should deal with the State level centre and inter-district centres. The centre should have proper facilities for communication activities. It should prepare the union catalogues of books, reports and periodicals held by all the institutional libraries of the district. It should provide current indexing and abstracting services including SDI, subject bibliographies, subject union catalogues and information retrieval on request.

Institutional Unit

The base level of the system would be located in the institution. The activities include:

(i) library with all the required documents and equipments for the functioning of the parent body;
(ii) an accession list of books and periodicals;
(iii) inter-library loan;
(iv) communication with district centre and concerned institutions of the State; and
(v) preparation and display of the list of publications and the services of the information units at higher levels (District, State and National Information Centres).

Operational Techniques

The survey and interview reveal and recommend that NISE should be designed to accommodate both traditional and modern methods of technology for handling of information and operating services to the users keeping in view the existing financial, manpower and physical resources in the country. Traditional methods will have to be adopted for utilising the existing strength and skills of manpower due to the paucity of financial resources. Modern technology will have to be adopted for utilising the internal and external information bases to provide quicker and fuller services to the users. The system will have to be based upon highly developed reprographic equipment, telecommunication facilities and computers. Parallel with the development of new techniques and their application to information work, manual methods will have to be continued, traditional skills will have to be utilised and expanded. Information staff will have to be trained both in traditional and modern machine-based methods.

Computer applications must be very carefully planned and designed for preparation of large-scale indexes of information sources, the utilisation of foreign information services and the organisation of data banks and data retrieval. Computer applications may be applied first of all to library operation and later on to information retrieval.

Coverage

The NISE should cover education in its broadest sense, including educational information, information for population, public health, employment, economic development of the country, sociology, culture, physical education, environment, rural development, psychology, scientific and technological development and policy, international understanding, and other fields closely related to education and on the application of research results and technical knowhow.

As a consequence, the NISE has to handle not only traditional and conventional sources of information (books and periodicals) but also non-conventional sources like research reports conference proceedings, government documents, monographs, newspapers, reference works, dissertations and theses, survey reports, audio-visual materials, museum objects, abstracts, indexes state-of-the-art, literature review, digests, bibliographies, maps, atlases and data belonging to various fields.

Priority should be assigned to basic statistics, curriculum materials, teaching and training methodologies, research findings, policy making and management of education, case studies on education etc.

The coverage would fall in the following pattern of priority:

(i) Current Indian literature (complete)
(ii) Retrospective Indian literature (substantially)
(iii) Current foreign literature (substantially)
(iv) Retrospective foreign literature (marginally)
(v) Literature belonging to third world (substantially)
(vi) Literature belonging to 1st world (substantially)
(vii) Literature belonging to 2nd world (marginally)

In addition to this, NISE has to arrange the establishment of data banks for the storage and retrieval of numerical and other data from the fields of education, economics, statistics, demography, labour, employment and training of various professions and vocations etc. making use of existing foreign and indigenous data sources or extracting data from other information sources.

First priority should be assigned to providing information needed to planners and administrators in the decision-making process at all levels in a convenient form.

Functions and Services

The functions are dependent on various factors, such as the network topology, the resources, the geographical area covered, the type of member libraries and the technology utilized to perform the functions.

The need to study functions is crucial to the design of library network. The functions to be performed by a network determine its physical structure as well as its logical organisation. To know the functions of an information system is important for designing a cost-effective network and to be able to make valid judgements regarding their performance. It is believed that designing networks to fit a specific set of functions is preferable to designing functions to fit a specific network. The impact of a function performed by a network upon other functions performed within the member libraries, or by another network utilized by the member libraries, is also important to the design and evaluation of library networks.

Networks currently perform an array of functions involving numerous activities, a variety of technological methods, a diversity of human expertise and solving of a plethora of problems.

Network functions fall into three primary classes:

(A) those that serve the patrons directly;
(B) those that serve the member libraries directly and the patrons indirectly, and
(C) those that support the network structure.[9]

(*A*) Functions that serve the patrons, directly would include:

(i) Inter-library loan. It relates to the photocopying and delivery of materials;
(ii) Inter-system reference. It depends upon a communication sub-system;
(iii) Inter-system referral. Its bases are a file of resources and the communication system; and
(iv) Continuing education for professionals within the network, or for patrons in general.

(*B*) Functions that serve the library interests directly and the patrons indirectly would include:

(i) *Co-operative acquisitions*

We believe the function of cooperative acquisitions is critical to any successful library network. The term 'cooperative acquisition' is used to cover all types of acquisition programmes e.g. joint ownership, centralized purchasing, specialised areas of acquisition etc. The joint ownership in the present Indian conditions is not feasible. The concept of centralized purchasing was given a try by State Trading Corporation (STC) in the field of foreign periodicals acquisition earlier but the venture did not prove successful. For our purpose the 'co-operative acquisitions' mean only the last programme i.e. specialised areas of acquisition. In other words an existing subject area strength is recognised, and the member library with that strength is encouraged to collect comprehensively in this area; or alternatively areas are assigned to the member libraries so that collection of each member library is comprehensive in its own field.

Co-operative acquisitions cannot be effectively implemented without an effective inter-library loan system because the fear of not being able to borrow when required, would defeat its purpose. Co-operative acquisition will also fail if an adequate delivery system does not exist.

Though in the present situation of existing inter-library loan system and inadequate delivery system, the co-operative acquisition programme is difficult to succeed, yet an effort will have to be made to identify the special collection strength for particular participant libraries with the mutual consent and agreement among the member institutions of the information system. Inspite of its difficulties, the concept is plain and it is possible to make a headway.

(ii) The Technical Processing

It involves procedure for acquisition, cataloguing and other means of resource identification and location, and circulation control systems.

For this the proposed system would standardize the practices in all these areas of activities so that participation among the network members becomes easy and smooth and service to the patrons becomes comfortable.

(*C*) Functions that support the network activities include:

(i) Evaluation activities such as compilation of statistics, analysis of performance and user evaluation studies;
(ii) Staff and user training activities;
(iii) The determination of costs and setting of fees, if any; and
(iv) Communication activities such as publications, the holding of meetings etc.

The functions range from the very common inter-library loan to the less common function of serving as a clearing house for materials. The following functions/services for the proposed network have been derived from the survey of users through a questionnaire which was subsequently supplemented by a personal interview:

(i) Inter-library loan;
(ii) Reference;
(iii) Referral (referring requests or request to another library);
(iv) Bibliographic access;
(v) Publications (newsletters, digests, compendium, reviews);
(vi) Union lists (serials, reference books, reports, Govt. documents etc);
(vii) Literature searching;
(viii) Abstracting/indexing;
(ix) Compilation of educational data and projections;
(x) System should also take the microfilming keeping in view the shortage of space and delivery problems;

(xi) Translation services. (from foreign languages to English and from regional languages to English, Hindi and in the desired regional language);

(xii) Photocopying;

(xiii) Standardization (establishing minimum standards: information system should develop standards for acquisitions, circulation, inventory control, cataloguing and processing);

(xiv) Delivery (transmission or transportation of package of information);

(xv) Communication (establishing and maintaining channels of communication among members of the network); and

(xvi) Continuing education (training of users, library staff and patrons: how to use network capabilities).

The broad features of the model are outlined in the foregoing chapter and the legal framework and operational details are to be worked out while implementing the model. Further this is not a rigid model and requires constant revision according to the changing user needs which need to be identified through periodic surveys.

REFERENCES

1. Haksar, P.N. (1985) Foreword to *Education in India (1781-1985)*. Policies, Planning and Implementation by Kuldip Kaur. Chandigarh: Centre for Research in Rural and Industrial Development.
2. Kent, Allen. (1979). Network anatomy and network objectives In *Structure and Governance of Library Network* by Allen Kent and Thomas J. Golvin. New York: Marcel Dekker, Inc., p.4
3. Kapoor, M.N. (1984). Information Management In *Educational Management in India*. New Delhi: NIEPA, p.100
4. *ibid.*, p.97
5. Montgomery, K. Leon and Dowlin, C. Edwin. (1979). The Governance of Library Networks; purposes and expectations In *Structure and Governance of Library Network* by Allen Kent and Thomas J. Golvin. *op. cit.*, p. 179
6. Avram, Henriette D. (1979). Governance of Library Networks: A call for action In *Structure and Governance of Library Network* by Allen Kent and Thomas J. Golvin. *Op. cit.*, p. 222
7. Stevens, Charles H. (1977). *Governance of Library Networks. Library Trends*, Fall, p. 222
8. Williams, James G. and Flynn, Roger. (1979). Network topology; functions of existing networks In *Structure and Governance of Library networks* by Allen Kent and Thomas J. Golvin. *Op. cit.*, p. 51

RESUME

The importance of education in all aspects of National development has been recognised by economic planners long time back as education is a resource as well as a factor of production. The age-old idea that education is some kind of social service performed by a welfare state is no longer valid and today education is the most critical input into the entire process of social, economic, political and cultural transformation of a nation.

Education is the most powerful tool for change. As such, educational system of India must actively promote that value system and outlook which is consistent with the kind of society we wish to achieve. In the fast changing world of today no education system can be frozen into a mould. It would need periodic revision and change to enable the education to grapple with social, economic and technological changes.

The development of sound education policies, plans and programmes requires a variety of information. A constant flow of information, to and from all groups taking part in the educational enterprize, such as policy makers, planners, administrators, teachers, educators, teachers and members of the community at large, is required to achieve the goals set for our educational system.

India being a vast and diverse country, its information needs in education are not only huge but also complex. The out-dated methods of collection, processing and dissemination of information in education followed in India cannot cater to the modern needs of the society. Hence the need to study the existing infrastructure and design a modern information system for education in India. Keeping the above in view the present study is undertaken: (i) to study in brief the existing education systems of India, U.K. and U.S.A.; (ii) to study the existing information systems of these three countries in the field of education; (iii) to make a study of user needs and preferences through a survey and on the basis of these to evaluate the effectiveness of the existing information services, programmes and products in India, keeping in view the availability of such facilities in UK and USA;

and (iv) to evolve a model for the National Information System for Education in India.

The study has been undertaken on the hypothesis that an efficient and comprehensive educational information system equipped with modern information technology can contribute to a great extent to the rapid growth of research and development activities in the field of Indian education.

Education Systems in U.K., U.S.A. and India

This chapter covered in the first place the general background of the countries, physical features, demographic cultural and economic aspects. Next the educational objectives of the governments, policies of education, administration, education structure and finance have been discussed. Within the education system the general education, childhood, primary, secondary, vocational and higher education stages have also been discussed. Non–formal and adult education, teacher education, special education and educational research of the three countries are the other aspects forming the subject matter of the chapter.

The basic objectives of education in all the three countries i.e. U.K., U.S.A. and India are almost common. In U.K. the emphasis is on developing rationality, respect for moral values and instilling the importance of unity and interdependence of life on the planet whereas in U.S.A. the effort is to provide an opportunity to all children to stretch their minds to full capacity, to develop the ability to adapt to the changes in the society and in general to increase the quality of life. In India the objectives of education are intertwined with the goal of life itself i.e. the self-fulfilment and therefore development of all such human faculties which help achieve this goal.

In England, all education, including technical education is financed by Department of Education (DES) while in India some professional and technical institutions are financed by the Department of Education (Ministry of Human Resource Development) while others are either under Ministry of Industry, or Ministry of Agriculture or some are even under the Ministry of Labour. Diffusion of sources of funding and lack of coordination among the concerned organisations is also a reason for the uneven progress of technical and professional education in India. In U.S.A., though Federal Government is not directly responsible for education, its contributions in the area from time to time are notable. The system of land grants for technical and vocational institutions, is a very strong force behind the successful wide-spread network of technical and vocational institutions all over the country. In U.S.A. there is coordination and co-operation among the industrialists and educational authorities while in India no such links exist.

In U.K. and India, there are not many choices in combinations of a particular course of study while in U.S.A., studies are divided into units and a student can take a fixed number of units, not necessarily from cognate or allied fields. An American student can offer a major in physics with history, Spanish language, beauty culture and psychology as minors.

In U.K. students are admitted after a public examination at the age of eleven and those who aspire to enter a university, need to sit for a university entrance examination. In India admission is on the basis of the school tests. Here, students are examined at every stage and every year. There are no public examinations at the close of High Schools in U.S.A. Some universities conduct the entrance examinations while some others do not.

Educational Information Systems in U.K., U.S.A. and India

The salient features of the educational information systems existing in U.K., U.S.A. and India are studied for formulating an efficient and suitable National Information System in Education for India (NISE). The third chapter outlined the micro-level units of the system i.e. libraries such as public libraries, National library and academic libraries. The library co-operation and networking, the existing library networks and the educational information networks constituted the main theme of this chapter.

Today, compared with other countries, a high standard of voluntary cooperation exists within the various libraries of the UK national network, public library membership is free and the tickets of one authority are accepted by other authorities. Public reference libraries are open and free of charge to all. Public, university and special libraries cooperate and a more responsible National Library Service with a unified control is in operation.

The original library systems of the 'Northern Regional Library System, West Midlands, Wales and Manmouthshire, the South-East, the East Midlands, the North-West, Yorkshire, and the South-West provide a united regional front with the help of union catalogue coordinating with the NCL.

Development in library co-operation, particularly in the special libraries resulted in the publication of many works of co-operative effort such as British National Bibliography, the National Foundation of Educational

Research's Technical Education Abstracts, British Technology Index and British Humanities Index etc.

Co-operation by negotiation has been established with foreign libraries. Redistribution and exchange have been conducted through the British National Book Centre and the National Central Library had undertaken the publication of the British Union catalogue of periodicals (BUCOP), which has made possible the identification of periodicals in all fields of knowledge.

The interlending system in U.K. is operated at National level, regional level and local level through British Library Lending Division, Regional Library Networks and Local Co-operative Scheme respectively. Some of the organisations and services for the networking are: The London and South Eastern Library Region (LASER); Machine Readable Catalogue (MARC); British Library Automated Information Service (BLAISE); Cataloguing-in-Publication; UKMARC current, UKMARC retrospect, Research in British Universities, Polytechnics and college, British Education Index, Birmingham Libraries Co-operative Mechanization Project (BLCMP), South West Academic Libraries Co-operative Automation Project (SWALCAP) and Scottish Libraries Co-operative Automation Project (SCOLCAP) etc.

The Educational Policy Information Centre (EPIC) situated at the National Foundation for Education Research in Slough, Bedfordshire is the National Centre for U.K. EPIC, the UK National unit, is a link to Education Information Network in the European Community (EURYDICE). Out of EPIC has grown the project for the Education Management Information Exchange (EMIE). The aim of the system is to serve the education policy makers.

In U.S.A. library cooperation movement is said to have started in 1853, when Charles Jewett suggested the use of stereotype plates to produce a national union catalogue. The history of on-line networking started with such projects as shared cataloguing between the Columbia, Harvard and Yale medical libraries. In 1968 came the creation of the weekly MARC tape services at the Library of Congress. In 1971 UCLC went on line followed by Bibliographic Automation of large libraries (BALLOTS), Research Libraries Information Network (RLIN), the Washington Library Network etc.

Some other important networks are Research Libraries Group (RIG), South Eastern Library Network, inc. (SULINET), New England Library Information (NELINET). In USA Networks, at the National, Regional and State level are in a very strong position and are functioning very well.

In the field of education, Educational Resources Information Centre (ERIC) is a nation-wide, decentralized, on-line information network for acquiring, selecting, abstracting, indexing, storing, retrieving and disseminating the most significant and timely educational information and related reports. It consists of a co-ordinating staff in Washington DC and 16 clearing houses operated in conjunction with professional organisations across the country. It offers a wide coverage of material in almost any education-related field.

ERIC has been designed to accomplish three main objectives: (i) to guarantee ready access to the world's English language literature relevant to education, (ii) to generate new information products by reviewing, summarising and interpreting current information products on priority topics, and (iii) to infuse information about educational developments and research findings.

Inter-University Educational Information Processing Network (EDUNET) is a nation-wide inter-university educational information processing network. This pilot network was designed to evaluate and assist education, particularly higher education. Through EDUNET, faculty, staff and students at 150 colleges and universities in the United States and several foreign countries can gain access to about two-dozen computers on campuses other than their own. EDUNET is a facilitating network established to enhance the quality of instructional and research computing and to expand the opportunities for computer based resource exchange among institutions of higher education and research.

In India education and development of libraries have been the divided responsibility of Central and State Governments. There is only a voluntary co-operation among the individual libraries and that is limited only to inter-library loan and consultation of library by the individual readers. The borrowing facilities are extended within the same city and through personal approach. The postal rates are prohibitive and delivery of parcels is not quick and safe which in turn discourages the inter-lending arrangements. There is no co-operation among public, academic and research libraries. The possessive nature of the librarians and their personal responsibility towards the safety of the collection stand in the way of co-operation.

Due to lack of efficient transport, communication and modern information technology, library networking has not been developed. In the recent past some efforts have been made in this direction but they are limited to science and technology and social sciences fields. No efforts have been made for the development of educational information system. Only Department of Education (Ministry of Human Resource Development) is the source of statistical information in the field of education.

Methodology

In order to design a suitable National Information System for Education in India, the following information users were identified: educational planners, administrators, teachers, teacher educators, researchers in education and librarians/documentalists in educational organisations. These users belong to all the relevant educational organisations/institutions of the nation such as Ministry of Human Resource Development (Department of Education – Division of Planning), State Departments of Education; Planning Commission - Education Division; National Council of Educational Research and Training (NCERT); State Councils of Educational Research and Training (SCERTs)/State Institutes of Education (SIEs); National Institute of Educational Planning and Administration (NIEPA); Teacher Training Colleges; Universities–Departments of Education; Colleges and senior secondary schools. The total respondents number 355.

An information schedule based on scanning the records of libraries of relevant institutions was prepared for the users of information in education. With the help of this information schedule a tentative questionnaire was developed. It was distributed for 'try out' and after getting suggestions and observations a final questionnaire was drafted. Further, information on the general background of the identified users, their needs, demands and preferences for establishing the information system for education in India was elicited through the pre-designed questionnaire followed by a selective personal interview.

Sample Procedure

Keeping in view the objectives of the study, a select group of experts, who, in their discharge of day to day work, have to depend upon the information system in education, was identified. These experts were working in different institutions. So the selection of the respondents is made in two stages. In the first stage a purposive selection of a sample of institutions was made. After their selection, the respondents were selected at random from among the lists of experts working in them. The purposive approach to sampling was adopted. The purposive selection approach is similar to the rural socio-economic surveys carried out by National Sample Survey Organisation (NSSO) in India.

Analysis and Interpretation of Data

The fifth chapter 'Analysis and Interpretation of Data' covers classificatory and study variables of the respondents. The classificatory variables cover the academic and professional qualifications of the respondents, their nature of work, experience, institutions where they work, time devoted to their subjects, possession of personal libraries and number of books in them, reading of journals and sources of availability of journals to them while study variables include use of library, literature, resources of his information centre, views on National Information System for Education in India (NISE)–its objectives, status, finance, organisational set up, nodal points for cooperation, operational mechanism, services to be rendered by the proposed system, language of the NISE and presentation of regional language materials etc.

An Information System–Concept, Design and Functions

The sixth chapter deals with the different aspects of an information system such as: An Information Network; National information System; Need of an Information System; Basic Characteristics and Objectives; Membership and components of an information system; Types of Information Network; Functions, Organisational units, design consideration and evaluation of an information system. The understanding of the concept, design and functions of an information system, particularly the National Information System/Information network is a *sine-qua-non.* Therefore, the characteristics, objectives, components etc. of such a system are carefully studied. This chapter provided the insights to build up a model of National Information System for Education in India.

National Information System for Education in India–A Proposed Model

The seventh and concluding chapter presented the model which dealt with the objectives, planning and coordination, governance, financing etc. of the National Educational Information System for Education. The functions and services to be rendered, the organisational units of the information network, their interlinking with other networks of the nation dealing with allied subjects, the linkage with international education system and organisation such as Unesco and International Bureau of Education (IBE) etc. are outlined. The organizational, financial, functional and other aspects of the model are presented in detail and its suitability to the Indian context is emphasized.

Under the existing system of collection of educational statistics, Ministry of Human Resource Development (Department of Education) obtain certain basic data from the State Governments which is collected annually on census basis. The responsibilities for collection of educational statistics largely rest with Ministry of Human Resource Development (Department of Education), Office of Registrar General, the Institute of Applied Manpower Research, the National Sample Survey Organisation (NSSO) National Council of Educational Research and Training (NCERT), National Institute of Educational Planning and Administration (NIEPA), University Grants Commission (UGC); Planning Commission and other similar agencies.

India has an abundance of recorded information; there is no shortage of data even in the field of education. However, this precious resource is concentrated in relatively few locations often virtually inaccessible to potential users and is lying largely untapped, as there is no formal system of dissemination like regular publications for general use. Office reports are prepared but these are used for only official purposes which is restricted to a limited number. There is no regular indexing and abstracting services in the field of education. At some places such services are available but they are irregular, meant only for in-house consumption and limited in scope as they reflect only the sources available in the institution library. Thus, the challenge is more to find the means for making these resources available to more people through an effective identification, location and distribution system, in addition to filling the gaps in the information.

The Centre, and the States should finance the project. It can be a central government suppported scheme.

Membership of NISE: In the education field, potential network members are easily identifiable. At the national level are the libraries of various institutions/organisations working under the administrative control of the Department of Education, Ministry of Human Resource Development, UGC, AIU, NCERT, NIEPA, Directorate General of Adult Education and all other institutions dealing with education activities at the national level. At the State level are State Departments of Education, SCERTs/SIEs, Directorates of Education, Universities having Department of Education, Teachers Training Colleges, organisations dealing with adult and non-formal education and institutions dealing with education at State level. At the district level are the libraries of the Chief Education Officer, DEO for school sector and DEO for adult/non-formal education sector, resource centre for open school, District Vocational Training Centre, DIET and all other offices dealing with education activities at the district level. At the lower level, the membership of the network can be extended to village education committees adult education centres, NFE centres, schools and colleges etc.

The National Information System for Education is planned and coordinated keeping in view the maximum utilization of the existing resources and its objectives are similar to that of a subject based network.

It will be controlled by a governing body consisting of representatives from Ministry of Human Resource Development, Department of Education, State Departments of Education, Ministry of Finance, Planning Commission and experts from Library/Information Science and educationists etc.

Operational Mechanism : The NISE should be designed to accommodate both traditional and modern methods and technology for handling of information and operating services to the users.

Organisational Units: Nodal points at different levels should be as follows:

National level	–	New Organisation
State level	–	SCERT
District level	–	Chief Education Officer
Institute level	–	Library

The nodal point at the national level should be a new set-up. Its activities should be classified and assigned to the following divisions viz. (i) National Education Library; (ii) Documentation Division; (iii) Translation Division; (iv) Publication Division; (v) Reprographic Division; (vi) Information Unit at Department of Education, Ministry of Human Resource Development; (vii) Regional Centres Division; and (viii) Adsministrative Division.

The proposed system should standardize the practices in all the areas of activity to facilitate easy and smooth participation among the network members and beneficial services to the patrons.

The proposed model is mainly based on the existing and perceived information needs in education in India as revealed by the survey and as viewed in comparison with the information systems in education prevailing in UK and USA. However, the paucity of resources and the overwhelming necessity to fully utilise the existing resources have guided the researcher to a pragmatic approach of suggesting a blend of traditional and modern technology in the operational methods, though this did impose some restrictions in the choice of organisational structure, services etc. While translating the model into practice, it is, therefore, necessary to incorporate such changes as warranted by the ground realities.

U.K. EDUCATION INFORMATION SOURCES

1. *British Education Index* - London: British Library Bibliographic Services Divison. University of Leeds, Education Library.
2. *Guide to the Literature of Education*. London: University of London, Institute of Education Library (Education Libraries Bulletin Supplement).
3. *Sociology of Education Adstracts*. Q. Carfax Publishing Co.
4. *Education Authorities Directory and Annual*. Mersthan: Redhill, School Government Publishing Co. Ltd.
5. *Education Yearbook. London*: Councils and Education Press, Ltd.
6. Great Britain. Department of Education and Science. Annual *Statistics on Education,* London: HMSO.
7. *Education Statistics for the United Kingdom*. London: HMSO.
8. SFIA Education Trust. *The Parent's Guide to Independent Schools*. Annual. Berks: Hobsons Press Kanbridge.
9. *Technical Education Abstracts*. Q. Carfax Publishing Co.
10. National Institute of Adult Education. *The Year Book of Adult Education*. Annual. Leister: National Institute of Adult Education.
11. Great Britain. Central Statistical Office. *Annual Asbtracts of Statistics,* London: HMSO.
12. Great Britain. Central Statistical Office. *Regional Statistics. Annual*. London: HMSO.
13. *Contents Pages in Education*. Monthly.Carfax Publishing Co.
14. *Educational Technology Abstracts*. Q. Carfax Publishing Co.
15. *EUDISED R&D Bulletin*. Q. K.G. Saur. Verlag.
16. *Higher Education Current Awareness Bulletin*. F.N. University of Aston-in-Birmingham.
17. *Research into Higher Education Abstracts*. 3/Yr. Carfax Publishing Co.
18. *School Organization and Management Abstracts*. Q. Carfax Publishing Co.

APPENDIX–B

U.S. EDUCATION INFORMATION SOURCES

1. *Education Index.* N.Y: H.W. Wilson. Monthly (except July & August) cumulated quarterly and annualy (Sept.-June).
2. *Resources in Education.* Washington: M&Annual Cumulation. Educational Resources Information Centre (ERIC) US Government Printing Office.
3. *Current Index to Journals in Education.* M. Educational Resources Information Centre (ERIC).
4. USA. Bureau of the Census. Statistical Abstracts of the United States. Washington, D.C. Government Printing Office. Annual.[1]
5. *Educational Administration Asbstracts.* Q. Stage Publications.
6. *Exceptional Child Education Resources.* Q. Council for exceptional children.
7. *Higher Education Abstracts.* Q. Claremont Graduate School.
8. *Journal of Abstracts in Internationals Education* Q. University of Toledo, College of Education.[2]
9. *Dissertation Abstracts International Series A – The Humanities and Social Sciences (M).* UMI Dissertation Information Service. Ann Arbor, Michigan.

The above listed publications are the basic educational information sources in the United States of America which are available throughout the country.

INDIAN EDUCATIONAL INFORMATION SOURCES

A. Bibliographical Services

(1) *Bibligraphy of Doctoral Thesis. (1935-58).* Inter–University Board of Indian and Ceylon. (Now known as Association of Indian Universities), New Delhi.

The bibliography contains Ph.D. theses accepted in the Indian universities in Arts and Sciences during 1935 to 1958. The Association publishes Research in Progress in 'University News'(F) to report about the research work taken up by scholars registered with Indian universities. for doctoral degrees. In collaboration with ICSSR, the Association has also taken up publication of annual bibliographies of Ph.D. theses accepted in Indian universities in Social Science and Humanities and in Physical and Biological Sciences.

A programme of retrospective bibliography has been launched to compolete a record of Ph.D., D. Litt. and L.L.D. theses accepted by Indian universities from 1857 onwards in various disciplines like Social Sciences, Humanities, Physical Sciences and Biological Sciences. The work is intended to be completed in 24 volumes. Fourteen volumes have already been published.

(2) *Catalogues of Government of India Publications.* Delhi, Director, Publications Division, Controller of Publication , Registrar General, Ministry of Human Resource Development and Lok Sabha Secretariat issue separate lists of their publications. The catalogues are arranged subject-wise.

(3) *Committees and Commissions in India.* Comp. & ed. by Virendra Kumar, Delhi, Concept Publishing Company 10 volumes. The work provides information on subjects like bibliographical data of the committees and commission, the Chairman, members and conveners etc. Appointment, terms of reference, contents and recommendations are given. Volumes 1-9 cover the period of 1947-69. The 10th Volume, covering the period of 1970-73 was published in 1975.

(4) *Committees and Commissions on Indian Education 1947-77:* a bibliography by A.N. Patra. New Delhi, N.C.E.R.T.

(5) Development of Education in India: A Historical Survey of

Educational Documents before and after Independent, A. Biswas and S.P. Agrawal, New Delhi, Concept. Publishing Company, 1986, 936p.

(6) Educational investigations in Indian Universities (1939-1961). New Delhi: N.C.E.R.T., 1963 (Memeographed) : It is a list of theses and dissertations approved for doctoral and Masters Degree in Education. The list has been divided into three parts:

I. Doctoral theses;

II. Thesis in full satisfaction of the requireemnts for M.Ed. degree;

III. Dissertations in partial satisfaction of the requirements of the M.Ed. degree (inclusive of M.A. in Education at Calcutta University).

In each part theses and disserations are arranged according to the universities and under each university alphabetically according to the names of the scholars.

(7) *Educational Investigations in Indian Universities (1962-66)* compiled by Satnam Singh. New Delhi: N.C.E.R.T., 1968.

This volume is in continuation of the earlier volume which covered the period from 1939-61. This volume has the same arrangement as its predecessor and lists theses and dissertations accepted in Indian universities in the field of education for Ph.D., D.Phil, D.Litt. and M.Ed.

(8) *Government of India Publications (1982).* by Mohinder Singh. New Delhi: Buduas Press.l 1982.

(9) *Guide to Reference Materials on India.* Compiled by N.N. Gudwani and K. Navalani. Jaipur: Saraswati Publications. 1974, 2 volumes.

The guide is arranged subject-wise. Most of the subject entries have been further arranged according to forms like Bibliographies, Asbtracting and indexing services, Reviews and Surveys, Catalogues and Directories, Enclopaedias. Directories, yearbooks, statistics, who's who etc. An exhaustive author cum subject index has been provided at the end. Vol.2 contains references to educational materials.

(10) *Indian National Bibliography.* Central Reference Library, Calcutta. (Monthly issues and Annual cumulations).

An authoritative bibliographic record of current publications in the major languages of India received by the National Library, Calcutta, under the provisions of the delivery of books and Newspapers (Public Libraries) Act (Act 2 of 1954 as amended by Act 99 of 1956).

(11) *Indian Periodicals: An annotated guide*. Compiled and edited by N.N. Gidwani and K. Navalani. Jaipur: Saraswati Publications, 1978: It coverns 6858 entries of current periodicals published in English language.

(12) *Indian Periodicals in Print,* ed. by H.N.D. Gandhi, et. al.Delhi: Vidya Mandal, 1973. 2 volumes.

(13) *Library of Congress Accession List*: India. (Quinquennial Cumulations). New Delhi: Library of Congress office.

(14) *Library of Congress Accession List:* South Asia. (Monthly). New Delhi: Library of Congress Office.

(15) *National Bibliography of Indian Literature*: 1901-1953. New Delhi. Sahitya Akademi. : To fill in the gap the Sahitya Akademi stepped in with a programme of compiling a retrospective bibliography of Indian publications in 12 (out of 14) Indian languages covering the period 1901-53. Volumes in Assamese, Gujarati, Telugu and Tamil have been published since.

(16) *Press in India (Annual).* New Delhi: Office of the Registrar of Newspapers, 2 parts. : Part II of the report contains a state-wise catalogue of newspapers. The newspapers in each state have been listed by periodicity and by language. Full particulars such as address, place of publication, names of publisher, printer, editor, subscription rate etc. are given. An index is also provided at the end.

(17) *Publication of Government of India* by S.P. Agrawal and Pushpa Rani Sharma, New Delhi, Concept Publishing Company, 1993. 2 vols.

(18) *Research Project Reports in Social Sciences Documentation Centre: An annotated Bibliography*. New Delhi: Social Science Documentation Centre (Now Known as National Social Science Documentation Centre), I.C.S.S.R., 1984.

The compilation includes the abstracts of research reports sponsored by I.C.S.S.R. Each abstract has following 3 parts:

(i) The aim of the project;
(ii) Methods of investigation and scope; and
(iii) Conclusions and suggestions.

Research projects completed upto 1980 have been included.

(19) *Second Historical Survey of Educational Development in India*

select Documents, 1985-1989, by J.C. Aggarwal and S.P. Agrawal, New Delhi, Concept Publishing Company, 1991.

(21) *State Governments Publications in India*-1947-82 by Mohinder Singh. Delhi: Academic Publications, 1985. 2 volumes. Publications of all the States and Union Territories of India published upto 1982 have been included in this bibliography.

(22) *Survey of Research in Education* ed. by M.B. Buch. Baroda: Centre of Advanced Study in Education, Faculty of Education and Psychology, M.S. University of Baroda.

First Survey, published in 1974 covers the research work completed upto 1972 and includes abstracts of Ph.D. theses as well as research reports of other institutions like N.C.E.R.T., S.I.Es and various university departments of education. The survey also presents a review of literature to identify research trends. The Second survey covers the period lof 1972-78. The 3rd Survey covers the period of 1978-83 and has been published by NCERT in 1986.

(23) *Survey of Research in Technical Education* , edited by M. Mukhopadhyaya and others. Bhopal: Technical Teachers' Training Institute, 1980 : The volume contains abstracts of studies in Technical Education. Studies are arranged under seven areas of technical educationand under each area alphabetically by authors of the studies.

B. Indexing and Abstracting Services

(1) *Current Literature in Education: Index of Articles selected from periodicals received in NCERT,* DLDI (Memeographed) (Q.). New Delhi: NCERT.

(2) *Guide to Indian Periodical Literature* (A.). Gurgaon: Indian Documentation Service.

(3) *ICSSR Research Abstracts.* (Q.). New Delhi: Indian Council of Social Science Research.

(4) *Index India* (Q.). Jaipur: University of Rajasthan.

(5) *Index to Indian Periodicals: Sociology and Psychology* edited by Nirmal Rupraill and K.G. Tyagi. New Delhi: National Social Science Documentation Centre. (ICSSR), 1987.

In this publication 35 periodicals in sociology, published in English, have been indexed, right from their respective vol.I to 1970. The Index is in two parts – Subject Index and Author Index.

(6) *Indian Dissertation Abstracts* (Q.). New Delhi, I.C.S.S.R.
(7) *Indian Education Abstracts* (Q.). New Delhi, Ministry of Education and Social Welfare (ceased).
(8) *Indian Education Index* (1947-1978), edited by K.G. Tyagi. General Editor S.P. Agrawal. New Delhi: Acharan Prakashan, 1980. (A joint undertaking of the Indian Council of Social Science Research, New Delhi and the Indian Institute of Education, Pune).
(9) *Indian Library Science Abstracts* (Q). Calcutta: Indian Association of Special Libraries and Information Centres (IASLIC).
(10) *Indian Press Index,* Delhi: Delhi Primary Library Association.
(11) *Indian Writings on Education, 1979-1986*; An Indicator to Indian Educational Journals, Grouped by 2465 Subject Descutors by S.P. Agrawal New Delhi, Concept Publishing Company, 2 volumes.

The indexing and abstracting services mentioned above fall into three categories:

(i) Retrospective
(ii) Current
(iii) Ceased publication.

Services at S.No. 5 and 8 are retrospective services to fill the gap for the period when no such services existed. Services at S. No.1-4,6,9 & 10 are current services. Many of them are irregular or behind the schedule. Department of Library, Documentation and Information, N.C.E.R.T. is bringing out an indexing service in memeographed form for limited circulation (S.No.1). Service mentioned at Sl. No. 7 is ceased publication.

Many of these services are not exclusively meant for education but are of general nature covering a large number of disciplines.

In conclusion it can be said that no regular documentation service worth the name in the field of education is being provided to the readers by any agency.

C. Sources of Educational Statistics

The responsibility for collection, collation and dissemination of information is primarily that of the Ministry of Human Resource Development–Department of Education. In this task it is supported by various agencies like University Grants Commission for higher education, Bureau of Technical education Education for technical and other ministries like Ministries of Agriculture, Health and Labour for agricultural, medical and vocational and occupational aspects of education respectively.

In India, the scope of educational statistics covers three major areas:

(i) Census statistics concerning the educational characteristics of the population;
(ii) Current administrative statistics related to educational institutions and finance; and
(iii) Ad hoc statistics collected in connection with studies of educational problems.

The major sources and organisations dealing with Educational Statistics can be mentioned as under:-

(i) Union Ministry of Human Resource Development-Department of Education

- (a) Education in India–vol.I (Numerical Data) Annual
- (b) Education in India–vol.II (Financial Data) Annual
- (c) Education in India–vol.III (Examination REsults) Annual
- (d) Selected Educational Statistics Annual
- (e) Pay Scales of School Teachers in India Annual
- (f) Selected Information on School Education in India Annual
- (g) Analysis of Budgeted Expenditure on Education Annual
- (h) Analysis of Annual Plan
- (i) Directory of Institutions for Higher Education in India Biennial
- (j) A Handbook of Educational and Allied Statistics Biennial
- (k) Educational Statistics District-wise Quinquennial
- (l) Indian Students going abroad and Foreign Students studying in Indian Universities and Institutions Quinquennial
- (m) Trends of Expenditure on Education ad hoc

(n) Enrolment Trends in States ad hoc

(ii) State Departments of Education

Concerning with state requirements on the similar lines as of Central Government on the prescribed formats issued by Ministry of HRD-Deptt. of Education.

(iii) University Grants Commission

(a) The University Development in India - Basic Facts and Figures Annual

(b) Thematic Studies ad hoc

(iv) National Council of Educational Research and Training (NCERT)

(a) All India Educational Survey – Comprehensive Data related to school education Quinquennial

(b) Yearbooks 1-4

(c) Thematic Studies ad hoc

(v) Directorate General of Employment and Training (DGE&T)

(a) A Handbook on Training Facilities (Institutional Training) ad hoc

(b) Data on Industrial Training Institutes and Employment Exchanges.

(vi) Census of India

(a) Census Report. Decennial Contents: (i) levels of education, (ii) type, (iii) rural/urban, (iv) sex, (v) State/Union Territory.

(vii) National Sample Survey Organisation (NSSO) NSS Reports for Data on socio/economic aspects of population, level and round wise.

(viii) Technical /Professional Bodies

(include Indian Council of Agricultural Research (ICAR); Directorate General of Health Services (DGHS); Medical Council of India; Dental Council of India; Indian Pharmacy Council, Indian Nursing Council, Indian Council of Social Science Research; etc).

They collect and maintain the data on

- intake/enrolment and outturn
- Annual Reports
- Thematic Studies ad hoc

(ix) Planning Commission

Annual Plans; Five Year Plans.

(x) National Institute of Educational Planning and Adminisstration (NIEPA)
– Educational Planning and Administration Surveys and Studies ad hoc
(xi) Central Statistical Organisation (CSO)
– Income and other related statistics of various economy sectors (for State and National)
(xii) Institute of Applied Manpower Research (IAMR)
– Area manpower surveys; vocational and technical education surveys.
(xiii) Association of Indian Universities
– Studies in educational problems of higher education, etc.
(xiv) Research Institutions in the field of Education and Related Disciplines.
– Thematic Studies & surveys ad hoc
(xv) Specially designed surveys for specific purposes ad hoc

REFERENCES

1. National Institute for Educational Research – Tokyo (1983). *Educational Information - Problems and Issues and Strategies for resolving them*: Report of a regional workshop 1-23 February p.10.
2. India. Ministry of Education and Culture. 1982. Report of the high level committee to review the educational statistics system in India. New Delhi, Ministry of Education and Culture, p.6-20
3. Kapoor, M.M. 1982 *Integrated Information System for Educational Management: A suggested model for India*. Paris, Unesco, p. 36
4. Saluja, M.R. 1972. *Indian Official Statistics System*. Calcutta, Statistical Publishing Society, Chapter XI , p, 251-265
5. Srivastava, A.B.L. and Hiriyanniah, K.N. 1977. *Education Statistics in India*. In National Seminar on Social Statistics Organised by Central Statistical Organization, Bombay, Allied, Vol.II p. 501
6. Institute of Applied Manpower Research, (n.d.). *Data Sources and items of Information on Educational Statistics in India*. New Delhi: IAMR, memographed.

APPPENDIX–D

INTERNATIONAL EDUCATIONAL INFORMATION SOURCES

BIBE Belletin International Bulleten of Bibliography on Education. Madrid, Unesco BIBE Project.

Commonwealth Universities Yearbooks. London, Association of Commonwealth Universities.

United Nations. Department of International Economic and Social Affairs, *Statistical Yearbook.* New York, Annual.

Statistical Yearbook. Paris, Unesco, annual.

Study abroad: International Scholarships and Courses. Paris Unesco. Bi-annual.

Ulrich's International Periodicals Directory 1986-87 (1986). New York: R.R. Bowker, p.526-557.

Unesco list of Documents and Publications and Annual Cumulation, Paris, Unesco. Q.

Walford, A.J. *Walford's Concise Guide to Reference Material op.cit.,* pp.63-66, 96-103.

The World of learning. London, Europe Publications. Annual.

INDEX

CICIL LIST

CONCEPTS IN COMMUNICATION, INFORMATICS & LIBRARIANSHIP

(CICIL)

General Editor: **S.P. AGRAWAL**

CICIL-1 Development of Library Services in India: Social Science Information
S.P. Agrawal Rs. 150

CICIL-2 Development of Documentation in India: Social Science Information
S.P. Agrawal Rs. 250

CICIL-3 UNESCO and Social Sciences: Retrospect and Prospect
S.P. Agrawal and **J.C. Aggarwal** Rs. 250

CICIL-4 INDIANA : A Bibliography of Bibliographical Sources
M.K. Jain Rs. 200

CICIL-5 Dimensions of Library and Information Science: Kaula Festschrift
V. Venkatappaiah (Eds.) Rs. 600

CICIL-6 Book Numbers: Some Indian Methods
M.P. Satija and **S.P. Agrawal** Rs. 100

CICIL-7 National Policy for University Libraries in India: Problems and Perspectives
N.B. Inamdar and **L.S. Ramaiah** (Ed.) Rs. 250

CICIL-8 Media Utilisation for the Development of Women and Children
B.S. Thakur and **Binod C. Agrawal** Rs. 150

CICIL-9 Terrorism: An Annotated Bibliography
Susheela Bhan (Ed.) Rs. 275

CICIL-10 Transnational Library Relations: The Indo-American Experience
M.B. Konnur Rs. 175

CICIL-11 Geography of Marketing and Commercial Activities in India (Documentation on Research Information)
R.S. Dixit Rs. 130

CICIL-12 Information India 1988: Global View
S.P. Agrawal and **J.C. Aggarwal** Rs. 200

CICIL-13 Women's Education in India: Historical Review, Present Status and Perspective Plan
S.P. Agrawal and **J.C. Aggarwal** Rs. 360

CICIL-14 Cultural Communication in India: Role and Impact of Phonograms
J.M. Ojha Rs. 220

CICIL-15 Second Historical Survey of Educational Development in India: Select Documents 1985-1989
S.P. Agrawal and **J.C. Aggarwal** Rs. 490

CICIL-16 Documentation Encyclopaedia of UNESCO and Education
J.C. Aggarwal and **S.P. Agrawal** Rs. 800 (set of 2 parts)

CICIL-17 Attitude Towards Information: A Study of Post-Graduate Teachers and Researchers in Social Sciences
N.G. Satish (in press)

CICIL-18 Librarianship and Bureaucratic Organisation: A Study in the Sociology of Library Profession in India
P.K. Jayaswal Rs. 175

CICIL-19 Literature Search
K.A. Isaac Rs. 150

CICIL-20 Child Education in India: Index to Scholarly Writings in Indian Educational Journals and Newspapers since independence
S.P. Agrawal and **Naresh Kanta** Rs. 100

CICIL-21 Lok Sabha and Vidhan Sabha Elections in India 1989 & 1990: Process and Results with Comparative Study of Manifestos
S.P. Agrawal and **J.C. Aggarwal** Rs. 250

CICIL-22 Islamic Studies in India: A Survey of Human, Institutional and Documentary Sources
Mohamed Taher Rs. 180

CICIL-23 Panchayati Raj: An Annotated Bibliography
N.B. Inamdar, N.G. Satish and **Anil Takalkar** 290

CICIL-24 Information India 1989-90: Global View
S.P. Agrawal and **J.C. Aggarwal** Rs. 500

CICIL-25 First Handbook of Psychological and Social Instruments
Udai Pareek and **T. Venkateswara Rao** Rs. 500

CICIL-26 Educational and Social Uplift of Backward Classes: At What Cost and How? Mandal Commission and After
S.P. Agrawal and **J.C. Aggarwal** Rs. 275

CICIL-27 Mass Media and New Horizons: Impact of TV & Video an Urban Milieu
H.R. Trivedi Rs. 180

CICIL-28 Indian Writings on Education : An Indicator to Indian Educational Journals Grouped by Subject Deseriptors 1979 to 1986 (in two parts)
S.P. Agarwal Rs. 900 (per set)

CICIL-29 Nation in Crisis
S.P. Agrawal and **J.C. Aggarwal** Rs. 200

CICIL-30 Information India 1990-91: Global View
S.P. Agrawal and **J.C. Aggarwal** Rs. 500

CICIL-31 Development of University Libraries in India after Independence
O.P. Gupta Rs. 270

CICIL-32 Handbook on Child : With Historical Background
Pramila Pandit Barooah Rs. 320

CICIL-33 Weaker Section in Indian Society : Undiscovered Past, Uncertain Present and Unpredictable Future : Index to Writings in Indian Scholarly Journals and 10 National Newspapers Classified under 1500 Descriptors 1886-1990
S.P. Agrawal and **Rajeev Kumar Sharma** Rs. 600

CICIL-34 Communication Informatics and Librarianship in India : An Introductory Guide to Publications Based on a Survey of Libraries in Capital City of India
S.P. Agrawal and **Pushpa Rani Sharma** Rs. 720

CICIL-35 Problems of Collection Development in Special Libraries
M.S. Sridhar Rs. 225

CICIL-36 National Information Resources for Social Sciences in India : Mobilisation, Dispersal and International Enhancement
S.P. Agrawal Rs. 225

CICIL-37 Modern History of Punjab : A Look Back into Ancient Peaceful Punjab Focusing Confrontation and Failures Leading to Present Punjab Problem, and a Peep Ahead : Relevant Select Documents
J.C. Aggarwal and **S.P. Agrawal** Rs. 400

CICIL-38 India Information Sources : Economics and Business
Kyllikki Ruokonen and Manohar Lal Rs.

CICIL-39 Educational Planning in India : With a Slant to Educational Financing and Administration, Vol. 1, Reports of Committees and Commissions, Five Year Plans, Statistical Tables
J.C. Aggarwal and **S.P. Agrawal** Rs. 650

CICIL-40 Integrated Library System : Two Case Studies : Latin America and India
Maria Luiza Rigo Pasquarelli, Rosaly Favero Krzyanowski, Ines Maria M. Imperatriz and **S.P. Agrawal** Rs. 160

CICIL-41 Social Science Information in India: Effort towards Bibliographical Control
S.D. Vyas Rs. 300

CICIL-42 Higher Education in India Since Independence: U.G.C. and Its Approach
O.P. Gupta Rs. 360

CICIL-43 Government and Politics in India: A Bibliographical Study of Contemporary Scenario Chronicling Rajiv Gandhi Era
S.P. Agrawal and **Rajeev Kumar Sharma** Rs. 500

CICIL-44 Second Handbook of Psychological and Social Instruments
D.M. Pestonjee Rs. 300

CICIL-45 Development/Digression Diary of India; 3D Companion Volume to Information India: 1990-91
S.P. Agrawal Rs. 200

CICIL-46 Development/Digression Diary of India; 3D Companion Volume to Information India: 1991-92
S.P. Agrawal Rs. 300

CICIL-47 Information India 1991-92: Global View
S.P. Agrawal and **J.C. Aggarwal** Rs. 500

CICIL-48 Committees and Commissions in India 1974, A Concept's Project, Compiled by a team of professionals guided by Virender Kumar (Vol. 12) Rs. 450

CICIL-49 Committees and Commissions in India 1975, A Concept's Project, Compiled by a team of professionals guided by Virender Kumar (Vol. 13) Rs. 450

CICIL-50 Committees and Commissions in India 1976, A Concept's Project, Compiled by a team of professionals guided Virender Kumar (Vol. 14) Rs. 450

CICIL-51 Committees and Commissions in India 1977, A Concept's Project, Compiled by a team of professionals guided by Virender Kumar (Vol. 15) (in four parts) Rs. 450 each

CICIL-52 Committees and Commissions in India 1978, A Concept's Project, Compiled by a team of professionals guided by Virender Kumar (Vol. 16) (in two parts) Rs. 450 each

CICIL-53 Subject Guide to Communication, Informatics and Librarianship in India (Based on a Survey of Library Holdings in Capital City of India)
S.P. Agrawal and **Pushpa Rani Sharma** Rs. 400

CICIL-54 Restructurring of Library and Information Science Curriculum
A. Tejomurty Rs. 250

CICIL-55 Committees and Commissions in India 1979, A Concept's Project, Compiled by a team of professionals guided by Virender Kumar (Vol. 17) (in two parts) Rs. 450 each

CICIL-56 Committees and Commissions in India 1980, A Concept's Project, Compiled by a team of professionals guided by Virender Kumar (Vol. 18) (in two parts) Rs. 450 each

CICIL-57 Third Historical Survey of Educational Development in India
S.P. Agrawal and **J.C. Aggarwal** Rs. 700

CICIL-58 Model Library Legislation
Velaga Venkatappaiah Rs. 400

CICIL-59 Indian Library and Information Science Literature (1990-91)
Sewa Singh Rs. 525

CICIL-60 Librarianship and Library Science in India
Mohamed Taher and **Donald Gordon Davis, Jr**. Rs. 350

CICIL-61 Comprehensive Glossary for Library & Information Science by **O.P. Gupta** Rs.300

CICIL-62 Information India 1992-93:
S.P. Agrawal and **J. C. Aggarwal** Rs. 500

CICIL-63 Automation of Libraries and Information Science
R.K. Shukla Rs. 250

CICIL-64 Modern History of Jammu and Kashmir
J.C. Aggarwal and **S.P. Agrawal** Rs. 1500 (per set of 2 vols.)

CICIL-65 Library and Information Science: Emerging Trends:
Sister M. Esperanza, A. C. Rs. 250

CICIL-66 Mental Retardation in India (A Bibliography)
S. Venkatesan and **V.G.D. Vepuri** Rs. 275

CICIL-67 Information Management in Health Science Libraries in India
R.P. Dixit (*Foreword* **Dr. Uton Muchtar Rafei**) Rs. 550

CICIL-68 Information Behaviour of Scientists and Engineers:
M.S. Sridhar Rs. 500